NELSON RODRIGUES: SELECTED PLAYS

NELSON RODRIGUES
Selected Plays

Translated by Daniel Hahn, Susannah Finzi
and Almiro Andrade

OBERON BOOKS
LONDON

WWW.OBERONBOOKS.COM

Contents

A Note from the Cesgranrio Foundation

It was with great enthusiasm and a firm commitment to Brazilian culture that the Cesgranrio Foundation received the invitation to assist with the project of translating and promoting the work of Nelson Rodrigues in the UK.

Nelson is a national treasure, a writer of a subtle and powerful dramaturgy, able to reveal the obvious in surprising ways. Exporting his work is not an easy task. The strength of his words lies precisely in revealing characteristics very much connected to the 'Brazilian way of being', our relationships and our social conventions. However, the masterly way that Nelson takes our soul into the stage makes his work universal and deserves to be known and recognized outside of Brazil.

The Cesgranrio Foundation, one of top investors in the Brazilian theatre, could not resist supporting this project of promoting our culture abroad, through one of the greatest exponents of our theatre.

At this moment our foundation prepares for the construction of a third theatre venue and has just launched an undergraduate theatre course. For over five years we have been taking theatrical performances to students who live in 'favelas' (Brazilian slums) and we also promote the top Brazilian theatre award. How could we not get involved with this challenge of translating Nelson into English? The author's genius honours our theatre with a unique quality in the country and the world. We want to be part of this historical moment, presenting here a part of Nelson, a part of our theatre, and a part of the huge diversity that we call Brazil.

It is for this same reason that, with unique satisfaction and great honour, the Cesgranrio Foundation has also sponsored the sculpture of Nelson Rodrigues that today stands, with all its strength and vigour, in Copacabana, in the marvellous city of Rio de Janeiro.

Hooray Brazilian Theatre! Hooray Nelson Rodrigues!

Carlos Alberto Serpa de Oliveira
President of the Cesgranrio Foundation

Exporting Nelson Rodrigues

The comment we heard the most, when telling people about our project was: "it's about time!". Yes, it is. It is about time for the English-speaking world to finally meet Nelson Rodrigues, the most important Brazilian playwright of all time.

The unique universe of Nelson Rodrigues was first published in English in 1998, in two volumes, sponsored by the Brazilian government and published by FUNARTE, in a collection organised by Joffre Rodrigues and translated by him, Toby Coe and Flávia Carvalho. It was a limited edition, launched mainly in Brazil and at the time not really known outside the country.

In 2015 I met Sacha Rodrigues in London. As grandson of Nelson Rodrigues, he was in the UK with the mission of "exporting" the work of his grandfather, inspired by what his father, Joffre Rodrigues, had tried to do seventeen years before. By coincidence, at the time I was directing *Wedding Dress*, using Joffre's translation, with my BA World Performance students at East15 Drama School, in the UK. Our meeting quickly turned into a meeting of souls with one aim: to rediscover Rodrigues' words, in English, in an attempt to bring his peculiar way of portraying the deepest human self to a wider audience. We then started a journey that took almost four years of hard work and endless online meeting between Rio de Janeiro and London, in an attempt to turn our dreams into reality. With the important support from the Nelson Rodrigues Estate, Oberon Books, East15 – University of Essex, King's College and many passionate people who Sacha would call "the Rodriguean knights", things gradually started to move forward. And finally, thanks to *Fundação Cesgranrio, Turbilhão de Ideias Entretenimento* and the Embassy of Brazil in London, you now have this book in your hands.

As a starting point we had the twelve plays curated by Joffre Rodrigues and published by FUNARTE. From those, in a tough selection process where we wanted to maintain a general panorama of Nelson Rodrigues' style and themes, we ended up choosing seven. They were all newly translated by Susannah Finzi, Almiro Andrade and Daniel Hahn who we believe have managed to rediscover the precious "Rodriguean" spirit we were looking for.

It is with honour and immense pleasure that we finally unveil, for all interested English speakers, the world of Nelson Rodrigues. It's about time!

Ramiro Silveira & Nelson Vinicius 'Sacha' Rodrigues
Project Curators and Organisers

Introduction

by Luís Artur Nunes

NELSON RODRIGUES (1912–1980) was born in Recife, Pernambuco and raised in Rio de Janeiro, where he initiated a lifelong career as a journalist. That was how he earned a living. His newspaper columns made him well-known and he also wrote a great deal of fiction which was later published in book format. However his main artistic contribution was a remarkable body of work as a playwright.

When his first play, *A Mulher sem Pecado* (The Woman With No Sin) premiered in 1942, the performing arts in Brazil were extremely conservative and limited mostly to comedy of manners, melodrama and music-hall. *The Woman With No Sin* introduced new themes and theatrical procedures which the author would develop for a total of seventeen plays. Such dramatic output established the modernization of Brazilian theatre.

The great novelty of his first creation for the stage was the presentation of the life of the mind, as the remembrances and fantasies of its demented protagonist, Olegário, are concretely enacted a number of times throughout the play. In his second work, *Vestido de Noiva* (Wedding Dress, 1943), Rodrigues would continue this investigation. Most of the action now takes place in the traumatized psyche of the heroine, Alaíde, who agonizes in a hospital after being run over by a car. The accident happened as the result of a succession of vicious conflicts involving jealousy and betrayal in her married life. The script sets up three "planes": memory, hallucination and reality. The meanderings of thoughts, reminiscence and dreams prevail most of the time over the stark context of external reality. Only by the second half of the last act after the protagonist's death, the real world, up to that point reduced to brief sparse scenes, outweighs the other planes. And still it is often haunted by fragments of the subjective realm.

By means of such counterpoint we watch the gradual emerging of a story of emotional violence and bitter social commentary.

Wedding Dress took Brazilian theatre by storm. It was produced by an amateur company from Rio de Janeiro, Os Comediantes, and staged by Polish director Zbigniew Ziembinski, one of the many European theatre professionals who had fled from the Second World War, who brought the Brazilian stage up to date with the trends of the contemporary avant-garde.

In spite of the overwhelming acclaim of his second play, Nelson Rodrigues was to be subsequently execrated by audiences and critics and banned by the official censorship. His next four plays dealt with outrageous subjects such as incest and family murder as an attempt to delve into the mythic realm of the collective unconscious. The style would greatly depart from strict realism, favouring instead poetic atmosphere, anti-illusionistic devices like choruses and masks, and stage images infused with symbolism. He describes this veering of content and form with the following words:

"With *Wedding Dress* I met success; with the following plays I lost it forever. (…) I stepped onto a path that can lead me anywhere but to success. Which path is that? My answer is: a theater that can be defined as "unpleasant". In a word, I am writing an "unpleasant theater", "unpleasant plays". In such category I include *Álbum de Família* (Family Portraits), *Anjo Negro* (Black Angel) and the recent *Senhora dos Afogados* (Lady Of The Drowned). Why are these unpleasant plays? As I said, because they are pestilent fetid works, capable in and of themselves of infecting the audience with typhus and malaria."[1]

Family Portraits (1945) displays actual behaviours derived from the irrational drives of the human soul. Each character plays out the strongest urges and wildest fantasies from the deep recesses of his/her inner self. Inside the microcosm of a single family, father, mother, sons, daughter and sister-in-law

---

1   *Dionysos*, #1, Serviço Nacional de Teatro, Ministério da Educação e Cultura, October, 1949.

are bound by ties of love, hate, sexual attraction and murderous impulses. It is a sort of primeval family depicted here, hence the mythic undercurrent of the text. Their actions suffer neither restraint nor guilt. Everything is possible in this magic world where the most forbidden desires come true. As the play progresses we watch in awe the relentless explosions of such powerful energy.

Black Angel (1946) takes up from *Family Portraits* the theme of moral transgression and the parading of high emotionalism, paroxysm and flamboyant physical action. But it adds to that quite a compelling ingredient: the race issue. The main dramatis personae are a couple formed by a black man and his white blonde wife. *Black Angel* also departs from the previous play in the sense that its characters lack the guiltless single-mindedness of their predecessors. There is a sort of moral ambiguity in the protagonists. Black Ismael and white Virginia are continuously split between opposing impulses towards spiritual elevation and self-debasement, symbolized respectively by the metaphors of "whiteness" and "blackness". However politically incorrect these images may be, they express nonetheless deeply rooted cultural concepts.

Senhora dos Afogados (Lady Of The Drowned, 1947) is also a family drama full of incestuous feelings and predatory actions in the life of an aristocratic clan living by the ocean, which functions as an ominous metaphor to an all-engulfing death. A chorus of neighbours wearing masks occasionally interacts with the main characters, but mostly provides commentary to the dramatic events they are witnessing.

We can add *Doroteia* (1949) to the list of spectacular flops of the playwright who once had been the greatest promise of Brazil's modern theatre. *Dorotéia* does not rely on poetic atmosphere as much as the three plays that followed *Wedding Dress*. Pervaded by a toxic sense of humour instead, it plunges deeply into the realms of the absurd and the grotesque. It is interesting to note that it was written a few years before Ionesco's *The Bald Soprano* and Beckett's *Waiting for Godot*, which established the Theatre of the Absurd as a new dramatic movement. Nelson Rodrigues's penchant for radical innovation is here once again reaffirmed.

Sábato Magaldi, – the first and still the most insightful critic to probe into the complexities of Rodrigues's drama – named the four "unpleasant plays" as the "mythic cycle", as opposed to other two categories: the "psychological plays" (in which *The Women With No Sin* and *Wedding Dress* fell) and the "carioca tragedies" – carioca being the term applied to all things related to the city of Rio de Janeiro – which produced detailed illustrations of the social milieu and a harsh criticism of society's illnesses.

Of course the utter rejection to the "mythic plays" was painfully frustrating to the once acclaimed dramatist. In his next theatre work, two years after *Dorotéia*, *Valsa Nº 6* (Waltz # 6, 1951), he tries a brief return to the scrutiny of the stream of consciousness. Once again the drama takes place inside a person's mind. In *The Woman With No Sin* we see only figments of Olegário's imagination popping up in scattered moments, and in *Wedding Dress* Alaíde's mental activity commands the course of the action, leaving a much smaller part to the "plane of reality". *Waltz # 6* goes even further: the character's subconscious fills up the totality of the play. But this is a monologue, albeit certainly not a traditional one. The only speaker is a fifteen-year old girl, Sônia, who, just like the main character of *Wedding Dress*, in the beginning is unsure of her past and even of her very identity and gradually retrieves them through the reenactment of the circumstances that led to her tragic demise. But instead of conjuring up on stage the characters and incidents of her story, real or delusional, (which is in fact what Alaíde does), she actually acts them out all by herself: parents, relatives, neighbours, the family doctor, her love affair with an older married man and her very death by murder in a last scene that informs us she had been dead all along. Through Sônia's voice and body we see and hear not only herself but the whole world around her. The process of digging out a coherent story out of the apparent puzzle of disparate images and events is the same in both plays. So is the dream-like atmosphere, which led many scholars to see a certain kinship with surrealism and expressionism in Nelson Rodrigues's theatre.

However *Waltz # 6* did not bring back the long awaited appreciation of audiences and critics. Perhaps it seemed too odd a theatrical experience watching a dead girl dramatize her tragic short life while punctuating her narrative with outbursts of despair as she runs to her piano and convulsively plays shreds of Chopin's vertiginous waltz.

Yet although Rodrigues remained a failure as a playwright in the eyes of the public and of the intelligentsia, he was nevertheless reaping massive popularity as a newspaper columnist. He signed a daily column in the tabloid "Última Hora" named *A Vida como ela É…* (Life As It Is…). In reality these were short stories, pieces of pure fiction, but pretending to pass for extracts of everyday reality, an anthology of faits divers of sorts, in the sense that they offered a faithful account of suburban life in Rio with its popular types and characteristic mores. Scandals, adultery and passion crimes were the basic plot material. One should not forget that carioca suburbia is not inhabited by the affluent as in many countries. Especially in those days it was rather the home of the underprivileged and the destitute.

Life As It Is… was so successful that it even caused an increase in the newspaper sales. Therefore, according to Sábato Magaldi, it was almost inevitable for Nelson Rodrigues to abandon his "unpleasant theater" and the examination of weird troubled psyches and begin to shape his new plays in the direct and accessible manner of his allegedly journalistic slices of life.

His first experiment in the new realistic mode was *A Falecida* (The Deceased Woman, 1953). On the surface it is a straightforward story about a suburban wife leading a wretched life with her absent unemployed husband. Her enormous frustration makes her nurture an obsession for some form of high-flown compensation. Seeing herself as prone to disease and expecting to die soon, she fantasizes about a sumptuous funeral: a lavish casket carried in a richly decked coach pulled by feathered horses. A sort of transcendence in death to atone for a paltry life. However the protagonist unexpectedly dies in the second act, still having managed to obtain the money to pay for her spectacular funeral rites. Act 3 thus disrupts the linear narrative and shows in flash-backs her manipulation of adultery in order to obtain the funds she needed, and in present time how the cuckolded husband gets his revenge by sabotaging her dream.

Perdoa-me por me Traíres (Forgive Me For You Betraying Me, 1957), another carioca tragedy, also disturbs conventional dramatic structure by turning the second act into a long flash-back exposing the past events as justification to the present ones. It also prepares Act 3, which picks up the main plot and provides closure after a last spectacular reversal. Tragic endings have become a rule since Nelson Rodrigues's very first play. Thoroughly realistic as it may seem, *Forgive Me For You Betraying Me* rekindles the mythical idea of the eternal return. The sins of lust and extreme violence that happen in the past recur in the present within the same family.

Notwithstanding the new predominant naturalistic approach, the playwright never abdicated entirely from making incursions into the sphere of subjectivity or from utilizing poetic imagery with mythic overtones. Nor did he give up experimentation with dramatic and scenic procedures. Myth and introspection (to a lesser degree), ingenious handling of plot structure and innovation in stage effects continued to appear, but now framed within a very concrete social context. In this sense, the new cycle of realistic plays is not an ensemble of mere docudramas about misery and corruption in Brazilian society. Through a combination of outer and inner aspects of human existence illustrated with modern and inventive theatrical tools, it constitutes an ultimate synthesis of the Rodriguean universe.

The most striking example of Nelson Rodrigues's bold manipulation of narrative techniques in the realistic cycle is *Boca de Ouro* (Golden Mouth, 1959). He borrows a Pirandellian scheme: the same story is retold three times, one for each act. The three versions differ largely in facts and implications according to the fluctuations of the narrator's state of mind. Similarly *Otto Lara*

Resende ou Bonitinha, Mas Ordinária (Otto Lara Resende or Pretty, Yet A Slut, 1962) confuses the veracity of the main dramatic incident – a case of violent rape – suggesting false variants of it up to an ending that exposes the truth in a totally unexpected (and catastrophic, as usual) fashion.

The plot of *Os Sete Gatinhos* (Seven Little Kitties, 1957) on the other hand unfolds quite straightforwardly in time with few changes of locale. It presents a dysfunctional family of poverty-stricken suburbans. An underemployed father, a sexually frustrated mother and four daughters also with low jobs devise a fantasy scheme to compensate for their dismal lives. The girls prostitute themselves in order to make extra money to provide for the education of the youngest, Silene, just a teenager, protecting her from all the wretchedness in an expensive catholic boarding school. At a certain point the father even proposes to set up a "family brothel", acting as a pimp for his older daughters, who then could work more comfortably at home. The family sacrifices itself in a life of degradation so that one of them remains a virgin, pure and untainted "as in a church stained glass". Her purity would supposedly atone for the elders' frustrations and sins. Of course, nothing turns out as expected. Despite its crude realism, the play is suffused with mythical overtones as the image of the holy virgin conflicts with the ones of the fallen woman and of the father-corrupter.

Toda Nudez será Castigada (All Nudity Will Be Punished, 1965) also evolves as a linear plot once it is established early in the play that it is all but a long flash-back triggered by a recorded message from the suicidal protagonist. Like *The Seven Little Kitties* it also deals with the opposition between virtue and perversion. A respectable bourgeois tries to change his fiery sexual affair with a morbid self-destructive hooker into a decent marriage. Apparently to both of them a relationship based on erotic urges is by no means acceptable and must perforce be sanctified through a proper wedding. Evidently the stratagem does not hold together and precipitates an array of ignominious actions leading to fatal consequences.

Other realistic plays by Nelson Rodrigues are *Beijo no Asfalto* (Kiss on the Asphalt, 1960) and *A Serpente* (The Serpent, 1980), both of them shaped as straightforward stories unreeling in a fast relentless pace up to startling final reversals followed by a disastrous denouement. *Anti-Nelson Rodrigues* (1973), under a realistic sheen, is essentially an exercise on self-parody, as indicated by the title.

Viúva, Porém Honesta (Widow, yet Virtuous, 1957) constitutes an exception in Nelson Rodrigues's theatre. It is pure comedy in the farcical mode, displaying no realism whatsoever and playing with a number of creative narrative contrivances. Yet it is clearly an acid satire targeting the moral hypocrisies of society. Together with *Anti-Nelson Rodrigues* these are the only two Rodriguean plays with perfect happy endings.[2]

As a consequence of his now firmly established realistic phase, Nelson Rodrigues was reconciled with the general public and the cultural establishment. Despite the gain in accessibility and approval, his theatre continued to innovate in dramatic composition, reject superficial verisimilitude and experiment with daring theatrical procedures which, surprisingly enough, did not contradict – and even enhanced – his accurate portraiture of social reality. His themes and subjects did not become more palatable as he insisted on taboo topics, sensational and provocative situations, aberration, degradation and extreme violence.

In his social drama, Nelson Rodrigues, although avoiding direct political commentary, was undoubtedly intent on denouncing corruption, hypocrisy and depravity in modern urban society. However, aside from the bitter social criticism implicit in his slices of life, his real goal was to reflect on the misery of the human condition. All throughout his career as a playwright he was concerned – more than with the imperfections

---

2   *Otto Lara Resende or Pretty, Yet A Slut* has a double denouement. A tragic one for the "evil" characters and a happy (although rather artificial) ending for the loving couple.

of the world – with ethical issues regarding human existence. Human beings for him were doomed to be eternally torn apart between an aspiration to transcendental purity and a fatal attraction towards the ultimate debasement. But becoming more local in his detailed and colourful representation of his beloved Rio de Janeiro the journalist-playwright achieved a much wider acceptance together with an immense prestige and became Brazil's most important and influential theatre voice.

WEDDING DRESS

A Tragedy in Three Acts (1943)

By Nelson Rodrigues
Translated by Daniel Hahn

Characters

ALAIDE

LUCIA

PEDRO

MADAME CLESSI *(A coquette from 1905.)*

WOMAN IN A VEIL

FIRST REPORTER *(Pimenta.)*

SECOND REPORTER

THIRD REPORTER

FOURTH REPORTER

MAN FROM THE PAST

WOMAN FROM THE PAST

SECOND MAN FROM THE PAST

THE CLEANER *(Who looks just like Pedro.)*

MAN IN THE COAT *(Who looks just like Pedro.)*

CLESSI'S BOYFRIEND AND KILLER *(Who looks
just like Pedro.)*

WOMAN READING *THE EVENING DAILY*[1]

GASTAO *(Alaíde and Lúcia's father.)*

DONA LIGIA *(Alaíde and Lúcia's mother.)*

DONA LAURA *(Alaíde and Lúcia's mother-in-law.)*

FIRST DOCTOR

SECOND DOCTOR

THIRD DOCTOR

FOURTH DOCTOR

---

1 There are actually two newspapers: the *Daily* and the *Evening*. We
have here chosen to maintain the list of characters as it appears in
the editions of Nelson Rodrigues's almost complete plays and his
complete plays, published in 1965 and 1971, respectively, which
were revised by the author.

Act 1

(The stage is divided into three sections, representing three "planes" on which the action takes place. First plane: Hallucination; second plane: Memory; third plane: Reality. There are four arches on the Memory Plane; two side staircases. Black.)

(A car horn. The noise of violent skidding. The sound of breaking glass. Silence. A siren. Silence.)

ALAIDE'S VOICE: *(Through a microphone.)* Clessi . . . Clessi . . .

> *(Lights comes up on the Hallucination Plane. Three tables, three women who are outrageously made-up, wearing long, gaudy dresses. Low necklines. Two of them are dancing to the sound of an invisible record player, with a certain suggestion of homoeroticism. ALAIDE, a young lady dressed with sober good taste, appears in the middle of the stage. A grey dress and red handbag.)*

ALAIDE: *(Nervous.)* I'd like to speak to Madame Clessi! Is she here?

> *(She's speaking to the first WOMAN, who is sitting at one of three tables, playing solitaire. The WOMAN doesn't answer.)*

ALAIDE: *(In distress.)* Is Madame Clessi there? Can you tell me? *(Seemingly naïve.)* You won't answer! *(Sweetly.)* Don't you want to answer?

> *(Silence from the other WOMAN.)*

ALAIDE: *(Hesitantly.)* Then I'm going to ask . . . *(Pause.)* her, over there.

> *(She runs across to the dancing women.)*

ALAIDE: Excuse me. Madame Clessi. Is she here?

> *(The SECOND WOMAN doesn't answer either.)*

3

ALAIDE: *(Still sweetly.)* Oh! You don't answer either?

(She hesitates. She looks at each of the women. A MAN walks past, a servant in this household, in a striped t-shirt. He's carrying a rubber broom and a floorcloth. This same gentleman appears all over the play, in different clothes and with different personalities. ALAIDE runs over to him.)

ALAIDE: *(Winningly.)* Could you possibly tell me whether Madame . . .

(The MAN speeds up and vanishes.)

ALAIDE: *(With childish disappointment.)* He ran away from me! *(In the middle of the stage, addressing all of the women, a little aggressively.)* That's all I want. I just want to know if Madame Clessi is here!

(The THIRD WOMAN stops dancing and walks over to change the record on the record player. She mimes choosing a record – which nobody can see – and putting it on the record player, which is likewise invisible. A samba comes on to coincide with this latter movement. The SECOND WOMAN approaches ALAIDE, slowly.)

FIRST WOMAN: *(Mysterious.)* Madame Clessi?

ALAIDE: *(Visibly glad.)* Oh, thank God! Yes, Madame Clessi.

SECOND WOMAN: *(A masculine voice.)* The woman who died?

ALAIDE: *(Astonished, looking around at all the women.)* She died?

SECOND WOMAN: *(To the others.)* She didn't?

FIRST WOMAN: *(The one playing solitaire.)* She did. Murdered.

THIRD WOMAN: *(Her voice slow and muffled.)* Madame Clessi died! *(Abrupt and violent.)* Now get out!

ALAIDE: *(Drawing back.)* It's a lie. Madame Clessi hasn't died. *(Looking around at the women.)* What are you all looking at me like that for? *(Changing her tone.)* It's no use, I'm not going to believe you! . . .

SECOND WOMAN: She did die. She was buried in white. I saw it.

ALAIDE: But there's no way she could have been buried in white! It's not possible.

FIRST WOMAN: She looked so beautiful. Like a bride.

ALAIDE: *(Over-excited.)* A bride? *(Getting carried away.)* A bride – her? *(With an intermittent, hysterical laugh.)* Madame Clessi, a bride? *(Her laughter rises in a crescendo, develops into a sobbing.)* Stop that music! Goodness!

(The music cuts out. Lights up on the Reality Plane. Four telephones on the stage, everyone speaking at the same time. Great excitement.)

PIMENTA: Is that the *Daily*?

JOURNALIST: It is.

PIMENTA: This is Pimenta.

LOCAL RIO REPORTER: Is that the *Evening*?

PIMENTA: A woman's just been hit by a car.

EVENING JOURNALIST: What's up?

PIMENTA: Here in Glória, near the clock.

LOCAL RIO REPORTER: A lady's been run over.

DAILY JOURNALIST: In Glória, near the clock?

EVENING JOURNALIST: Where?

LOCAL RIO REPORTER: In Glória.

PIMENTA: The emergency services have already taken her away.

5

LOCAL RIO REPORTER: Kind of not too far from the clock. She was crossing the street in front of the tram.

EVENING JOURNALIST: The clock.

PIMENTA: The driver fled the scene.

DAILY JOURNALIST: Right.

LOCAL RIO REPORTER: The driver scarpered.

PIMENTA: Attractive, well dressed.

EVENING JOURNALIST: Did she die?

LOCAL RIO REPORTER: Not yet. But she's going to.

(Blackout. Lights up on the Hallucination Plane.)

ALAIDE: *(Leading the FIRST WOMAN by the arm over to one corner.)* That man over there – who's he?

(She points at a MAN who has just entered and who is looking at ALAIDE.)

THIRD WOMAN: Who knows! *(Changing her tone.)* He comes here on Saturdays.

ALAIDE: *(Terrified.)* His face is just like my husband's! *(She draws back, pulling the other woman with her.)* It's just the same face!

THIRD WOMAN: You're married?

ALAIDE: *(Gripped by uncertainty.)* I don't know. *(Doubtful.)* I've forgotten everything. I have no memory – I'm a woman without a memory. *(Surprised.)* But everybody has a past; I must have one, too – for crying out loud!

THIRD WOMAN: *(In a low voice.)* What you are, is crazy.

ALAIDE: *(Surprised.)* I'm crazy? *(Sweetly.)* How delightful!

SECOND WOMAN: *(Approaching her.)* What are you two talking about over there?

THIRD WOMAN: *(To ALAIDE.)* Is that the ring?

ALAIDE: *(Showing her finger.)* It is.

THIRD WOMAN: *(Looking at it.)* A wedding ring.

SECOND WOMAN: My sister's is more slender.

THIRD WOMAN: *(Sceptical.)* Fat or slender, makes no difference. *(She takes a few dance steps.)*

ALAIDE: *(Excited.)* Oh! Oh, God! Madame Clessi! Madame Clessi! Madame Clessi!

(The solitary MAN approaches. Alaíde moves away with the THIRD WOMAN.)

ALAIDE: He's coming! Tell him I'm not from here! Quick! Explain it to him!

THIRD WOMAN: *(Dancing samba as she speaks.)* Really, girl, what do you expect me to say!

THE MAN: Are you new here?

ALAIDE: *(With a complete change of attitude.)* No, I'm not new. What, you hadn't seen me before?

THE MAN: *(Serious.)* No.

ALAIDE: *(Excited, but pleasant.)* How odd! I've been here – let me see – it's been about three months now . . .

THE MAN: I remember perfectly now.

ALAIDE: *(Sarcastic.)* You remember me?

THE MAN: Ah yes, I do, I remember you.

ALAIDE: *(Sharply.)* Cretin!

THE MAN: *(Astonished.)* What?

SECOND WOMAN: *(Pacifying.)* I'm sorry, doctor. She's crazy. *(To ALAIDE.)* Madame isn't going to like that!

THE MAN: Why do you put a crazy woman here?

ALAIDE: *(Excited.)* Yes, a cretin! *(Challenging.)* Say you've seen me here before. Say it, if you dare!

THE MAN: *(Formal.)* I'm going to lodge a complaint with madame. It's not right.

SECOND WOMAN: *(To ALAIDE, reproachful.)* You see? I'm telling you!

ALAIDE: Say it! Have you seen me before? I ought to slap you . . .

THE MAN: *(Offering up his cheek.)* I'd like to see that.

ALAIDE: *(With an unexpected transformation.)* . . . but I don't want to. *(She moves from violence to sweetness.)* I'm smiling – see? It was nothing! *(She smiles sweetly.)*

THE MAN: Shall we go sit over there?

ALAIDE: *(Still smiling.)* I'm smiling, though I don't want to. Not at all. I'll go with you – and I don't even know why. That's just the way I am. *(Sweetly.)* Shall we go, my love?

THE MAN: *(Suspicious.)* Why are you in a different dress to the others? *(The others are wearing red, yellow and pink satin.)*

ALAIDE: *(Sweetly.)* Did you notice how I said "my love"? I'll say that again a few times – "my love" – and other worse things, too! Madame Clessi's taking her time! *(Changing her tone.)* But has she really died?

THE MAN: *(With a laugh.)* Madame Clessi died – fat and old.

ALAIDE: *(Carried away.)* Liar! *(Aggressive.)* Fat and old my arse! Madame Clessi was beautiful! *(Dreamily.)* Beautiful!

THE MAN: *(Still laughing and sitting down on the floor.)* She had varicose veins! She groaned as she walked, dragging her slippers!

ALAIDE: *(Stubborn.)* A woman who's fat and old and covered in varicose veins isn't loved! And she was so loved! *(Ferocious.)* You liar! *(ALAIDE slaps the MAN, who stops laughing abruptly.)* *(The THIRD WOMAN sambas over, and caresses the MAN's head.)*

FIRST WOMAN: He's telling the truth. Madame had varicose veins.

ALAIDE: *(Dreamily.)* After her death, they put her in a wedding dress!

FIRST WOMAN: Such nonsense getting buried in a wedding dress!

ALAIDE: *(Distressed.)* Madame Clessi! Madame Clessi!

THE MAN: *(Getting up, serious.)* I'm going now. I've had my face slapped, and enough is enough.

ALAIDE: *(With nervous friendliness.)* Oh! You're leaving already! Do you want my phone number?

THE MAN: *(Ignoring her.)* I've never been so happy! I got slapped and I didn't react! *(With exaggerated formality.)* If you'll excuse me.

ALAIDE: *(Running after him.)* Don't leave like this. Stay a little longer!

THE MAN: Goodbye, madame. *(He exits.)*

(The THIRD WOMAN *dances with ostentatious sensuality. The* SERVANT *goes past, once again, with the broom, the floor cloth and bucket.)*

ALAIDE: *(Fed up.)* Oh, God – not him, too!

FIRST WOMAN: Who?

ALAIDE: That man there. He looks just like my fiancé. My fiancé's eyes, his nose – they're always after me. Everyone looks just like him.

(Two tables and three women disappear. Two WOMEN *take two chairs. The two tables are raised upward. A* WOMAN *appears on the stairs. In a corset, a feathered hat. An elegance that is antiquated, from 1905. Attractive. The light comes up onto her.)*

ALAIDE: *(With an impressed sigh.)* Ah!

MADAME CLESSI: You want to talk to me?

ALAIDE: *(Approaching, fascinated.)* Yes, I do. I did . . .

MADAME CLESSI: I'll put a record on. *(She heads over towards the invisible record player,* ALAIDE *following her.)*

ALAIDE: You didn't die, madame?

MADAME CLESSI: I'll put on a samba. This one isn't very good. But we'll have it anyway.

(A samba surges up.)

MADAME CLESSI: You see how fat I am, how old and full of varicose veins and money?

ALAIDE: I read your diary.

MADAME CLESSI: *(Sceptical.)* You did? Impossible. Where!

ALAIDE: *(Assertive.)* I really did. Let me die now if that's not the truth.

MADAME CLESSI: Tell me how it starts, then. *(CLESSI is talking with her back to ALAIDE.)*

ALAIDE: *(Remembering.)* Want to see? This is how it goes . . . *(Slight pause.)* "Yesterday Paulo and I went to Paineiras . . ." *(Happy.)* That's how it starts.

MADAME CLESSI: *(Evocative.)* It is. That's right.

ALAIDE: *(Troubled.)* I don't know how you could have written that! How you could have been so brave! I wouldn't have dared!

MADAME CLESSI: *(Relaxed.)* But that's not all. There are other things.

ALAIDE: *(Excited.) I know. There's a lot more. I became . . . (Anxious.)* My God! I don't know what's up with me. It's something – I don't know. Why am I here?

MADAME CLESSI: Are you asking me?

ALAIDE: *(Changeable.)* Something happened, in my life, that brought me here. When did I hear your name for the first time? *(Pause.)* I'm starting to remember.

(The previous CUSTOMER with an umbrella, hat and coat enters. He seems to be adrift.)

ALAIDE: That man! He looks just like my fiancé!

MADAME CLESSI: Forget about that man! How did you first hear my name!

ALAIDE: I remember now! *(Changing her tone.)* He's looking at me! *(Changing tone again.)* It was in a conversation I overheard when we moved. That same day, between my dad and mum. Let me remember how it went . . . I know! Dad was saying "And the whole business just ended up . . .'

(Lights out on the Hallucination Plane. Lights up on the Memory Plane. Alaíde's FATHER and MOTHER appear.)

FATHER: *(Continuing her sentence.)* "… in a wild orgy."

MOTHER: And this all happened here?

FATHER: Here – but so what?!

MOTHER: Alaíde and Lúcia living in Madame Clessi's house. Alaíde's room was the one she used to sleep in, I'm sure of it. Best room in the house!

FATHER: Let the woman go! She's dead already!

MOTHER: Murdered. Didn't the newspaper say?

FATHER: It did. Long before I'd even dreamed of meeting you for the first time. The crime got everyone talking. They printed a photo.

MOTHER: Up in the attic there are some pictures of her, a suitcase full of clothes. I'll get the whole lot burned.

FATHER: Do that.

(Lights out on the Memory Plane. Lights up on the Hallucination Plane.)

ALAIDE: *(Concerned.)* Mum said something about Lúcia. But who's Lúcia? I don't know. I don't remember.

MADAME CLESSI: So you all went to live there? *(Nostalgic.)* The house must be very old now.

ALAIDE: It was, but Pedro . . . *(Excited.)* I remember now: Pedro. He's my husband! I'm married. *(Changing her tone.)* But that Lúcia, oh God! *(Changing her tone.)* I think I'm under a death threat! *(Frightened.)* He's coming over here. *(She's talking about the solitary man who is approaching.)*

CLESSI: Leave it.

ALAIDE: *(Animated.)* Pedro had the whole thing re-done, and painted. It was good as new, that house. *(Changing her tone.)* Oh! I ran up to the attic, before my mum could have everything burned!

CLESSI: And?

ALAIDE: That's where I saw the suitcase – with the dresses, the suspenders, the pink corset. And I found the diary. *(Entranced.)* Oh, it was so beautiful!

CLESSI: *(Loud.)* You want to be like me, do you?

ALAIDE: *(Vehemently.)* Yes, I do. Yes.

CLESSI: *(Getting carried away, shouting.)* To have the reputation I had. The life. The money. And then get murdered?

ALAIDE: *(Abstract.)* I went to the library to read all the newspapers from that time. I read everything!

CLESSI: *(Transported.)* They printed so many stories about the crime! There was one reporter who wrote something quite beautiful!

ALAIDE: *(Moving away abruptly.)* Wait, I'm remembering something. Wait. Let me see! Mum telling Dad.

(Lights out on the Hallucination Plane. Lights up on the Memory Plane. FATHER and MOTHER.)

MOTHER: Oh, Lord! I actually thought I'd seen a body there – I've been so nervous. And these hallways! Madame Clessi's ghost could be wandering round here . . . and . . .

FATHER: Stop your ridiculous obsession with souls! The woman's dead, and buried!

MOTHER: Right . . .

(Lights out on the Memory Plane. Lights up on the Hallucination Plane.)

CLESSI: What is it?

ALAIDE: Nothing. Something I remembered, but it's not important. *(Loud.)* I do want to be like you, madame. To wear a corset. *(Sweetly.)* I think corsets are so elegant!

CLESSI: But what about your husband, your father, your mother and . . . Lúcia?

MAN: *(To ALAIDE.)* Murderer!

(Lights out on the Hallucination Plane. Lights up on the Reality Plane. An operating theatre.)

FIRST DOCTOR: Pulse?

SECOND DOCTOR: One-sixty.

FIRST DOCTOR: Rugine.

SECOND DOCTOR: Just look at the state of it!

FIRST DOCTOR: Try osteosynthesis!

THIRD DOCTOR: Look at this.

FIRST DOCTOR: Sutures in bronze.

(Pause.)

FIRST DOCTOR: The bone!

THIRD DOCTOR: We've got to go all the way now.

FIRST DOCTOR: If it doesn't work, it'll have to be an amputation.

(The noise of surgical implements.)

FIRST DOCTOR: Hurry!

(Lights out on the operating theatre. Lights up on the Hallucination Plane.)

MAN: *(To ALAIDE, sinister.)* Murderer!

CLESSI: *(Shocked.)* What?

MAN: *(Pointing.)* Her! Murderer!

CLESSI: *(To ALAIDE.)* You?

ALAIDE: *(Extremely nervous.)* Don't ask me anything. I don't know. I don't remember. *(A lament.)* If only I knew, at least, who Lúcia was!

MAN: *(Anguished.)* Is there nobody around? I want a beer!

ALAIDE: *(Panicking.)* He wants to arrest me! Don't let him!

CLESSI: *(Astonished.)* You . . . you're the killer? You?

ALAIDE: *(Desperate.)* Yes, I am. I am – there you go!

MAN: *(Complaining.)* For God's sake! There's nobody around to serve me. *(Anguished.)* No one! *(He looks at ALAIDE.)* Murderer!

ALAIDE: *(Pathetic.)* I'm the killer. I killed my fiancé.

MAN: She said "I killed my fiancé". It's true. I saw it.

ALAIDE: You did not! There was nobody there. There was no one around! And it wasn't my fiancé. It was my husband!

CLESSI: *(Flighty.)* Husband or fiancé, makes no difference.

ALAIDE: *(Hysterical, to the man.)* Now take me, arrest me – I'm a murderer.

MAN: I'm not arresting you. It's nothing to do with me! *(Anguished.)* There's really no one around to serve me? *(Melancholy.)* No one!

CLESSI: Excuse me, senhor, do you look like Alaíde's husband?

ALAIDE: He does. He's going to say he doesn't, but he does.

MAN: *(Serious.)* I do . . .

(The MAN moves away. The table disappears. The MAN carries off the chair.)

MAN: When you want to carry the body, I'll help. *(Exit.)*

ALAIDE: He's there. There.

CLESSI: *(Marvelling.)* He who?

ALAIDE: *(Quietly.)* My husband.

CLESSI: Alive?

ALAIDE: Dead.

(Alaíde leads CLESSI. She points at an invisible corpse.)

ALAIDE: See?

CLESSI: I see. But can you? . . .

ALAIDE: I can. Look at those feet. The way they're all . . . twisted. *(She mimes accordingly.)*

(A car horn, the noise of a skid. An ambulance. ALAIDE and CLESSI are motionless.)

CLESSI: But why'd you do that?

ALAIDE: *(Excited.)* He was good, he was very good. Good all the time and everywhere. I was disgusted by his goodness. *(She thinks, checks.)* I don't know, I was disgusted. I'm starting to remember everything, just the way it was. That day I said to him: "I wish I was Madame Clessi, Pedro. How about it?"

(Lights out on the Hallucination Plane. Lights up on the Memory Plane.)

PEDRO: You're still joking around about that.

ALAIDE: What do you mean, joking? I'm serious!

PEDRO: Don't make me angry, Alaíde!

ALAIDE: What would you do?

PEDRO: I don't know. *(Quickly.)* I'd kill you.

ALAIDE: *(Sceptical.)* Hardly. You'd never have the nerve!

PEDRO: *(Looking at her.)* Right. I wouldn't.

ALAIDE: Didn't I say? But how about if I ran away, if I did turn myself into a Madame Clessi?

PEDRO: I have no idea, Alaíde! No idea!

ALAIDE: *(Perverse.)* Oh, so that's your answer? Well you ought to know . . .

PEDRO: What? . . .

ALAIDE: *(Maliciously.)* Not telling! *(She hums the "Blue Danube" waltz.)*

PEDRO: *(Shouting.)* Tell me now. Tell me!

ALAIDE: *(Maliciously.)* Tell you what?

PEDRO: So why did you mention it!

(Blackout. Lights up on the Hallucination Plane. ALAIDE is there already.)

ALAIDE: *(In a sinister and unexpected tone.)* There's somebody who wants to kill me.

CLESSI: I know. What I want to know is how you killed Pedro. How did it happen?

ALAIDE: Interesting – I'm remembering a woman, but I can't see her face. She's wearing a veil. If only I could recognise her! . . .

CLESSI: Forget the woman in the veil. How did you kill him?

ALAIDE: *(Tormented.)* I can smell flowers, a lot of flowers. It's actually making me nauseous. *(Changing her tone.)* How did I kill him? I'm not even sure. My head's so tangled up! I'm starting to remember. I've just forgotten the reason. I was so crazy that day.

(Blackout.)

ALAIDE'S VOICE: *(From the darkness.)* Crazy with hatred. Maybe it was because of the woman in the veil. I still don't know who she is, but I know I should remember. Pedro was reading a book.

(Lights up on the Memory Plane. PEDRO is reading a book.)

ALAIDE: *(Provoking.)* Are you never going to finish that book?

PEDRO: Come on, sweetheart, I've only just started!

ALAIDE: *(With some annoyance.)* With those books of yours, you forget I even exist!

PEDRO: *(Appeasing.)* Don't be silly! *(He gets up, he wants to kiss her.)*

ALAIDE: *(Pushing him away.)* Stop that! No – I've told you, no!

(PEDRO insists.)

ALAIDE: *(Hurt.)* I don't want to! Go on, read your book! Go!

PEDRO: *(Kidding around.)* Shan't!

CLESSI'S VOICE: *(Microphone.)* Who's that woman in the veil?

PEDRO: Don't be like that, Alaíde!

ALAIDE: *(Vehemently.)* Don't be like what? You don't even notice I exist and now you come at me with all this pretence!

PEDRO: *(Affectionate.)* Stop behaving like a child! Come here! Just one little kiss!

ALAIDE: *(Intransigent.)* No! I won't. No! Stop it. *(Threatening.)* Pedro! *(She pushes him away.)* I'm going to read too!

PEDRO: What?

ALAIDE: *(Mysterious.)* You have no idea! A diary! The diary of a great woman!

(Blackout.)

ALAIDE: *(In the darkness, into the microphone.)* He didn't know why I'd changed. Changed so much. How could he have known it was a ghost – the ghost of Madame Clessi – who was driving me crazy?

CLESSI'S VOICE: *(Microphone.)* And not just my ghost. And what about the other two ghosts? The woman in the veil's, and Lúcia's?

ALAIDE'S VOICE: I'll see about that later. *(Changing her tone.)* If he only knew he was going to die! . . .

(Lights up on the Memory Plane. PEDRO is reading.)

ALAIDE: *(Provoking.)* Pedro. *(She says his name in a song-song fashion, emphasising each syllable: PE-DRO; there is silence from PEDRO.)* Oh! So that's how you're going to be – huh!

PEDRO: *(Without turning around.)* Who told you to do that?

ALAIDE: I didn't do anything!

PEDRO: You pushed me away!

ALAIDE: I did! I don't like you! I stopped liking you a long time ago! Ever since the day we got married . . .

PEDRO: *(Getting up and moving towards her.)* Silly little thing!

ALAIDE: I mean it!

(The two of them look at each other.)

ALAIDE: *(Turning her back.)* I like someone else.

PEDRO: *(Apprehensive.)* Alaíde! Listen to what I'm telling you!

ALAIDE: *(Pointed.)* That's right, I do. I like somebody else. Why're you looking at me like that?

PEDRO: *(With something like a threat.)* Don't say another word, Alaíde!

ALAIDE: At least you must be thinking, "If she liked somebody else, she wouldn't say." Am I right?

PEDRO: Am I really supposed to pay any attention to what you're saying?!

ALAIDE: *(Ironic.)* Oh – no! *(Getting worked up.)* You were wrong to say you would never kill your wife! . . . A husband who gives a life-time guarantee is finished.

PEDRO: *(Irritated.)* Don't provoke me, Alaíde.

ALAIDE: I'm going to leave you, run away from this place! I want to be free, darling! Free! So great!

PEDRO: *(Grabs her impulsively by the arm, twisting her wrist, harshly.)* Didn't I tell you not to provoke me? Didn't I?

ALAIDE: *(Desperate.)* Ow, ow! I was joking, Pedro – ow! Ow!

PEDRO: *(Darkly.)* Never joke like that again, never in your life! You hear?

ALAIDE: *(Wild with pain.)* For the love of God, Pedro – ow. No, Pedro! I swear . . .

(PEDRO lets go. ALAIDE hides her hurt arm behind her back.)

ALAIDE: *(Panting.)* You hurt me! I was only joking . . .

(PEDRO turns his back on her. With a trembling hand, he lights a cigarette. He turns back to ALAIDE.)

ALAIDE: *(Dropping her bracelet.)* Pedro, I've dropped my bracelet. Would you get it for me? Would you?

(PEDRO moves to pick it up. He bends down. With diabolical speed, ALAIDE grabs hold of an invisible iron, or something of the kind, and, possessed, starts hitting him. PEDRO falls in slow motion.)

(Blackout.)

ALAIDE'S VOICE: *(Microphone.)* I hit him back here, I think it was on the base of his skull. He jerked around before he died, like a dog that's been run over.

CLESSI'S VOICE: *(Microphone.)* But how'd you get hold of the iron?

ALAIDE'S VOICE: *(Microphone.)* Who knows! It just appeared! *(Changing her tone.)* Sometimes I think he might be alive. Oh God, I don't know anything! I never thought it would be so easy to kill a husband.

(Lights up on the Hallucination Plane. ALAIDE and CLESSI are sitting on the floor in the place where supposedly the invisible corpse is lying. The two of them are looking at it.)

CLESSI: Shall we carry him? *(Caressing the dead body, presumably his head.)* Poor man!

ALAIDE: A dead man's always good, because you can leave him somewhere and when you come back he's still in the same position.

CLESSI: Can you really smell flowers?

ALAIDE: *(Agitated.)* Shall we carry him? *(Changing her tone.)* But oh God, where to? There isn't anywhere!

CLESSI: We'll hide him under the bed.

ALAIDE: *(Desperate.)* But he can't stay there for the rest of his life. The cleaner – when he comes to tidy the room, he'll find him.

CLESSI: It's even worse here. The police might show up.

ALAIDE: *(Tortured.)* So let's get going, shall we?!

CLESSI: *(Explaining.)* Look, I'll pull one arm, and you pull the other.

ALAIDE: It's less hard work if we drag him.

(Each pulls the arm of an invisible corpse, dragging him along. It's a considerable effort. They are panting.)

ALAIDE: *(Panting.)* He's so heavy! *(The two women stop. They act as though they are laying the victim's body carefully down on the ground. CLESSI steps over the corpse.)*

CLESSI: *(Sitting down on the ground.)* Don't you feel sorry for him now?

ALAIDE: *(Excited.)* Sorry for him, me? Not at all! I don't feel anything for him but hatred. *(Changing her tone.)* Oh God, what was it he did again? *(Confused and distressed.)* What was it?

CLESSI: I don't know, child.

ALAIDE: *(Distressed.)* I can't seem to remember. But he did something, I'm sure of that. At the very least, I know the woman in the veil's something to do with it! . . .

CLESSI: And Lúcia, too.

(The MAN with the coat and umbrella enters. He approaches. The two women look at each other, without saying a word.)

MAN: *(Close to ALAIDE.)* Murderer!

(The characters freeze, totally silent. The noise of a skid. A shout. An ambulance.)

ALAIDE: Why are you looking at me like that? Haven't you ever seen me before? *(Changing her tone.)* Arrest me, then! Go on, what are you afraid of? *(To CLESSI.)* Did you hear a shout? Shall we go to the police?

MAN: Murderer!

(Blackout. Lights up on the Memory Plane. Four NEWSPAPER SELLERS, one in each of the arches.)

FIRST NEWSPAPER BOY: Take a look! The *Evening*! The *Daily*! The woman who killed her husband!

SECOND NEWSPAPER BOY: Get your copy here – it's the *Evening*! The *Daily*! Tragedy in Copacabana!

THIRD NEWSPAPER BOY: The *Evening*! *Daily*! What's-her-name died!

FOURTH NEWSPAPER BOY: *Daily*! Violent article! Read all about it!

FIRST NEWSPAPER BOY: Woman who swallowed a brick! Only in the *Daily*!

(The four young NEWSPAPER SELLERS repeat the above cries, all at the same time. Blackout. Lights up on the Hallucination Plane.)

ALAIDE: *(Distressed.)* Dad and Mum and everybody is going to read the newspapers. They're going to print my picture!

MAN: Why did you kill your husband?

CLESSI: *(Intervening.)* He was a very bad man! Oh, you can't imagine, senhor!

ALAIDE: *(Vehement.)* He wasn't bad at all! If anything, he was very good! *(Excited.)* Noble!

CLESSI: Silly girl! You've ruined everything!

ALAIDE: But I can't remember why I killed him – I can't remember.

MAN: I know.

ALAIDE: So tell me.

MAN: There's a woman involved. *(In confidence.)* A woman in a veil. She has a veil covering her face. You understand?

ALAIDE: *(Surprised.)* A woman in a veil? *(Lively.)* But you must know who she is, then, senhor – you have to know! Tell me!

MAN: I'm not saying. *(Taking his leave of them.)* If you'll excuse me. Goodbye! *(Before disappearing.)* Remember your wedding! *(Exit.)*

(Blackout. Lights up on the Reality Plane. At the editorial desk and house.)

WOMAN: *(Shouting.)* Who's this?

THE DAILY JOURNALIST: *(Eating a sandwich.)* It's the *Daily*.

WOMAN: *(Shrill.)* I'm one of your readers.

THE DAILY JOURNALIST: Very good.

WOMAN: I live in an apartment here in Glória! I saw a horrible accident!

THE DAILY JOURNALIST: A woman getting run over.

WOMAN: It was all the driver's fault. The way those cars come down this way, you wouldn't believe it! And just think about people who have children! . . .

THE DAILY JOURNALIST: Of course!

WOMAN: By the time she'd seen him, it was already too late! The *Daily* should publish a complaint about the terrible way people use cars!

THE DAILY JOURNALIST: We'll do that! *(He hangs up.)*

WOMAN: *(Still speaking.)* Thank you – really!

(Blackout. Lights up on the Hallucination Plane. ALAIDE and CLESSI in the same place. But lying there on the floor, there really is a man – the usual one. Different clothes.)

ALAIDE: *(Troubled.)* What was it about my wedding? He said, "Remember your wedding".

(The sound of the Wedding March. ALAIDE gets up. She makes a movement as if picking up the train of her wedding dress. She straightens it up.)

CLESSI: Beautiful dress! Whose idea was it?

ALAIDE: *(Transported.)* I saw it in a movie. Only the floral crown is different. Everything else is just like it was on the tape.

(Alaíde walks over to the Memory Plane, where the lights come up.)

PEDRO: *(Getting to his feet naturally and also moving into the Memory Plane.) (He pulls out his pocket watch.)* It's nearly time. We have to go quickly; there's another wedding after ours.

ALAIDE: You mean another wedding's going to get to use our decorations?

PEDRO: Forget about it. It doesn't matter.

ALAIDE: Oh! Pedro!

PEDRO: What is it?

ALAIDE: *(Unexpected.)* I forgot it's bad luck for the groom to see the bride beforehand. It's really bad! *(She turns around.)*

PEDRO: That's just childish! There's no point now! I've already seen you!

ALAIDE: *(Entreating.)* Go, Pedro, just go!

(Enter Alaíde's MOTHER.)

ALAIDE: *(Like a sleepwalker.)* Oh, Mum, what about the bouquet?

CLESSI: Can't be your mum.

(The MOTHER reverses out.)

CLESSI: She only showed up later! And are you really in your bedroom without anybody else around, Alaíde? A bride always has people near her. What? You might not remember, but there has to have been somebody beside your mother! Remember.

(The "Wedding March". ALAIDE mimes touching up her make-up. Alaíde's FATHER and MOTHER enter, dressed to go out.)

FATHER: All set?

ALAIDE: Almost. Are they really going to play Gounod's "Ave Maria", Dad?

FATHER: They are. I've already told them at the church.

MOTHER: Here's dona Laura.

ALAIDE: *(Turning.)* Oh! Dona Laura.

D. LAURA: How are you?

(They kiss.)

ALAIDE: *(Cheerful, showing herself off.)* So how's your daughter-in-law looking? Very ugly?

D. LAURA: Beautiful. Delightful!

ALAIDE: Look, Dad . . . – sorry, dona Laura.

D. LAURA: Don't mention it, my dear.

ALAIDE: *(To her FATHER.)* Either Gounod's "Ave Maria", or if not, then Schubert's. I insist. Nothing else will do.

FATHER: I know.

D. LAURA: Schubert's or Gounod's, either one is very pretty. Oh!

(D. LAURA seems to have noticed somebody she hadn't seen before. She turns to this invisible person and kisses her, presumably on the forehead.)

D. LAURA: I'm sorry, I hadn't seen you.

(A pause for a reply nobody hears.)

D. LAURA: *(All smiles.)* When's yours?

(Pause for another reply.)

D. LAURA: *(Wicked.)* What nonsense! Come now, I don't believe you! So young, so full of life.

FATHER: *(To ALAIDE, who is ready.)* Well, let's go, then!

(D. LAURA makes some gesture towards the invisible person and joins ALAIDE.)

D. LAURA: Careful with the train!

(D. LAURA picks up the imaginary train and hands it to ALAIDE.)

ALAIDE: *(Taking one last look.)* I don't need anything else?

MOTHER: *(Also looking.)* Nothing. I don't think so.

FATHER: *(Impatient.)* It's already late. Let's go down.

(The "Wedding March". Blackout.)

END OF ACT 1

Act 2

(The second act opens to black. ALAIDE's and CLESSI's voices in the microphone.)

CLESSI: There's no way there wasn't anybody else.

ALAIDE: *(Getting impatient with her own memory.)* But I can't remember, Clessi. My memory's so bad! . . .

CLESSI: Look, Alaíde. Before your mother came in, when you asked for the bouquet, was somebody there? Apart from Pedro?

ALAIDE: *(Disoriented.)* Before my mum came in?

CLESSI: Yes. There must have been someone else. I've already told you – a bride is never left all alone like that when she's getting dressed!

ALAIDE: *(As though straining her memory.)* Before mum came in . . . I'm just thinking . . . Let me see . . .

(Lights up on the Memory Plane. ALAIDE, who really is dressed as a bride, is sitting on a stool. The imaginary mirror has now transformed into a real mirror, a large one, almost the size of a person. The floral crown is not yet on. ALAIDE is alone.)

CLESSI: *(Microphone.)* Oh! Want to see something? Who was it dona Laura kissed on the forehead, after she talked to you?

(At the mirror, ALAIDE is touching up her make-up, tidying her hair, moving closer to the mirror and away again etc.)

CLESSI: *(Microphone.)* Oh – another thing! Who was it that dressed you? Was it your mother? No? Well, exactly, Alaíde!

(A dim half-light. A WOMAN enters, almost by magic. She has a veil covering her face. Lights revert to normal.)

CLESSI: *(Microphone.)* Didn't I say there had to be more people? Look! *(Changing her tone.)* The woman in the veil!

ALAIDE: *(Nervous as befits a bride.)* Did you find it?

WOMAN IN THE VEIL: No. I went through everything!

ALAIDE: *(Tortured.)* But I left the white thread in your room! Did you check in the chest of drawers?

WOMAN IN THE VEIL: *(Reticent.)* I did. I couldn't find anything.

ALAIDE: In the bottom drawer?

WOMAN IN THE VEIL: There, too.

ALAIDE: *(Impatient, touching up a detail of her make-up.)* You're being so odd!

(The WOMAN IN THE VEIL tries to straighten up something on ALAIDE's shoulder.)

ALAIDE: Would you call Mum a moment?

(Silence.)

ALAIDE: *(Turning around.)* Would you call her?

WOMAN IN THE VEIL: *(Turning her back.)* No. I'm not calling anybody. *(Aggressive.)* Go get her yourself!

ALAIDE: *(Hurt, she slowly applies some blusher; she turns again to the WOMAN IN THE VEIL.)* There's something wrong with you!

WOMAN IN THE VEIL: *(Her back turned.)* Me? Nothing wrong with me. Nothing. *(Turning to face ALAIDE, quick and harsh.)*

You know perfectly well! *(Violently.)* You know and you still ask!

ALAIDE: *(Getting to her feet and picking up her train.)* That's enough. I'll go call her myself.

(The woman in the veil, with a decisiveness that is quick and strange, positions herself in front of ALAIDE.)

ALAIDE: *(Amazed.)* What's this? *(Changing her tone.)* I don't think you're quite right in the head!

WOMAN IN THE VEIL: *(Forceful.)* Sit there. *(The two women face up to one another.)* You're not calling anyone!

(Alaíde sits down mechanically on the stool, looking in amazement at the WOMAN IN THE VEIL; the WOMAN seems quite excited.)

ALAIDE: *(Naïve.)* But I need some white thread!

WOMAN IN THE VEIL: First we're going to talk! *(Sarcastic.)* White thread!

ALAIDE: You really want to talk now! Now?

WOMAN IN THE VEIL: *(Getting worked up.)* Why not! Why shouldn't it be now? What of it? *(Changing her tone.)* I've never told anyone, I've never said anything, but now you need to hear me!

ALAIDE: *(Shouting.)* People can hear you! Talk quietly.

WOMAN IN THE VEIL: *(Getting worked up.)* So you think you could steal my boyfriend and just leave it at that?

ALAIDE: *(Somewhere between entreating and intimate.)* You're not going to do anything.

WOMAN IN THE VEIL: *(Contemptuous.)* Oh, you're afraid! *(Ironic.)* Of course you are. Even at the church door it's still not too late for a wedding to be called off.

ALAIDE: *(Braver now.)* Not mine.

WOMAN IN THE VEIL: *(Coming closer.)* Not yours – poor thing! *(Changing her tone.)* Yes, yours! Just don't push me, Alaíde, don't you push me.

ALAIDE: *(Standing up.)* Then don't speak to me in that tone!

WOMAN IN THE VEIL: *(Aggressive.)* I will, I will – and if you're in any doubt, I'll make a scene right now. Right here – want to see?

(Silence from ALAIDE.)

ALAIDE: *(Quietly.)* What do you know?

WOMAN IN THE VEIL: If I said – Alaíde – I'd be surprised, very surprised, if this wedding went ahead.

(Alaíde and the WOMAN IN THE VEIL freeze. Then blackout.)

CLESSI: *(Microphone.)* You stopped when the woman in the veil said "I'd be surprised . . ."

(The lights come up. Only ALAIDE and the WOMAN IN THE VEIL, in the same position as the previous scene.)

CLESSI: *(Microphone, continuing.)* . . . very surprised, if this wedding went ahead!"

ALAIDE: But what did I do to you? Tell me! To make you like this?

WOMAN IN THE VEIL: *(Getting worked up.)* What you did? You hypocrite!

ALAIDE: So tell me what it was!

WOMAN IN THE VEIL: You mean you didn't know I was in a relationship with Pedro?

ALAIDE: *(Increasingly indignant.)* That, "a relationship"? A flirtation, just a meaningless flirtation!

WOMAN IN THE VEIL: *(Outraged.)* You're telling me that was a flirtation. Think you can convince me of that?

ALAIDE: *(Stubborn.)* It was.

WOMAN IN THE VEIL: *(Violent.)* And that time he kissed me in the garden, that was just a flirtation too?

ALAIDE: I don't know anything about any kiss! What kiss?

WOMAN IN THE VEIL: See what you're like? You saw everything! You came out onto the terrace then you went straight back in again. But you saw it!

ALAIDE: *(Desperate.)* I won't allow you to come here reminding me of these things! He's my fiancé!

WOMAN IN THE VEIL: *(Perverse.)* Did you see it, or didn't you?

ALAIDE: No!

WOMAN IN THE VEIL: You did!

ALAIDE: *(Pathetic.)* Why didn't you object earlier? Why didn't you say something at the time?

WOMAN IN THE VEIL: Because I didn't want to. I wanted to see how far you'd go. *(Changing her tone.)* I waited till this moment.

(There is a knock on the door.)

ALAIDE: *(Panicking.)* It's Mum!

MOTHER: *(From the door.)* Alaíde!

WOMAN IN THE VEIL: *(Quiet and determined.)* Let me get this.

MOTHER: Will one of you open up?

WOMAN IN THE VEIL: *(Loudly.)* Coming! *(To ALAIDE, quietly.)* You stay there. Remember what I said: I'll make a scene!

(The WOMAN IN THE VEIL heads towards what is presumably a door.)

WOMAN IN THE VEIL: *(Naturally.)* We'll call for you soon. Not long now.

MOTHER: What are you doing in there?

WOMAN IN THE VEIL: Alaíde's nearly ready.

MOTHER: Open up. I want to see.

WOMAN IN THE VEIL: *(Playfully uncompromising.)* No. Only when everything's done.

MOTHER: You girls!

WOMAN IN THE VEIL: In five minutes – alright?

MOTHER: Get a move on, then.

(The WOMAN IN THE VEIL comes back to ALAIDE.)

ALAIDE: *(Warning.)* Mum must be suspicious.

WOMAN IN THE VEIL: Doesn't matter. Let her be suspicious! *(Changing her tone.)* If you weren't the monster you are.

ALAIDE: *(Quickly.)* And you're so much better, are you?

WOMAN IN THE VEIL: *(Pathetic.)* At least I've never married your boyfriends! I've never done what you did to me: take away the only man I've ever loved! *(With all the dramatic dignity she can muster.)* The only one!

ALAIDE: That's nothing to do with me! He chose me over you – simple as that!

WOMAN IN THE VEIL: What do you mean, chose you? You took advantage of the month I was laid up in bed, you chased after him, threw yourself at him. It's shameful!

ALAIDE: *(Sarcastic.)* So why didn't you do the same thing?

WOMAN IN THE VEIL: I was sick!

ALAIDE: Why didn't you do it afterwards? Is it my fault you don't know how to win a man . . . or win one back? That you're not woman enough – is it?

WOMAN IN THE VEIL: *(Aggressive.)* I've never had your shamelessness.

ALAIDE: *(Quickly.)* And who cares about being shameless when you love someone?

WOMAN IN THE VEIL: *(Fed up.)* Well, there's no point arguing about all that.

ALAIDE: *(Aggressive.)* There really isn't!

WOMAN IN THE VEIL: But there's just one thing I want you to know. Your whole life you've stolen all my boyfriends away from me, one by one.

ALAIDE: *(Ironic.)* Such a persecution complex!

CLESSI: *(Microphone.)* So, you stole the woman in the veil's boyfriends? *(A pause for a reply from ALAIDE that nobody hears.)*

CLESSI: *(Microphone.)* And you also don't remember anything! Try to get a look at her without her veil. She can't be a woman without a face. There has to be a face under that veil.

(A pause for another unheard reply.)

CLESSI: *(Microphone.)* You'll remember soon enough, Alaíde.

(Blackout. Lights up on the Reality Plane. An operating theatre.)

FIRST DOCTOR: Pulse?

SECOND DOCTOR: A hundred and sixty.

FIRST DOCTOR: *(A request.)* Callipers.

SECOND DOCTOR: Nice body.

FIRST DOCTOR: Curette.

THIRD DOCTOR: She's married – look at the ring.

(The noise of surgical implements.)

FIRST DOCTOR: This is where the amputation happens.

THIRD DOCTOR: It'd take a miracle.

FIRST DOCTOR: Saw.

(The noise of surgical implements.)

(Alaíde's memory in total disintegration. Images from the past and present jumble together and are superimposed. Recollections no longer follow any chronological sequence. Lights out on the Memory Plane. Lights up on the side stairs. Two men have appeared at the top of the steps, each holding two votive candles; they come down, slowly. The light follows them. One of them is fat, with a substantial belly, somewhat advanced in years; he has huge black whiskers, a top hat; the other is a teenager, lyrical and thin. Both are in black, dressed as if in 1905. They position the four candles; they light them. After which they greet each other and go to kneel down beside an invisible corpse. The make the sign of the cross, moving in perfect unison. The two gentlemen are in the Hallucination Plane.)

(Lights up on the Memory Plane. ALAIDE and the WOMAN IN THE VEIL.)

36

WOMAN IN THE VEIL: *(Continuing what she was saying.)* But with Pedro, you made a mistake. *(A vertical light on each group.)*

ALAIDE: *(Getting to her feet and crossing between the candles, with an air of debauchery; the vertical light follows her.)* I'm going to marry him one hour from now, my dear.

WOMAN IN THE VEIL: That's just why I'm saying you've made a mistake. Because you're getting married!

ALAIDE: *(Ironic.)* Oh, really? I had no idea!

WOMAN IN THE VEIL: You stole my boyfriends. But I'm going to steal your husband. *(Pointedly.)* That's all!

ALAIDE: *(With restrained rage.)* Keep on hoping!

(ALAIDE turns to the mirror and the WOMAN IN THE VEIL stands behind her.)

WOMAN IN THE VEIL: You'll see. *(Changing her tone.)* It's not stealing exactly.

ALAIDE: *(Ironic.)* Things are getting better, then.

WOMAN IN THE VEIL: You might die, my dear. Doesn't everybody die?

ALAIDE: Are you saying you might kill me?

WOMAN IN THE VEIL: *(More seriously now.)* Who knows? *(Changing her tone.)* *(Quietly.)* You think I couldn't kill you?

(Lights up on the Hallucination Plane where a woman is already standing – corseted, wearing a dress from 1905 – who makes the sign of the cross over the invisible coffin. This lady, having greeted the two gentlemen present takes a little handkerchief out of her bag and cries silently. Lights up on the Memory Plane.)

ALAIDE: *(Assertive.)* You wouldn't have the nerve. No chance!

WOMAN IN THE VEIL: Maybe I wouldn't have the nerve to kill. But I do for this!

(She slaps ALAIDE. ALAIDE recoils, her hand on her cheek. Lights up on CLESSI and the BOYFRIEND. CLESSI on a récamier. The boyfriend, in a khaki school uniform. The lad looks just like Pedro. The Memory Plane.)

CLESSI: *(Affectionate and maternal.)* I like you because you're a child! Such a child!

THE GUY: *(Begging.)* Are you going? Shall we go to the picnic tomorrow?

CLESSI: *(Careless.)* Where is it?

THE GUY: It's on Paquetá. Everybody's going, on the ten o'clock boat . . .

CLESSI: No.

THE GUY: *(Pleading.)* It's Sunday tomorrow!

CLESSI: *(Ignoring him.)* So fair! And seventeen years old! Women should only ever love boys who are seventeen years old!

THE GUY: *(Still entreating.)* Don't change the subject! Are you going? *(Angry.)* I'm not going to ask again!

CLESSI: *(Sweetly.)* No, not tomorrow. I have an engagement.

THE GUY: *(Wheedling.)* And what about that thing I said?

CLESSI: I don't remember! What?

THE GUY: *(Wheedling.)* Do you want to die with me? Make a pact like those two lovers in Tijuca?

CLESSI: *(Still tender.)* Lovely! Look how fine his hair is!

(Lights up on ALAIDE and the WOMAN IN THE VEIL.)

ALAIDE: *(Superior.)* Say whatever you like. *(Provoking.)* I'm the one who's getting married, aren't I? So it doesn't matter.

WOMAN IN THE VEIL: Another thing: you believe he's only yours, don't you?

(A superior silence from ALAIDE.)

WOMAN IN THE VEIL: You really shouldn't believe that, you know! You know that boyfriend I've got myself, you know who he is? I've come to talk to you about him so many times! To tell you, oh God, about every little detail! *(Ironic.)* Well, guess what: that boyfriend was your fiancé. He was your fiancé!

ALAIDE: *(Sharply.)* That's a lie! I don't believe you!

WOMAN IN THE VEIL: *(Superior.)* If you say so. So it's a lie!

ALAIDE: *(Assertive.)* He would never, ever give in to you like that!

WOMAN IN THE VEIL: *(Irritated.)* But that's not the important thing.

ALAIDE: *(Aggressively.)* Liar!

WOMAN IN THE VEIL: The important thing is that you're going to die. I don't know how, but you are, and then I . . . I'm going to marry your widower. And that's that. Totally natural, a woman marrying a widower.

(ALAIDE sits down. She sinks her face into her hands. Lights up on the Hallucination Plane.)

BEARDED MAN: *(With a sweeping gesture, orating with a full, deep voice.)* She's unrecognisable.

WOMAN FROM THE PAST: And a blade to the face, too!

BEARDED MAN: *(Describing the blow.)* All the way across here!

ROMANTIC BOY: *(Lyrical.)* She was so beautiful – you wouldn't know it!

(The woman approaches the invisible coffin and mimes the lifting of a sheet that's covering the face of an invisible corpse. Lights up on ALAIDE and the WOMAN IN THE VEIL.)

ALAIDE: *(Threatening.)* I'm going to tell Pedro what you said!

WOMAN IN THE VEIL: If you do, just wait and see what a scene I'll make! Just try it!

(A knock on the door.)

WOMAN IN THE VEIL: Who is it?

MOTHER: It's me!

WOMAN IN THE VEIL: Nearly there now.

MOTHER: You must be joking!

WOMAN IN THE VEIL: *(Begging cynically.)* Just a tiny bit longer. Then we will call you. Alright?

(Lights up on the Hallucination Plane. Another conversation beside the fantasy coffin, while the WOMAN IN THE VEIL walks back to ALAIDE.)

WOMAN FROM THE PAST: What time is it?

BEARDED MAN: *(Consulting his pocket watch.)* Three in the morning.

ROMANTIC BOY: *(Pathetic.)* I thought it was later.

BEARDED MAN: *(Laboriously pulling a huge handkerchief out of the back pocket of his trousers; he blows his nose noisily.)* All because she didn't want to go on a picnic.

WOMAN FROM THE PAST: Apparently, they'd agreed to die together. And when the time came, she didn't want to. So then he . . .

BEARDED MAN: I heard it was the thing with the picnic.

WOMAN FROM THE PAST: *(Philosophical.)* People say so many things! You can never tell!

(Lights up on the Memory Plane. The WOMAN IN THE VEIL approaches ALAIDE, having picked up the floral crown.)

WOMAN IN THE VEIL: *(Coldly.)* What about the crown?

ALAIDE: *(Drawing away.)* Leave it, I'll put it on myself.

WOMAN IN THE VEIL: I'll do it. I've already done everything else. Might as well do this, too.

ALAIDE: *(Looking at her bitterly.)* That's why you asked Mum if you could dress me.

WOMAN IN THE VEIL: *(Violently.)* That's why.

ALAIDE: *(Tearful.)* And I didn't suspect a thing, I'm such a fool! And Mum let you!

(The WOMAN IN THE VEIL wants to put on the crown.)

ALAIDE: *(As if trying to escape some kind of repulsive contact.)* And don't you touch me!

(A knock on the door.)

WOMAN IN THE VEIL: *(Exasperated.)* Oh, for God's sake! Are you serious?

ALAIDE: *(Darkly.)* So you wish me dead!

PEDRO: *(From the door.)* Alaíde!

WOMAN IN THE VEIL: *(Changing her tone.)* Pedro!

ALAIDE: *(Changing her tone.)* We'll be right there, Pedro! *(To the WOMAN IN THE VEIL, harsh.)* Go open it.

WOMAN IN THE VEIL: *(Quietly.)* Don't say a word about what I said. Or else you know what'll happen!

(The two women exchange a quick glance. The WOMAN IN THE VEIL goes to open the door. ALAIDE puts on the crown.)

PEDRO: *(Cheerful.)* Dona Lígia is outraged. She says you two have locked yourselves in here and you won't let anybody else in.

CLESSI: *(Microphone.)* What on earth have they done to you!

ALAIDE: *(Naturally.)* My mum's talking nonsense!

(The WOMAN IN THE VEIL is keeping quiet, keeping her distance.)

PEDRO: *(Leaning down.)* Just one little kiss!

ALAIDE: *(Still looking in the mirror.)* Are you offering one or asking for one?

PEDRO: Asking for one.

ALAIDE: *(Primly.)* You'd only ruin my make-up. And also . . . *(ALAIDE points at the WOMAN IN THE VEIL.)*

PEDRO: *(Cynical.)* She's pretending she can't see us!

WOMAN IN THE VEIL: Actually, I think I'll just leave!

ALAIDE: *(Dripping with irony.)* She's so totally scrupulous, Pedro! You have no idea!

CLESSI: *(Microphone.)* If that were me, I'd break off the wedding!

WOMAN IN THE VEIL: *(Calculatedly slow.)* You remember what I said to you, Alaíde?

PEDRO: *(Curious.)* What was that?

ALAIDE: Nothing. Nothing important.

PEDRO: *(Perverse, to the WOMAN IN THE VEIL.)* Do you have a boyfriend?

WOMAN IN THE VEIL: *(Coldly.)* Why?

PEDRO: *(Cynical.)* No reason. You seem really odd!

WOMAN IN THE VEIL: I do. *(Perverse.)* I did. He's marrying someone else.

PEDRO: So the guy's a proper villain!

WOMAN IN THE VEIL: He is.

ALAIDE: *(Sarcastic.)* No matter. She still likes him anyway.

WOMAN IN THE VEIL: That's true, I do. It's none of anybody's business!

PEDRO: *(Already on his way out.)* Do let dona Lígia come in before she starts crying.

ALAIDE: *(Brusque.)* My mum's so silly. She still asks permission to come into her own daughter's bedroom! She just stands outside, begging!

PEDRO: It's nearly time. We have to go quickly; there's another wedding after ours.

ALAIDE: *(Complaining.)* You mean another wedding's going to get to use our decorations?

PEDRO: *(Careless.)* Forget about it. It doesn't matter.

ALAIDE: *(Complaining.)* Oh! Pedro!

PEDRO: What is it?

ALAIDE: *(Turning her back prudishly.)* I forgot it's bad luck for the groom to see the bride beforehand. It's really bad!

PEDRO: *(Good-humoured.)* That's just being childish! There's no point now! I've already seen you!

ALAIDE: *(Entreating.)* Go, Pedro, just go!

(They freeze, and ALAIDE and the WOMAN IN THE VEIL fall silent.)

CLESSI: *(Microphone.)* Fine. I know the rest, Alaíde. *(Changing her tone.)* What?

(She seems to hear an aside that nobody else can hear.)

CLESSI: *(Microphone.)* Oh, you skipped something else? What was it?

WOMAN IN THE VEIL: We're three cynics – me, you and him. But you're the worst, because you think you can stay innocent all the way to the end.

ALAIDE: *(With focused anger.)* I should just keep my mouth shut!

WOMAN IN THE VEIL: And him so natural, asking "Do you have a boyfriend?" What must he think of us, for God's sake!

ALAIDE: *(Disgusted.)* I know exactly what he thinks!

WOMAN IN THE VEIL: *(Vehement.)* That I'm perverted! That you're an idiot! *(Sarcastic.)* In any case, I'd much rather be a perverted than an idiot!

ALAIDE: *(Outraged.)* You think that's better! You even admit it!

WOMAN IN THE VEIL: *(Sarcastic.)* Of course! Isn't it? "Do let dona Lígia come in . . ." What a scoundrel he is, that fiancé you've got yourself.

ALAIDE: *(Ironic.)* But you still like him!

WOMAN IN THE VEIL: I do like him. I love him. But I like him even knowing that he is, and even *because* he is. But you . . . Oh God, I bet you don't even believe any of what I've told you.

ALAIDE: *(Enraged.)* And I don't!

(Blackout for the new characters to enter the Memory Plane.)

CLESSI: *(Microphone.)* Ah, so the woman dona Laura kissed on the forehead – the one you couldn't remember who it was – that was the woman in the veil? What was it the two of them said to each other at that moment, Alaíde?

(Lights up on the Memory Plane. The scene in ALAIDE's bedroom, at the moment when DONA LAURA, already all dressed up, is talking to another person, who is the WOMAN IN THE VEIL. Alaíde's FATHER and MOTHER are also present, also dressed for the ceremony.)

D. LAURA: *(To the WOMAN IN THE VEIL, who is drawn back slightly from the others.)* I'm sorry, I hadn't seen you.

WOMAN IN THE VEIL: Don't worry about it.

(D. LAURA kisses her on the forehead.)

D. LAURA: *(All smiles.)* When's yours?

WOMAN IN THE VEIL: It'll be a while yet! *(Changing her tone.)* *(With some bitterness.)* Never!

D. LAURA: *(Wicked.)* What nonsense! Come now, I don't believe you! So young, so full of life.

FATHER: *(To ALAIDE, who is ready.)* So let's go!

(The sound of the "Wedding March". D. LAURA makes some gesture towards the WOMAN IN THE VEIL and joins ALAIDE.)

D. LAURA: *(Solicitously.)* Careful with the train! *(She picks up the train, which she hands to ALAIDE.)*

ALAIDE: *(Taking one last look.)* I don't need anything else? *(Everybody looks, positioned as they were at the end of the first act.)*

MOTHER: *(Looking around her.)* Nothing. I don't think so.

FATHER: *(Impatient.)* It's already late! Let's go down!

(To the sound of the "Wedding March", the characters exit. The WOMAN IN THE VEIL remains, looking pathetic.)

(Dim lighting. The two men at the wake whisper to each other and move away slightly to have a cigarette. They light a cigarette on one of the candles and smoke.)

CLESSI: *(Microphone.)* So the woman in the veil didn't go?

ALAIDE: *(Ditto.)* No.

CLESSI: *(Ditto.)* Why not?

ALAIDE: *(Ditto.)* She didn't want to. Absolutely not. I don't know who it was told me later that while we were in the hall waiting to leave, my mum went back to fetch the woman in the veil.

(Normal lights up on the Memory Plane. Enter DONA LIGIA, hurrying. The woman in the veil is where we left her.)

MOTHER: Are you still there? Everyone's already downstairs!

WOMAN IN THE VEIL: I'm not going. I'm staying!

MOTHER: *(Surprised.)* What's up with you?

WOMAN IN THE VEIL: Nothing.

MOTHER: *(Suspicious.)* Did you two argue?

WOMAN IN THE VEIL: *(Impatient.)* I don't know, I don't know.

MOTHER: Let's go. Don't be like that.

WOMAN IN THE VEIL: I'm not going. It's no use. You're wasting your time.

MOTHER: *(Looking at her, shocked.)* But why aren't you going?

WOMAN IN THE VEIL: *(With focused anger.)* Because I'm not, for crying out loud! *(Changing her tone.)* *(Facing her.)* No way I'm going to the wedding of that woman!

MOTHER: *(Hurt.)* Oh! That's how you refer to her now, "*that woman*"?

WOMAN IN THE VEIL: *(Sarcastic.)* No other word for her!

MOTHER: What brought this on, so suddenly! And you such good friends!

WOMAN IN THE VEIL: *(Bitterly.)* Friends, us? God! How could anyone be so blind! *(Changing her tone.)* The very idea I'd go to that wedding, when I'm the one who should be the bride!

MOTHER: *(Panicking.)* Are you crazy?

WOMAN IN THE VEIL: *(Violent.)* Oh yes, senhora – yes, I am.

MOTHER: *(Taken aback.)* You love Pedro! *(Pause; the two women look at each other.)* So that's it?

WOMAN IN THE VEIL: *(Sarcastic.)* What did you think it was?

(Lights up on the Hallucination Plane. The woman from the past, standing beside the bier, raises the sheet to look at the invisible dead girl's face. She mimes a gesture of piety. ALAIDE and CLESSI appear at the top of one of the side staircases, sitting on a step. Shadows over the wake.)

CLESSI: You're starting to seem crazy!

ALAIDE: *(Next to Clessi.)* Me?

CLESSI: You're getting things confused! A wedding with a funeral! . . . Old fashions with new ones! Nobody wears a hat with feathers like that anymore, or that collar!

ALAIDE: *(Anguished.)* Everything's so jumbled up in my memory! I muddle things up, things that happened with things that didn't. The past with the present. *(A lament.)* It's all mixed up!

CLESSI: *(Impatient.)* You talk so much about that woman who died! So who is she, then?

ALAIDE: *(Tortured.)* That's the thing, I can't remember. I can't do it! All I can remember is that sitting vigil there was a lady with a feathered hat and a corset, and two men with moustaches, slicked-down hair and high collars.

CLESSI: That's very old-fashioned. So this must have been a long time ago.

ALAIDE: *(Struggling with her memory.)* I'm trying to see if I can remember anything else . . .

(The bearded man speaks, now, sitting on the floor with the woman from the past, really enraptured.)

BEARDED MAN: Clessi would never have imagined she'd be dead today!

CLESSI: *(At the top of the steps, standing up and coming down.)* Clessi . . . *(Shocked and afraid.)* Clessi! . . .

ALAIDE: *(Triumphantly, also standing up and coming down.)* I remember now! I remember all of it, every little bit! The name! It's you – the dead woman is you!

(ALAIDE and CLESSI walk over to the bier.)

CLESSI: *(Pointing at her own invisible corpse.)* *(Melancholy.)* You had no way of remembering that! And I was right here!

ALAIDE: *(Excited.)* Yes, that was it! I was so confused! But I know now. I read it all at the National Library. I saw all the news reports about the crime. The reporter described it all, even the people who sitting vigil in the small hours of the morning . . .

CLESSI: *(Melancholy.)* Were there a lot of people at my funeral?

ALAIDE: *(Getting carried away.)* Oh, lots! People started arriving in the morning . . .

CLESSI: *(Vain.)* How many, more or less?

(The BEARDED MAN comes up to the ROMANTIC BOY.)

BEARDED MAN: No one here but us?

ROMANTIC BOY: Just wait till seven o'clock! You'll see what it'll be like!

BEARDED MAN: *(Checking his pocket watch.)* It's still only four.

(CLESSI and ALAIDE are sitting beside the two candles.)

CLESSI: *(Sweetly.)* Funerals for little angels are always lovelier than grown-up ones.

ALAIDE: Then my mum said to the woman in the veil . . .

CLESSI: *(Reproachfully.)* We're talking about one thing and there you go showing up with something totally different!

(Lights up on the Memory Plane. DONA LIGIA and the WOMAN IN THE VEIL. The WOMAN IN THE VEIL yanks off her veil.)

MOTHER: I've already told you not to call your sister "that woman", Lúcia.

LUCIA: *(Getting very worked up.)* I will! That woman! That woman! That woman!

MOTHER: I'm calling your father. You have no respect for me!

LUCIA: *(Challenging her.)* Go ahead and call him! *(Changing her tone.)* He isn't going to hit me.

MOTHER: What a way to behave! Bringing down a curse on your sister's head!

LUCIA: Really, after what she did to me!

MOTHER: *(Going over to sit down on the stool, pathetic.)* We have children . . .

LUCIA: *(Interrupting her violently.)* And I asked to be born, did I?

MOTHER: *(Tearful, exploding.)* And this is what happens!

(Enter Alaíde's FATHER. DONA LIGIA gets up quickly. LUCIA assumes an attitude of discretion. Her FATHER is furious.)

FATHER: *(Shouting.)* Are you two coming, or aren't you?

MOTHER: I'm coming. *(Dissembling.)* I was just here having a chat . . .

FATHER: *(Grumpily.)* You think this is the time for a chat?! . . .

(DONA LIGIA exits.)

FATHER: And you? You aren't coming?

LUCIA: No. I'm staying.

FATHER: *(Surprised.)* Why?

LUCIA: I'm not feeling well. If I go, I'll pass out in the church.

FATHER: *(Furious.)* Fine.

(He exits. LUCIA sits down on the stool. Lights up on the Hallucination Plane.)

ALAIDE: *(Evocative.)* You were stabbed by a schoolboy.

50

CLESSI: *(Marvelling.)* So Lúcia and the woman in the veil are the same person!

ALAIDE: *(Still evocative.)* . . . a seventeen-year-old boy killed you. *(Abstractly.)* November 27th, 1905. I even retained the date!

CLESSI: *(Sweetly.)* Sisters hating each other so much! It's funny – I think it's kind of beautiful seeing two sisters who love the same man! I don't know why – I just do! . . .

ALAIDE: You do?

CLESSI: *(Serious.)* I do.

(The sound of a skid. A woman's scream. An ambulance. The characters are motionless.)

ALAIDE: Well, getting murdered by a boy is even more beautiful. A high school student! *(Changing her tone.)* Did he wear a khaki-coloured uniform?

CLESSI: *(Sweet and evocative.)* During the day, he did. Not at night.

ALAIDE: I would have liked to have loved a boy. Yours was seventeen? *(The other woman nods.)* He must have been very fair.

CLESSI: *(Troubled.)* Wouldn't it be good if every dead person got to see what they looked like? Did I look very ugly?

ALAIDE: The reporter said you didn't. He said you were beautiful.

CLESSI: *(Surprised.)* Did he really? But . . . *(A pause, as she looks lost.)* And the slicing of my face? *(Abstractly.)* A stabbing to the face isn't possible! It was a slashing with a blade, wasn't it? *(Changing her tone.)* I so wish I could have seen myself dead!

(She walks over towards the candles. She hesitates. The WOMAN FROM THE PAST mimes lifting an invisible sheet covering an invisible face.)

CLESSI: *(Astonished.)* The way dead people look! . . .

(She runs off with ALAIDE. The WOMAN FROM THE PAST exchanges a comment with her fellow wake attenders.)

WOMAN FROM THE PAST: Looks like she's smiling.

BEARDED MAN: *(With an expansive gesture, and depth to his voice.)* Anyone who dies is at peace.

WOMAN FROM THE PAST: Are you a spiritualist, senhor?

BEARDED MAN: *(With an even more expansive gesture.)* I respect all religions.

(Pause. The two of them kneel down, cross themselves, and get up again.)

WOMAN FROM THE PAST: *(Straightening out some part of her dress.)* I think I'm going.

BEARDED MAN: *(After looking off to the side, sly.)* Already?

WOMAN FROM THE PAST: It's late.

BEARDED MAN: *(Looking from side to side again.)* Do you live far?

WOMAN FROM THE PAST: Not terribly. But it's a very dark place. I get scared.

BEARDED MAN: *(Lascivious.)* I could go with you.

WOMAN FROM THE PAST: It's not worth it.

BEARDED MAN: *(With another gesture.)* I was going to leave anyway.

WOMAN FROM THE PAST: Well, in that case . . .

(The WOMAN walks over to the invisible coffin and makes a sign of the cross. She leaves with the BEARDED MAN.)

BEARDED MAN: *(Pausing on his way out; with a grave, deep voice.)* In fact, I'm against women walking all alone when it's so late.

(The romantic lad, annoyed, passes the invisible corpse, making a quick sign of the cross, and keeps walking. He's just about to leave the stage when he slaps his forehead, remembering the votive candles. He turns around and picks up two candles; the bearded man does the same. Blackout. Lights up on the Hallucination Plane. PEDRO and ALAIDE, as bride and groom, kneeling in front of the cross. A beam of vertical light. A recording of "Ave Maria", such as Rosa Ponselle's.)

LUCIA'S VOICE: *(Microphone, in a crescendo.)* I'll make a scene. If I just told them something I know! . . . Don't push me, Alaíde! I'm the one who should be the bride! You're a monster! The only man I ever loved! I've never married your boyfriends! I've never had your shamelessness! . . .

(A muted "Ave Maria". Suddenly, in bursts LUCIA, running onto the stage in a wedding dress.)

LUCIA: Pedro!

ALAIDE: You?

PEDRO: Ah, it's you, Lúcia. Finally!

(LUCIA hugs PEDRO. They speak almost mouth to mouth.)

LUCIA: It took me a while, my dear, because I had trouble finding the white thread.

ALAIDE: Where did you find it?

LUCIA: In the chest of drawers. It was in the bottom one.

ALAIDE: *(Triumphant.)* Didn't I tell you?! That's where I'd put it!

PEDRO: *(Cynical.)* If you'd arrived a little later the wedding would have happened!

LUCIA: *(Letting go of PEDRO, shouting, her fist raised, as in the communist salute.)* I'm the one who should be the bride! . . .

ALAIDE: *(Over-excited, her fist also raised.)* Liar! You liar! I stole your boyfriend and now he's mine! All mine!

LUCIA: *(Fist raised.)* She's confessed. At last! At least say it, scream it: "I stole Lúcia's boyfriend!!! . . .'

ALAIDE: *(Unbalanced.)* I won't say a thing! I don't want to!

(Blackout.)

CLESSI: *(Microphone, very slowly.)* Two brides! Interesting: two brides! But what did the priest say, when Lúcia showed up? Belgian lace, you ordered it – how much did that cost? Don't say – let's see if I can guess. I bet it was . . . about . . .

(Lights up on the top of one of the side staircases, on the Reality Plane. PEDRO, in his normal clothes, is talking to the doctor on duty. A vertical light on the two of them.)

PEDRO: *(Moved.)* My name's Pedro Moreira.

FIRST DOCTOR: Yes?

PEDRO: *(Moved.)* I'm the husband of this woman who's being operated on.

FIRST DOCTOR: Run over, wasn't she?

PEDRO: *(Distressed.)* That's right, doctor. Run over in Glória. I've only just heard. They called my office. *(Expectantly.)* Her condition: how is it, doctor? Very serious?

FIRST DOCTOR: *(Restrained.)* Well, her condition is not good.

PEDRO: *(Pathetic.)* It's not good? *(Changing his tone.)* But there's hope?

FIRST DOCTOR: There's always hope. They're doing everything they can.

PEDRO: *(Tormented.)* And did she suffer a lot, doctor?

FIRST DOCTOR: No. Not at all. She arrived in a state of shock. And she isn't going to suffer at all.

PEDRO: *(Shocked.)* A state of shock?

FIRST DOCTOR: That's right. For a person in an accident, that's a blessing. It's a big deal. The person feels nothing – nothing.

(Blackout. The curtain falls quickly.)

END OF ACT 2

Act 3

(The third act begins with the theatre in darkness. CLESSI and ALAIDE speaking through the microphone.)

CLESSI: *(Microphone.)* Maybe you didn't kill your husband.

ALAIDE: *(Microphone.)* But I remember! With an iron – I hit the base of his skull! Just here.

CLESSI: *(Microphone.)* Sometimes these things can be a dream!

ALAIDE: *(Microphone, pained.)* A dream – is that possible? My head's so upside-down! Maybe the whole thing was just wishful thinking!

CLESSI: *(Microphone.)* So what happened, in the church?

(Lights up on the Memory Plane. CLESSI and her BOYFRIEND are there, dressed in the style of 1905.)

ALAIDE: *(Microphone.)* I can't stop thinking about how much your boyfriend looks like Pedro!

(CLESSI and PEDRO are sitting down, on a récamier.)

CLESSI: *(In the same dress, but without a hat.)* Do you want to see my bunny-rabbits in the back yard?

BOYFRIEND: *(Coldly.)* No.

CLESSI: *(Sweetly.)* Some of them are so pretty! *(The two of them get up. He looks at her. Then he sits down again with his back to her. CLESSI walks off then comes back again.)*

CLESSI: *(Impatient and coquettish.)* Oof, you're such a child!

BOYFRIEND: So that's what you think!

CLESSI: *(Sitting down, listless.)* Well, aren't you?

BOYFRIEND: *(With focused anger.)* You think I am?

CLESSI: *(Languidly.)* You accepted money from me!
(Provoking.) You didn't want to do it, but you did!

BOYFRIEND: *(Amazed.)* But you were the one who put it in
my pocket! You insisted!

CLESSI: I'm just joking, you silly thing! That wasn't a big deal!

BOYFRIEND: *(Getting up.)* If you keep joking around with me
like that, one day . . .

CLESSI: *(Joking.)* You're going to hit me?

BOYFRIEND: *(Serious.)* Clessi . . .

CLESSI: Sit here!

BOYFRIEND: *(Sitting down.) (Quietly.)* You know what we
could do?

CLESSI: *(Stroking his hair.)* What?

BOYFRIEND: Guess.

CLESSI: Tell me.

BOYFRIEND: *(Quietly.)* Die together. *(The two of them are face to
face.)* Shall we?

CLESSI: *(Dreamily.)* You look so much like my son who died!
He was fourteen, but so well developed.

BOYFRIEND: *(Begging.)* Do you want to?

CLESSI: *(Sweetly.)* Look at me. *(She pauses, considering him.)*
Exactly his eyes! Just the same!

*(Blackout. The recording of a skid, a scream, an ambulance. Lights
up on the Hallucination Plane. PEDRO, ALAIDE and LUCIA in
bridal wear. A cross.)*

LUCIA: *(Furious, her fist raised.)* Say it loud so everyone can hear you: "I stole Lúcia's boyfriend!"

ALAIDE: I will say it!

LUCIA: Go on, then, I'd like to see you!

ALAIDE: *(Loud and clear.)* I stole Lúcia's boyfriend!

LUCIA: *(Excited.)* See, Pedro? She said it! She wasn't ashamed to say it!

ALAIDE: *(Aggressive.)* I'll say it as many times as you like!

PEDRO: *(Cynical.)* You two can argue as much as you want. It doesn't matter anyway.

ALAIDE: *(Reproachful.)* You shouldn't say that, Pedro. It's so cynical.

LUCIA: *(Sarcastic.)* Oh, so you're only just discovering now that he's a cynic! I'm so surprised!

ALAIDE: *(Pained.)* I've always known.

LUCIA: *(Contemptuous.)* So why did you take Pedro away from me?

ALAIDE: You're always going on about this taking-away business – taking him away! *(Enraptured.)* It's so good taking a boyfriend away from another girl. *(Ironic.)* And as for a sister's . . .

LUCIA: *(Boasting.)* You still believe he's only yours?

ALAIDE: I don't believe that. He is.

LUCIA: I've already told you he's both of ours, my dear! If you don't want to believe that, so much the better!

PEDRO: *(To LUCIA.)* You shouldn't say that! Alaíde didn't need to know!

ALAIDE: *(Pathetic.)* But I know now. Your suggestion has come too late.

(Enter the girls' mother. She is fanning herself.)

ALAIDE: *(Excited.)* A good thing you arrived, Mum.

D. LIGIA: *(Still using her fan.)* Arguing again!

LUCIA: *(Accusingly.)* Mum, it's her fault!

ALAIDE: *(Indignant.)* Me? You've got some nerve! . . . Mum, the two of them want me dead!

D. LIGIA: Don't think such things, child. You don't know what you're saying!

ALAIDE: *(Pathetic.)* When I die, they're going to get married, Mum! I'm sure of it!

PEDRO: You're acting crazy, Alaíde!

ALAIDE: *(To LUCIA.)* Repeat what you just said about mum!

LUCIA: *(Turning her back.)* Now she's wanting to complicate things for me with my mother! *(To ALAIDE.)* It's no use!

D. LIGIA: *(Fanning herself.)* Let's put an end to all this! It's most unpleasant!

ALAIDE: *(Mocking.)* She's scared! *(To LUCIA.)* Don't you want to tell her?

LUCIA: *(Determined.)* I will – I will tell her. It's very simple. I said . . .

ALAIDE: *(Ironic.)* Lost your nerve?

PEDRO: *(Looking around him.)* There's no chair. So I'm going to kneel down. Kneeling is restful, too.

(He kneels in front of the cross.)

D. LIGIA: *(Reproachful.)* You ought to have more respect for religion, Pedro!

(And she goes over to sit down, next to PEDRO, with her back to the cross.)

ALAIDE: *(To LUCIA.)* Are you saying it or not?

LUCIA: *(Somewhat reluctant.)* What I said, Mum, was that you . . . perspire a lot. So much! There, that's it! *(To ALAIDE.)* You see how I said it?

D. LIGIA: *(Fanning herself harder.)* Oh, my child! You were very brave . . . Oh, Lúcia!

ALAIDE: *(Enraged.)* But that wasn't all!

(Total darkness. CLESSI's voice in the microphone.)

CLESSI: Why did you stop talking about my story, Alaíde?

(A reply that nobody can hear.)

CLESSI: *(Impatient.)* I know that! Tell me about that later! But my conversation with him first! He was so like my son, so very like him! And those eyes, Alaíde! That way of smiling! What else did the newspaper say?

(Lights up on the Hallucination Plane.)

ALAIDE: *(Cruel.)* And the rest of the business, "that thing" you said?

D. LIGIA: *(Lifting one of her arms and fanning her armpits.)* That's enough, Alaíde! Enough! Oh God, my own daughter!

LUCIA: What "thing"?

PEDRO: *(Kneeling.)* Let her say it, dona Lígia. It's so interesting!

ALAIDE: *(Aggressive.)* You don't remember?

LUCIA: *(Decisive.)* I remember now! I also said, Mum, that when you start perspiring – you're my mother – but I can't bear it! I just can't. I need to leave!

(As she talks, she comes over towards DONA LIGIA and sits down beside her.)

ALAIDE: *(Triumphant.)* Exactly! You see, Mum?

(ALAIDE also comes over and sits down, beside PEDRO.)

(Blackout. Lights up on CLESSI and the BOYFRIEND.)

CLESSI: *(Insistent.)* Just accept it. Simple as that! Totally natural!

BOYFRIEND: *(Reluctant.)* No. I know what you're like.

CLESSI: But didn't your father stop your allowance because of me? Well? *(Changing her tone.)* Carry on like this you'll make me angry!

BOYFRIEND: *(Reluctant.)* Only for you to say "you accepted money from me" later? You think I've forgotten?

CLESSI: I was kidding! You really thought I was being serious?

BOYFRIEND: *(Defeated.)* I'll pay it back, then. Only on that condition.

CLESSI: Very well. What a boy! *(Changing her tone.)* Now go, son!

BOYFRIEND: *(Bitter.)* You don't have to drive me away. I'm going.

CLESSI: *(Conciliatory.)* You know why! The judge will be arriving soon!

BOYFRIEND: *(Jealous.)* You see?

CLESSI: What?

BOYFRIEND: *(Bitterly.)* I don't even have the nerve to complain, after I've accepted things from you.

CLESSI: *(Explaining.)* You know he's an old friend!

BOYFRIEND: *(Lively.)* And that's all? Swear it!

CLESSI: *(Categorical.)* Of course! He knew me when I was a little girl!

BOYFRIEND: *(In a sinister outburst.)* I'll end up killing you over that judge. You'll see!

(Enter the BOYFRIEND's MOTHER, dressed in the 1905 style.)

BOYFRIEND: *(Panicking.)* Mum!

(CLESSI gets to her feet.)

MOTHER: *(With focused anger.)* I knew it! I was so sure you were here!

BOYFRIEND: What are you going to do?

MOTHER: *(Firmly.)* Go home, Alfredo!

CLESSI: *(Gently.)* Go. Do as your mother says. *(The BOYFRIEND goes, after having received his MOTHER's blessing.)*

MOTHER: *(With an expansive gesture, conspicuously caricatured, with a tremor in her voice.)* And would you be Madame Clessi?

CLESSI: *(Humble.)* I am. Wouldn't you care to sit down?

MOTHER: No. I'm fine as I am. *(Highly exaggerated.)* I am the mother of Alfredo Germont.

CLESSI: *(Humble.)* I know.

MOTHER: *(With a tremble in her voice.)* And so you really have no conscience at all?

CLESSI: *(Shocked but gentle.)* Me?

MOTHER: *(Increasingly pathetic.)* Yes, you. Is this any way to behave? With a child?

CLESSI: *(Delicate and pained.)* But how is it my fault?

MOTHER: Fault! *(Changing her tone.)* A boy, a mere child, arriving home at two, three, four in the morning! Don't you see?

(Blackout. ALAIDE's voice.)

ALAIDE: *(Microphone.)* But I'm getting everything confused again, oh dear Lord! Alfredo Germont is the name from an opera! *La Traviata!* It was *La Traviata!* The guy's father came to challenge the girl! Everything's so messed up in my head, Clessi!

(Lights up on the Memory Plane. CLESSI and the boyfriend's MOTHER. The tone of the performances is different, but still caricatured.)

CLESSI: *(Whimpering.)* That man's eyes are undressing us!

MOTHER: *(With total lack of composure.)* You're exaggerating, Scarlett!

CLESSI: Rhett is unworthy of coming into a decent family home!

MOTHER: *(Crossing her legs, a total lack of good manners.)* Ashley, though, is too spiritual! It's just too much! I don't like them like that either.

CLESSI: *(Crying, resentful.)* Ashley has asked for Melanie's hand! He's going to marry Melanie!

MOTHER: *(Emphatic.)* If I were you, I'd prefer Rhett. *(Changing her tone.)* A hundred times better than that other one!

CLESSI: *(Tearful.)* I don't think so!

MOTHER: *(Sensual and descriptive.)* Oh, but he is, child! Did you see how strong he is? Like this! So strong!

(Blackout.)

ALAIDE: *(Microphone.)* You see, Clessi? Happened again. I think I'm describing your case, talking about what I read in the papers from then about the crime, and I find myself mixing everything up! I confuse *La Traviata . . . Gone with the Wind . . .* with your murder! Amazing. *(Pause.)* Isn't it?

(Lights up on the Memory Plane. CLESSI and the boyfriend's MOTHER now behaving normally.)

MOTHER: *(Threatening.)* This is the last time I ask you. Will you stop, or won't you?

CLESSI: *(Gently.)* Ask me for anything except that. Not that.

MOTHER: *(Aggressive.)* Then I'm taking the case to the police. And then we'll see.

CLESSI: *(Dreamily.)* I've cried so much! *(Changing her tone.)* I've never had a love of my own before. It's the first time. You, you've been in love, senhora, you'll understand.

MOTHER: *(Losing it.)* You're shameful!

CLESSI: *(With the same gentleness.)* I know I am. I know. *(Laughing and crying.)* If you saw how angry he gets when I talk about the judge!

MOTHER: *(Covering her face with her hand.)* My son involved with this depraved woman! With such a reputation!

CLESSI: *(In the same tone of abstraction, sits down.)* And when I put money in his pocket!

MOTHER: Liar!

CLESSI: *(Still sweetly.)* And he gets so awkward about accepting!

MOTHER: I'm going to speak to my husband! *(Threatening.)* Oh, if that's true!

(She makes as if to leave, but CLESSI's attitude changes and she screams violently.)

CLESSI: Look!

(MOTHER stops, astonished.)

CLESSI: Yes, you!

(Aggressively she approaches the MOTHER, who draws back, panicking.)

CLESSI: If you ever come to my house again, I'm going to chase you out myself!

MOTHER: *(The two women are face to face.)* *(Cowering.)* But what's this?

CLESSI: *(Violent.)* I'm not respectable, but I say what I think. I don't pretend. You hear me? Get out, now!

(The alarmed mother exits. Blackout. Lights up on the Reality Plane. A newspaper editorial desk and press room.)

FIRST MAN: *(Yelling.)* Daily!

SECOND MAN: *(Yelling.)* Get me Osvaldo!

FIRST MAN: That's me.

SECOND MAN: This is Pimenta. Note this down.

FIRST MAN: Go ahead.

SECOND MAN: Alaíde Moreira, white, married, aged 25. Resident of Copacabana Street. Look . . .

FIRST MAN: What is it?

SECOND MAN: She's important, this one. Rich folk. Wife of that guy, that industrialist, Pedro Moreira.

FIRST MAN: Yeah, I remember him. Go on.

SECOND MAN: Facial bones caved in. Compound fracture in the right arm. Generalised bruising. Critical condition.

FIRST MAN: . . . bruising. Critical condition.

SECOND MAN: The driver ran off. They didn't get his number. She's still on the operating table.

(Blackout. Lights up on the Hallucination Plane. ALAIDE and CLESSI are here, motionless. The noise of a skid. A woman's scream. An ambulance.)

CLESSI: What else did she say in the newspaper?

ALAIDE: She said you'd said "Get out, now." That she was scared she was going to be murdered!

CLESSI: She didn't mention the money I'd been giving him?

ALAIDE: It was the maid who told the reporter about the money!

CLESSI: *(Sarcastic.)* Imagine that!

ALAIDE: *(Nervous.)* He's coming this way, Clessi! It's Pedro!

CLESSI: But hadn't you murdered him?

ALAIDE: I thought I had. But it must have been a dream! Look at him!

(Enter PEDRO, in mourning clothes. ALAIDE goes up to meet him, smiling.)

ALAIDE: Will you excuse me, Clessi? *(To PEDRO, in mourning.)* Well, then, my love? *(They kiss.)*

PEDRO: *(Surprised, secretive.)* Who's she?

ALAIDE: *(As if apologising.)* Oh! Oh, right. I forgot to introduce you! Clessi, madame Clessi! This is my husband!

PEDRO: *(Pleasantly.)* Aren't you the lady who was murdered?

CLESSI: Of course.

ALAIDE: That's right. In 1905. The one I told you about, Pedro.

PEDRO: I remember perfectly. Your boyfriend was a high school student, right? He stabbed you?

CLESSI: *(Dreamily.)* During the day, he wore a khaki uniform. Not at night.

ALAIDE: Would you excuse us now, Clessi?

CLESSI: Of course.

ALAIDE: I need to talk to Pedro about something. Then I'll call you.

PEDRO: *(Cynically, to CLESSI, who is leaving.)* Do drop by anytime!

(Before leaving, CLESSI turns around to face him and gives a nod.)

PEDRO: *(Suddenly irritated.)* What's all this with you going around talking to Madame Clessi?

ALAIDE: *(Flustered.)* And what's the big deal about that, darling?

PEDRO: *(Vehemently.)* She isn't respectable! I don't want you around people like that!

ALAIDE: *(Getting carried away.)* She isn't respectable! And you're respectable? Are you? You think I don't know about any of it? You really believe that?

PEDRO: *(Astonished.)* That you don't know what?

ALAIDE: *(Excited.)* That you and Lúcia . . . *(Threatening.)* Yes, you and Lúcia! That you've been wishing me dead!

PEDRO: *(Turning his back on her.)* You're nuts.

ALAIDE: Nuts, me? You know I'm not! So I haven't been seeing anything, then?

PEDRO: *(Turning back to face her.)* What have you been seeing?

ALAIDE: The two of you whispering! I walk in *(Sarcastic.)* and you immediately change the subject, talk about something totally different, all totally natural.

PEDRO: *(Ironic.)* You've got some imagination, my love!

ALAIDE: Day and night, wishing me dead! And I know what for! So that you can marry each other after my death!

PEDRO: *(Adopting a tone.)* So you think . . .? Really . . .?

ALAIDE: *(Increasingly excited.)* You've already planned the whole thing! The whole crime! Murder, leaving no trace!

PEDRO: *(Sarcastic.)* A true perfect crime!

CLESSI: *(Microphone.)* What a pair! Planning a crime!

ALAIDE: *(Still over-excited.)* And on top of that you're still playing the innocent! But I'll catch the two of you – good and proper! You'll see!

(Enter LUCIA, like an apparition. She is in mourning clothes.)

LUCIA: Oh, you're both here?

ALAIDE: *(Triumphant.)* Aha! The accomplice has arrived! You're both so sure of my death that you're even in mourning already!

LUCIA: *(Innocent.)* What's going on?

PEDRO: *(Pointing at his forehead.)* Alaíde isn't quite right in the head!

ALAIDE: *(Trembling, to LUCIA.)* Come here and tell my husband what you said, "that thing" you said! The day of my wedding!

LUCIA: Am I supposed to know what you're talking about?

ALAIDE: You do know. You do! That insinuation of yours . . . That I might die!

LUCIA: *(Turning her back on her.)* You're dreaming, girl. I didn't say a thing.

ALAIDE: Coward! You're scared now! But you did say it – you said it to me!

PEDRO: But she denies it, Alaíde!

LUCIA: *(A different attitude.)* So I said it! There! I said it! So now what?

ALAIDE: *(Pathetic.)* So kill me! Why don't you both kill me? There's no one else here! Then you can hide my body underneath something! *(And as she speaks, the three of them move closer, their heads meeting.)*

(Heads lowered, following the rhythm of the words.)

PEDRO: *(Sinister.)* Not now! There's still time!

(When he finishes speaking, what remains is the impression of a plastic bouquet of heads. Blackout. Lights up on the Reality Plane: the noise of surgical implements.)

FIRST DOCTOR: Pulse?

SECOND DOCTOR: Can't say . . . Oh, she's not responding!

FIRST DOCTOR: She's finished!

THIRD DOCTOR: That's it!

(One of the DOCTORS is pulling a cover over a woman's face. The DOCTORS exit slowly, one of them removing his mask. "Funeral March". Blackout. Lights up on the Hallucination Plane. ALAIDE and CLESSI have their backs to the audience. ALAIDE holds a bouquet, with the microphone secreted inside it. Lights up on the Reality Plane: a bar and a newspaper editorial desk.)

PIMENTA: *(Yelling.)* That woman died.

REPORTER: *(Yelling and jotting things down.)* Which one?

PIMENTA: The one run over in Glória.

REPORTER: What else?

PIMENTA: She arrived here in a state of shock. She died without regaining consciousness; she didn't suffer at all.

REPORTER: You don't know that!

PIMENTA: Her sister cried so much!

REPORTER: You'd expect that from a sister!

PIMENTA: She's cute!

REPORTER: Who?

PIMENTA: The sister.

(Blackout. Lights up on the Reality Plane: LUCIA and PEDRO. LUCIA is crying. Wreaths. The Hallucination Plane is also illuminated.)

ALAIDE: Who could have died there, in that house?

CLESSI: Look! A whole fortune's worth of flowers!

ALAIDE: That's what rich people's funerals are like.

CLESSI: Mine had a lot of people at it, too, didn't it?

70

ALAIDE: That's what the newspaper said, at least.

(In the Reality Plane.)

PEDRO: *(Quietly.)* Lúcia!

LUCIA: *(With a start, getting up.)* What? What time is it?

PEDRO: It's three o'clock.

LUCIA: Stay away from me! Don't come any closer!

PEDRO: What's going on?!

LUCIA: *(With focused hatred.)* Never again! I never want anything to do with you, ever again! I swear it!

PEDRO: Have you gone crazy? What did I do?

LUCIA: *(Stubborn.)* I swore it before Alaíde's body.

PEDRO: *(Shocked.)* You did?

LUCIA: *(Decisively.)* I did. Yes, I did. Want me to go over to the living room and swear it again? *(She sinks her head into her hands.)* Yesterday, before she went out to die, we had a horrible argument!

PEDRO: *(Quietly.)* Did she know?

LUCIA: *(Pathetic.)* She did. She guessed what we were thinking. And I told her.

PEDRO: But she never mentioned it to me.

LUCIA: We argued several times. I threatened to make a scene. But yesterday, it was just horrible – horrible! You know what she said to me? "Even if I do die, I'll never leave you in peace!"

(LUCIA is speaking with her head in her hands. ALAIDE replies through the microphone hidden in the bouquet. The light falls into shadow, for the whole duration of this evocative piece of dialogue.)

ALAIDE: *(Her voice slow and dull.)* Even if I do die, I'll never leave you in peace!

LUCIA: *(Speaking quietly.)* You think I'm scared of spirits coming back from another world?

ALAIDE: *(Microphone.)* Don't kid around, Lúcia! If I die – I don't know if there's life after death, but if there is – then you'll see!

LUCIA: *(Sarcastic.)* See what, my dear sister?

ALAIDE: *(Microphone.)* You won't have a moment's peace, if you marry Pedro! I won't let you – you'll see!

LUCIA: *(Ironic.)* You're so sure you're going to die?

ALAIDE: *(Microphone.)* I don't know! You and Pedro are capable of anything! I might wake up dead and everyone would think it's a suicide.

LUCIA: Who knows? *(Changing her tone.)* Did I ask you to take Pedro away from me?

ALAIDE: *(Microphone.)* For God's sake, what did I do?

LUCIA: *(Sarcastic.)* Oh, nothing!

ALAIDE: *(Microphone.)* I did what a lot of women do. I took someone's boyfriend! A triviality, in other words . . . *(Vehemently.)* But not you! You and Pedro want to kill me. That's an actual crime, not what I did!

LUCIA: *(Irritated.)* But you won Pedro so hopelessly that he still chases after me all day long!

ALAIDE: *(Microphone.)* You know where I'm going now?

LUCIA: I don't care!

ALAIDE: I'm not going to tell you anyway – my dear sister! I'm going to have an adventure. A sin. Know what that is?

I'm going to visit a place, and what a place! Wonderful!
I've been there once before!

LUCIA: *(Sarcastic.)* I bet you have!

ALAIDE: *(Provoking.)* Last time I went, there were two women
there dancing. Women in long dresses, yellow and pink
satin. A record player. Look: you can tell Pedro if you like.
I don't care. It'd be good, actually.

LUCIA: *(Sarcastic.)* Liar!

ALAIDE: *(Microphone.)* Oh? Am I really?

LUCIA: *(Assertive, raising her voice.)* You are! You've never been
there. Never! The whole thing you're telling me – those
two women, the satin dresses, the record player – you just
read it all in a book that's upstairs! Want me to go get it?
Do you?

ALAIDE: *(Microphone.)* Fine, Lúcia. I didn't go, I was lying.
(Pained.)

LUCIA: *(Cruelly.)* You can go there and stay there!

ALAIDE: *(Microphone.)* Listen to me. Even if I die a hundred
times, you aren't going to marry Pedro.

(Lights back to normal.)

LUCIA: *(Overwhelmed, speaking to PEDRO now.)* Now, whenever
I think about Alaíde, I can only picture her in her
wedding dress.

PEDRO: *(Restrained.)* That's what she said, that's all?

LUCIA: *(Darkly.)* That's all. She predicted she was going to
die!

PEDRO: *(Somewhat ironic.)* We predicted it, too.

LUCIA: You say "we"!

PEDRO: *(Assertive.)* I do, because you did, too. *(Pause.)* You predicted it, and you wanted it to happen. We just didn't think about a car running her over. That's all.

LUCIA: *(Desperate.)* You were the one who put it into my head – that she should die!

PEDRO: *(Cruelly cynical.)* So she shouldn't have?

LUCIA: *(Desperate.)* You beast! You won't even wait till the body's been taken away! With the body right there, so close. *(She points in the direction of what must be the next room.)* And you say that!

PEDRO: *(Suggestive.)* Who's responsible?

LUCIA: *(Shocked.)* Maybe I am!

PEDRO: *(Vigorous.)* Yes, it's you!

LUCIA: *(Shocked.)* You've got some nerve . . .

PEDRO: I have. *(Vehement.)* Who was it that said, "You don't get to touch me till after you're married!" Who was it?

LUCIA: It was me, but that doesn't mean anything!

PEDRO: *(Definitive.)* It means everything! Everything! It was you who gave me the idea for the "crime"! You!

LUCIA: *(Afraid.)* You're so bad, so cynical, accusing me!

PEDRO: *(Vehement, but quiet.)* Either you or her had to disappear. I preferred it to be her.

LUCIA: *(Anguished.)* Having this conversation practically next to the coffin!

PEDRO: *(Still quiet.)* Didn't we study the "crime" in every detail? You never once protested! You're my accomplice!

LUCIA: *(Distractedly, shocked.)* They've sent so many flowers!

PEDRO: *(Insistent.)* And now you're getting cold feet because the body's still here!

LUCIA: *(Somewhat crazy.)* You remember what she was saying? About that "trivial thing" she'd done?

ALAIDE'S VOICE: *(Microphone.)* I'm much more of a woman than you are – I always have been!

LUCIA: *(Changing attitude.)* You're the reason I lost my soul!

PEDRO: *(Quickly.)* And you mine!

LUCIA: *(Sarcastic.)* You were never any good! You were always the same! Don't look at me, it's no use!

PEDRO: Fine. I'll talk to you later.

LUCIA: It's no use. I won't be yours, or anybody's. You're never going to touch me, Pedro.

PEDRO: You say that now!

LUCIA: I swore that not even a doctor is going to see my body.

PEDRO: *(Cruel.)* So she was so impressed by the women wearing yellow and pink. A record player! Two women, whoever they were, dancing!

LUCIA: *(Tearful.)* Don't talk like that! She's right there. She died.

PEDRO: *(Sarcastic.)* She was wild about any woman who behaved badly. She never stopped talking to me about Clessi. A madwoman!

LUCIA: *(Disgusted.)* You must be drunk to be talking like that!

PEDRO: *(Serious.)* Or mad . . . *(Grave.)* I'm not scared of madness at all.

(Blackout.)

LOUDSPEAKER: Pedro Moreira, Gastão dos Passos, wife and
daughter, Cármen dos Passos, Eduardo Silva and wife
(In absentia.), Otávio Guimarães and wife, are touched
and grateful for the presence of all those who have come
for the burial of their unforgettable wife, daughter, sister,
niece and sister-in-law Alaíde, and invite relatives and
friends for the Seventh-Day Mass, to be held on Saturday,
the 17th of this month, at the Candelária church, at 11 a.m.

(Lights up on the Reality Plane. LUCIA and her MOTHER.)

LUCIA: *(Like a madwoman.)* Did you see what they put in the
paper? "Alaíde Moreira, white, married . . ." *(Sarcastic.)*
White! . . . *(Muffled.)* "Compound fracture of the right arm.
Facial bones caved in . . ."

MOTHER: *(Shocked.)* Don't be like that, Lúcia!

LUCIA: *(Ignoring her and continuing.)* " . . . generalised
bruising. . ." "succumbing to her injuries . . ." *(Her voice
muffled.)* Oh Mum, I know it all by heart! By heart!

MOTHER: Oh, my child!

LUCIA: *(Astonished.)* Can you hear that, Mum? Her again!
She's come back – didn't I tell you?

MOTHER: It's nothing, child. Just your delusion.

LUCIA: *(Amazed.)* But I can hear her voice! Perfectly! Talking!

MOTHER: You're behaving like a child, girl!

LUCIA: *(With a strange expression.)* It was nothing. Silly.

ALAIDE: *(Microphone.)* "You always wished me dead. Always
– always."

MOTHER: When you go out of town, it'll all stop. The climate
up at the farm is an absolute wonder!

(Blackout. Only voices in microphones.)

FATHER: *(Microphone.)* What's up with Lúcia and Pedro?

MOTHER: *(Microphone.)* Nothing that I know of. Why?

FATHER: *(Microphone.)* Didn't you see yesterday?

MOTHER: *(Microphone.)* Oh, that?

FATHER: *(Microphone.)* Yes, that. It was weird.

MOTHER: *(Microphone.)* Maybe it was an accident.

FATHER: *(Microphone.)* Accident my foot.

MOTHER: *(Microphone.)* Lúcia's been so on edge! But I'll talk to her.

FATHER: *(Microphone.)* Don't get involved.

MOTHER: *(Microphone.)* She said this thing to me yesterday! Anyway . . .

(Lights up on the Reality Plane: Lúcia's FATHER and MOTHER, and DONA LAURA. LUCIA is arriving back from a trip.)

LUCIA: Mum! I've missed you so much!

FATHER: And I don't deserve that, I suppose.

LUCIA: Dad!

MOTHER: You're so much fatter, you have so much more colour – isn't that right, Gastão?

FATHER: Much.

D. LAURA: When one takes off one's mourning black, things are quite different.

LUCIA: Oh, dona Laura! I hadn't seen you there!

(Exeunt DONA LAURA and Lúcia's MOTHER.)

FATHER: *(Confiding.)* All sorted out?

LUCIA: What do you think, father?

FATHER: This one's up to you, child; you're the one who has to decide.

(Blackout. Lights up on ALAIDE and CLESSI, poetic ghosts. The two extremes of the Reality Plane are illuminated. Stage left is ALAIDE's tomb. Stage right is LUCIA, in a wedding dress, at the mirror, getting ready. An arrangement incorporating the "Wedding March" and the "Funeral March".)

LUCIA: Make it nice and tight, Mum.

D. LIGIA: It's very loose here!

LUCIA: Do you think Pedro's arrived already?

MOTHER: Dona Laura will come in when he arrives.

LUCIA: *(Retouching something in the mirror.)* I don't want him to see me till we're inside the church.

(Enter DONA LAURA.)

D. LAURA: May I see the bride?

LUCIA: Oh! Dona Laura!

(They kiss.)

D. LAURA: *(To Lúcia's MOTHER.)* You must be getting so flustered!

MOTHER: You can't imagine!

LUCIA: *(Coquettish.)* Am I looking very ugly, dona Laura?

D. LAURA: Beautiful! Delightful!

LUCIA: *(Holding out her arms.)* The bouquet.

(The music – funeral and festive – rises up in crescendo. When LUCIA asks for the bouquet, ALAIDE, like a ghost, advances towards her sister, up one of the side staircases, as if about to hand it over. CLESSI is coming up the other staircase. There is a vertical light following ALAIDE and CLESSI. Everyone is motionless, frozen in mid-movement. Then the whole stage is plunged into darkness leaving only a moon-like light on ALAIDE's tomb. Crescendo of the "Funeral March". Blackout.)

END OF ACT 3 AND FINAL ACT

FAMILY PORTRAITS
Tragedy in Three Acts

By Nelson Rodrigues (1945)
Translated by Almiro Andrade

Characters

THE SPEAKER

THE PHOTOGRAPHER

WEDDING GUESTS

WOMAN (in labour.)/TOTINHA

JONAS (Forty-five years old, bears a
slight resemblance to Jesus.)

DONA SENHORINHA (Jonas' wife, forty years old,
beautiful and young looking woman.)

GUILHERME (The couple's oldest son; A Mystic Creature.)

EDMUNDO (A young man, somewhat feminine.)

GLÓRIA (Fifteen years old, bears a striking
resemblance to Dona Senhorinha.)

TERESA (Glória's girlfriend.)

NONÔ (The possessed one.)

AUNT RUTE (Dona Senhorinha's sister, a spinster,
the kind of woman with no sex appeal at all.)

GRANDFATHER

GIRL

HELOÍSA (Edmundo's wife.)

MEN (Four, to carry the coffin.)

CHORUS[1]

---

1 Characters in *Italics* were not included in the list present in the
original, even though they are described within the play.

Act 1

SCENE 1

Open curtain: the first family album portrait – dated 1900.

JONAS and SENHORINHA, the day after their wedding. They both carry an emphatic comedic flair, common to old portraits. THE PHOTOGRAPHER is on stage making the technical-artistic arrangements needed for the intended pose. He pulls out all the stops to ensure everything is done to a tee, literally painting the town red – he moves SENHORINHA's chin, begging her for a photogenic smile. THE PHOTOGRAPHER himself assumes the naïve attitude, more compatible with a prude bride after her very first night. Every once in a while, he buries himself under the black cloth and looks through the lense to adjust the focus; back and forth, retouching SENHORINHA's pose. During this scene, a completely silent scene, a true ballet of the family portrait can take place. After a thousand and one pirouettes, THE PHOTOGRAPHER steps back, taking the camera with him as he walks away, until he completely vanishes. JONAS and SENHORINHA stand still, motionless for a moment: he, with his puffed up chest; she, bearing a false and nitwitted smile, either reminiscent of or perhaps contemporary to Francesca Bertini[1], or her alikes. We then hear THE SPEAKER's voice, which should bear the same traits as D'Aguiar de Mendonça's[2] voice, for example. IMPORTANT NOTE: THE SPEAKER, in addition to the heinous bad taste of his comments, makes sure to feed us with false information about the family.

THE SPEAKER is a kind of Public Opinion.

THE SPEAKER: *(Once THE PHOTOGRAPHER vanishes, whilst JONAS and SENHORINHA keep the pose.)* First family portrait.

---

1 Francesca Bertini was an Italian silent film actress. She was one of the most successful silent film stars in the first quarter of the twentieth century.

2 Radio announcer famous in Rio in the first half of the twentieth century.

1900. January 1st: Cousins, Jonas and Senhorinha, the day after their wedding. He, a twenty-five years old men. She, barely completed fifteen canty springs. Observe the shyness of the young betrothed woman. It's only natural – this is a bride who's only now become a wife; that always brings this up in a woman. Back then, a girl who dared to cross her legs was considered a hussy, perhaps even shameless – pardon my French.

They break the pose. JONAS tries to embrace SENHORINHA who, confirming THE SPEAKER's comments, reveals a hysterical chastity.

THE SPEAKER: *(Entranced.)* Such a winsome thing, to see chastity in a woman!

Bride and groom assume a more formal attitude, as they hear noises from the outside. WEDDING GUESTS enter and, without saying a word, throw rice at them. JONAS and SENHORINHA exit.

THE SPEAKER: The lovebirds flee to Jonas' little farm in São José de Colgonhas. Away from the hustle and bustle of the big city, they'll relish their honeymoon. Au revoir, Senhorinha! Au revoir, Jonas! Don't forget what says the Bible: "Be fruitful and multiply!"

Lights go off, THE SPEAKER is no longer heard: a new scene is then lit – the corner of a secondary school dorm room. A metal platform bed, with grids at the headrest, where – lying side by side – are GLÓRIA and TERESA, both in very thin layered, quite diaphanous nightgowns. They both look no older than fifteen years old. There is an atmosphere of idyll between the two girls.

TERESA: Do you swear?

GLÓRIA: I do.

TERESA: Swear to God?

GLÓRIA: Of course!

IMPORTANT NOTE: An imbalance must be observed between the two: TERESA's emotions are more active, more absorbing; whilst GLÓRIA's, although bowing to the idyllic atmosphere, appears to be more resistant.

TERESA: Then, show me it. But, hurry, the Sister can come in at any minute now.

GLÓRIA: *(Raising her head.)* I swear I...

TERESA: *(Correcting her.)* I swear to God...

GLÓRIA: I swear to God...

TERESA: ...that I will never marry...

GLÓRIA: ...that I will never marry...

TERESA: ...that I will be faithful to you til the day I die.

GLÓRIA: ...that I will be faithful to you til the day I die.

Pause. They look at each other. TERESA gently touches GLÓRIA's face with her nose. She squashes her nose against GLÓRIA's face.

TERESA: And that you won't even date anyone.

GLÓRIA: And that I won't even date anyone.

TERESA: *(In love.)* I swear to God too, that I'll never get married, that I'll love no one else but you, and that no man will ever kiss me.

GLÓRIA: *(Less tragic.)* Yeah right, I bet you will.

TERESA: *(Trembling.)* Hold my hand like this. *(Looking deep into her eyes.)* If you died, I don't even know what I would do!

GLÓRIA: Don't be silly!

TERESA: But I don't want you to die, never! Only after me. *(With a new expression, carrying a newly found beauty.)* Better yet, at the same time, together. You and me buried in the same coffin.

GLÓRIA: Would you really want that?

TERESA: *(In transit.)* It'd be so good, so, so good!

GLÓRIA: *(Practical.)* But it couldn't be in the same coffin – I don't think they'd allow that!

TERESA: *(Forever in love.)* Kiss me!

GLÓRIA kisses her on the cheek, slightly frivolous.

TERESA: Kiss my lips!

They kiss each other; TERESA, with absolute commitment.

TERESA: *(Grateful.)* We never kissed like that before – it's our first time!

GLÓRIA: *(As if still tasting the kiss.)* Interesting!

TERESA: *(Somewhat agitated.)* Did you like it, like, really like it?

GLÓRIA: A kiss like that is different, isn't it?

TERESA: You'll forget about me!

GLÓRIA: *(Frivolous.)* Silly!

TERESA: *(Carried away.)* You'll never find anyone who loves you like I do – I doubt it!

GLÓRIA: As if I didn't know that?

TERESA: *(Always making the first move.)* Kiss me again…

After a long kiss.

GLÓRIA: *(Uncertain whether she liked it or not.)* – Your lips are cold, I mean – wet.

TERESA: *(Happy.)* Obviously, silly. It's the saliva…

Lights go off on the small dorm room scene. A greater, more central space is now lit. Living room at JONAS' farmhouse. At first, the room is deserted; NONÔ comes to the window from the outside, and utters a dreadful, non-human cry, the cry of a wounded beast. Following this, two frightened women enter and look out the window: DONA SENHORINHA, dignified, haughty and extremely beautiful; and AUNT RUTE, SENHORINHA's sister, an old spinster, taciturn and cruel. DONA SENHORINHA seems older than in the portrait, as over twenty years have past since. After a while, the constant moan of a WOMAN in labour is heard from an outhouse nearby. A portrait of Jesus hangs on the wall.

AUNT RUTE: *(By the window, looking out.)* It's Nonô, once again!

With angst, DONA SENHORINHA also looks out the window whilst AUNT RUTE, with noticeable harshness, continues to speak.

AUNT RUTE: I'm familiar with his cries. Actually, it's not a cry. It's something else, I don't know what. More like a howl, perhaps. If I were you, I'd be ashamed!

DONA SENHORINHA: *(With suffering.)* Ashamed of what?

AUNT RUTE: Of having a son like him – is that not reason enough to feel shame?

DONA SENHORINHA: *(Still suffering.)* A disgrace, I say, like any other!

AUNT RUTE: *(Chastening her sister.)* Now how bizarre that the boy goes crazy and his first instinctive response is to take off his clothes and go live in the woods. Like an animal! Didn't you see him, not long ago, through the window, licking the ground? He must've hurt his tongue!

DONA SENHORINHA: *(In pain.)* Quite often, I wonder if the crazy ones feel no pain!

AUNT RUTE: Today, he's skulking outside this house, circling around us, like a mad horse!

DONA SENHORINHA: Nonô is much happier than me – that's a cinch. *(Always in pain.)* Sometimes, I'd love to be skulking in my son's shoes…

They've left the window by now. DONA SENHORINHA, sad, dignified, haughty, in a rather sober pain, tries to have her back to her sister at all times. AUNT RUTE bears a cruelty she cannot conceal.

AUNT RUTE: *(Sardonic.)* Skulking…. IN THE NUDE, naturally.

DONA SENHORINHA: *(Abstruse.)* My only consolation is that he doesn't forget us, his family. Almost every day he comes howling near here, as if he were calling for someone…

AUNT RUTE: *(Perverse.)* For you, perhaps?

DONA SENHORINHA: *(Somewhat violent.)* Nonô liked me, back when he was well, he adored me. *(Once again abstruse.)* He misses us… MISSES US! *(Taciturn.)* He misses his home…

AUNT RUTE: *(Vehement.)* Ha, his home! He never liked it here. He couldn't even stay more than half an hour in one of the rooms, or his own bedroom. He was always outside!

DONA SENHORINHA: I'd love it if he were to only miss me, just me – no one else!

The WOMAN in labour starts moaning once again, interrupting their conversation. JONAS enters: sort of a restive man, passionate, sensual lips, beard on point. His hair resembles Buffalo Bill, a kind of indweller that is. He bears a vague resemblance to Our Lord Saviour.

WOMAN: *(Always with a hoarse voice, heavy, the voice of someone who has suffered too much, who had to shout way too much.)*…

You, bastard – you crippled me... I damn you... You'll
pay for what you've done to me...

*JONAS, AUNT RUTE and DONA SENHORINHA look towards the
WOMAN's shouts.*

JONAS: *(Rispid.)* Is the doctor coming or what?

AUNT RUTE: *(Showing solicitude and tenderness when addressing
him.)* Like I said, he went to Três Corações to attend
another woman in labour.

JONAS: *(Taciturn.)* Unbelievable!

AUNT RUTE: *(Mellifluous.)* He'll only get here by tomorrow
morning or way into the night, at the earliest.

JONAS: *(Suffering.)* I think you two'd better settle this once
and for all.

DONA SENHORINHA: *(Without turning towards her husband.)*
Jonas.

JONAS: *(As if waking up, a bit surprised.)* That's me!

DONA SENHORINHA: *(Maximum seriousness.)* This girl,
Jonas...

JONAS: What about her?

DONA SENHORINHA: *(Doleful.)* She's nearly a child...

JONAS: *(Paying close attention to what he sees outside.)* I know.

DONA SENHORINHA: ...she's barely hit puberty – she's not
even fifteen years old. She didn't have any idea what it
meant to bear a child.

JONAS: *(Paying no attention to his wife.)* Nonô is possessed
today!

DONA SENHORINHA: Why did you have to pick her, not another?

JONAS: *(Addressing AUNT RUTE.)* What about that thing I asked you, Rute?

AUNT RUTE: *(Lit up.)* All solved.

DONA SENHORINHA: *(Without noticing that no one is paying attention to her.)* Do you think this is fair?

JONAS: *(To DONA SENHORINHA; holding back his wrath.)* I do.

DONA SENHORINHA stops, as if returning to her senses; she lowers her head without, however, losing her dignity.

DONA SENHORINHA: Jonas, this girl should not be having children!

JONAS: *(Somber.)* Yet, she is. You're the only one who's making a fuss out of this. *(Violent.)* That doctor, that stupid doctor!

AUNT RUTE intervenes; cajoling, soothing, trying to soften JONAS' reactions. DONA SENHORINHA sits near the window.

AUNT RUTE: *(Mysteriously.)* I have another one. You've met her.

JONAS: *(Interested.)* Has she already been here?

AUNT RUTE: *(Excited.)* Yes, she has – that day! You kept looking at her – I noticed!

JONAS: *(Stretching his legs, sensually.)* – What's she like, more or less?

AUNT RUTE: She's got a lot of men chasing after her – if you could see her now! *(Pointing at the WOMAN's outhouse.)* There's only one thing: she's not like this one – with narrow hips! She's got a lot more hips, but never mind – it doesn't really matter. If I were a man, I wouldn't think twice. *(In confidence.)* I saw her skinny-dipping in the little lake!

JONAS (Somewhat disappointed.) Big hips – but… are they really big, way too big?

AUNT RUTE: *(As if admiring.)* A body like no other, my dear! *(Making gestures.)* Her breasts, everything!

JONAS: Is she married? Because if she is, I'm not interested!

AUNT RUTE: Ha, married! She's only engaged, but her fiancée… *(With absolute disdain.)* now she swears like sailor. The words she uses! And she does it out loud, in front of everybody.

JONAS: *(Somber with desire.)* Tell me her name… How old is she?

AUNT RUTE: *(Changing her tone.)* Really young – she's only sixteen. Besides, she's one of those who gives it as good as she takes. She hits her fiancée; better yet, they say he likes it.

JONAS: Is she "pure"?

AUNT RUTE: *(Categorically.)* Obviously! She's got this going for her but no one gets with her all the way. She just teases them – such a smart girl!

JONAS: How about this swearing for no apparent reason? Is she crazy?

AUNT RUTE: Crazy, ha! No way!

DONA SENHORINHA: *(Without paying any mind to what she is saying.)* I do believe loving a crazy person – is the only kind of pure love!

DONA SENHORINHA says this while looking outside, somewhat sweet.

JONAS: *(Looking towards DONA SENHORINHA appearing impressed; as if full of fear.)* 'Cos if she's crazy, I don't want her! *(As if, talking to himself.)* The one I had was enough. *(In extreme distress.)* The crazy ones are incredible *(Lowers his voice.)*; making love, they can be frightening!

The WOMAN in labour starts moaning again; this time, she also speaks in full sentences.

WOMAN: ... give me something for the pain... I can't take it anymore, Dear Lord...Oh Little Flower, St. Teresa!

JONAS: What about her?

AUNT RUTE: *(Avid.)* What about her what?

JONAS: Is she into it?

AUNT RUTE: Of course! Everybody is in on it as well – the grandfather – she hasn't got a father nor a mother – and the fiancée. *(Lowers her voice.)* I promised them you'd look after her family. She said you were a real man – A REAL MAN! And, above all else, her pride, her vanity. You know what all these women are like!

JONAS: *(Suffering retrospectively.)* Not all of them! Remember that one – Açucena – she wanted nothing to do with me!

AUNT RUTE: That one was different: she was from the city – well educated. I'm saying different from the people here *(With emphasis.)* here in the countryside.

During the dialog, DONA SENHORINHA is looking outside in silence.

JONAS: *(On fire.)* Then, make it happen. But, hurry!

DONA SENHORINHA's apathy is shattered.

AUNT RUTE: I'll take a peek outside.

AUNT RUTE exits.

DONA SENHORINHA: I could tell you I'm your wife…

JONAS: *(Sardonic, interrupting.)* Like that would do any good!

DONA SENHORINHA: … I could complain about you hosting a woman in this house to have your bastard child…

JONAS: *(Threatening.)* Don't play fool with me!

DONA SENHORINHA is interrupted by the arrival of AUNT RUTE and, following behind, the GRANDFATHER of her husband's new conquest. He is an old man with a biblical beard; he also rests his weight on a cane as one of his legs is bandaged with rags, due to a conspicuous case of elephantiasis.

AUNT RUTE: *(Picking up from where she left off.)* Hurry, uh!

GRANDFATHER: *(Obdurate.)* Just a quick word, I swear.

Promptly, the GRANDFATHER makes a wide and all-encompassing greeting gesture.

GRANDFATHER: Good afternoon to you all. *(No one answers.)*

JONAS: *(Taciturn.)* What's happening here?

AUNT RUTE: He's the grandfather, Jonas. The girl's grandfather. The one I told you about.

GRANDFATHER: I just came to pay my respects, "Seu" Jonas. I bet you don't even remember me, but I can't blame you, you were so young! You, "Seu" Jonas, peed all over me many a times, plenty! You rode on my hunchback too. All in jest, of course. But, if you want to once again, please, sir! I'm here whenever you want to!

AUNT RUTE: Enough, Tenório.

AUNT RUTE tries to pull the old man away.

GRANDFATHER: I brought you my granddaughter. I'm a man of my word. You did good, "Seu" Jonas, not going for those ones at Mariazinha Bexiga's bawdy house. Scabby bunch of whores! Now, like my granddaughter – there is no other! I assure you, she's clean, you won't find a scab on her. Except for that time her heel nearly gone rot, but that was a long time ago.

Under no circumstances, does the old man show any intention of leaving.

GRANDFATHER: May the Good Lord bless you with good health. Dona Senhorinha, too. If my granddaughter is disrespectful, pay no mind in calling me. I'll give her a good belting!

Pulled by AUNT RUTE, the patriarchal GRANDFATHER exits.

JONAS: *(As if falling into a trance; he addresses no one; AUNT RUTE comes back, without him noticing.)* I like these shameless girls. Not women; girls. Fourteen, fifteen years old. Foulmouthed. *(With angst.)* To be honest, I never understood why women can't swear like us. It makes no sense, right? *(With absolute dignity, almost suffering.)* In a conversation, during a meal, with the Last Supper hanging on the wall and the lady of the house swearing like a sailor!

Turns to AUNT RUTE; he seems mad.

DONA SENHORINHA: *(Vehement, cruel.)* Glória doesn't swear! Glória doesn't use swear words! She's just a girl, a fifteen-year-old girl!

JONAS: *(Recovering his senses.)* Glória's a saint... She's like a porcelain angel, a china doll...

AUNT RUTE: *(As if to wake him up.)* How about the girl?

JONAS: *(Still in complete angst.)* I wanted a fifteen-year-old girl, pure, who never felt desire! Who'd never said a swear word!

Once again, JONAS addresses AUNT RUTE, still making no sense at all.

JONAS: Rute, I want that old man's granddaughter, here, today!

DONA SENHORINHA: *(Laconic and cold.)* Not today. It can't be today.

JONAS: *(Approaching AUNT RUTE.)* You're the only one, Rute, the only one I have in this house! You're the only person who cares for me, who does anything, EVERYTHING for me!

AUNT RUTE: *(Passionately.)* EVERYTHING!

JONAS: *(With the same sweetness, almost musical.)* The only one capable of infamies – of any kind! Even capable of a crime! *(Turns to DONA SENHORINHA with sudden rancour.)* But this whole house hates me. I feel it! That crazy son of mine, Nonô…

DONA SENHORINHA: *(Harsh.)* Don't you lay a hand on Nonô!

JONAS: *(Violent.)* Completely mad! The only human trait he's shown has been his hate for me, for his father! When he leaves the woods and sees me in the distance, he throws rocks!

DONA SENHORINHA: When he was sane, you used to hit him with a belt!

JONAS comes closer to DONA SENHORINHA, who turns her profile to him as if to avoid facing him.

JONAS: *(Talking to himself.)* Edmundo can't stand me…

DONA SENHORINHA: Wasn't it you who threw him out of the house, three days after his wedding?

JONAS: *(Ignoring the interruption.)* Guilherme can't stand me, either! *(Violent, trying to face DONA SENHORINHA.)* Neither can you! When we're face to face, you turn your face away from me. You try to pass yourself as a martyr, when you should be on your knees, at my feet, kissing my boots!

AUNT RUTE returns and watches the dialogue, fascinated.

JONAS: *(Unexpectedly sweet.)* Not you, Rute. Always steady. I'm sure that, if I became a leper, maybe my wife and sons would beat me to death. But you wouldn't mind, you'd not find it disgusting. Not at all.

AUNT RUTE: *(Persuasive.)* Don't get too excited, Jonas. It's bad for you, getting that excited.

JONAS: *(Shouting.)* But they got me all wrong. I am the Father! The Father is sacred; the Father is the LORD! *(Out of his mind.)* From now on, I'm going to read the Bible every day before dinner, especially the chapters which speak of family!

JONAS' excitement seems to drain him; he falls into a chair, stretching his legs.

DONA SENHORINHA: *(From the corner where she is.)* This woman can't come in here, Jonas!

DONA SENHORINHA is mortally cold.

AUNT RUTE: *(Sardonic.)* My sister's trying to give you orders!

JONAS: Leave her with me! *(Changes his tone.)* I now insist that you bring this girl in, Rute.

AUNT RUTE: *(Exultant.)* Don't worry.

DONA SENHORINHA gets in AUNT RUTE's way to stop her from leaving.

DONA SENHORINHA: *(On the verge of humiliating herself.)* Rute, you're my sister.

AUNT RUTE: *(Cutting.)* Don't bother.

DONA SENHORINHA: *(Between authoritarian and supplicant.)* When Mother died, she asked you to take care of me. Like any older sister would. You promised her, Rute, you swore!

AUNT RUTE: *(Hard.)* So what?

DONA SENHORINHA: *(Supplicant.)* Send that woman, that girl back. God may punish you!

AUNT RUTE: Who cares.

DONA SENHORINHA: *(Further humiliating herself.)* Just for today, Rute. You know I don't mind. I've already put up with so much! But, not today, because Glória's coming… Glória.

JONAS: *(In panic.)* Glória!

DONA SENHORINHA: … something happened to Glória at school, I don't know, but she'll be here today or tomorrow.

JONAS: *(Standing up, disturbed.)* What happened to her? Tell me! You're hiding something from me. What is it?

DONA SENHORINHA: Your guess is as good as mine. The telegram only says she's coming – a telegram from the Mother Superior.

JONAS: *(Tormented.)* Dear Lord, what happened to her?

DONA SENHORINHA: *(As if talking to herself.)* You only seem to behave yourself, whenever Gloria's here. You seem to treat me better, like you're someone else entirely. She's the only person in the world you seem to pay an ounce of respect to. *(In transit.)* Glória's so pure, she believes in people, she sees no evil! She doesn't know love exists, she doesn't have the faintest idea about what love is. She thinks it's friendship!

JONAS: *(Suffering.)* She's not of this world. While she was having her holy communion, I had a dreadful feeling!

DONA SENHORINHA: *(Vehement.)* She doesn't need to know, she can't suspect a thing! *(With sadness and sweetness.)* She confessed to me once that looking at you, with your beard like that, and your hair, it was just like looking at Our Lord and Saviour, Jesus Christ!

JONAS: *(As if touched by distrust.)* Wait, is she arriving today or tomorrow?

DONA SENHORINHA: *(Upset.)* I'm not really sure, either today or tomorrow!

JONAS: *(Shouting.)* Tell me!

DONA SENHORINHA: *(Lowering her head, humiliated.)* I suppose, tomorrow.

JONAS: *(Cruel, rekindling his desire.)* Tomorrow, eh? So, Rute, bring the girl now! *(Changing his tone, enigmatic.)* As Glória is on her way, now I really need those girls more than ever!

DONA SENHORINHA: *(Interposing once more.)* Wait, Rute; there's more to it, Jonas.

JONAS: What is it?

DONA SENHORINHA: *(Utterly mortified.)* Edmundo's here.
Edmundo's just arrived!

JONAS: *(Surprised.)* On his own or with his wife?

DONA SENHORINHA: On his own.

JONAS: *(Wrath in crescendo.)* I could've tried to tolerate it if he
came with his wife…But on his own! You were concerned
with Edmundo, not with Glória. Who gave Edmundo the
right to come into my house like that? I told him never to
come back. NEVER!

DONA SENHORINHA: *(Humiliating herself.)* He came to see
me, Jonas, to see you!

JONAS: *(Bestial.)* Pass.

DONA SENHORINHA: That other time, you two had a fight
because of me, because of the way you treated me. I don't
want you two to fight because of something like that. If he
had any idea! He's already suspicious of you!

DONA SENHORINHA addresses AUNT RUTE.

DONA SENHORINHA: *(Savage.)* Look at me! I'm begging
you, do you hear me? – so we stop something worse from
happening!

AUNT RUTE: Worse than what? What could he do to Jonas?
Jonas is far more of a man than Edmundo will ever be,
that's for sure. That day, Jonas gave him a beating like
I've never seen a man give another. And he ran from it, in
front of everybody!

DONA SENHORINHA seems intimidated by her sister's violence.

AUNT RUTE: *(To JONAS.)* I'll be right back with the girl,
Jonas!

DONA SENHORINHA: Shameless!

AUNT RUTE: *(Surprised.)* What?

DONA SENHORINHA: You!

JONAS: Pay no mind, Rute!

AUNT RUTE: *(Overtaken by wrath, as well.)* Who's shameless here? Me? No, you are! No man has ever touched me!

DONA SENHORINHA: *(Calmer, cruel.)* Because they didn't want you – you're not even a woman!

AUNT RUTE: Thank God, I still haven't done what all of them do, or want to! What you did!

DONA SENHORINHA: *(Bestial, again.)* You have no hips, nor breasts, nothing! *(With suitable mimicry.)* You're as flat as a wooden board! This way it's easy to be modest, my dear! I'd like to see you say that being pretty, a desirable woman! Having all men going crazy, closing in on you! That's the kind of virtue worth bragging about!

JONAS: *(Interfering.)* Don't go there, Rute!

AUNT RUTE: *(Resentful.)* Now, only if she listens to what I have to say... *(To DONA SENHORINHA.)* You're the real virtuous one, aren't you? And what about that night, eh? Probably, you've forgotten all about that night by now, for sure!

DONA SENHORINHA remains silent.

AUNT RUTE: *(Possessed, entirely.)* But there's something you don't know. I lied when I said no man had ever touched me.

DONA SENHORINHA: *(Sardonic.)* Ah, so there was one...?

AUNT RUTE: *(Painfully, as if transfigured by the blissful memory.)* It was only once. He was drunk, but I paid no mind to it. NO MAN HAD EVER LOOKED AT ME BEFORE.

None, not even the blacks. It was a drunkard's frolic – I know. But the matter of fact is I'VE BEEN LOVED. He even kissed my lips, as if I were one of those very desirable women. That man *(Changing her tone, violent.)* IS YOUR HUSBAND!

JONAS: *(With some resentment.)* You shouldn't have told her!

AUNT RUTE: *(Without hearing him.)* That's why I like him. I knew it had only been that one time – it wouldn't happen again, Sod's law. But it was so good! Now, whatever he wants from me, I do it with gusto. He wants me to get him girls, thirteen, fourteen, fifteen year-olds; not a problem. Only virgins; but of course! To me, he's a saint and that's that!

AUNT RUTE covers up her face with one of her hands. DONA SENHORINHA is motionless, rigid. Finally, JONAS seems impressed with his sister-in-law's confession.

JONAS: *(To DONA SENHORINHA, with resentment.)* Did you ever love me like that? There was a time when… But not even then would you ever be capable of something like this *(Serious, as if making a legitimate complaint.)* you, yourself finding women – especially virgins – for the man you love; ME. No woman does that.

DONA SENHORINHA: Would you rather have me do it?

JONAS: *(Approaching his wife.)* Why do you have to put up this act? *(With increasing wrath.)* You said something about being shameless. *(With sinister candour.)* Now tell me; there is someone like that in here. But who's that?

DONA SENHORINHA: *(Tormented.)* I have no idea.

JONAS: *(Advancing as she tries to recoil.)* Yes, you do. Who is that?

DONA SENHORINHA: *(Evasive.)* The three of us.

101

JONAS: Say it.

DONA SENHORINHA: *(Cornered.)* Me. I'm the one who's shameless – that's me!

Only then, slowly, DONA SENHORINHA, JONAS and AUNT RUTE exit. The lights are dimmed. The stage is empty. The WOMAN in labour is heard moaning and speaking.

WOMAN: I gave him the time of day, I believed his sweet talk... Oh, if I only knew it was going to hurt this much... May death catch you!... and here comes the pain. Oh, God!

Darkness at centre stage. Lights back on the Family Album. Second portrait. Same PHOTOGRAPHER, thirteen years later. Same camera, same mise-en-scène. The whole family: JONAS and DONA SENHORINHA, now with their four children: GUILHERME, EDMUNDO, NONÔ and GLÓRIA, this last one on DONA SENHORINHA's knee. The two younger boys are dressed as sailors; GUILHERME, the eldest, wears a school uniform. THE SPEAKER enters, fatuous as per usual.

THE SPEAKER: Second family portrait. 1913. A year before the so called "crazy pandemonium". Senhorinha, no longer a shy and nervous bride; now, a fertile mother. From her marriage to Jonas were born, from oldest to youngest, Guilherme, Edmundo, Nonô and Glória. Ah, and there are still those who are against the institution of marriage!

The portrait is taken. JONAS kisses DONA SENHORINHA's forehead and, only then, picks up his daughter, GLÓRIA.

THE SPEAKER: A mother like that is a timely example for those modern girls who insist on drinking fizzy pops straight out of the bottle!

Lights on the main room of JONAS' farmhouse. A GIRL with an untamed kind of beauty is leaving a bedroom. She runs by, leaving the door open. After a moment, JONAS leaves through the same door, still fiddling with his belt. The GRANDFATHER enters, as his granddaughter runs off stage.

GRANDFATHER: All good, "Seu" Jonas? All to your liking?

JONAS: *(Taciturn.)* Kind of.

GRANDFATHER: That's good, then. Believe me, "Seu" Jonas: don't go fiddling with Mariazinha Bexiga's girls because you'll catch something for sure.

GRANDFATHER stands in front of JONAS as if about to leave; JONAS doesn't say a thing.

GRANDFATHER: Anything you need, just give us a shout. At Mariazinha Bexiga's, they seem to be at each other's throats. *(Stops, giving one last shot.)* My dearly departed missus was real chummy with your old man…

JONAS: *(Explosive.)* You old bastard! Get the hell out, before I… Well!

GRANDFATHER: *(In panic.)* All right! All right!

The GRANDFATHER exits. DONA SENHORINHA enters, with her beautiful sadness.

JONAS: *(With irritation.)* Were you spying on me?

DONA SENHORINHA: *(Ironic.)* Me? As if I cared about what you do!

JONAS: *(Vile.)* But did you see the girl?

DONA SENHORINHA: Not that I meant to, she passed by as I came in.

JONAS: *(Approaching DONA SENHORINHA, analysing her as if she were an exotic beautiful animal.)* She's more interesting than you.

DONA SENHORINHA: *(With desperate irony.)* Of course! She's got more hips, larger breasts... She sweats more and I barely produce any sweat!... She's filthy, I'm not! But you need women like that, don't you? You like them!

JONAS: *(Changes his tone.)* The worst thing is I can't find one, I simply can't... I feel the urge of hurting them, even choking them! They're filthy pigs and so am I! *(Collapses, exhausted.)*

DONA SENHORINHA: Edmundo quarrelled with Heloísa – they're separated. Welcome your son, Jonas!

As soon as DONA SENHORINHA begins the last sentence, EDMUNDO enters.

DONA SENHORINHA: *(Pathetic.)* I hope he doesn't see that woman that just left!

EDMUNDO: *(Young, handsome, somewhat feminine.)* I saw some woman...

DONA SENHORINHA: *(In panic.)* You promised me, Edmundo!

JONAS: *(Sardonic.)* And that wasn't a woman; that was a girl...

EDMUNDO: *(Obstinate, to DONA SENHORINHA.)* Who's that woman?

DONA SENHORINHA: Nobody, Edmundo.

JONAS: *(Yelling.)* I am talking. *(Another tone of voice.)* I see it as a character flaw, really shameful, someone who is thrown out of a house, CAST OUT, not only comes back but BEARS THE WORLD'S MOST CYNICAL LOOK!

EDMUNDO: *(Ignoring his father, as if he didn't exist.)* Mother, who is she, Mother?

DONA SENHORINHA: It doesn't matter – it's so silly.

EDMUNDO: *(To DONA SENHORINHA.)* How can you stand THIS?

DONA SENHORINHA: *(Imploring.)* This has nothing to do with you, Edmundo, stay out of it!

EDMUNDO: A long time ago I witnessed certain things, but I was just a child… Now, you're telling me that all of this happens here, inside our house, right in front of your nose! You see it all, you bear through it and you say nothing! Why – that's what bothers me – WHY?

JONAS: *(Ironic, to his wife.)* Tell him why, explain it!

EDMUNDO: I don't want this to go on, I REALLY DON'T!

DONA SENHORINHA: *(Sweet.)* Edmundo, would you do something for me?

EDMUNDO: What they're doing to you should not be done to the worst of women!

DONA SENHORINHA embraces EDMUNDO. She shakes him, as if to wake him up.

DONA SENHORINHA: Will you do what I ask you? Tell me – will you?

EDMUNDO pauses; he seems perplexed.

EDMUNDO: *(Suddenly, in transit.)* I will!

DONA SENHORINHA: *(Sweet, looking straight into his eyes.)* Remember when you were little: go and ask for your father's blessing!

EDMUNDO: *(Retreating, aghast.)* No, not that!

DONA SENHORINHA: *(Loving.)* It's me who's asking you – me! Let's stop being silly here!

EDMUNDO: *(Revolted.)* You're completely insane!

JONAS starts to boil up.

JONAS: *(Pacing through the room from one side to the other.)* I've cast him out… I gave him a beating… He ran from me - he's not a man… *(Evidently referring to EDMUNDO, who doesn't seem to be affected by his father's words.)*

AUNT RUTE enters.

EDMUNDO: This is going to end badly!

AUNT RUTE: *(Sardonic.)* What's going to end badly? What are you talking about?

EDMUNDO: *(Cutting.)* I'm not talking to you. The only thing I can feel towards you is repugnance, disgust.

AUNT RUTE: *(Thrilled.)* Good one – "This is going to end badly". Are you threatening Jonas, are you? Did you forget the beating he gave you?

JONAS: Let it go, Rute! I'm the Father here! *(Talking to himself.)* How dare you criticise me – a lowlife who has just abandoned his wife! Why couldn't he be like Guilherme, who's still there, firm at the seminary, ready to become a priest! I know why: because Guilherme's cold. Not really cold: feminine, perhaps.

EDMUNDO: I'm cold too.

JONAS: *(In wrath.)* Cold, yeah right! *(Exploding.)* Talk to me! Talk straight to me, be a man! *(Changing his tone, directly to EDMUNDO.)* You're like me – you think about women, day and night. Someday, you'll kill someone over a woman!

EDMUNDO: I think about ONE WOMAN, which is something totally different! Just ONE!

JONAS: *(Exultant.)* You admit it – you think about a woman. *(Passionately.)* Same thing, thinking about all of them.

EDMUNDO: This is different. *(Filled with hate.)* I don't chase after those countryside whores, those ones, that might carry diseases and God knows what else! *(Gravely.)* I have now and only have ever had one love!

JONAS: *(Sardonic.)* It's not your wife? Or is it?

EDMUNDO: No.

DONA SENHORINHA: *(Fascinated.)* Then, who is it?

JONAS: Say it!

EDMUNDO: *(Lowering his head, in all seriousness.)* I won't say. *(To DONA SENHORINHA, looking straight into her eyes, lowering his voice.)* Maybe you'll know, someday.

JONAS: *(Violent.)* You don't fool me. You could only feel hate towards me – since you were a child. Someday, I know, you'll kill me, maybe in my sleep. But I'm making my own arrangements.

AUNT RUTE: Who this boy thinks he is to kill you, Jonas?

JONAS: I'm telling everyone that, if one day you find me dead, you can count on it: it wasn't an accident, nor was it natural causes – MY SON KILLED ME. *(Almost no change in his tone of voice.)* But I know you fear me – fear and hate me. But the fear is stronger. *(With perilous sweetness.)* Isn't that so, Edmundo? Isn't the fear stronger?

EDMUNDO seems fascinated.

JONAS: Come closer, just a minute.

DONA SENHORINHA: *(Panicking.)* Go Edmundo. It's me who's asking you to!

EDMUNDO: *(Immobile.)* No, not that! Never!

JONAS: Come take your blessing, Edmundo! *(With heinous sweetness.)* From your Father!

DONA SENHORINHA: *(Impressed by her son's humiliation.)* If you don't want to, Edmundo, don't go... I can't really ask you to humiliate yourself... Edmundo, don't go!

EDMUNDO battles against his own weakness; still, he walks towards JONAS as if a higher power emanated from him.

EDMUNDO: *(Not directing his speech to his father.)* When I was a little boy, he humiliated me, beat me... Once, I was forced to kneel on corn kernels... *(With despair.)* But I'm not a little boy anymore...

Slowly, EDMUNDO walks towards his father.

DONA SENHORINHA: *(Hysterical, with both hands covering her ears.)* No, Edmundo, no!

EDMUNDO: Why do they make boys ask for their father's blessing? Boys should only get their mother's blessing... A woman's hand is totally different... It doesn't have any hair or those thick sweaty veins.

As if entirely taken over, EDMUNDO bows quickly and kisses JONAS' hand.

EDMUNDO: There. I did it. I kissed my father's sweaty hand.

END OF ACT 1

Act 2

SCENE 1

Third portrait of the album. Glória's portrait, at her holy communion. She is on her knees, hands in prayer, etc. The PHOTOGRAPHER instructs the young girl in the mystical pose she should assume; for that, he kneels, puts his hands in prayer also and rolls his eyes. After this, he gets up and contemplates the result of his instructions. He is about to take the portrait when he slaps his forehead, remembering she needs the prayer book and the rosary; he fetches them for her and she assumes the final pose. DONA SENHORINHA is present, but takes no part in the portrait; she is only there to keep her daughter company.

THE SPEAKER: Quoting the Renaissance Pastoral Romance, Maiden and Modest, Glória has received an irreproachable education. The innocence shines through her angelic countenance. Mother and daughter complement each other.

The portrait is taken. Mother and daughter embrace, showing utter tenderness.

THE SPEAKER: A Mother is always a mother.

DONA SENHORINHA pays the PHOTOGRAPHER, who responds by making a wide gesture of eternal gratitude. DONA SENHORINHA distances herself.

THE SPEAKER: If Dona Senhorinha is a devoted mother, then Glória is an obedient and respectful daughter.

The lights go off on the portrait scene. Living room at the farmhouse. No one on stage. The WOMAN in labour starts to moan again.

WOMAN: *(Hoarse due to the shouting.)* Help me, I can't take anymore... Oh, my Virgin Mary, by Saint Theresa! I'm not going to make it! Oh!

EDMUNDO and DONA SENHORINHA enter; they seem to be coming from a stroll.

EDMUNDO: You endure so much – there must be a reason, some kind of explanation I'm not aware of.

DONA SENHORINHA: *(Painfully.)* No reason at all.

EDMUNDO: It would be so much better if, in every family, someone just killed the father!

DONA SENHORINHA: What would you want me to do?

EDMUNDO: *(Passionately.)* Why didn't you kill yourself?

DONA SENHORINHA: *(Pathetic.)* There's still time. *(Changes her tone.)* Do you want me to kill myself?

EDMUNDO: *(In fear.)* No!

DONA SENHORINHA: *(Meek and sad.)* See? You don't even think before you speak! EDMUNDO: *(Obsessed.)* Should you ever die, I don't even know! I don't want you to die, ever! *(Changes his tone.)* I can't even think of you dead! *(Touching his mother's face.)* I prefer you alive, even if, one day, you decided to join Mariazinha Bexiga's brothel!

DONA SENHORINHA: What nonsense!

EDMUNDO: *(Painfully, talking to himself.)* Sometimes, I think, I imagine you working as one of Mariazinha Bexiga's girls! Missing a front tooth! Drinking beer!

JONAS enters. His face still bears the customary cruel expression.

JONAS: *(Approaching EDMUNDO.)* You haven't explained yet why you left Heloísa.

EDMUNDO: *(With sudden shame.)* We had irreconcilable differences.

JONAS: *(Walking away, as if talking to himself.)* I just don't understand Guilherme... How can he be that cold – he's flesh of MY FLESH.

DONA SENHORINHA: *(In transit.)* Guilherme was so... *(Not knowing what to say.)* Since he was a little boy, he was always at church...

JONAS: He has to be like me!

DONA SENHORINHA: *(Sweet.)* Always with his little prayer book.

JONAS: He cannot possibly be devoid of lust!

DONA SENHORINHA: *(Happy.)* He used to love angel prints!

JONAS: *(Exultant.)* But I know what's going to happen – I BET YOU! Guilherme will show up one day and say: " I left the seminary!"

GUILHERME enters in time to hear his father's last words.

GUILHERME: I left the seminary...

JONAS: *(Astounded.)* There he is! *(Pauses; possessed, to everyone.)* Didn't I tell you? I just said it... *(Gasping.)* God's confirmed my words... *(Pointing at a Jesus portrait.)* It was God! Yes, God. God!

JONAS walks towards GUILHERME.

JONAS: *(Grabbing GUILHERME'S lapel.)* I know why you left the seminary; why you gave up on priesthood...

JONAS addresses his wife, exultant.

JONAS: Yes, I know! To seek freedom – to go after some prostitute!

DONA SENHORINHA: *(Lamenting.)* God will smite you, Guilherme! God will smite you!

JONAS: Who is she?

GUILHERME: *(Sombre.)* I don't want, nor do I care about any prostitute.

JONAS: *(Fills the stage with his voice.)* Liar! And to think I felt an ounce of respect for you! To the point that I didn't feel comfortable around you! I THOUGHT YOU WERE THE ONLY PURE ONE IN THIS FAMILY!

GUILHERME: What about Glória?

JONAS: *(Correcting himself, promptly.)* I meant, the only pure man. *(To the others.)* Didn't I tell you he was COLD? Didn't I?

GUILHERME, with his hands interlaced behind his back, doesn't seem to pay any mind to the others' presence.

JONAS: *(As if talking to himself.)* I like young women, really young ones *(Nervous chuckle.)* and you – none of you – have any idea WHY! *(To GUILHERME, aggressive.)* What about you, eh? *(Changes his tone.)* Now you're just like me, like that one over there *(Points at EDMUNDO.)*, who's left his wife…

JONAS approaches DONA SENHORINHA. She doesn't face him.

JONAS: … like this one over here!

EDMUNDO: Leave my Mother out of this!

DONA SENHORINHA: *(Sardonic.)* Like Glória, too!

JONAS: *(Adrift.)* Not Glória! Glória is the only one – do you hear me? – the ONLY ONE who's escaped! Glória's the very portrait of an angel!

DONA SENHORINHA: *(Ironic.)* I don't know about that!

JONAS: *(To GUILHERME.)* I hope what happened to Nonô, who's gone mad, doesn't happen to you too. For sure, it was for thinking too much about women! Now, he licks the soil, he's developed an obscene love for the soil... love-making love! *(Intense, face to face with GUILHERME.)* Let me tell you just one thing: No girls! Nor very young women either – do you hear me? Never!

The WOMAN in labour starts to moan again.

JONAS: Where's that bloody doctor!

GUILHERME: She's one of yours, right?

EDMUNDO: *(Painfully.)* Mother has told me it isn't!

JONAS: *(In one breath, to EDMUNDO.)* I've let you stay here because you asked for my blessing... But stay out of it, or I'll throw you out of here again!

Another moan from the WOMAN in labour.

DONA SENHORINHA: *(Exploding.)* This is horrible!

JONAS: *(Agitated.)* You are not far from it, either!

DONA SENHORINHA: *(Not noticing the interruption.)* She's got no hips!... She's got the hips of a child!...

JONAS: *(Restless, possibly remorseful.)* If it wasn't me, it would've been someone else!

DONA SENHORINHA: Such narrow hips!

JONAS: Why's that my problem? Is it my fault she's got no child bearing hips?

GUILHERME walks toward the door of the WOMAN's outhouse, and speaks from there.

GUILHERME: Do you know what: I should do to this one what I did to that mute girl! *(Heinously joyful.)* Do you remember, Father – the MUTE ONE?

JONAS: *(Somewhat fearful.)* I don't know what you're talking about.

GUILHERME: Oh yes, you do. The one who couldn't speak, a little bit stupid – cross-eyed! *(Wildly joyful.)* Yes, that's right – she was CROSS-EYED!

AUNT RUTE passes by carrying a big pot of water to the WOMAN's outhouse; she looks at the scene for a moment. She leaves the pot at the WOMAN's outhouse and returns, curious.

GUILHERME: Everybody showed respect for the mute one… Nobody got frisky with her.

JONAS: *(Fearing his son.)* Me neither!

GUILHERME: *(Violent.)* Yes, you did… You couldn't spare even the mute one…

JONAS: *(To the others, defending himself.)* Just because she was a mute, is she any less of a woman? Just because she's a cripple?

GUILHERME: Then, she'd been made pregnant. She came crawling, in labour – SHE WANTED TO HAVE THE BABY IN THIS HOUSE… I caught her on her way here.

Everyone in the room seems fascinated by GUILHERME's story. He lowers his voice, showing his suffering in his expression.

GUILHERME: When she saw me, she seemed to know – she feared me. *(Changes the tone, ruthless.)* She tried to run – but I stepped on her belly, I kicked her in the kidneys!…

GUILHERME says those things as if inebriated. Tired and in awe, he stops himself.

JONAS: *(With suffering.)* Murderer!

GUILHERME: I don't mind!

> *GUILHERME looks at Jesus' portrait. He speaks, suddenly grave and manful.*

GUILHERME: As God is my witness, I'm not sorry for what I did! *(Savage.)* I should do the same with the one out there!

JONAS: *(Obsessed.)* MURDERER!

GUILHERME: They're all bitches!

> *The WOMAN in labour moans and speaks.*

WOMAN: I'm gonna die! Jesus Mary Joseph – I am going to die!

> *AUNT RUTE, who'd just been to the WOMAN's outhouse, returns.*

DONA SENHORINHA: What about the contractions?

AUNT RUTE: Getting worse.

DONA SENHORINHA: I'll go check.

> *DONA SENHORINHA goes to the WOMAN's outhouse.*

JONAS: *(Somber.)* You sons of mine, all you want is to criticise me! If you only knew my reasons – a big REASON – for doing what I do – ... and a lot worse!

DONA SENHORINHA: *(Reappearing.)* Rute, come here a second.

AUNT RUTE: Not now.

DONA SENHORINHA: Edmundo, would you be a lamb and help your mother?

> *EDMUNDO exits.*

GUILHERME: *(To JONAS.)* Are you finished? Or do you have anything else to say?

JONAS: Yes, I'm finished! Now, I'm leaving... Self-righteous pricks like you really have me up to here – do you hear me? UP TO HERE! Good-bye!

JONAS attempts to leave, stumbles, and is stopped by GUILHERME.

GUILHERME: Where do you think you're going? You're not leaving!

AUNT RUTE: Who are you to give your father orders?

GUILHERME: You're the one who's getting out of here, now!

JONAS: *(In awe.)* What did she do?

AUNT RUTE: *(Mournful.)* I didn't do anything – not a thing!

GUILHERME: You're the real damned soul in this house. *(More aggressive.)* Don't you answer back to me: GET OUT!

DONA SENHORINHA reappears and approaches AUNT RUTE.

AUNT RUTE: *(Retreating, in fear.)* Only if Jonas wants me to, if he tells me to!

GUILHERME: *(Holding her wrists.)* You want to be dragged out?

DONA SENHORINHA: *(Intervening.)* Go, Rute, go!

AUNT RUTE frees herself, violently.

AUNT RUTE: *(To DONA SENHORINHA.)* Who asked for your opinion?

DONA SENHORINHA: Rute, think of Mother...

AUNT RUTE: *(Aggressive.)* Mother? What for? *(Changing her tone.)* I promised her, I swore to Mother... *(Cynical.)*

Who cares? She never liked me. It was always all about you, you! She had an indecent infatuation for your looks. She used to watch you take your bath, dried your back! Now tell me: WHY HASN'T SHE EVER CARED TO WATCH ME TAKE A BATH?

DONA SENHORINHA: *(Extremely shocked.)* You must be going mad!

AUNT RUTE: *(In a crescendo.)* Mother, Father, everyone! No one ever liked me, no one! Once, in Belo Horizonte, I remember going out with you...

GUILHERME twists AUNT RUTE's wrist so abruptly, she is made to have her back to him.

GUILHERME: Shut your mouth!

AUNT RUTE: *(Despite the pain.)* ... a bunch of men would come whisper things in your ear – obscenities most times! But when it was my turn, not even a miser black, not even a street beggar, would care to say a word to me – A WORD! You're breaking my arm, ouch!

GUILHERME lets go of his old aunt.

AUNT RUTE: *(Possessed.)* I'm trying to say, every woman has a man who desires her, even if it's a nigger, a sweaty nigger, everyone BUT ME!

DONA SENHORINHA: *(Leaving.)* So, am I to blame here? You were not graced with looks, and I'm the one to blame?

AUNT RUTE: Since I was a little girl, I envied your beauty. *(Accusatory.)* But it should be immoral to be as beautiful as you, because no man comes near you without thinking of YOU KNOW WHAT!

AUNT RUTE stops and covers her face with one hand.

GUILHERME: *(Ironic.)* Go ahead, carry on!

JONAS: *(Shouting.)* Enough!

GUILHERME: Carry on, because after this you're leaving and you are never to come back!

AUNT RUTE: *(Almost hysterical.)* Are you all throwing me out?

GUILHERME: You bet!

AUNT RUTE: But I have nowhere else to go!... I have no other relatives, nothing!... Do you want me to starve to death?

GUILHERME: Who cares?

AUNT RUTE: *(In a crescendo.)* You can't do this to me. *(Yells.)* I KNOW ALL THE FAMILY SECRETS! I KNOW why Guilherme and Edmundo came back – I KNOW. I know why Nonô went crazy – why they sent Glória to boarding school!...

AUNT RUTE grabs JONAS, who shows no reaction.

AUNT RUTE: Jonas, don't let them do this to me!

JONAS: If you say another word about Glória, the things I'd to you – you know, you know! How can you be so ugly!

AUNT RUTE: *(In awe.)* You are all against me. *(Lowering her voice.)* Against me and against you, Jonas. Are you going to allow this, Jonas?

AUNT RUTE holds JONAS by the shoulders, desperately. JONAS shows no reaction.

AUNT RUTE: At least say something! Talk to me!

JONAS: I don't have any desire for you! *(Changes his tone.)* I can't stand women I feel no desire for... THAT'S WHY I'VE ALWAYS HATED MY MOTHER AND SISTERS... *(Suffering, yet with the greatest dignity imaginable.)* I don't know, I can't understand how a man tolerates his own mother, unless…

JONAS abruptly turns to AUNT RUTE, without hiding his rancour.

JONAS: If only you weren't as ugly as you are! This nasty, with acne all over your forehead! You're worse than ugly – A WOMAN WHO SHOULD NOT BE DESIRED UNDER ANY CIRCUMSTANCE!

AUNT RUTE ignominiously embraces JONAS' legs.

AUNT RUTE: How am I to blame for that – how?

JONAS: *(Cruel.)* Even the mute one, even with her crossed-eyes, I desired her!

AUNT RUTE: You desired me once!

JONAS: *(Implacable.)* I was drunk, totally drunk!

AUNT RUTE: *(Recoils.)* I know what you all want – you want me to kill myself! You want me to throw myself in the lake. *(Hysterical.)* But if I die, I'll throw a curse over every single one of you, the entire family!

DONA SENHORINHA reappears, also hysterical.

DONA SENHORINHA: Rute! Either you come help me or I'll stop and let this woman die!

DONA SENHORINHA quickly returns to the outhouse and AUNT RUTE follows her, as if sleepwalking.

JONAS: *(With a kind of delayed remorse.)* I've lost count of how many girls she got for me! *(Lighting up.)* and VIRGINS!

JONAS stands up and gets a small, thick whip from a cabinet. He hits the furniture with it.

JONAS: *(Like an old-fashioned father.)* When a son rebelled against my father, he used THIS! Once I raised my voice to him – then, he hit me with it. He got me right here – left me a massive gash, IT BRUISED ME!

GUILHERME: *(Laconic.)* Glória was expelled from school!

JONAS: *(Amazed.)* Glória did what? She was expelled? Have you gone mad?

GUILHERME: *(In absolute pain.)* Expelled!

JONAS: *(Dizzy.)* But... What did she do? What was it?

GUILHERME: *(Cold, merely informative.)* The day before yesterday, they called me to her school... Then, one of the priests told me that Glória and some other girl there...

JONAS: *(Overexcited.)* Stop the innuendos! Tell it to me straight!

GUILHERME: *(No reaction.)* She and the girl were sending each other letters... They found a bunch of them...

JONAS: *(Not understanding.)* Letters?

GUILHERME: They were always together... and, even before that day, one of the nuns saw the two of them talking, late at their dormitory... She heard their whole conversation! They were talking about dying together and, by the end...

JONAS: What happened at the end?

GUILHERME:... they KISSED EACH OTHER ON THE LIPS!

JONAS: *(After a pause, triumphant.)* So, I now know what CONCLUSIONS they've reached! They and YOU, as well. *(Terrible.)* How indecent of you – ALL OF YOU, indecent!

GUILHERME: They had no doubt – the situation was CRYSTAL CLEAR!

JONAS: *(Agitated.)* You can't comprehend the innocence between the two girls. You're a bunch of dirty old dogs!

GUILHERME: *(Informative once more.)* The priest then said they'd reached a conclusion regarding the KIND OF FRIENDSHIP between the two… that they wouldn't tolerate such thing… that the only solution would be to EXPEL THEM BOTH!

JONAS: Why didn't you punch one of them dogs?

GUILHERME: *(Always cold.)* I brought you one of the letters I stole.

GUILHERME takes the letter out of his pocket.

GUILHERME: *(Reading.)* It says things like: "Glória, my love, yesterday was so good! I couldn't sleep, thinking! I know what we DID is a sin, but it doesn't matter, etc." And it ends like: "From the one who'll love you always til death and who'll never betray you – Teresa".

JONAS: *(Like a beast.)* It's the same old story. In fact, exactly what they did to Joan of Arc!

GUILHERME: Now, listen to me: I came ahead of her, Glória should arrive any moment now, today, tomorrow, I'm not sure. I want you to agree with me on this: SHE WON'T ENTER THIS HOUSE!

JONAS: She won't enter this house – what are you talking about? Why wouldn't she?

GUILHERME: *(Vehement.)* Because this house is unworthy of her – BECAUSE YOU CAN'T EVEN CONTROL YOUR URGES NEAR YOUR OWN DAUGTHER! *(Overexcited.)* You taint, you soil everything you touch – the house, the furniture, the walls, everything!

JONAS: How about you? Are you any better than me? My son? Just as lustful as I am!

GUILHERME: *(Triumphant.)* I used to! I used to be as lustful as you – used to. But not anymore – never again!

JONAS: Sure, never again! WE WERE BORN THIS WAY; WE'LL DIE THIS WAY!

GUILHERME: If you only knew what I did! *(Changes his tone.)* Listen, Father, when I went to the seminary, I was just like you and this whole family; I could barely sleep at night, in there. I had to run away, I couldn't stand it.

AUNT RUTE leaves the WOMAN's outhouse carrying a few things, and approaches them.

AUNT RUTE: You'll bite each other's heads off, tear each other apart, both of you, all because of women. *(Towards the outhouse.)* Edmundo is over there, he won't budge – he's mesmerised by the whole thing. You're all just...

AUNT RUTE exits, returning to the WOMAN's outhouse.

GUILHERME: *(As if he hadn't been interrupted.)* One night, at the seminary, it was very hot. I decided to cut it off – a mutilation wound – the blood drenched the sheets.

JONAS: *(Not understanding immediately.)* Mutilation wound?

GUILHERME: *(Abstract.)* After this VOLUNTARY ACCIDENT, I've become someone else, as if I didn't belong to this family anymore. *(Changing his tone, completely.)* Glória cannot come into this house!

JONAS: *(Disoriented.)* Your mother will take care of her!

GUILHERME: Not even Mother! She's a MARRIED WOMAN, she knows LOVE – she's not PURE. She's not worthy of Glória – only I am, after the ACCIDENT!

JONAS: But Glória is everything to me! She's the only thing I have in life!

GUILHERME: *(Not paying attention to him.)* You do well in humiliating Mother. She needs to PURGE her sins, because she desired love, she got married. Because a woman who has loved once – husband or not – should never leave her bedroom. She should stay there, like lying in a tomb. Married or not. Good-bye!

DONA SENHORINHA reappears from the door of the WOMAN's outhouse.

DONA SENHORINHA: She's going to die, Jonas – her hips are too narrow!

Darkness at centre stage. Lights back on the Family Album. Fourth portrait, same PHOTOGRAPHER. DONA SENHORINHA and AUNT RUTE, adopt a pose like the ones in the preceding portraits, extremely artificial. This time, the PHOTOGRAPHER does not intervene. Once more, we are graced by the same stupid comments from THE SPEAKER.

THE SPEAKER: Dona Senhorinha is not only wife and mother *aussi*; she's a sister, also, as devoted as the best of them. Throughout Rute's illness, she remained by her sister's bedside, like a dedicated diligent guardian angel. She didn't even sleep! We live in an utilitarian age, when affection like this, humble and pure, is only found elsewhere. On the other hand, Rute, who is the oldest out of the two, is equally affectionate. These are the results of a patriarchal upbringing!

The portrait is taken, the pose is undone; the stage goes dark again. A new scene lights up: the interior of a small local church. The altar is completely decorated. Immense portrait of Our Lord Saviour Jesus Christ, totally disproportionate – it takes the whole space between the floor and the ceiling. IMPORTANT NOTE: instead of the face of Our Lord Saviour, what we see is the cruel and bestial face of Jonas. It is evident that the portrait, given its size, reflects GLÓRIA's psychological condition. She comes in with GUILHERME. GLÓRIA's first reaction: she looks mesmerised at the false Jesus. There had been a storm. GLÓRIA is soaking wet and so is GUILHERME. GLÓRIA is such a beautiful young woman.

GLÓRIA: *(With surprise, and some fear.)* Where's Dad? Didn't you say he was waiting – here?

GUILHERME: He's coming. He'll be here soon!

GLÓRIA is facing the picture, charmed by it. She kneels down and prays. During her prayer, GUILHERME raises his hand to caress his sister's head but stops the gesture in time.

GUILHERME: You've taken so long!

GLÓRIA: *(Shivering, paying no attention to his comment.)* Who does HE look like?

GUILHERME: *(Troubled.)* We need to get you out of these clothes – look at you! You'll catch a death!

GLÓRIA: It's so similar!

GUILHERME: Last year, because of a storm like this, that girl died of pneumonia… *(Changes his tone.)* Look, I've found a place, here! Just behind here!

GUILHERME is standing beside the altar.

GLÓRIA: *(Still impressed with the false Christ.)* – I've never seen anything like it! What a resemblance! *(She's still shivering, arms crossed over her chest.)*

GUILHERME: *(Calling her, in angst.)* Come on! Here, behind the altar – it's a big hollow! You can take off your clothes, let them dry – put them back on later!

GLÓRIA: *(Only then making sense of what her brother says.)* In there? *(Big shiver.)* But people can come in!

GUILHERME: Of course not! In this weather?

GLÓRIA: But it'll take a while for them to dry!

GUILHERME: *(Agitated.)* But you can't stay like that – wet. YOU CAN GIVE ME YOUR CLOTHES, I'LL DRY THEM, AND GIVE IT TO YOU IN NO TIME!

GLÓRIA: *(Going into the hollow behind the altar.)* I've got the shivers!

GUILHERME: You've caught a cold, at the very least.

GLÓRIA: Where's Daddy? What's keeping him?

GUILHERME: He'll be here any minute now!

GLÓRIA: This little church brings me so many memories!

GUILHERME: Glória, there's SOMETHING you should know...

GLÓRIA: *(Not paying attention to him.)* Can't you see the resemblance – NONE AT ALL?

GUILHERME: What?

GLÓRIA: Look at the portrait, closely... – can't you see the resemblance – don't you think it looks just like him?

GUILHERME: What do you mean?

GLÓRIA: Isn't the face of Jesus Christ the same as Daddy's, same expression, TO A TEE?

GUILHERME: *(After a pause.)* Hand me your clothes so that I can put them to dry.

GUILHERME is noticeably possessed by a great sense of anxiety.

GLÓRIA: No need!

GUILHERME: Why not? It's something – SO NATURAL!

GLÓRIA: It's okay! I'll dry them myself!

GUILHERME: All right then... *(Lowers his voice.)* But, it's no big deal. I'm not like THEM.

GLÓRIA: I didn't catch that. What did you say?

GUILHERME: *(In a low voice, so GLÓRIA won't hear him.)* If THEY saw your arms, just your bare arm – NAKED – holding up your clothes to dry – they'd be in awe. Father, for sure!

GLÓRIA: Speak up!

GUILHERME: *(Still quiet.)* But I'm different. *(Raising his voice.)* Glória, it's safe for me to be here – alone with you. Even if I were the last man on earth and you, the last woman.

GLÓRIA: What do you mean, Guilherme?

GUILHERME: *(In pain.)* I suffered an ACCIDENT.

GLÓRIA: You know, I've been noticing something different about you!

GUILHERME: I've gained so much weight... I'm turning into a blob... *(Looks at his hands, disgusted.)* My hands are so sweaty!

GLÓRIA exits the hollow behind the altar; her dress is wrinkled, from attempting to dry it.

GUILHERME: *(Resentful.)* But you didn't dry your clothes at all!

GLÓRIA: Just the dress!

GUILHERME: *(With angst.)* Just the dress? You should dry everything… Take off all your clothes and dry them completely… If not, you'll catch a cold, at the very least.

GLÓRIA: Where's Daddy?

GUILHERME: What was IT like? You and that girl?

GLÓRIA: Who, Teresa?

GUILHERME: Why did you do… IT?

GLÓRIA: *(In pure angst.)* I didn't do anything!

GUILHERME: *(Supplicant.)* Tell me… EVERYTHING! You should never feel any shame in front of me – NONE.

GUILHERME holds both of GLÓRIA's hands. Almost like a satyr.

GUILHERME: Can you feel my heart – how it's beating fast!

GLÓRIA: Do we really need to talk about it?

GUILHERME: *(Puffed up with rage.)* Tell me!

GLÓRIA: *(Crying.)* If you only knew, the effort I have to make not to think about IT! *(Vehement.)* I'm sure, I know it in my heart; she's going to kill herself!

GUILHERME: *(Lowers his voice.)* Tell me – the two of you did it – in pure INNOCENCE?

GLÓRIA: *(As if talking to herself.)* She begged me for us to die together. She wanted me to throw myself between train carriages with her. *(Sweet and in transit.)* It would run us over…

GUILHERME: *(Astounded.)* God wouldn't want that!

GLÓRIA: *(As if still talking to herself.)* She was hurt – so hurt! All because I told her…

GUILHERME: *(Desperate.)* Told her, what?

GLÓRIA: ... that every time we kissed, I'd close my eyes and see Daddy's face, as clear as day. As if it were this portrait I see here, to a tee.

GLÓRIA points at the fake portrait of Jesus Christ.

GLÓRIA: *(Suffering.)* So hurt! She stopped speaking to me. She'll die mad at me – I know it.

A scream is heard, somewhat non-human, the cry of a wounded beast, out in the storm.

GLÓRIA: Did you hear that?

GUILHERME: Pay him no mind – it's just Nonô!

NONÔ's maniacal laughter is heard, surrounding the small church.

GLÓRIA: *(Cold passed the shivers.)* It's so sad having a mad relative! Maybe they'd be better off dead.

GUILHERME: He's happy with the rain. He loves the rain – rolls around in the puddles...

GUILHERME shows no transition, face to face with his sister, putting on another satyr-like expression.

GUILHERME: You know he lives in the woods – UNCLOTHED?

GLÓRIA: Teresa told me a man's body is something disgusting!

GUILHERME: She's right.

GLÓRIA: What she forgets is many women love it, with gusto!

NONÔ's laughter is heard even louder.

GUILHERME: One of the Sisters told me that, once, you and the other girl...

GLÓRIA: *(Stopping her brother.)* If you only knew how innocent it was, what we did! *(Puffed up with wrath.)* Now, that Sister starts telling everyone that I, we... *(Covers her face with one hand.)* She had it in for us. She only liked teacher's pets! *(Suffering.)* If it wasn't for Daddy, if I didn't need to see Daddy – I'd be under the train by now. I swear I'd be – I give you my word!

GUILHERME: Glória, we have run away from here, fast.

GLÓRIA: *(Backing off.)* What's going on? What are you hiding?

GUILHERME: *(Passionately.)* Run away somewhere far! I've given this a lot of thought! No house, no walls, no rooms. Only the ground we live in! And we wouldn't mind the rain!

GUILHERME changes his tone; seems to be talking to himself.

GUILHERME: Even when we make love! No bedroom, no bed! On the ground, the ground we live in!

GUILHERME changes his tone once again; now to GLÓRIA.

GUILHERME: We're different from the others. Let me look at you.

GLÓRIA: *(Trying to change the subject.)* What about Daddy, uh? What's keeping him?

GUILHERME: What about Daddy? ANYWHERE WITH AN OUNCE OF DECENCY, DADDY WOULD BE IN A CAGE. He's even killed people!

GLÓRIA: Liar!

GUILHERME: Yes, a killer. He killed... a woman from the village. She was A MUTE – and cross-eyed!

GLÓRIA: It can't be true!

GUILHERME: *(Laughing like a demon.)* She'd been made pregnant. She came crawling, about to give birth, really in labour… Then, Daddy stepped on her belly. *(Jubilant.)* He stepped on the baby, the mute woman, all of it!

GLÓRIA: *(Leaning against the altar.)* Carry on with your lies, carry on!

GUILHERME: *(Cruel.)* One of his boots was covered in blood. He had to have it cleaned with benzene – with a cloth soaked in benzene, but the stain wouldn't go away.

GLÓRIA: *(Beast-like, accusatory.)* I know what you are – you're as malicious as that Sister! You see evil in everything!

GUILHERME: *(Wheezing.)* What he does to mother…

GLÓRIA: I never noticed anything! Daddy's always treated Mum quite well… !

GUILHERME: *(Quick and ironic.)* To your face! He tries to behave himself when you're at the house… You're still the only person he respects; who still carry, under his eye, some sort of consideration. But with anyone else! He does the filthiest things in front of whoever is there to see it. It's like he has to boast his manhood! Mother has to put up with all sorts of things.

GLÓRIA: *(In pain.)* All of you always take Mother's side – but not me, NO!

GUILHERME: I give you my word of honour!

GLÓRIA: I never told anybody, always hid it, but I'll say it now – I don't like Mum. I can't love her – she's evil; I can sense she's capable of killing a person. I always feared being left alone with her! Feared she'd kill me!

GUILHERME: Father's worse.

GLÓRIA: *(In transit.)* Not my Daddy! When I was little, I
    didn't like to go to church... I only started to like it – I
    remember it perfectly – only when I saw, for the first time,
    a portrait of Our Lord and Saviour, Jesus Christ... Like
    that one over there, only smaller – of course! *(Disfigured by
    her emotions.)* I was in awe with the RESEMBLANCE!

GUILHERME: What's this resemblance you see?

GLÓRIA: *(Entrapped by her own ecstasy.)* I collected portraits...
    The happiest day of my life was when I had my holy
    communion – I even had a portrait made!

GUILHERME: *(Laughing like a beast.)* If that Sister learnt
    of this! If she saw you talking like this... She'd see that
    THAT THING WITH THAT GIRL WAS NOTHING
    compared to this!

GLÓRIA: *(Desperate.)* What I feel for Daddy is so pure, so
    beautiful, that Sister wouldn't understand it. Neither would
    you, nor Mum, no one!

GUILHERME: *(Bestial.)* Are you sure?

GLÓRIA: *(Back with her senses, changing her tone.)* No, I can't
    be sure. But whatever it is, it doesn't matter. I don't care
    about what anyone else thinks. I don't even care what
    I think!

GUILHERME: I have to save you – WHATEVER IT TAKES!

GLÓRIA: And even if it's all true... If Daddy stepped on that
    woman's belly... If he does whatever he does to Mum...
    Even if he's the Devil incarnate. *(Her excitement wanes off;
    sweet, once again.)* Even so, I'd still love him. I'd adore him!

GUILHERME: *(In pain.)* There's just one thing you don't
    know!

GLÓRIA: Where is Daddy?

GUILHERME: Do you know why I went away to become a priest? Why I decided to give up on everything?

GLÓRIA: *(Backing off.)* I really don't care!

GUILHERME: *(Intense.)* BECAUSE OF YOU!

GLÓRIA: *(Lowers her voice.)* Liar!

GUILHERME: *(Beast-like.)* Because of you, sure! *(Like a satyr.)* You were just a little girl back then... still, I couldn't even look at you, all my thoughts were about you... *(Pathetic.)* I couldn't handle it, couldn't take it anymore!

GLÓRIA: *(Fearful.)* Now I see why you wanted me to go over there, in the back... WHY YOU WANTED ME TO TAKE OFF MY CLOTHES AND GIVE THEM TO YOU TO DRY...

GUILHERME: *(In awe.)* It wasn't like that – I swear!

NONÔ's laughter is louder, closer.

GLÓRIA: *(Rancorous.)* You think I hadn't noticed the look on your face. Your eyes popped when you said Nonô was wandering around here – UNCLOTHED?

GUILHERME: *(Terrified.)* I'm telling you! You can only say those things because you don't know about the ACCIDENT... *(Lowers his voice.)* the voluntary accident! I'm not like that anymore...

GLÓRIA: *(Crying.)* Dear Lord, I hate you so much right now!

GUILHERME: I don't want him to see you! Come with me! I'll take you to a nice place – A LOVELY PLACE!

GUILHERME rushes toward GLÓRIA who backs away until she reaches the altar.

GUILHERME: Or, if you prefer, we can do what your friend wanted, we'll throw ourselves between train carriages, HOLDING ONTO EACH OTHER!

GLÓRIA: Daddy has got no chest hair, not even one!

GUILHERME: For the last time – COME WITH ME!? Please, say you'll come, please!

GLÓRIA: No!

GUILHERME: You'll never be his – NEVER!

GUILHERME pulls out a gun and fires twice at GLÓRIA. She collapses, on her knees, both hands covering her wounded stomach.

GLÓRIA: *(Squirming, in pain.)* When I was little… I thought Mum could just die… Or else, Daddy could run away with me… *(Rolls over.)* Ah, the pain!

GLÓRIA dies.

END OF ACT 2

Act 3

SCENE 1

The third act begins with the fifth portrait of the family album. NONÔ is a taciturn young boy, incredibly built for his age. DONA SENHORINHA stands next to him, beautiful and decorative as per usual. The PHOTOGRAPHER dances around NONÔ who seems hostile towards the reputable portrait-maker. The PHOTOGRAPHER seems to be in a discrete panic. NONÔ resembles Lon Chaney Jr[3].

THE SPEAKER: Fifth family portrait. On this occasion, Nonô was only thirteen, but seemed much older! Very well developed for his age! By painful coincidence, this portrait was taken the day before he'd gone mad. A thief had entered Dona Senhorinha's bedroom and, due to the natural shock of such situation, Nonô had his better judgment obliterated. What a difference between a son like that and our beach rats who only care about playing volleyball in the sand. Poor Nonô! Nowadays, science's made so much progress and, who knows, he might benefit from Cardiazol convulsion therapy, some ECT or the likes of it?

The lights go off on the portrait scene. Living room at the farmhouse is lit up. JONAS is alone on stage. He goes to a cabinet, picks up a gun from one of the drawers, examines the barrel and puts it in his trousers. The WOMAN in labour starts to moan again.

JONAS: *(To himself.)* I knew that, sooner or later... *(Suffering.)* But what does he take me for?

---

3   Creighton Tull Chaney (February 10, 1906 – July 12, 1973), known by his stage name Lon Chaney Jr., was an American actor known for playing various roles in many horror films, such as Count Alucard (Dracula spelled backward.), Frankenstein's monster in The Ghost of Frankenstein (1942), and the Mummy in three Universal motion pictures at the time.

DONA SENHORINHA appears, somewhat fearful and seems physically exhausted. She wipes her forehead with the back of her hand, attempting to dry her sweat. She hears JONAS' words and is in awe as she approaches.

DONA SENHORINHA: *(Trying to hide her startle.)* – What's wrong?

JONAS: *(Fed up.)* That boy… But he'll get what's coming for him!

DONA SENHORINHA: I have a bad feeling about this!

The WOMAN in labour starts to moan once again. DONA SENHORINHA is beside herself, in angst. She moves toward the outhouse; and, yet again, moves back toward her husband.

DONA SENHORINHA: Can't you see she's dying, Jonas!

JONAS: *(Also a little fearful.)* You're been hysterical!

DONA SENHORINHA: *(Yielding to despair.)* This time I'm serious. *(Changing her tone.)* She should never have been a mother. She's not wide enough – she has no hips whatsoever.

JONAS: *(Looking towards the outhouse.)* How come nothing like that ever happened to you?

DONA SENHORINHA: *(Somewhat boasting.)* Thank God, I've always been very lucky delivering my children…

JONAS: *(Agitated.)* That's right!

DONA SENHORINHA: *(Transported to the past.)* … a lot of women have tears, have to have surgery. Not me, never!

The WOMAN in labour moans loudly, again.

DONA SENHORINHA: *(To herself, with pride, caressing her stomach.)* The doctor said my measurements were perfect… That I had textbook childbearing hips…

WOMAN: – … 'Seu' Jonas… Call for 'seu' Jonas, please…

JONAS: *(In a mix of awe and fear.)* There must be a way. Having kids should be the easiest thing to do here… There are those who, just by standing up, right at work – POP a baby out! Almost no one dies of labour!

DONA SENHORINHA: She should've been taken to surgery.

JONAS: *(Irritated.)* You and your surgeries!

JONAS, changing his tone, goes face to face with his wife.

JONAS: Do you want to know something? I think you're wishing her dead.

DONA SENHORINHA: Do you think?

JONAS: *(Choosing his words with care, in a pathetic plea.)* But I really don't want her to die – I DON'T!

JONAS changes his tone once more; now sweet and sad.

JONAS: She was just a girl – quite bony in here *(Pointing at his hip.)* she had absolutely no desire; she was just curious…

EDMUNDO leaves the WOMAN's outhouse. She starts to moan, calling out to JONAS.

WOMAN: *(Already in dyspnea.)* 'Seu' Jonas… "seu' Jonas!

JONAS, in a sudden move, rushes toward the outhouse.

JONAS: *(Faking congeniality.)* Hey, Totinha! How are things here?

TOTINHA: *(In dyspnea.)* I think it's time, 'seu' Jonas – I'm GOING…

JONAS: *(Always trying to seem cheerful.)* Don't be silly, Totinha! You're going nowhere!

TOTINHA: *(In rancor, full of angst.)* No need for me to be here… *(Stops, she's suffocating.)* … suffering…

JONAS: Don't say that!

TOTINHA: … but I blame it all on you!

JONAS: This will only make things worse!

TOTINHA: *(In a uppermost effort to articulate a full sentence.)* Hear my words, 'seu' Jonas, – GOD SHALL SMITE YOU!

JONAS shuts the door violently, kicking it or something similar by the sound of it. DONA SENHORINHA and EDMUNDO are facing the outhouse, minding the full conversation.

DONA SENHORINHA: *(In a sudden fit of despair.)* I can't take it anymore, Edmundo! I just can't!

EDMUNDO: *(Passionately, pointing at the outhouse.)* When I was in there, it occurred to me you went through the same thing. *(Lowers his voice.)* It felt like it wasn't Totinha in there, going through the contractions, in such horrid pain; but you!

DONA SENHORINHA: *(After a pause.)* Perhaps one day, I don't know! Oh, if I weren't religious! If I didn't believe in God. *(Stopping in front of her son.)* There are things I think about, things I'd like to do, but I don't know if I'd have the courage!

DONA SENHORINHA expresses great despair.

DONA SENHORINHA: There's something I have to do – I wonder if I can?

DONA SENHORINHA and EDMUNDO look at each other, in silence, astonished, somewhat in fear. They are startled by AUNT RUTE, who leaves the outhouse banging the door shut, as abruptly as JONAS. She passes by them with a sombre expression of rancour.

AUNT RUTE: *(Walking by them.)* Deadlock.

AUNT RUTE whizzes by and disappears.

DONA SENHORINHA: My God, I can't believe this!

EDMUNDO: And you put up with him!

DONA SENHORINHA: *(Holding her son's face with both hands.)* I fear, Edmundo – that you'll be like that, too.

EDMUNDO: Like that? What do you mean?

DONA SENHORINHA: *(Hesitant, trying to find the right words.)* I mean, chasing after women, a new one every moment, almost every instant!

EDMUNDO: *(In a boyfriend's plaint.)* Is that what you think of me?

DONA SENHORINHA: *(Vague.)* The things I've seen!

EDMUNDO: *(Vehement.)* I'm a man of only one woman! Up to now, I've only loved one!

DONA SENHORINHA, taken completely by angst, finds support in her son's words.

DONA SENHORINHA: Do you swear?

EDMUNDO: Of course!

DONA SENHORINHA: *(Lowers her head toward her hands.)* Oh, if I could only believe you!

EDMUNDO: I've sworn, haven't I?

DONA SENHORINHA: And this woman, who is she?

EDMUNDO: *(Vehement.)* Do you want me to tell you?

DONA SENHORINHA: *(After hesitating.)* I do.

EDMUNDO: *(Answering with a question.)* What difference does it make?

DONA SENHORINHA: Don't tell me, then.

EDMUNDO: *(Vehement.)* But you do know who I'm talking about, don't you?

DONA SENHORINHA: *(As if talking to herself, but incredibly sweet.)* I think so! *(Changes her tone.)* I think I know, I've always had an idea, but I could be wrong!

DONA SENHORINHA, in an unexpected impulse, holds her son's face once again; at first looking at him passionately, then with an abrupt wrath.

DONA SENHORINHA: I really don't care!

EDMUNDO: I doubt it!

DONA SENHORINHA: *(Poignant and obsessed, both her hands pressing each cheek.)* You're just like him!

DONA SENHORINHA looks toward the WOMAN's outhouse.

EDMUNDO: *(Slowly.)* How about you?

DONA SENHORINHA: *(Instinctively fearing the question about to be asked.)* What about me?

EDMUNDO: Do you love anybody?

DONA SENHORINHA: *(Closing herself up.)* I'm married!

EDMUNDO: That's your answer?

DONA SENHORINHA: I don't know, I don't know! *(Changing her tone, in transit to a different frame of mind.)* Things here are going to get a lot worse – Glória's on her way… *(In a new tone.)* She could never stand me, Edmundo. Never! *(Finding yet another tone of voice.)* When she was born and they said – it's a GIRL- I had a feeling she'd be my enemy. *(Distressed.)* I was right!

EDMUNDO: Glória doesn't really matter!

DONA SENHORINHA: *(Feeling misunderstood.)* That's what you think!

EDMUNDO: But he does. *(Points to the outhouse.)*

DONA SENHORINHA: Both of them!

EDMUNDO: Mother, this can only result in a utter disgrace. I can't even look at that man anymore. Sometimes, I think there might be only one solution!

DONA SENHORINHA: *(In panic.)* What do you want to say, Edmundo?

EDMUNDO: *(As if talking to himself.)* This has been a long time coming – since I was a boy! I remember once – it was after lunch. We had guests over. He whispered something to you...

DONA SENHORINHA: *(Not fully comprehending.)* When?

EDMUNDO, as if he's reliving his own memory.

EDMUNDO: *(Ignoring the interruption.)* ... he said something. Then, he got up – he went ahead of you, you followed him. *(Suffering.)* Even though I was only a child, I understood everything. If you knew how angry I was, what I really wanted to do to him!

DONA SENHORINHA: *(Covering her face with one hand.)* Dear Lord, how absurd!

EDMUNDO: I remember, they hadn't even served dessert yet. *(Vehement.)* He asked for it in front of everyone, because his desire can't wait!

The storm outside makes itself heard.

DONA SENHORINHA: *(Sweet and enigmatic.)* One day, I'm going to tell you something… Then, on that day!… It's one of my life's secrets. *(Slowly, intentional.)* SOMETHING VERY INTIMATE!

EDMUNDO: So tell me, now, this instant!

DONA SENHORINHA: *(With a new attitude, abstract toward EDMUNDO.)* The things I've been through, here, in this house, with that man!

EDMUNDO: *(Looks at the outhouse.)* Did you think I hadn't noticed it?

DONA SENHORINHA: *(To herself.)* The other day, just because I said – POWDER ROOM- so natural, isn't it? He made me say the other word; the one that feels so ugly to me! In front of everyone!

EDMUNDO: Mother, you have to get out of here!

DONA SENHORINHA: Ah, if only I could!

EDMUNDO: You have to leave him! *(Holding his mother's hands between his.)* We could go somewhere no one would even know us. I know places like that!

DONA SENHORINHA: He'd come after us! Not out of love, but just out of spite.

EDMUNDO: *(Slowly, in a special tone.)* Maybe if we could, or if only I could…

They look at each other; DONA SENHORINHA seems to understand EDMUNDO.

DONA SENHORINHA: *(Overcome by fear.)* No Edmundo. I don't want it that way.

EDMUNDO: Maybe THIS is the only way!

DONA SENHORINHA: *(Overtaken by her nerves.)* You must swear to me you'll never, ever, never try… THIS! *(Changing her tone, as if, despite it all, the idea fascinated her.)* Or, if you were to try it, don't try it face to face! He could find a way to defend himself! *(Taking her son's hands.)* Behind his back – do you understand me?

Beside herself, DONA SENHORINHA falls in love with the idea; as if making a full plan for the perfect crime.

DONA SENHORINHA: Behind his back and it has to be in a controlled environment – in a way he couldn't fight back. For instance: WHEN HE'S ASLEEP…

Tired, DONA SENHORINHA stops. Totally fascinated with the crime, she continues.

DONA SENHORINHA: When he's asleep, it'd be so easy. He wouldn't fight back. He wouldn't even have time to cry for help.

Nearby, NONÔ's inhuman cries are heard.

DONA SENHORINHA: *(Changing her tone.)* Nonô, again. *(In pain, like the most damned amongst women.)* You see, Edmundo – I can't – I can't run away with you!

EDMUNDO: *(Supplicant.)* Yes, you can! Come with me!

DONA SENHORINHA: I'll never have the courage to leave Nonô! It's impossible! *(Changing her tone, as if falling in love.)* You can't imagine how he gets, every time he sees me, from far away! It's something else!

EDMUNDO: Do you see Nonô a lot? Do you actually look at him?

DONA SENHORINHA: *(Closing her eyes without noticing her son's angst.)* Sometimes, when I go out. Or else, from the window!

EDMUNDO: *(With rancour.)* I don't want you to see, to look at him!

DONA SENHORINHA: *(Not understanding.)* He's my son!

EDMUNDO: *(Suffering.)* He goes around with nothing on… *(Makes a gesture symbolising nudity.)* And he has a body that'd impress any man – so not to mention, any woman!

DONA SENHORINHA: *(Abstract.)* I like him the way he is – HANDSOME! Olive skinned! *(Somewhat bestial.)* He's lost his mind – but no one can take away the beauty of his physique. He was born with it!

EDMUNDO: You like Nonô more than you like me.

DONA SENHORINHA: *(Not paying attention to him.)* I can't abandon Nonô. It isn't in me.

EDMUNDO: *(Changing his tone, passionately.)* Mother, sometimes I feel as if the world was empty, and no one else existed except for us. I mean, you, Father, me and my brothers. As if ours was the one and only family. *(In a kind of hysteria.)* That way, love and hate would all have to be born from us. *(Returning to his senses.)* But no, no! *(Changing his tone.)* – I think the man should never leave his mother's womb. He should stay there, forever, all curled up, facing up, facing down, sideways, I don't know.

EDMUNDO kneels at DONA SENHORINHA's feet.

DONA SENHORINHA: *(In fear.)* No, Edmundo, no!

EDMUNDO: Heaven, not the one that comes after death; the real heaven, the one before I was even born – was your womb…

Always on his knees, EDMUNDO plunges his head – facing the audience – into his mother's womb.

143

EDMUNDO stands up. We hear the door to the outhouse open and JONAS returns, while the WOMAN's voice is heard, cursing. IMPORTANT NICETY: JONAS is fastening his belt and only finishes doing so when he approaches his wife.

WOMAN: *(As usual, her voice is hoarse.)* You devil... What's yours... is coming for you...

JONAS approaches with an evil expression. He stops, expecting the WOMAN's curse to reach an end.

WOMAN: *(In dyspnea.)* You're evil...

DONA SENHORINHA: Hear that?

WOMAN: I'm gonna curse you plenty!

DONA SENHORINHA: *(To JONAS.)* What the hell is happening in there?

JONAS: She's lost it!

WOMAN: You and your family!

JONAS: She said I had a daughter; that my daughter would get knocked up... *(Changing his tone.)* So I hit her in the mouth, like this... *(Shows the back of his hand.)*

AUNT RUTE, upright and stiff, scuttles by on her way to the outhouse. She goes straight in and out of stage.

JONAS: *(Fed up.)* Let her die!

AUNT RUTE: *(Reappears, excited.)* She's all whirled up, contorted, convulsing!

DONA SENHORINHA: *(Laconic.)* Eclampsia!

JONAS: *(Objective.)* She's done for!

DONA SENHORINHA: I'll go check!

DONA SENHORINHA wants to go, but EDMUNDO protests.

EDMUNDO: Don't go! I don't want you to!

JONAS: Why wouldn't she?

EDMUNDO: *(Hysterical, without hearing JONAS, talking to DONA SENHORINHA.)* Why can't he go? *(Confronting his father.)* – Yeah, you! You're the one responsible for all this! *(In a special tone, face to face with his father, full of both hatred and pain.)* And, what's worse, the girl's dying. *(Lowers his voice, in awe.)* How could you!

JONAS: *(Sombre.)* Go, Senhorinha, go!

EDMUNDO: *(Almost hysterical.)* If she does, it's because she really is shameless!

DONA SENHORINHA faces her husband, cowardly.

DONA SENHORINHA: *(Lowers her voice.)* I'm going, Jonas!

EDMUNDO: *(To his mother.)* If you go, I'll never speak to you again, never!

DONA SENHORINHA stops.

EDMUNDO: *(Talking to himself.)* A man who spends his life corrupting girls… While Mother, Mother is a SAINT!

JONAS starts laughing like a beast.

JONAS: SAINT!

JONAS goes face to face with DONA SENHORINHA; he laughs even harder.

JONAS: *(Pointing at her.)* He called you a saint!

JONAS stops laughing abruptly; savage, talking to DONA SENHORINHA.

JONAS: Are you a saint? Say it; I want to hear you say it: are you?

EDMUNDO: *(Supplicant.)* Answer him, Mother! Say it: I am!

DONA SENHORINHA: *(Lowering her head, in a cold impulse.)* I am!

JONAS grabs DONA SENHORINHA.

DONA SENHORINHA: *(Dominated by her husband.)* No!

JONAS: *(Triumphant.)* Now tell him what happened... *(Suddenly changing his tone, almost sweet.)* Your son has the right to know!

EDMUNDO: *(Lost.)* Don't let you be dominated by this man, fight back!

JONAS: *(Sweet as a demon.)* Tell him about that day – THAT NIGHT... *(Always sweet.)* tell him!

DONA SENHORINHA doesn't respond.

JONAS: *(Speaking for his wife.)* I'd gone to Três Corações – came back early... I saw a shadow leaving our bedroom... I chased him and fired, but he ran away. I went into the bedroom, you confessed. You just didn't want to say who it was. I slapped you, beat you...

DONA SENHORINHA: You beat me!

JONAS: You only told me who the next day. *(To his son, changing his tone.)* Guess who?

EDMUNDO: *(In fear.)* I don't know...

JONAS: Teotônio!

EDMUNDO: *(In absolute awe.)* The reporter?

JONAS: The reporter! The editor-in-chief of 'Arauto de Colgonhas'! The guy, who had a hump, everybody said was fake... *(JONAS is overwhelmed by the pain.)* If it was anybody else, I'd understand! But that man, she'd gone too far!

DONA SENHORINHA: You never showed me any love!

JONAS: *(Overexcited.)* Yes, I did. Up to that night; not after. Nor love nor anything close to it.

DONA SENHORINHA: Edmundo, he made me call Teotônio the next day *(In the deepest awe.)* and he killed him in my bedroom! As if he were a dog!

JONAS: I killed him!

DONA SENHORINHA: That's when my living hell began. *(To EDMUNDO.)* Every day, in front of other people, your father would slap my hips – and he'd say – FEMALE IN HEAT!

EDMUNDO: I'd do the same thing!

JONAS: But not even that – you weren't even a FEMALE IN HEAT… never was… not with me, at least. Neither you nor any other woman I had. *(To himself, with extreme dissatisfaction.)* They all left me more anxious than before – sick, sick to my stomach, missing something, I don't even know what. *(Affirming hysterically.)* Women can't even be FEMALES IN HEAT!

JONAS talks to EDMUNDO.

JONAS: What astonishes me the most is that she has always been COLD! Never reacted. Not even flinch. She seemed dead!

DONA SENHORINHA: *(In a kind of hysteria, to her son.)* Did you hear – what he just said? That I was COLD!

EDMUNDO doesn't react.

DONA SENHORINHA: *(Triumphant.)* That was the secret – the SOMETHING VERY INTIMATE I was going to tell you, my son, I've always been COLD!

JONAS: *(Sardonic.)* So should I or shouldn't I bring women here?

EDMUNDO: Mother, tell me he's lying!

DONA SENHORINHA: I can't deny it. It's all true!

EDMUNDO: Deny it, for the love of God!

DONA SENHORINHA: *(Raising her head, very dignified.)* I had a lover!

EDMUNDO makes an unexpected gesture: he bows quickly and kisses JONAS' hand.

JONAS: I have one real love. But that one's untouchable…

EDMUNDO and DONA SENHORINHA observe, in awe, each of JONAS' gestures.

JONAS: *(Before leaving.)* I'm going out – to kill a man.

JONAS exits the room with absolute dignity. IMPORTANT NOTE: two shots are heard from afar. AUNT RUTE reappears, somewhat excited.

AUNT RUTE: A candle – she's about to make the passage!

EDMUNDO and DONA SENHORINHA seem to not hear her, absorbed as they are by their own emotions.

AUNT RUTE: *(Not understanding their indifference.)* A candle – so she can hold as she makes the passage!

EDMUNDO and DONA SENHORINHA don't answer. AUNT RUTE backs away, looking at her sister and nephew in awe.

DONA SENHORINHA: *(Sardonic, face to face with her son.)* Why all that playing nice?

EDMUNDO: *(Waking up.)* What do you mean?

DONA SENHORINHA: *(Cruel.)* You asked for your father's blessing?

EDMUNDO: *(In his turn, sardonic.)* Is that how you saw it?

DONA SENHORINHA: *(Frivolous.)* How else could I look at it? Was it fake?

EDMUNDO: *(With violence.)* No!

DONA SENHORINHA: *(With the same affirmative tone.)* Yes, it was! *(Face to face with her son.)* Between you and him *(Slowly, emphasising each word.)* there cannot be anything – there can never be anything! *(Violent.)* Only HATE!

EDMUNDO: You're nothing but a female in heat!

DONA SENHORINHA: So why did you leave everything – your wife – and come here?

EDMUNDO: I'm going back to Heloísa!

DONA SENHORINHA: *(Challenging.)* I dare you!

EDMUNDO: *(Laconic.)* Female in heat.

DONA SENHORINHA: *(Changes her tone.)* Are you saying that what he told you was worth nothing?

Pause, as the two of them look at each other, as if they were complete strangers.

DONA SENHORINHA: *(Lowering her voice.)* That I had always been cold?

EDMUNDO: *(In his own obsession.)* FEMALE IN HEAT!

AUNT RUTE reappears; she approaches them.

AUNT RUTE: *(Funereal and laconic.)* She passed. *(Pause.)* The baby's head didn't even crown.

DONA SENHORINHA at that moment, very dignified and beautiful, goes to the cabinet, gets a candle from a drawer and moves toward the outhouse where the WOMAN died.

AUNT RUTE: *(Absolutely stiff.)* Now the candle's useless.

DONA SENHORINHA appears to not hear anything; she keeps going. AUNT RUTE and EDMUNDO are left alone.

AUNT RUTE: *(Stiff.)* I'm leaving this place, still don't know where to. I'm going to walk, and keep walking until I fall. But before I go, there's something I need to tell you… *(AUNT RUTE comes even closer to EDMUNDO.)* – I heard everything. Now, here's something you don't know: ever since that night – seven years ago – Jonas never touched her again.

EDMUNDO: Who cares?

AUNT RUTE: She's waiting for you – she's sure that you're going after her. YOU CAN GO.

EDMUNDO, as if not having any willpower whatsoever, obeys. AUNT RUTE observes, with a triumphant expression. The outhouse door screeches, as it closes slowly. Then, the lights go off over the end of the first scene of Act 3.

Sixth portrait of the family album. JONAS poses, taciturn, as if dead inside. The PHOTOGRAPHER seems to move heaven and earth trying to get a suitable pose out of him. But JONAS seems to be made of stone. The PHOTOGRAPHER is justifiably fuming as he, ultimately, will have to produce a portrait by any means available.

THE SPEAKER: Sixth family portrait. The last portrait of Jonas, dated July 1924. The day before, he had sent a telegram to President Artur Bernardes saying he considered the São Paulo revolution reprehensible and unpatriotic. Congenital civility did not suit him. Two days later, just as luck dictates, fate took three children of this Plutarchian Hero. Unable to bear this painful blow, Jonas hung himself from a lintel. Others will say his wife killed him. Gossip flew about, rampant. People with little or nothing to themselves, real busybodies. Right when Jonas was being considered for candidacy to the Senate House in the next legislature. Let us pray for the eternal rest of his soul!

The lights go off on the portrait scene. The small church near the farmhouse is lit up. The portrait of Jesus that, to GLÓRIA's eyes, was so huge and disproportionate, now is reduced to its real size. Two coffins on stage: in one of them is EDMUNDO's body; in the other, GLÓRIA's. Candles are lit. DONA SENHORINHA is alone, mourning her son. She's still so beautiful in her severe sadness, even wearing her mourning clothes. After a little while, HELOÍSA, EDMUNDO's wife, comes in. She's also in mourning clothes. DONA SENHORINHA, in her pent up pain, seems not to sense HELOÍSA's presence in the small church.

HELOÍSA: *(After kneeling by EDMUNDO's coffin and praying briefly; she speaks somewhat in fear.)* Just now, there was a terrible accident at the train tracks: a man fell between two of the train carriages…

DONA SENHORINHA remains stolid and silent, as if she were three thousand miles away.

HELOÍSA: *(After overcoming a kind of repugnance, she kisses EDMUNDO's face rapidly; she seems to regret what she's done immediately.)* Why did you call me?

DONA SENHORINHA remains stolid. No answer.

HELOÍSA: *(After hesitating.)* If you ask me, he could've died as many times as he wanted.

HELOÍSA seems surprised by her own words.

HELOÍSA: *(Covering her face with one hand.)* God in Heaven, I don't know what I'm saying!

DONA SENHORINHA: *(With the greatest possible economy of gestures; her voice slightly hoarse.)* Edmundo is dead!

HELOÍSA: *(Turning, quick and aggressive.)* And I am the one to blame – am I?

DONA SENHORINHA: *(As if talking to herself.)* He killed himself, in front of me.

HELOÍSA: He's always been an odd person, a complete stranger to me – always. I only came because my family thought I should, they begged me to…

HELOÍSA continues, as if confiding a secret.

HELOÍSA: Daddy said it wouldn't look good – people would notice.

DONA SENHORINHA: *(Perking up, pathetic.)* Nobody notices anything around here. This is a god-forsaken place!

HELOÍSA: *(Approaching DONA SENHORINHA, in a mysterious and provocative tone.)* Would you like to know something Edmundo once told me?

DONA SENHORINHA: *(Closing herself up.)* I don't want to know anything!

HELOÍSA: *(In a kind of triumph.)* Oh, do I sense fear?

DONA SENHORINHA: *(As if rising to the challenge.)* Fear of what? There's no fear!

HELOÍSA and DONA SENHORINHA stand next to each other, face to face.

HELOÍSA: He told me – EVERYTHING!

DONA SENHORINHA: *(Quick and awake.)* I doubt that!

HELOÍSA: *(Ironic.)* But I didn't even say what it was?

DONA SENHORINHA: Well, I just thought out loud!...

HELOÍSA: *(Resolute.)* Well, he told me he had married me...
(Interrupts herself.)

DONA SENHORINHA: *(Secretly fearful.)* What else?

HELOÍSA: ... he had married me to run away from a woman,
some woman from here.

DONA SENHORINHA: *(Somewhat insecure.)* What else are you
making up about him?

HELOÍSA: He had to forget this woman. He thought maybe
with me...

DONA SENHORINHA: *(Pretending to be very serene.)* Did he say
who it was?

HELOÍSA: *(Sardonic.)* Is that what you care about – the name?

DONA SENHORINHA: *(Irritated.)* Did he tell you or not?

HELOÍSA: *(Torturing.)* Not with the exact words, but...

DONA SENHORINHA: *(With violence.)* You know nothing!
(Goes on, disdainfully.) You have no idea!

HELOÍSA: *(Abstract.)* Three years we lived together
(Passionately.) Three years and he never – do you hear
me? - never touched me...

DONA SENHORINHA: *(Fascinated.)* You're serious, never?

HELOÍSA: *(Lowers her head, talking to herself.)* NEVER!

DONA SENHORINHA: *(Approaches HELOÍSA, looking straight into
her eyes.)* Not even on your wedding night?

HELOÍSA: *(Letting go, as if sleep-talking.)* When he wanted
to and came to me, the memory of the "other" made it

153

IMPOSSIBLE! Then, he'd say: "Heloísa, 'She' won't let me!" I remember this once, I tried everything...

DONA SENHORINHA: *(Perturbed.)* What do you mean "everything"?

HELOÍSA: EVERYTHING a woman can try, the most incredible things!

DONA SENHORINHA: *(Devoured by curiosity.)* You did... and?

HELOÍSA: *(Vehement.)* I don't know, I lost all my inhibitions! What else could I do? At the beginning he was... But then, the memory of the "other"... I was so humiliated – I really was! The funny thing is he always said he thought my body was beautiful!

DONA SENHORINHA: *(Feverish, unable to keep to herself.)* The "other's" might have been better!

HELOÍSA: I asked if it was. But he told me it wasn't that, it wasn't a matter of looks.

DONA SENHORINHA: Looks are important, quite important!

HELOÍSA: He said he was born to love this woman, and only her. That he couldn't, he wouldn't desire any other woman.

DONA SENHORINHA: *(Thankful.)* He said that, did he?

DONA SENHORINHA, in an unexpected impulse, goes to her son's coffin, and kisses EDMUNDO's face.

DONA SENHORINHA: *(Returning, in a peculiar cold way.)* His eyelashes are so long! He had such a beautiful mouth, a young girl's breath, really nice, he never smoked!

HELOÍSA: *(Evocative.)* Once, Edmundo said: "I can only be fully realised, sexually speaking, with this woman".

I thought it was a funny way of saying it: "… sexually speaking".

DONA SENHORINHA: *(Nostalgic.)* He used words like that!

HELOÍSA: *(Progressively more exalted.)* One night, he couldn't take it anymore: he told me the secret, the woman's name, everything!

DONA SENHORINHA: *(Becoming exalted herself.)* That's a lie – he wouldn't tell you that! *(Staggering in her choice of words.)* It was a secret.

HELOÍSA: *(Quick and cruel.)* A FAMILY SECRET!

DONA SENHORINHA: *(Backing off, in fear.)* No! No!

HELOÍSA: *(Jubilant.)* I meant nothing to him. Edmundo could only love and hate people in his own family. He didn't know how to love, or hate anybody else!

DONA SENHORINHA: *(Savage, letting the mask slide off slightly.)* I already knew that.

HELOÍSA: And so?

DONA SENHORINHA: That means nothing!

HELOÍSA: *(Decisive.)* That means everything!

DONA SENHORINHA: Who cares!

HELOÍSA: Don't you think this woman Edmundo loved is very cheap, quite vulgar – extremely vulgar?

DONA SENHORINHA: *(Ironic.)* Who's to say?

HELOÍSA: *(Changing her tone.)* Edmundo also told me that his sister… *(Points at GLÓRIA's coffin.)* … that one over there, thought the father looked just like – extremely like Our Lord and Saviour Jesus Christ. *(She goes to EDMUNDO's coffin.)* I imagine my husband thought of you *(Dragging out her words.)* as a some kind of HOLY MARY!

DONA SENHORINHA seems to be scared by HELOÍSA's ferociousness.

DONA SENHORINHA: *(Taciturn.)* I've never seen such resentment!

HELOÍSA: *(Looking closely at EDMUNDO's face.)* I didn't feel a thing when I heard Edmundo had died, nothing at all. I felt a lot more for that stranger's death, the man who fell under the train; a lot more!

DONA SENHORINHA: *(Severe.)* That doesn't matter!

HELOÍSA: *(Somewhat hysterical.)* Now, tell me why you spend so much time over there, with your son, and leave your daughter, abandoned, like that?

DONA SENHORINHA looks over at her daughter's coffin with a cruel expression.

HELOÍSA: Tell me why? *(Extremely violent.)* Just because he's a man?

DONA SENHORINHA: *(Closed off.)* I don't need to justify myself to you!

HELOÍSA: At least be a hypocrite! Say you liked your daughter! Did you?

DONA SENHORINHA: *(Positive.)* No! *(With sudden vehemence.)* I never liked her! And she never liked me!

HELOÍSA: Cynical!

DONA SENHORINHA: *(Lowering her head.)* I am!

HELOÍSA: At least, you could pretend you did.

DONA SENHORINHA: *(As if talking to her dead daughter.)* I didn't like her, not even when she was born. One time, many years ago, I almost drowned her in that little lake. But as I was doing it, people arrived and I froze – I came so close!

DONA SENHORINHA seems to have won over her daughter-in-law, now.

DONA SENHORINHA: I'm sick and tired of not talking, of hiding for so long what I feel, what I think. They can say what they want. But I praised the heavens when I learned of my daughter's death!

HELOÍSA: The whole family's like that. That Nonô, the mad one, walks around the woods, naked – like an animal. Picking up dirt, rubbing it on his face, his nose, his mouth!

DONA SENHORINHA: *(In pain.)* He has such a beautiful body!

HELOÍSA: *(Desperate, walking towards the door, facing DONA SENHORINHA.)* I'm leaving – I can't stay here a minute longer.

HELOÍSA reaches for the door and speaks as hysterically as possible.

HELOÍSA: You can keep your son – you can make of him all you want.

DONA SENHORINHA regains her reputable serenity. A little later, four MEN come in. The lights are dimmed; they bring torches. They're going to take EDMUNDO's coffin. They're black, with big feet, naked from the waist up. Their trousers have the hems rolled up to the middle of their legs. DONA SENHORINHA's calm is shattered. She seems overtaken by fear and impatience, as she commands the MEN.

DONA SENHORINHA: Quickly, before he gets here!

Before the MEN close the coffin, DONA SENHORINHA kisses her son's forehead. The four MEN are about to take Edmundo away.

The greatest visual impact must be achieved in this particular scene. Once the coffin leaves, the lights go off on stage.

Last portrait of the family album: the esteemed PHOTOGRAPHER's old studio; EDMUNDO and HELOÍSA prepare for a pose. It's obvious they can't even pretend to have a natural atmosphere of well-being. HELOÍSA, cold, hard, as if her husband is a complete stranger. He is not warm toward her either, incapable of smiling. This is the scenario in which the baffled PHOTOGRAPHER must try and take the portrait. THE SPEAKER should completely ignore the obvious psychological state shown by the young couple. In his opinion, EDMUNDO and HELOÍSA live in a strange kind of matrimonial bliss.

THE SPEAKER: Seventh portrait of the album. Heloísa and Edmundo's honeymoon. Those in favour of divorce should see this as an example: the faces of the couple are mirrors of unparalleled happiness. Only the perfect marriage can provide such healthy and uplifting joy. When Edmundo died riddled with an insidious malady, Heloísa almost went insane with the pain. She only wedded again three years later, by the way, to a Baptist preacher who makes a point of praying before every meal.

Lights go off on the portrait of the family album for the final time. DONA SENHORINHA is in front of GLÓRIA's coffin. She doesn't know what to do. JONAS comes in, with the expression of a man who has lost everything in life.

JONAS: Why are you here? What are you doing?

DONA SENHORINHA: I don't know, I don't know. *(Changing her tone, after hesitating; more resolute.)* I was waiting for you.

JONAS: *(As if talking to his daughter's dead body.)* I looked for Guilherme everywhere. To kill him. But I couldn't find him anywhere; they told me he took the train.

DONA SENHORINHA: *(With a perfectly neutral tone.)* Jonas, I can't stand you anymore.

JONAS: *(Without paying attention to his wife.)* So I went to Mariazinha Bexiga's brothel… She got me the worst woman there – one that's probably rotten all over… *(Fed up, he approaches his wife, going face to face.)* I wanted to see if I could forget all this. If I could stop thinking about the most vulgar woman in the whole world. *(With an air of madness.)* But it was useless! I'm like Guilherme, after his accident.

DONA SENHORINHA: *(Serene.)* I won't live with you anymore, Jonas!

JONAS: I'll never be able to want another woman!

DONA SENHORINHA: *(Abrasive.)* Do you want to listen to me or not?

JONAS: *(Without paying attention to anything.)* Since Glória started to grow up, something interesting happened: when I kissed another woman, I closed my eyes and saw her face!

DONA SENHORINHA: *(Aggressive.)* Jonas!

JONAS: *(Waking up.)* What is it?

DONA SENHORINHA: *(Dry.)* I'm leaving you.

JONAS: *(Finding it difficult to understand.)* You're leaving me? *(Violent.)* Then leave damn it! Who's stopping you? The only thing I owe to you is my daughter.

DONA SENHORINHA: *(Quick and decisive.)* And I owe you – my sons – the men of my life.

DONA SENHORINHA seems to find focus.

DONA SENHORINHA: The men, my sons – Edmundo, Nonô… Except for Guilherme, the one over there in the coffin stole him from me.

DONA SENHORINHA takes a note from her breast.

DONA SENHORINHA: Edmundo wrote me letters, such beautiful letters! This one has a line that says – let me see, ah! – this part… "only you exist in the whole world. I wanted so much to go back to be what I was, a seed in your womb".

JONAS: You pig!

DONA SENHORINHA: *(Defensive.)* The comparison is beautiful - just beautiful! He always had a way with words.

Slowly, JONAS approaches DONA SENHORINHA who backs away, in fear.

JONAS: For the first time, I'm noticing something about you.

DONA SENHORINHA: About me – what?

JONAS: *(Transfigured into a satyr.)* Senhorinha, you look like Glória – you remind me of her! You have some of her features – your mouth, the same way of looking at me…

DONA SENHORINHA: *(In a panic.)* No!

JONAS: *(Obsessed.)* Yes, you do.

DONA SENHORINHA leans against the altar; she can't back away any further.

JONAS: I shouldn't have made a point of dressing Glória after she died. *(In a lament.)* Why did I do that? *(Changing his tone.)* You look just like Glória…

JONAS is at the peak of his sexual tension. He presses DONA SENHORINHA's face between his hands.

JONAS: You and those girls Rute got me – only girls, who had shown no desire whatsoever. Once, a fifteen year old died; the funeral party crossed the soccer field, the game stopped... I saw the girl in the coffin – she looked like my daughter. Every girl has something of Glória, but she mustn't have wide hips...

JONAS presses DONA SENHORINHA in his arms.

JONAS: When she was growing up, only girls existed in the world for me. Not women, but girls, so many! Twelve, thirteen, fourteen, fifteen year-olds!

JONAS tries to kiss DONA SENHORINHA; she fights back.

DONA SENHORINHA: No!

JONAS: You look just like Glória!

DONA SENHORINHA: *(Freeing herself.)* I should be untouchable to you – after I had a lover!

JONAS: It doesn't matter!

DONA SENHORINHA: And it wasn't Teotônio!

JONAS: *(Tormented.)* It was. I killed Teotônio!

DONA SENHORINHA: You killed him in vain. I said it was him because I couldn't think of another name. I needed – do you hear me? – to save the real one!

JONAS: More lies!

DONA SENHORINHA: *(Lost in her own thoughts.)* I told Edmundo who it was. When he found out, he cursed me... *(Spasmodic.)* He called me a name thinking it would offend me, but I liked being called that by him!

JONAS: *(With DONA SENHORINHA in his arms.)* Glória! Glória!

DONA SENHORINHA: *(Suffering.)* Then he killed himself, in front of me!

JONAS: *(Shouting at her, trying to pull her away from her abstraction.)* Senhorinha, I need a daughter – NEED – do you understand me?

DONA SENHORINHA: Do you want to know my lover's name? The real name?

JONAS: *(Obsessed.)* I want a daughter like Glória!

JONAS caresses his wife's shoulders, traveling all over her body.

DONA SENHORINHA: *(Lost again in her thoughts.)* I was so happy when you killed Teotônio. I breathed: Nonô is safe! *(Sweet.)* He went insane with happiness; he couldn't stand so much happiness!

JONAS: *(Affirmative.)* Now that Gloria's dead, what do I care about your lover's name?

For a moment, JONAS' sexual tension wanes off. His voice is low and, at this moment, he exists only in the plane of the past.

JONAS: When I was done killing Teotônio – I looked at you and realized you meant nothing to me, nothing at all. Even our bed seemed different, not the same – as if it were some strange bed, unknown – an ENEMY bed! That's when I started to hate you, because I didn't desire you anymore... *(After a pause, passionately.)* But I should've known, since Glória was born, you weren't my love!

DONA SENHORINHA: *(With the same passion.)* Well, I KNEW FOR SURE who I was meant to love, when Guilherme, Edmundo, Nonô were born!

JONAS: I could've sent for Glória at school, but I'd put it off, I was afraid. When you love, you should possess the woman and kill her. *(Suffering.)* Guilherme was right: a woman should never leave the bedroom alive; not the woman – nor the man.

DONA SENHORINHA: Murderer!

JONAS: *(Without hearing her, in a kind of fear in hindsight.)* I didn't want to do that to Glória; I'm sure she'd ask to die with me. *(As if cold.)* But I was afraid!

DONA SENHORINHA: Edmundo was afraid, and got married; Nonô was afraid, and went insane... *(Vehement, defiant.)* But me, no!

JONAS: *(With sacred despair.)* But the father has the right. If he wants, he can even strangle, squeeze his daughter's neck like this!

DONA SENHORINHA: I didn't want to forget; I didn't want to run away; I wasn't afraid or ashamed of anything. *(Possessed.)* I didn't put my sons in the world to hand them over to another woman!

JONAS: *(Changing his tone.)* Listen; pay attention to what I'm going to tell you – if we have a daughter, I'll name her Glória!

DONA SENHORINHA: Another girl, no! I don't want that!

JONAS: *(Dominating her.)* If you don't want it, I'll kill you, right here! I'll kill you!

DONA SENHORINHA: *(Overcome with terror.)* No, Jonas, no!

JONAS: Glória!

DONA SENHORINHA: Not here, no!

JONAS: Of course, here! Right here! Or out there! *(Caresses his wife, savage.)* As I call you Glória!

JONAS presses his wife's face between his hands; then, he makes a sudden gesture of repulsion.

JONAS: It doesn't feel right – it's not working for me!

DONA SENHORINHA: What is it?

JONAS: *(Somewhat obscure.)* My daughter died. *(Slowly.)*
ALL THE DESIRE I HAD IN THIS WORLD HAS
VANISHED FROM ME!

*DONA SENHORINHA, disgusted, starts rubbing her mouth with
the back of her hand.*

DONA SENHORINHA: *(Insulting.)* If you only knew how you
always disgust me, how all men disgust me!

*DONA SENHORINHA changes her tone, to an attitude of almost
adoration.*

DONA SENHORINHA: *(Caressing her own stomach.)* I can only
love my sons.

JONAS: You were always disgusted by me – you hated
me! You've always wanted me dead, you and all of my
children, except for Glória! Why didn't you kill me – why
don't you kill me now? *(Approaching DONA SENHORINHA
who backs off, terrified..)* Do you want to? I'll let you! It's so
easy! All you have to do is to pull the trigger…

*JONAS takes out the gun that he would have used to kill
GUILHERME. DONA SENHORINHA is terrified.*

DONA SENHORINHA: No, Jonas, no!

JONAS: Here! Take it!

*DONA SENHORINHA accepts the gun, but it's as if the gun makes
her nauseated.*

JONAS: *(Shouting.)* Now, shoot me! *(Out of his mind.)* Shoot!
Go on – is it fear I sense? For the love of God, shoot me!

*DONA SENHORINHA can't make up her mind, overcome as she is
by terror. But then, NONÔ's cry is heard, as if he was pleading for
something.*

DONA SENHORINHA: Nonô is calling – I'm going for good.

DONA SENHORINHA pulls the trigger twice; JONAS is shot. He falls, fatally wounded.

JONAS: *(With a final gasp.)* Glória!

DONA SENHORINHA leaves to meet NONÔ and start a new life. JONAS dies.

CHORUS: Suscipe, Domine, servum Tuum in locum
Sperandae sibi salvationis a misericordia tua. Amen.
Libera, domine, animan servi tui ex omnibus periculis
inferni, et de laqueis poenarum, et ex omnibus
tribulationibus. Amen. Libera, domine, animan servi
tui, sicut liberasti henoch et eliam de communi morte
mundi. Amen.[4]

The CHORUS diminishes, without having to finish the funeral prayer.

END OF ACT 3 AND FINAL ACT

---

4 Receive, O Lord, Thy servant, have mercy on us here at the place
of things we hope to be saved from. Amen. Redeem, O Lord, Thy
servant's soul, leaving it out of all the dangers of hell, and from the
bonds of the penalties, and, out of all the troubles. Amen. Deliver
Thee, the soul of Thy servant as Enoch and Elias were delivered
from the common death of the world. Amen.

BLACK ANGEL
Tragedy in Three Acts

By Nelson Rodrigues (1946)
Translated by Almiro Andrade

Characters

ISMAEL
VIRGÍNIA
ELIAS (The Blind Man.)
ANA MARIA
THE AUNT
Female COUSINS
THE MAID (Hortênsia.)
BLACK MEN (From the cemetery.)
The barefoot BLACK WOMEN (Chorus.)

The action takes place anytime, anywhere.

Act 1

SCENE 1

ISMAEL's house. A set with no realistic features. On the ground floor, a wake takes place. The little "angel's" coffin – made out of white silk – with four lit candles, really long and slick ones. Sitting in a semicircle, there are ten BLACK WOMEN whose prophetic functions are quite conspicuous, at times: their premonitions are always imbued with very sad forebodings. They pray a lot, they are always praying, mainly Hail Mary's, Our Father's. ISMAEL, the Great Black Man, is standing up, rigid, in mourning. Throughout the play, he wears a very starched white linen suit, Panama style, and patent-leather shoes. Upstairs, with her back to the audience is VIRGÍNIA, the white wife, very fair; she is in mourning clothes. Two beds, one of which looks normal. The other one is broken, half of the sheets hanging out, pillow on the floor. A long and stylized stairway. The house has no roof so the night might enter it and claim its inhabitants. In the background, there are high walls which grow in pace with the increasing loneliness of the Great Black Man.

BLACK WOMAN: *(Sweet.)* Such a strong boy, such a beautiful boy!

BLACK WOMAN: *(Pathetic.)* Dead, all of a sudden!

BLACK WOMAN: *(Sweet.)* Lil' brown baby boy, lil' brown baby!

BLACK WOMAN: Brown?! No, he was not brown!

BLACK WOMAN: Kind of a Mulatto in disguise!

BLACK WOMAN: *(Controversial.)* Black!

BLACK WOMAN: *(Controversial.)* Brown!

BLACK WOMAN: *(Controversial.)* Mulatto!

BLACK WOMAN: *(In panic.)* Oh Dear Lord, I'm scared of black people! I'm scared, scared!

BLACK WOMAN: *(Smitten.)* Such a sweet, sad, polite little boy!

BLACK WOMAN: *(Enchanted.)* He knew he'd die, it is as if he called for it... death!

BLACK WOMAN: *(Sorrowful.)* He's the third one to die. Here, none of them make it!

BLACK WOMAN: *(Lamenting.)* None of them boys make it!

BLACK WOMAN: Three already died. Same age. God holds a grudge against them!

BLACK WOMAN: The angels, the angels are the ones with a grudge!

BLACK WOMAN: Or his mother's womb is cursed!

BLACK WOMAN: *(Accusing.)* White woman with a black womb!

BLACK WOMAN: *(Lamenting.)* God must like children. He takes the little ones for Himself! So many little boys die so young!

BLACK WOMEN: *(All together.)* Hail Mary, full of grace... *(The prayer is lost in an unintelligible murmur.)* Our Father who art in Heaven... *(Also lost in a murmur.)*

BLACK WOMAN: *(Frightened.)* And he drowned in such a shallow bath!

BLACK WOMAN: No one saw it!

BLACK WOMAN: Does anyone know if it was suicide?

BLACK WOMAN: *(Screaming.)* Children don't kill themselves! They don't kill themselves!

BLACK WOMAN: *(Sweet.)* But it would've been so beautiful if a little boy killed himself!

BLACK WOMAN: The black man lusted after the white woman!

BLACK WOMAN: *(Screaming.)* Oh! God kills all our lust!

BLACK WOMAN: *(Lamenting.)* The white woman also lusted after the black man!

BLACK WOMEN: *(All together.)* Life be damned! Love be damned!

All voices come to a halt. ISMAEL enters to look at his son's face. Upstairs, in the bedroom, VIRGÍNIA kneels. Outside, a young beggar appears; he moves, tottery, with a staff. It is soon made obvious that he is a BLIND MAN, with bright curly hair; his face bears a quasi-feminine sweetness. Right after that, four BLACK MEN appear. They are surprised at the BLIND MAN's presence. They are bare-chested, wearing straw hats, smoking cigars.

BLACK MAN: *(Somewhat playful.)* Are you gate-crashing, blindie?

BLIND MAN: *(Surprised.)* The gate was open.

BLACK MAN: You're taking a gamble, pal. The Man wants no whites coming in.

BLACK MAN: You might get hurt.

BLACK MAN: See these walls? Oh, right, you're blind! Well: he fenced the whole property. Walls everywhere. So no one can come in. And if the visitor insists, he takes them down. He shot one the other day, didn't he?

BLACK MAN: He did, indeed!

BLACK MAN: Just because the visitor, a white visitor, insisted on having a look!

BLIND MAN: Then, it is him.

BLACK MAN: What did you say?

BLIND MAN: Just thinking out loud.

BLACK MAN: And if we're here it's because we're from the cemetery. You know what I mean, don't you? The cemetery? Oh, right, you're blind! Small cemetery, but kind of neat; for what it is, it delivers. As I was saying – we are taking the son of the man there. The boy died.

BLACK MAN: All of a sudden.

BLIND MAN: Tell me – is he called Ismael?

BLACK MAN: The Doctor? Yeah. And what a doctor!

BLIND MAN: He's black, isn't he?

BLACK MAN: But he knows what he's doing! *(To the others.)* Am I lying?

BLACK MAN: There's no one like him!

BLACK MAN: What did I say? Great Doctor!

BLACK MAN: But a word of advice; do not mention blacks, he goes off the wall!

BLIND MAN: *(To himself.)* He thinks he's white, can't get over the idea. *(Changing his tone, to the black man who talks most.)* When did the kid die?

BLACK MAN: Calling four men to carry this coffin, when one alone could do the job.

BLACK MAN: I'm with you.

BLACK MAN: *(To the BLIND MAN.)* Isn't that so, pal? Why do they need four of us on the casket, when the dead's this tiny? It weighs nothing!

BLIND MAN: What about the wife?

BLACK MAN: That one, uh, son! No one really sees her!

BLIND MAN: Are they doing well?

BLACK MAN: If they are at each other's throats, no one really knows!

BLIND MAN: I'm asking – are they well off?

BLACK MAN: Loaded! They're so well-off, he takes no house calls, nor books any appointments!

BLIND MAN: She's got to be a woman of colour. Or am I being too hasty?

BLACK MAN: You are! White like no other. She's something else. I met her when she was still single, still a school girl. Afterwards, haven't seen her no more!

BLIND MAN: *(To himself.)* Of course, she had to be white! *(Changes his tone.)* I'd like to speak to him!

BLACK MAN: *(Alarmed.)* To the Doctor?

BLACK MAN: Wouldn't go there if I were you!

BLIND MAN: I'm a relative, not a really close one. I'll make my way in.

BLACK MAN: This way, straight ahead. Do you want me to go with you?

BLIND MAN: I am fine on my own, thanks.

The BLIND MAN walks, with difficulty, using his staff. He talks to himself.

BLIND MAN: There has been a death in this house, and you wouldn't even notice. I do not hear crying, not even a wail. There's no much fuss for the death of a child.

The four BLACK MEN wait for the BLIND MAN to disappear into the back of the house. Their cigars fill the room with smoke.

173

BLACK MAN: It's time!

BLACK MAN: The man said noon. Too early still.

BLACK MAN: *(Lying down on the ground and resting his head on both hands.)* I don't buy this whole talk of being the Doctor's relative.

BLACK MAN: How do you know he's not a relative of the Doctor's wife?

ISMAEL leaves the living room presumably towards his wife's bedroom; but his chosen path coincides with the one taken by the BLIND MAN. During all the pauses, we hear fragments of 'Our Father's and 'Hail Mary's from the chorus of BLACK WOMEN.

BLIND MAN: *(To himself.)* I hear nothing. Surely, when it's time to take away the casket, there's going to be at least a wail.

ISMAEL: *(After contemplating the BLIND MAN, in silence.)* Who asked you here?

BLIND MAN: *(Towards ISMAEL, dubious.)* Ismael, give me your hand.

ISMAEL, unmoved, silent, lets the BLIND MAN approach.

BLIND MAN: I've been looking for you for so long and I've lost my way so many times!

The BLIND MAN finds his brother, touches him, searching for his brother's hand.

BLIND MAN: I heard your son just died. Talk to me, Ismael, talk!

ISMAEL: Who sent you?

BLIND MAN: I'm here on my own volition. Aren't I your baby brother, youngest in our family?

ISMAEL: Someone must have sent you!

BLIND MAN: She sent me *(Lowers his voice.)* your mother! *(Changing his tone.)* I was not supposed to tell you; I wasn't going to, at least not now, just because your son will be buried today. But you're still brutally hard *(Holds ISMAEL'S hand; he remains static.)* even your hand, your knuckles, they are as hard as a rock!

ISMAEL: Is it money you want?

BLIND MAN: *(Slightly pleading.)* Will you at least admit I am your brother? Say, "You are my brother, Elias!"

ISMAEL: *(Obdurate.)* How much, for you to leave right now, to never come back?

ELIAS: At least let me kiss your son.

ISMAEL: No!

ELIAS: *(Pleading.)* It won't cost you a thing! As you won't let me, tell how he died at least; how did it happen?

ISMAEL: *(In free fall towards detachment.)* God has tainted my life, I know He did, it has to be Him. No one knows how it happened: Virgínia was distracted for a moment, just for a second, and the boy disappeared. *(Agitated.)* He was nowhere to be found. *(As if amazed by the thought.)* Then, I remembered: the bath! I ran – he was there lying at the bottom of the bath, so quiet – and dead. But the water was so shallow, as high as a child's waist. He couldn't have drowned there!

ELIAS: He must have been a beautiful child!

ISMAEL: He's the third one to die. They all die. *(With vehemence.)* They never make it – do you get it? – they never do. None of them, none! *(Changes the tone.)* You shall not see my son! I do not want anyone to see him. Except for me and his mother – the two of us, no one else! Now leave and never come back!

ELIAS: *(Also with vehemence.)* Had I kissed your son, perhaps your mother's words would have been wiped clean.

ISMAEL: Then speak.

ELIAS: You know your mother has become a cripple, right?

ISMAEL: I heard word of it.

ELIAS: Before I left, she made me promise…

ISMAEL: I know.

ELIAS: … and I swore I'd come to say to you just these words: "Ismael, your mother sends her curse!"

ISMAEL: You have passed on her message…

ELIAS: It's not a message. It's a curse.

ISMAEL: So let it be a curse. Now, the door's right there, even though you cannot see it.

ELIAS: I came to stay, Ismael.

ISMAEL: *(With a sinister humour.)* And you expect me to let you stay?

ELIAS: I have nowhere else to go.

ISMAEL: Would you rather I throw you out? Drag you out? Or have you lost your fear?

ELIAS: I was full of fear when I was a little boy. Back then, you'd beat me because I wasn't your mother's son, because I was the son of a white woman with a white man. But not today. Perhaps, the fear will return tomorrow…

ISMAEL doesn't answer. He has his back to ELIAS who, obviously, doesn't see him.

ELIAS: *(Pleading.)* I'll stand there in a corner like an animal, quiet, silent; I won't bother anyone – I swear!

ISMAEL remains silent. ELIAS speaks to himself, with a certain sadness and sweetness.

ELIAS: I don't have to talk to anyone, I don't have to see anyone. I talk to myself, I laugh, have fun all by myself – it's so good when there's no one around!

At this point, ISMAEL is far away from his brother who carries on talking and making gestures in the wrong direction. ISMAEL picks up a whip.

ISMAEL: *(Striking a piece of furniture with the whip.)* You know what this is?

Instinctively, ELIAS turns in the right direction. His face expresses terror.

ELIAS: I do. That short plaited whip that my father gave you.

ISMAEL: Do you want to feel it on your flesh?

ELIAS: *(With a courage full of despair.)* You can't hit a blind man! You wouldn't dare!

ISMAEL: Leave my house!

ELIAS: I will, but sooner or later you'll have to answer to God.

ELIAS walks, with difficulty, towards the front door.

ISMAEL: *(Once the other reaches the front door.)* Elias!

ELIAS: *(With an expression that exudes hope.)* Yes?

ELIAS turns around, as if dazzled by what he has heard.

ISMAEL: *(Still harsh.)* In honour of my son who died, I'll let you stay here; but only until tomorrow, not even a single day more. There's a bedroom at the back of the house; stay there and don't leave the room!

ELIAS: I won't leave, Ismael.

ISMAEL: Water, food, everything will be brought to you. And another thing: I have a wife. Don't you even dream of speaking to her. It is as if she was from heaven and you, from earth; not earth, no, you're from the mud.

ELIAS: Do you want me to promise?

ISMAEL: Makes no difference.

ELIAS: *(Sweet.)* I can help carry your son's coffin. I can hold a handle.

ISMAEL: I don't want you laying a finger on my son's coffin!

ISMAEL goes up the stairs; enters VIRGÍNIA's bedroom. Downstairs, in the wake, the murmur of praying becomes more pronounced. ISMAEL stops right behind VIRGÍNIA, who is, once again, standing.

ISMAEL: Since yesterday you've been like this, in this position.

VIRGÍNIA: I've been kneeling plenty of times.

ISMAEL: But you haven't let your hair down, haven't even slept.

VIRGÍNIA: My eyes are burning.

ISMAEL: Fever.

VIRGÍNIA: *(Rectifying.)* A sleepless night.

ISMAEL: Our son is alone.

VIRGÍNIA: I sensed you weren't in the living room anymore. *(Turning toward her husband.)* Since yesterday, I've been waiting – waiting on what, dear Lord?

ISMAEL: You were waiting on me, Virgínia.

VIRGÍNIA: *(In awe.)* Waiting on you! Who else would I be waiting on? You're the only one who comes in, you're the only one who leaves. The world has been reduced to the both of us – you and me. Now that YOUR son is dead.

ISMAEL: *(Somewhat vehement.)* But wasn't that what you wanted? When that happened, over there *(Points at the bed next to them.)* what did you say?

VIRGÍNIA: I don't know; I don't remember, and I don't want to.

ISMAEL: You said you wanted to get away from everything, from everyone; you wanted no one else to see you, no one to even look at you. Or am I wrong?

VIRGÍNIA: After what happened right there – if someone saw me, if someone even looked at me, I'd feel naked…

ISMAEL: So I told you about those mausoleums for rich people, the ones that look like small houses. And what did you say to me?

VIRGÍNIA: *(Mechanical.)* I said: "I'd like to be in a place like that, but ALIVE. A place where no one would be allowed in. So I could hide my shame."

ISMAEL: That's what I wanted, too. And I need this place, this life. For this reason I've put up all those walls, so that no one could enter. Stone walls, high stone walls.

VIRGÍNIA: *(With astonishment, turning toward her husband.)* The world reduced to you and me, and a son between us – a son who always dies.

ISMAEL: Always.

VIRGÍNIA: I've already forgotten about other men, I feel as if there's only one face in the whole world – yours – as if all men had only a single set of features – yours. *(Changes her tone.)* Ismael, your boys have the same face as you.

VIRGÍNIA comes closer to look closely at her husband's face.

VIRGÍNIA: No matter how many more come our way, their faces will be your face.

ISMAEL: Why do you say "your" sons?

VIRGÍNIA: *(With contained violence.)* Because they are "yours"!

ISMAEL: Ours!

VIRGÍNIA: *(After a pause, plunging her face into her hands.)* THEY ARE OURS! *(Changing her tone, to herself.)* They're also MINE! *(Agitated, to her husband.)* Ismael, they're also MINE! *(Caressing her stomach.)* Here is where they all came from! *(Holding her husband by both of his arms.)* This one who just died, the one who's down there – was MY son. *(Somewhat feral.)* So much like you, it was as if you were watching me through his eyes.

ISMAEL, without a gesture, without a word, observes the hysteria which takes over his wife.

VIRGÍNIA: The other day – do you hear me? – I remembered a face, but I didn't know who it belonged to, I couldn't remember the name. There was no way to make sense of it. Then, later, I remembered – it was Jesus, it was the face of our Lord, Jesus Christ.

VIRGÍNIA holds her face between her hands. She's being devoured by despair. She walks around the room whilst ISMAEL remains unmoved.

VIRGÍNIA: *(Pleading.)* Ismael, I want you to get me a picture of Jesus! Jesus doesn't have your face, he doesn't have your eyes – he doesn't, Ismael!

ISMAEL: No – no one is allowed in here.

VIRGÍNIA: But it's just an image, Ismael, a picture, a print –
I'll put it right there, on the wall. Isn't that a great place?
Right here, Ismael! If you prefer, I won't even look, it's
enough for me to know that there's a new face in the
house. Please, Ismael?

ISMAEL: *(Holding her.)* I don't want to, I don't want you to!
I chose to live here, I built these walls; I saved up money,
a lot of money; I don't allow anyone into my house – all
because I am running away. I'm running away from the
desire of other men. I had those windows made so high,
so very high, for this very reason – so you had to forget,
so those memories you had within your mind would die
forever. *(With an absolute passion.)* Virgínia, look at me,
right here! I did all this so that there was only me. Do
you understand that, now? No other faces exist, no white
faces! – there's only my face, the black one…

VIRGÍNIA: *(Dolorous.)* If it were not for Hortênsia, who
sometimes talks to me, I wouldn't know anyone else
existed, except for us… Will you do this for me?

ISMAEL: No!

VIRGÍNIA: *(More aggressive, in a crescendo.)* Do you fear that the
Christ in the picture will be looking at me?

ISMAEL has his back to her.

VIRGÍNIA: If it were a blind Christ, it wouldn't matter. But
there's no blind Christ!

ISMAEL: I don't want you to, I don't want to… *(Astonished.)*
Not a Christ like that; light-skinned, delicate features …

VIRGÍNIA: *(Pleading.)* Let me walk in the garden then, like
I used to? Late at night. I need to see the stars. I can go
with you!

ISMAEL: There are no stars anymore.

VIRGÍNIA: *(Not hearing him.)* Just now, I remembered that they exist or have existed. It's been a while since I last thought about them. They were gorgeous, weren't they?

ISMAEL: Your place is here. Why do you speak of everything else but the child down there? Why don't you think about him?

VIRGÍNIA: *(As if enchanted.)* He must be like this *(Emulating the hand gesture.)* both hands bound together, like two sisters, a couple of twins...

ISMAEL: Since he died, you wouldn't look at him, you haven't looked at our son once!

VIRGÍNIA: *(With fear.)* If I saw him now, I'd never get rid of the memory!

ISMAEL: The coffin is on its way out. Won't you cry? Not even a single tear?

VIRGÍNIA: I can't! I want to, but I can't.

ISMAEL: Because he's black. Black.

ISMAEL walks toward the door. VIRGÍNIA sits on the bed. ISMAEL locks the door from the outside. VIRGÍNIA screams, frightened.

VIRGÍNIA: *(Running towards the door.)* You're locking me in?

ISMAEL: It's what's needed.

VIRGÍNIA: *(Pleading.)* But what for? Haven't you always let me wander round the house? *(Sweet.)* So nice to see walls other than these ones; the living room walls, the hallway... So nice, the tables, chairs and not just these two beds, the sheets... *(Vehement.)* My only source of joy was to change my surroundings, moving from one room to the other; going up and down the stairs. *(Desperate.)* Why are you locking me in, Ismael? Why?

ISMAEL: I'll tell you later.

VIRGÍNIA: Wait. *(With resentment.)* I don't want any more
    sons. None at all – do you hear me? – never again!

ISMAEL: *(Getting close to the door.)* The only want that matters
    is mine. And I want another son, Virgínia!

VIRGÍNIA: *(Desperate.)* Not mine!

ISMAEL: Yes, yours! A son of yours who does not die like the
    others. Because the next one will not die – this I swear,
    Virgínia!

VIRGÍNIA: But don't you understand it cannot be? That I
    cannot go on having children like this? I'm so tired of
    death, so sick of seeing children die. *(Changing her tone,
    with a deaf voice.)* Death makes me sick to my stomach, it
    makes me nauseous! *(In a rush.)* Having children just to
    see them die!

ISMAEL: I'll be back.

VIRGÍNIA: *(In a loud cry.)* No, Ismael, no! Show respect for
    the day! *(Changing her tone, surprised.)* I don't want to get
    pregnant of a son, not on the same day the other one is
    being buried! It is as if the one who died came back into
    my womb and started to rot inside me! *(Pleading.)* Okay?
    Not today!

They look at each other.

VIRGÍNIA: Why do you look at me like that? *(In a low voice.)*
    I see it in your eyes, the desire. But you won't get any
    from me – not today – even if I have to kill myself; and
    I will kill myself in front of you, Ismael!

*VIRGÍNIA falls on her knees, plunging her face into her hands. The
four BLACK MEN, who are outside, go around the house and appear
by the living room door. ISMAEL comes down. The four BLACK MEN*

accompany him. They take away the coffin. VIRGÍNIA gets up and seems to follow all the movements of the men, downstairs. The four BLACK MEN carry the coffin and leave the house, with ISMAEL leading the way. Then, in a kind of frenzy, VIRGÍNIA picks up a small bell and rings it frenetically.

END OF SCENE 1

SCENE 2

The curtain opens with VIRGÍNIA in the same position and performing the same action, meaning, ringing the small bell. There is, however, something different in the scene. The BLACK WOMEN have left the living room and now appear sitting in a semicircle, in the white woman's bedroom. Suddenly, VIRGÍNIA stops, as if overcome by exhaustion. At the same time, the BLACK WOMEN start to speak.

BLACK WOMAN: *(Lamenting.)* The mother didn't even kiss her dead son!

BLACK WOMAN: Only young virgins should be holding the handles.

BLACK WOMAN: She didn't kiss her son because he was black!

BLACK WOMAN: They are gorgeous things, the virgins!

BLACK WOMAN: He's blond, the white brother of the black husband.

BLACK WOMAN: And their hips are so generous!

BLACK WOMAN: A woman should never cease to be a virgin!

BLACK WOMAN: Even when they marry, even when they have children. Dear Lord! Cursed are all white women who despise the blacks!

After the last line, once again, the murmur of the BLACK WOMEN's prayers is heard whilst their nimble and expert fingers count the rosary. VIRGÍNIA starts ringing the bell again, in a mad frenzy.

VIRGÍNIA: *(Suddenly serene.)* I thought you weren't coming – it took you so long!

THE MAID: I was outside…

VIRGÍNIA: Is it gone?

THE MAID: The burial?

VIRGÍNIA: Yes.

THE MAID: They've left, Dona Virgínia. Just now.

VIRGÍNIA: *(As if talking to herself.)* So Ismael's only back late at night! Thank God, I'm getting some rest. It's so good when he's not here! *(To THE MAID, changing her tone.)* Open the door!

THE MAID: I'm sorry, Dona Virgínia, but I can't. Dr. Ismael left orders not to open the door.

VIRGÍNIA: *(In a lament.)* Why am I being locked in here – why?

THE MAID: I don't know, Dona Virgínia, but I imagine it's because of the Doctor's brother…

VIRGÍNIA: Who?

THE MAID: The Doctor's brother, who got here this morning.

VIRGÍNIA: Brother? But what kind of brother?

THE MAID: The white kind…

VIRGÍNIA: *(In awe.)* White?

THE MAID: Blind – he can't see a thing…

VIRGÍNIA: *(Euphoric.)* Blind? He's blind, is he? *(To herself.)* Can't see… *(Vehement, to THE MAID.)* I have to talk to this man, Hortênsia!

THE MAID: *(In panic.)* Hold your horses, Dona Virgínia!

VIRGÍNIA: Open this door, right now!

THE MAID: The Doctor said not to; he left orders!

VIRGÍNIA: *(Possessed.)* Cheap black whore, nigger! *(Suddenly nice.)* Please, Hortênsia, open it!

THE MAID: I can't, Dona Virgínia!

VIRGÍNIA: *(Pleading.)* Hortênsia, do you remember what I did for you that time – for your daughter? You said she was in trouble, that she had screwed up, she had lost her way. Did you or did you not?

THE MAID: I did, I'd never deny it. I could never thank you enough for it.

VIRGÍNIA: *(Sweet, persuasive.)* Then I gave you the money to save your daughter from that kind of life. I thought – do you hear me? – that black women must suffer more than others, they are more humiliated. I don't know, perhaps just for being black, I think in comparison a woman of colour must be, generally speaking, more tainted. You gave your daughter the money. But she didn't want to come back, she preferred to stay where she was. Am I lying?

THE MAID: No.

VIRGÍNIA: So, open the door. I'm not asking for anything else - just for you to open the door.

THE MAID: I'm so sorry, Dona Virgínia…

VIRGÍNIA: *(Very agitated.)* I can give you money, lots of money! All the money I have, all I've ever saved up! You can leave here and never come back!

As if possessed, VIRGÍNIA goes to a drawer and picks up numerous banknotes.

VIRGÍNIA: Take it! It's all yours!

THE MAID: You're ruining me, Dona Virgínia!

VIRGÍNIA: Open it!

THE MAID opens the door, not before scooping up the banknotes that were on the floor.

VIRGÍNIA: Thank God! *(After THE MAID has picked up the last banknote.)* Now, go tell this man I want to talk to him, but hurry!

THE MAID goes downstairs with her small fortune. VIRGÍNIA, alone, as if by instinct, fixes her hair. She looks at her own image in the mirror for a while. VIRGÍNIA, thinking out loud.

VIRGÍNIA: *(Astonished.)* I spoke of a blind Christ, and his brother had already arrived, from afar, I don't know where from, but he was already there...

ELIAS appears at the door of the central living room, guided by THE MAID.

THE MAID: It's here. She'll be right in.

ELIAS: If he finds out! If he shows up out of a sudden – he'll kill me...

VIRGÍNIA comes in. She stops herself, looking at the blind man, in awe. Instinctively, ELIAS turns around towards his sister-in-law, nervous with the prolonged silence.

ELIAS: Are you the lady of the house?

VIRGÍNIA: Yes, I am.

ELIAS: Did you send for me, madam?

VIRGÍNIA: I did. Sit down!

ELIAS: *(Whose behaviour displays an almost feminine shyness.)* I'm sorry, I'm blind, madam. Did you know that?

VIRGÍNIA: No, I did not. Ismael had not told me. He mentioned you once, without going into any details…

Pause. VIRGÍNIA starts a gesture as if caressing the air, but hides her hand quickly.

ELIAS: *(Unsure and sweet.)* Are you beautiful, madam?

VIRGÍNIA: Stop calling me madam.

ELIAS: So?

VIRGÍNIA: Do you think I am?

ELIAS: I've been told you were.

VIRGÍNIA: I am indeed.

VIRGÍNIA stretches her hands out to ELIAS, as if pleading for something. Soon, however, she interrupts the gesture.

ELIAS: Ever since you came in, I knew you were beautiful.

VIRGÍNIA: *(Caressing herself.)* Not many women are as beautiful as me. If you could see it for yourself, you'd know I'm not lying.

ELIAS: *(Sweet.)* I can imagine.

VIRGÍNIA: But, at the same time, it's good that you're blind. If you weren't blind, I'd feel shame. I couldn't be here with you. Not like this. I can put my hands over yours *(Reach for his hands.)* and I don't see anything wrong with it.

ELIAS: Your hands are so soft!

VIRGÍNIA: *(With suffering.)* If only you knew how I miss seeing a face other than his! And a white one?!... Thank God, I'm not blind. I can stay like this, looking at you, until I've had my fix; and I think I'd never get enough! *(Pleading.)* Let me run my fingers over your face? Please, humour me. *(Stroking his face with her hands.)* I'm touching you as if I was the one who's blind! Your features are so delicate!

ELIAS: *(Restless.)* What if he comes in?

VIRGÍNIA: There is no danger. It'll be a while. He won't be back till dawn. Please, talk to me. For eight years no man has spoken to me. And a white man, I can't even remember when. It was only him. You two never saw eye to eye, did you?

ELIAS: He doesn't like me.

VIRGÍNIA: Nor you him?

ELIAS: Nor I. And you?

VIRGÍNIA: Me?

ELIAS: Do you like your husband? *(Silence.)* Answer me. Do you? *(Silence.)* He cannot be liked... Since he was a boy, he's been carrying this shame; no, not shame: he literally hates the colour of his skin. A man like that is forever tainted. We are what we are. I believe that not even a leper should deny his own leprosy.

VIRGÍNIA: *(Landing her hands over his.)* What you're saying pleases me so much! How can you be Ismael's brother?

ELIAS: Stepbrother.

VIRGÍNIA: Ah, I should've known!

ELIAS: My father was from Italy and, after my mother died, he got together with Ismael's mother...

VIRGÍNIA: I hear you.

ELIAS: *(Passionately.)* When Ismael was younger, he wouldn't drink cachaça because he thought cachaça was a black man's drink. He never got drunk. And he killed the desire he felt for black or even mulatto women – he did, the ever so sexy Ismael. He never forgave me for being born a son of white folks, not a black like him. When I went to live in his house, he was already a young man and I was just a boy. Ismael would be mean to me, he'd beat me up. I truly feared him; *(As if looking around, or rather, turning his head from one side to the other, as if he could see.)* and, even to this day, I do – I fear him – like the fear you'd have of an animal, of a beast!

VIRGÍNIA: *(Standing up and pressing ELIAS' head against her bosom.)* I rather like it knowing that you fear him, that you're like this, so delicate with your slender waist...

ELIAS: You do like me, don't you? Despite the blindness...

VIRGÍNIA: *(Changing the tone.)* How did you become blind?

ELIAS: *(Lamenting.)* It was fate; something was wrong with my eyesight and Ismael, who was looking after me, switched the medication. Instead of using the prescribed medication, he used something else... I lost sight in both eyes... Even after I became blind, he'd torment me. He studied so hard to be better than the white people around us, he wanted to be a doctor – just out of vanity, pure vanity. Do you know what he did with São Jorge? He took São Jorge's image off the wall and threw it out the window – just because he is the patron of black Brazilians. All of a sudden, he just took off, right after telling his mother: "I'm black because of you!" *(Sweet, pleading.)* You've heard what I had to say. Now, tell me – do you like him? *(Silence.)* Do you?

VIRGÍNIA: *(Obsessed.)* He switched the medication on purpose…To blind you!… *(Changing her tone.)* Do I like him? No… I don't…

ELIAS: Do you hate him?

VIRGÍNIA: *(Unsure.)* I hate him…

ELIAS: Do you fear him?

VIRGÍNIA: *(Unsure.)* Fear? *(Changing her tone, VIRGÍNIA stands up, walks around, whilst ELIAS becomes disoriented, not knowing in which direction to turn.)* His perspiration is in every nook and cranny of this house, rotting on the walls, in the air, on the sheets, on the bed, in the pillows, even on my skin, my breasts *(Holding her head tight between her hands.)* And in my hair, Dear Lord!

VIRGÍNIA smells her cupped hands, as if wanting to find in them the smell which had been cursed over and over, and over again.

ELIAS: So why did you marry him? I've been told you were white, not even olive-skinned, but white, really white.

VIRGÍNIA: *(As if in transit.)* Really white, really fair-skinned. *(Changing tone.)* We who love blend sweat with sweat. *(Asks avidly.)* Tell me if his sweat stayed with me, if it's in my flesh? Or is it just my imagination?

With an expression of suffering, VIRGÍNIA first offers her hands, then her arms and, finally, her shoulders so that ELIAS, who's already stood up, can smell them.

ELIAS: *(As if in transit.)* It's just your imagination!

VIRGÍNIA lowers her head, in a sudden burst of shame.

ELIAS: *(Aggressive.)* But if you dread the thought of…

VIRGÍNIA: *(Interrupting, abruptly assertive.)* I do!

ELIAS: … why did you marry him?

In his despair, ELIAS digs his nails into VIRGÍNIA's arms.

VIRGÍNIA: You're hurting me!

ELIAS: *(Softly, speaking closer to her ear.)* I fear you might be beautiful but meretricious! Tell me you're not, that you can have feelings – tell me!

VIRGÍNIA: *(Full of sorrow.)* I will tell you – if you only knew! It happened right here. This house used to belong to my aunt, who raised me. My parents had died. Auntie was a widow – so cold and mean, I don't know how a woman like that could exist. She had five daughters, all spinsters, except for the youngest, who was soon to be married. She was the only one who had a chance of not dying a virgin…

As she talks, VIRGÍNIA walks away.

ELIAS: *(Pleading.)* Stay near me!

VIRGÍNIA: *(Sweet.)* Yes, I am here. *(Changing her tone.)* Everyone in the house hated me. Because I was fifteen, because I was way too pretty – beautiful! All eyes were always on me. When I was getting dressed, I was always being watched. That's when Ismael showed up, first as a doctor, then as a friend. "Black, but very distinguished", they said; and, on top of all that, a doctor. In small towns, that means a lot. He fell in love with me…

ELIAS: *(Sweet and restless.)* And you fell for him too?

VIRGÍNIA: I swear I didn't. I swear on everything most sacred. I feared the desire in his eyes. I already had the feeling that making love with a man like that would be the same as being violated every day.

ELIAS: It has always been his dream, to violate a white woman.

VIRGÍNIA: I was in love with my baby cousin's fiancé. I never said anything to anyone. He was the one, the only one. You remind me of him. Especially your mouth – delicate soft lips. Not my husband's vengeful mouth! One night, my cousin's fiancé arrived earlier than expected. I was alone. It was all so sudden! We didn't say a word; he grabbed me and kissed me. Nothing else, except his hands running all over my body...

ELIAS: You never should've desired another man – never...

VIRGÍNIA's narrative develops now in a crescendo.

VIRGÍNIA: At that moment, the bride to be and my aunt arrived. Just in time to see everything. And they did; and didn't say a word. They watched us until it was over. When the kiss was over, my cousin's fiancé ran away, forever. My aunt locked me in the room... *(Now, in a lower voice.)* The bride to be locked herself up in the bathroom. It took her so long to come out that they went in to check on her. *(Astonished.)* She had hung herself, Elias, with a rope so thin I don't know how it withstood the weight of her body...

ELIAS: *(In a lament.)* Only men should hang themselves; not women...

VIRGÍNIA: *(Without hearing him.)* And there I was. At night, Ismael came to pay us a visit. He was the only outsider; no one else had been informed. Later that night, I heard footsteps. My door was opened – it was him, sent by my aunt. I cried for help. He tried to cover my mouth with his hand – I screamed like a woman in labour... *(Changing her tone.)* If you could see it, I'd show you...

The lights in the rest of the room go dim; only the bed where VIRGÍNIA was violated is fully lit. All the signs of a violent struggle can be noticed: the support at the bottom of the bed has fallen off; half the sheets are off the bed; there's a pillow on the floor; a small bedside lamp is broken.

VIRGÍNIA: *(Pointing at the bed.)* No one else has slept there since... The bed remains as it was; they didn't change the sheets, didn't pick up the pillow nor the crystal crucifix that was broken that night...Everything is as it was eight years ago... Ismael doesn't want me or anyone else to touch anything... The other bed, the one that's a double size, came later. But my bed, my maiden bed, remains there, forever and ever... And it will remain there after my death.

ELIAS: The fiancé of the cousin who died must've been handsome...

VIRGÍNIA: *(Resentful.)* It was because of her, my aunt. She called Ismael, showed him the stairs and said: "Let her scream, let her scream..." Ismael bought the house and, the next day, she and the three virgins moved out. They came back thirty days later, for the marriage. And now, when a son of mine is born or dies – she and her daughters come to watch the birth, or the funeral... They want to see if the son who's born or who dies is black... *(Astonished.)* Today, they haven't showed up yet. But they will; I'm sure they will; they'll always come...

ELIAS: *(Astonished.)* Because of you, the bride killed herself...

The cursed room is no longer lit.

ELIAS: Why didn't you die? A woman who is taken – *(Lowers his voice.)* taken this way – should not carry on living...

VIRGÍNIA: *(With fear.)* Dying, never. I can't die. *(Like a maniac.)* Never. *(Desperate.)* If I died, he'd not bury me,

I'm know that for sure. He'd leave my body on that bed, hoping that despite my demise I'd keep on having children *(Slowing down.)* black children…

ELIAS: Dead women can't have children…

VIRGÍNIA: Maybe… *(Disoriented.)* Who knows? I surely don't; I don't understand anything anymore.

ELIAS: If you'd let me, I'd save you!

VIRGÍNIA: I don't see how!

ELIAS: *(Holding her tight.)* Let's run away!

VIRGÍNIA: I can't. If I ran away, his stench wouldn't leave me; it's ingrained in my flesh, in my soul. I can never be free! Not even death will set me free!

ELIAS: May that black brother of mine forever be damned.

VIRGÍNIA: *(Sweet.)* You can save me, but not like that. There's another way. And if you do what I ask you to do, I'll fall on my knees and thank you, I'll kiss the footprints your shoes have left on the floor.

ELIAS: *(Carried away.)* You know, don't you? That I'll do anything, everything!

VIRGÍNIA: I do. I sensed that from you.

VIRGÍNIA caresses ELIAS's face and hair. They fall on their knees, facing each other.

ELIAS: You're driving us both crazy.

VIRGÍNIA: If we are not already there.

ELIAS: What do you want from me?

VIRGÍNIA: Remember what I said? That your lips were delicate and soft? Give me a kiss?

They kiss each other passionately. ELIAS stands up, bringing VIRGÍNIA up with him. VIRGÍNIA frees herself from him and moves away, turning her back to ELIAS. Then she turns to him.

VIRGÍNIA: *(Resentful.)* I've already had three sons; none of them white. That's why they die – because they are black.

ELIAS: And if they were white? Wouldn't they die as well?

VIRGÍNIA: *(Imperative.)* If they were white, they wouldn't. I swear they wouldn't die. If a white child doesn't come next time – it'll be another one I bring to death. Do you hear me?

ELIAS: Yes.

At this moment, four women, who are Virgínia's AUNT and COUSINS, appear in the garden. THE AUNT, the kind of woman in which all geniality has died. The COUSINS are spinsters who drag through life an unwanted virginity.

VIRGÍNIA: And don't forget I'm really pretty, beautiful! Here are the stairs! Up there, straight ahead, there's a door… It's unlocked.

VIRGÍNIA goes upstairs and reappears in the bedroom. ELIAS goes up right after her. They meet each other, embrace and kiss. The curtain drops as THE AUNT and COUSINS go around the house.

END OF ACT 1

Act 2

Same setting. VIRGÍNIA and ELIAS are standing by the door. VIRGÍNIA fixes her hair. Her attitude is imbued with post-amorous fatigue. ELIAS, sweet as ever. VIRGÍNIA's double bed is now as messy as her maiden bed - pillow on the floor; the sheets half off the bed. The BLACK WOMEN go downstairs and form a semicircle, near the small and decorative tub in which the boy drowned. They run their rosaries through their fingers; they pray. THE AUNT and spinster COUSINS are in the living room. Although the sun is still shining elsewhere, night falls in spite of all the clocks; therefore, it is a sad and premature night.

COUSIN: *(As if in a lament.)* In other houses, the sun is still shining. Not in this one, it's already night here.

THE AUNT: Did you hear something?

COUSINS: *(Unison.)* No.

THE AUNT: Voices?

COUSINS: Where?

THE AUNT: *(Restless.)* Upstairs.

COUSINS: *(To one another.)* Voices upstairs.

THE AUNT: Two voices.

COUSINS: *(In a lament, always as if in a lament.)* There's no one home. They're at the cemetery.

THE AUNT: I heard something.

COUSIN: We got here too late.

COUSIN: We missed the funeral.

COUSIN: This house is tainted.

COUSIN: No flowers on the floor.

COUSINS: *(Ominous.)* At a funeral, there's always a flower left behind.

COUSIN: Always.

COUSIN: A flower floating on the floor.

THE AUNT: I thought I heard a voice. Or a couple of them. A man and a woman.

Upstairs, in the bedroom, ELIAS embraces VIRGÍNIA but she pushes him away violently.

THE AUNT: It must be my nerves.

Back, upstairs.

VIRGÍNIA: Now, go.

ELIAS: It's still early.

VIRGÍNIA: It's late.

ELIAS: You're not the same anymore. Suddenly, you changed. I feel you changed.

VIRGÍNIA: He'll be here soon. Any minute now, he'll walk in.

ELIAS: So why did you call for me? You shouldn't have called for me. I was about to leave tomorrow. I'd never come back. *(Sweet.)* Show me your hands…

VIRGÍNIA offers her hands mechanically; ELIAS kisses one and, then, the other but VIRGÍNIA remains cold.

VIRGÍNIA: *(Impatiently.)* You can't stay in this house. Not a single minute more.

ELIAS: You're cold, absolutely cold.

VIRGÍNIA: It's the fear.

ELIAS: I no longer fear.

VIRGÍNIA: *(Aching.)* Yes, you do. I can feel it on your hands, in your mouth – fear… *(Looks around.)*

ELIAS: There's no fear. That was all before I met you. But now, everything's changed. And if you want me to – do you?

VIRGÍNIA: I don't!

ELIAS: I'd stand right here, in this bedroom. On my feet. Facing the door.

VIRGÍNIA: This is madness!

ELIAS: *(Continuing.)* Then, he arrives…

VIRGÍNIA: And kills you.

ELIAS: And kills me.

VIRGÍNIA: For the love of God, what for?

ELIAS: *(Passionately.)* I can't live without you anymore, I don't want to. Without the woman who I've never seen, who I'll never see, this absolute stranger…

While ELIAS says these words, he touches VIRGÍNIA as if trying to recognise her.

VIRGÍNIA: Please, for the love you say you feel for me – leave.

ELIAS: No!

VIRGÍNIA: You don't know Ismael! He could end up sending you away and killing me instead…

ELIAS: No, not you!

VIRGÍNIA: Why not? I've never seen him smile. He's so cold, so hard. His hands are as hard as a rock. *(Anxious.)* And you? Would you like to see me dead?

ELIAS: *(In free fall towards detachment.)* It would be so good if you died; this way, neither he nor any other man – no one else would ever lay hands on you…

Downstairs, between THE AUNT and the COUSINS.

THE AUNT: The funeral's taking so long!

COUSIN: They had no flowers!

COUSIN: The cemetery is really far away!

THE AUNT: Not that far!

COUSIN: It is, mum!

COUSIN: It's not like Virgínia to go to the cemetery!

THE AUNT: Today, she finally did!

COUSIN: Or could she still be here?

Back upstairs.

ELIAS: *(Daydreaming.)* Could you ever imagine yourself dead? *(Holds both of VIRGÍNIA'S arms.)* I could – but not by his hands; no, not his – my hands could kill you. No hate, no viciousness – out of love; so no one would ever cherish you and you'd never desire anyone yourself – your mouth forever at rest, your breasts at rest, and your hips at peace, so innocent…

ELIAS kneels and, caught up in his delirium, caresses VIRGÍNIA, who lets him adore her without as much as a gesture, motionless.

ELIAS: It wouldn't be bad to die like that – I swear! It'd be good– can't you see how good it would be?

VIRGÍNIA: *(Aching.)* I can.

ELIAS: You'd be pleased by it…It'd be such a sweet thing just like the death of a young girl; not a woman's death, but a girl's, on the day of her first communion…

VIRGÍNIA: Ismael dreams of a death like that, more or less like that…

ELIAS: *(Sweet.)* I should be your killer, not him – me!

ELIAS stands up and searches for VIRGÍNIA with his hands, who doesn't say a word. VIRGÍNIA leans against the wall, motionless. ELIAS moves very close, brushes past his sister-in law but doesn't find her, doesn't sense her.

ELIAS: *(Sweet.)* Don't hide from me. I'm not a killer. I don't feel like a killer and this wouldn't be a crime. I wouldn't kill just anyone, only you…

Gradually, ELIAS's sweetness turns into excitement and, finally, wrath.

ELIAS: Virgínia, where are you? I wouldn't bury you, either. I'd stay with you, close to your body, ever faithful, my desire satisfied, without making a sound, not a sound… I'd lie down next to your body… *(Disoriented.)* But where are you? Are you hiding from me? *(Resentful.)* You don't want me? You'd prefer that nigger. *(Pleading again.)* Forgive me but speak! Virgínia! Virgínia!

ELIAS turns his head in every direction, lost in his darkness.

VIRGÍNIA: Go away!

ELIAS: First, listen!

VIRGÍNIA: Leave!

ELIAS: You can't send me away like this, not after what happened…

VIRGÍNIA: Nothing happened!

ELIAS: Just now…

VIRGÍNIA: You're hallucinating!

ELIAS: You gave yourself to me… you were mine!

VIRGÍNIA: *(Changing her tone.)* I was yours but I was cold –
    cold, as if made of ice – couldn't you tell I was cold!

ELIAS: You went crazy…

VIRGÍNIA: It was all an act!

ELIAS: You're lying!

VIRGÍNIA: It's so easy to pretend! Any woman can do it.
    (Absolutely cruel.) Leave, I never want to see you again. If
    you show up around here, if you come back – I'll tell on
    you, I'll tell him everything!

*Pause. ELIAS goes to the door. From there, he turns around and
speaks.*

ELIAS: I'll wait for you in my room. I won't leave. Never.
    But, if you don't come – if you don't want to – then…
    goodbye!

ELIAS waits for an answer.

ELIAS: Goodbye.

Nothing.

ELIAS: At least say – "Goodbye". That's it. I don't ask for
    much.

*VIRGÍNIA, with her back to him, remains silent. She faces up and
shows her expression immersed in absolute sadness.*

VIRGÍNIA: Goodbye.

ELIAS goes downstairs at the same moment that THE AUNT appears in the middle room. She stops a moment, dazed. After the blind man leaves, THE AUNT goes up the stairs and into the bedroom, just as VIRGÍNIA is picking up the pillow. VIRGÍNIA leaves the pillow on the floor. They look at each other in silence.

COUSIN: Shall we go upstairs?

COUSIN: Mum might not like it.

COUSIN: So what?

COUSIN: Not now.

COUSIN: Just for a peek.

COUSIN: Virgínia was luckier than the rest of us.

COUSIN: Well, I don't think so!

COUSIN: I wouldn't want a black husband!

COUSIN: Me neither!

COUSIN: Yeah.

COUSIN: The only one of us, who got engaged, died!

COUSIN: Her trousseau was ready and all paid for.

COUSIN: Shall we?

COUSIN: All that beautiful linen!

COUSIN: Shall we?

COUSIN: I'm not going. I'll stay here.

The COUSINS go in search of THE AUNT. They go upstairs and into the bedroom at the moment in which, without uttering a word, THE AUNT picks up the sheets, the pillow and starts making up the bed.

COUSIN: What happened?

THE AUNT: *(Making up the bed, to VIRGÍNIA.)* Have you nothing to say?

VIRGÍNIA: *(With her back to THE AUNT and facing the audience.)* NOTHING!

THE AUNT: On my way up here, I saw a man going down the stairs…

VIRGÍNIA: *(Quick.)* My brother-in-law.

THE AUNT: A blind man.

VIRGÍNIA: *(Confirming.)* Blind…

THE AUNT: And that's all he is, your brother-in-law?

VIRGÍNIA: That's all.

THE AUNT: Do you swear?

VIRGÍNIA: I swear.

THE AUNT: Swear on your son who's being buried today?

VIRGÍNIA hesitates for a moment; she turns around, facing THE AUNT and with her back to the audience; they are face to face, really close.

VIRGÍNIA: On my son…

THE AUNT: *(In a controlled fury.)* Why are you lying?

VIRGÍNIA: *(Aching.)* I'm not!

THE AUNT: Why are you so conniving? Why do you have to always hide the truth? – ever since you were a little girl…

VIRGÍNIA: I've sworn!

THE AUNT: Are we supposed to trust you because of that? *(Without change.)* Did he come into your bedroom?

VIRGÍNIA: No!

THE AUNT: He did!

VIRGÍNIA: He came here just to talk to me. He stood in the hall...

THE AUNT: Shameless! I know he came in here, and he stayed quite a while!...

VIRGÍNIA: *(Quick.)* If you already knew – why torment me with questions? I'd like to be left alone now, please; to pray...

THE AUNT: *(To herself, in transit.)* Praised be the Lord for me arriving late here! If it wasn't for that, maybe I'd never have found out you have a lover...

VIRGÍNIA: *(Astonished.)* No!

THE AUNT: *(Still absorbed by her rationale.)* I wouldn't have made up your bed... I made it up myself...

VIRGÍNIA: *(Desperate.)* But I don't have a lover!

THE AUNT: What about that man?

VIRGÍNIA: *(Passionately.)* He's not a lover! It was just once, a moment, over so quickly. It only lasted for a second. And he'll never touch me again, I give you my word for it – with God as my witness! *(Changes her tone, sweet, pleading.)* If you knew why I gave myself to him, if you knew why – I swear there's a reason! God, who sees what's in my heart, who sees what's in my flesh, knows it wasn't out of mere desire...

THE AUNT: It was desire, pure desire! Since you were little, that's who you are!

VIRGÍNIA: *(In transit.)* If you knew how happy I feel. Today my bed is pure – a virgin can now lie in it with no fear; a virgin, a little girl... He's a man who only had me once, just once, and I don't see that as a lover – he's

not a lover – understand? I was the one who called for
him – me, do you hear me? – he didn't know me and
I didn't know him; and if it wasn't something so pure,
I wouldn't have called for him, I wouldn't have taken him
by the hand like a boy!

THE AUNT: You confess it was all your doing?

VIRGÍNIA: *(Still in awe.)* I confess!

THE AUNT: Confess to me. *(Quick.)* And to your husband,
too?

VIRGÍNIA: *(Horrified.)* No, not my husband!

THE AUNT: *(Triumphant.)* But I'll tell him everything!

VIRGÍNIA: *(In a panic.)* Ismael?

THE AUNT: Yes, Ismael. He'll hear about your lover…

VIRGÍNIA: *(In a lament.)* He's not my lover!

THE AUNT: A lover who didn't know you and who you didn't
know. A lover you called for, a lover you seduced, who
was brought by the hand to your bedroom. I'll tell him
everything, I'll tell your husband!

VIRGÍNIA: No, not my husband!

THE AUNT: Listen – you came into my house and led us to
our disgrace. My daughter killed herself because you stole
her fiancé. Are you or are you not responsible for her
killing herself?

VIRGÍNIA: *(Lowering her head.)* I don't know about that.

THE AUNT: I've been waiting for this moment for a long time.
I'd keep telling myself: "She'll pay for it; she has to pay for
it. Or there is no God'. When your first son died, I thought
I'd had my vengeance. Vengeance for what you did to my

daughter. But soon I saw it wasn't so, you didn't suffer, you didn't like your babies, the sons of Ismael. I even told you girls, didn't I?

COUSIN: You did!

COUSIN: She doesn't like her sons!

COUSIN: She doesn't even mourn their deaths!

THE AUNT: *(Approaches VIRGÍNIA, who retreats with early signs of fear.)* You do hate your sons; don't you, Virgínia? *(Almost sweet, as if asking her niece to hate.)* Do you?

VIRGÍNIA: I don't.

THE AUNT: Don't deny it, Virgínia. You know you hate them...

VIRGÍNIA: *(Not knowing what she says anymore.)* The sons of Ismael...

THE AUNT: *(Going down her own memory lane.)* I kept on waiting. Sooner or later, I'd have my revenge...

VIRGÍNIA: *(Hysterical.)* You got your revenge that day, when you locked up the house and told Ismael to go upstairs!

THE AUNT: It wasn't enough. It was too easy, far too easy on you... You still owe me... And I'm not even sure what Ismael did to you was an act of revenge. *(Vehement.)* I can't tell. *(To VIRGÍNIA.)* I swear, if a man did to my daughter – what Ismael did over there *(Points to the broken bed.)* – I'd thank him – I swear! If you could see the state my daughter is in, the one who's downstairs – if you could hear what she says, see what she does...

At this exact moment, the COUSIN who THE AUNT is referring to, assumes a series of erotic postures, like holding her breasts with both hands, expressing profound sexual anxiety.

THE AUNT: She's nearly insane. And I can't do anything about it – do you understand? And her sisters – these here – are going the same way. *(Suddenly ferocious.)* But I'd rather they go crazy! Better crazy than dead. I don't want them to die *(Without transition, horrified.)* My daughter downstairs…

COUSINS: *(In a lament.)* We too, mum.

THE AUNT: … and these two, are going to die virgins, because you're a slut. *(Violent.)* I'm going to tell your husband everything; I'll tell him not what you told me, but what I saw!

VIRGÍNIA: I just stole your daughter's fiancé…

THE AUNT: You've tainted all of us!

VIRGÍNIA: But, Auntie, Ismael can't find out. It's important that he doesn't. I'll do whatever you want. Whatever you want me to do – tell me! I'll do anything!

THE AUNT: I don't want anything. It's my turn, now… I'll wait for your husband, Virgínia…

THE AUNT and COUSINS leave. VIRGÍNIA remains in the bedroom. THE AUNT and COUSINS make comments on their way down. They wait for ISMAEL in the living room.

COUSIN: Virgínia has a lover!

COUSIN: A lover.

COUSIN: Just wait till her husband finds out!

COUSIN: You think he'll kill her?

COUSIN: Course!

THE AUNT and COUSINS reach the living room; addressing the CRAZED COUSIN.

COUSINS: *(Together.)* Virgínia has a lover!

COUSIN: I said it first.

COUSIN: Did not!

COUSIN: Did too.

COUSIN: Mum, didn't I say it first?

THE AUNT: Girls, behave!

COUSIN: *(Unbalanced.)* I remember that night. Did Virgínia scream!

COUSIN: Mum's going to tell on her, aren't you, mum?

THE AUNT: I am.

COUSIN: *(As joyous as a half-wit.)* Yay, good!

THE AUNT: I'll only leave this house after having told him.

The COUSINS are on pause. ISMAEL comes in. He goes straight to VIRGÍNIA's bedroom.

ISMAEL: Why is the door open?

VIRGÍNIA: It was my aunt who arrived with my cousins. She opened it. Did you not speak to them?

ISMAEL: No.

VIRGÍNIA: Ah! *(New approach, sweet.)* I was waiting for you. Let's go for a walk outside; just for a while… A short stroll – shall we?

ISMAEL: Not today.

VIRGÍNIA: Please. I'm begging you.

ISMAEL: No, because my brother's in the house.

VIRGÍNIA: Your brother? Oh, the one who is blind? He is
   blind, isn't he? You didn't say a thing when you left for the
   funeral.

ISMAEL: He arrived this morning.

VIRGÍNIA: Well, let's stay here then. It's better this way.
   We can have a chat.

ISMAEL: You seem different.

VIRGÍNIA: Me?

ISMAEL: Almost loving.

VIRGÍNIA: *(In a kind of euphoria.)* I am, aren't I?

ISMAEL: We've been married for eight years. And you've
   never shown any kind of love, or a simple gesture, even a
   gentle touch...

VIRGÍNIA: You as well, you almost never talk to me.

ISMAEL: *(Holding her by the shoulders.)* But today I feel you as if
   you were someone else entirely, not the same person.

VIRGÍNIA: *(Aching.)* I am not the same, Ismael.

ISMAEL: *(Low.)* Did you forget I'm black?

VIRGÍNIA: I hardly ever remember you're black, to be
   honest, I always forget – I swear. Sometimes I have to look
   very, very hard at you and I can't decide if you're black or
   not. There are also times when I think the world has only
   blacks and I'm the only white one. And then there are
   times when I think I am black, too. Would you still love
   me if I were black?

ISMAEL: I never told you – isn't it true? – that I loved you,
   right? Did I?

VIRGÍNIA: Never.

ISMAEL: *(Exasperated.)* Virgínia, I have to think about you and not my son; no one but you. *(Changing his tone.)* Now, say it– I have to know the truth – do you feel horrified by me?

VIRGÍNIA: *(After a moment of silence.)* No.

ISMAEL: *(Affirmative.)* You do!

VIRGÍNIA: *(Desperate.)* I don't!

ISMAEL: Why do you lie? For eight years, every night, the same thing that happened in that maiden bed, has happened in ours. For eight years, you've screamed as if it was the first time; and I still have to cover your mouth. I'm your husband, but when I come near you, I feel like I'm going to violate a woman. You're that perpetually violated woman – because you don't want it, you don't give yourself to me… You see my desire as a crime. Do you?

VIRGÍNIA: My body is yours, it has always been yours and it'll be forever yours, time and time again. But, for the love of God, don't ask me any questions! Forget all that happened, everything that has happened, everything. Because today – can't you see it? can't you feel it? – I'm loving or the closest I can be to it…

VIRGÍNIA rests her head on her husband's chest.

VIRGÍNIA: I do not fear you…

ISMAEL: You do. I know you do. *(Changing his tone.)* Why did you hate my sons?

VIRGÍNIA: *(Retreating.)* I didn't hate your sons!

ISMAEL: You did. Even before they were born, while they were still in your womb – you already hated them. Because they were my sons… Look at me! Am I lying?

And because they were black and looked like me. You even said so yourself – they had my face…

VIRGÍNIA: *(Looking at her husband's facial traits.)* They did have your face…

ISMAEL: They died because they were black…

VIRGÍNIA: *(In terror.)* It was fate.

ISMAEL: *(Still holding back.)* Because they were black. *(New tone.)* – You thought I didn't know?

VIRGÍNIA: *(Retreating, in a whisper.)* No, Ismael, no!

ISMAEL: What you did to my sons?

VIRGÍNIA: *(Terrified.)* Nothing – I did nothing…

They look at each other.

ISMAEL: You killed them. *(Lowers his voice.)* Murdered them. *(With controlled violence.)* It wasn't fate: it was you, your hands, those hands…

Instinctively, VIRGÍNIA looks down and examines her own hands.

ISMAEL: One by one. This last one, the one we buried today, you yourself took him by the hand. You didn't say a harsh word, you didn't scare him; you couldn't have been sweeter. Near the tub, you even kissed him; then, you looked around. You didn't see me, up there, watching you… After that, you were quick and straight to the point – you had already killed two – you covered my son's mouth, so he couldn't scream… You only ran off once he was lying still at the bottom of the tub…

VIRGÍNIA: *(Ferociously accusatory.)* So, why didn't you shout? Why didn't you stop me?

ISMAEL: *(Cutting.)* So it's true?

VIRGÍNIA: *(Astonished.)* It is.

ISMAEL: You gave poison to the other two...

VIRGÍNIA: *(Harsh.)* Yes.

ISMAEL: Because they were black.

VIRGÍNIA: *(Abandoning herself.)* Because they were black. *(With sudden vehemence.)* But if you knew all along, why didn't you stop me?

ISMAEL: *(With a somber tone, incredibly charged.)* I didn't stop you because your crimes brought us even closer; and because I want you even more now, knowing you to be a murderer – thrice a murderer. Do you hear me? *(With the greatest pain.)* Bare-handed murderer of my sons...

VIRGÍNIA: *(Savage.)* I wanted to rid my house of black boys. Destroy them, one by one, until not a single one was left. I didn't want to have to caress a black son... *(Weird.)* Ismael, they must be destroyed, all of them...

ISMAEL: Listen. You will have another son.

VIRGÍNIA: I know.

ISMAEL: Black, like the others.

VIRGÍNIA: I know that too.

ISMAEL: But this one won't die.

VIRGÍNIA: *(As if daydreaming.)* No, not this one.

ISMAEL: Not because you won't feel the desire to kill him. But because I don't want you to. The others, I had let you, but not this one... You will never bring him up with your hate...

VIRGÍNIA: Ismael, I swear – in God's name – in the name of the sons that I *(Lowers her voice.)* killed – I swear this one

will live and that he'll have my love... I want another
son... You'll find me a new woman today – one who no
longer fears, who's no longer repulsed by you, who won't
be violated, not today, not ever... Touch me. See how I
don't avoid you? Or maybe you don't like making love
like this? Perhaps you need me to fear you... Perhaps you
need to feel the taste of blood on your teeth.. I give you
my body to rack... I love you, I've never told you, but
I love you... I only ask you one thing – don't talk to my
aunt! Throw that witch out of here! Her words bite!...

ISMAEL: *(Abstract.)* You are yet to love me. I know it, for
sure... First, you have to love a son of mine... A black
son... Then, and only then, you'll love your black
husband... the Negro...

VIRGÍNIA: But I do love you, Ismael!

ISMAEL: *(Violent.)* So why now do you want a new son, if you
hated all the others?

*THE AUNT, who has left the living room, reaches, at this moment,
the bedroom door.*

ISMAEL: Why?

THE AUNT: Because it won't be yours, Ismael!

Suspense among the three.

THE AUNT: She has a lover, Ismael! Your wife has a lover!

VIRGÍNIA: *(Beyond herself.)* Lies! I don't have a lover; I never
had a lover!

THE AUNT: She does! It's your brother, Ismael, the one who's
blind... She gave herself to him!

VIRGÍNIA: *(Hysterical.)* Believe your wife, Ismael, not this
witch...

ISMAEL: *(Holding her by the shoulders.)* You have a lover...

VIRGÍNIA: I don't!

ISMAEL: You do!

VIRGÍNIA: I give you my word!

ISMAEL: And Elias, of all men...

THE AUNT: He's not to blame, Ismael. It wasn't his fault. She went after him, brought him up here, by the hand... Your brother's blind, he can't see. He would've tripped on the steps.

ISMAEL: You went after him...

THE AUNT: She betrayed you to have a white son.

ISMAEL: *(Losing track of everything and everyone; talking to himself.)* This is my punishment... I've always hated being black. I despised my black man's sweat, but I shouldn't... I only desired the wombs of white women... I hated my mother because I was born of colour... I envied Elias because of his white flesh... Now, it's payback... A black Christ has tainted my flesh... All because I despised my sweat...

VIRGÍNIA, frantic, trying to tear her husband away from his day-dream.

VIRGÍNIA: I wanted a son who could live, not a dead one... A son who didn't have to die...

ISMAEL: *(Waking up, violent, addressing THE AUNT.)* You can go – now. And don't ever come back. You and your daughters.

Without saying a word, still quite dignified, THE AUNT leaves the bedroom. She goes to meet the COUSINS in the living room.

CRAZED COUSIN: *(In a lament.)* She has a husband, and a lover!

THE AUNT: Today, she'll pay!

COUSIN: Will she die?

COUSIN: Of course!

COUSIN: She has to!

COUSIN: I bet you!

COUSIN: Such a shameless slut!

THE AUNT: She's always been one!

CRAZED COUSIN: I'll help carry the coffin!

THE AUNT and COUSINS make these comments as they leave. In the bedroom, VIRGÍNIA is in bed, devastated. ISMAEL, standing up, seems petrified. The BLACK WOMEN, in a semicircle, speak near the tub.

BLACK WOMAN: Deadly water!

BLACK WOMAN: That seems so innocent!

BLACK WOMAN: It killed a child!

BLACK WOMAN: Oh, Lord, let the next one be a white son!

BLACK WOMAN: As fair as daylight!

BLACK WOMAN: That won't die like the others!

BLACK WOMAN: And no one would say this tub had already killed one.

BLACK WOMAN: Or more than one.

BLACK WOMAN: No one would say it.

BLACK WOMAN: Forgive, Dear Lord, this cold and dark water!

BLACK WOMAN: And make the next one be a white son, not even brown, but white, very fair.

The BLACK WOMEN's voices are lost in a prayer-like murmur.

ISMAEL: I built these walls, locked you in a room. And while I was burying my son – you opened the door, called for a man you'd never seen before.

VIRGÍNIA: *(As if daydreaming.)* I only opened the door.

ISMAEL: Just now, you said – for the very first time – that you loved me.

VIRGÍNIA: *(Cold.)* I did.

ISMAEL: Say it again.

VIRGÍNIA: Did you believe me?

ISMAEL: Do you love me?

VIRGÍNIA: Do I have to answer?

ISMAEL: Yes or no?

VIRGÍNIA: *(Retreating ever so slightly, in a crescendo.)* No. You know very well I don't. You know I am repulsed by you, always was, always have been, and that I can't stand anything you touch…

ISMAEL: Is that all?

VIRGÍNIA: *(Dignified.)* That's all.

ISMAEL: And your lover?

VIRGÍNIA: *(Seems lost, hesitates, but soon snaps out of it.)* He escaped. I said: "Run! Run!" He must be far away by now, very far away *(Passionately.)* praise be the Lord!

ISMAEL: *(In a crescendo.)* Your lover is far, far away. But his son is here; his son didn't escape. *(Laughs, brutally.)* Let your lover run away. *(Stops laughing, abruptly.)* But his son is here, within my reach, I can almost caress him…

And ISMAEL actually caresses his wife's belly.

ISMAEL: Do you see where this is going?

VIRGÍNIA: *(In early signs of panic.)* Yes.

ISMAEL: And you have no fear?

VIRGÍNIA: *(Ferociously, covering her belly with her hand, as if defending her future child.)* You won't touch this son – never, you hear me – never! I won't let you. He's mine, not yours! He's white – white!

ISMAEL: *(With savage joy.)* Wasn't it you who killed my sons?

VIRGÍNIA: Me?

ISMAEL: Yes, you. One by one. Didn't you kill them? Well, your one – his one – I'll kill him too *(With a madman's joy.)* and in the tub, Virgínia, over there. *(Points in the direction of the tub.)* I'll wait the nine months – it's nine, isn't it? – and even if it were more – a year – I'd wait. *(Sweet.)* Nothing will happen to you. Or to Elias. But him. *(Points to his wife's belly.)* He's still shapeless – he has no flesh yet – but he's already doomed!

Delirious, VIRGÍNIA runs toward the door; ISMAEL goes after her and drags her back by the wrists.

ISMAEL: *(As if both demanding and pleading.)* I have the right – don't I? – To drown this child – or don't you agree? If you're a murderer, I can be one, too… can't I?

VIRGÍNIA: *(Holding on to him.)* No, Ismael, no! I was mad when I said you repulsed me! My words don't obey me anymore. I don't know what I say, what I think! I'm mad, Ismael, completely mad! I needed to have a son – a son that wasn't yours – but I didn't sin, I swear I didn't sin. I swear, not by the sons who died, but by this one *(Touches her own belly.)* – this one here. If you only knew, if you could imagine my innocence and… Elias's. Do you want to know? If he ravished me every day, I'd remain pure, my soul would be untouched. If he killed me – and he wanted to kill me – he'd be as pure in crime as he is in love… His crime wouldn't be cruel, but more like a dream… I didn't know, I couldn't even imagine that an innocent love like that could exist and that a woman could give herself to a man without guilt. Do you understand me? I feel no guilt – no guilt at all! *(In pure bliss forgetting, for a moment, her husband's presence.)* I think he had never known love, had never known a woman. *(Face to face with ISMAEL.)* I think I was the first…

ISMAEL: *(Still holding her.)* Look at me! If it had only been desire…

VIRGÍNIA: It wasn't!

ISMAEL: … just desire, pleasure, I could forgive or forget.

VIRGÍNIA: Then forgive and forget, Ismael!

ISMAEL: But it was more than desire…

VIRGÍNIA: Much more!

ISMAEL: Looking at you, I can see you won't forget this man. He showed you a love no other man can show you. Not even me.

VIRGÍNIA: *(In a whisper.)* No! No! *(Desperate.)* I'm losing myself in my words. They say what I don't want them to say!

ISMAEL: *(As if trying to convince her.)* Since this man has run away – the son must pay, his son.

VIRGÍNIA is out of her mind; her incoherence is absolute.

VIRGÍNIA: My son, no. My son is not guilty of anything, Ismael. I don't love this man. If I called for him, it was because of this son, so I could have this son… I don't care about your brother. And he's not pure; he's not innocent… If I said that, it was to deceive you; I believed, this way, you'd not feel so betrayed… But he only knows how to love like you do, like all men do – making the woman a prostitute… *(In an ultimate effort to convince her husband.)* I swear I hated him, I hated myself, *(Hysterical.)* hated the bed, the pillowcase, the sheets, everything!

VIRGÍNIA plunges her face into her hands, in a fit of tears.

ISMAEL: I believe you!

VIRGÍNIA: *(Raising her head.)* So, you forgive my son?

ISMAEL: No.

VIRGÍNIA: Suppose I gave you proof? Suppose I could show you – proof that this man means nothing to me? *(Changes her tone, slowly.)* I lied when I said he ran away. He's downstairs, in the room you gave him, waiting for me… Just a few steps away…

ISMAEL: *(In a savage joy.)* Downstairs; he's still here? He didn't run away?

Quickly, ISMAEL gets a gun. VIRGÍNIA watches fascinated all his movements.

VIRGÍNIA: *(Approaching him.)* He should pay, not my son. He was the one who took me…

ISMAEL: You won't suffer, if he dies?

VIRGÍNIA: Not at all! I even want it. After all, I was the one who told you he was still here!

ISMAEL takes a few steps but stops.

ISMAEL: *(Lit up.)* Maybe you could go downstairs and called him yourself? He'd be happy to come. You say – let me see – say I didn't come back, I'm spending the night out… He's pure, his heart's sweet, he won't suspect a thing. He'll follow you up here. And then I'd like to see, with my own eyes, what kind of man he is, who loves like an angel; whose desire is neither sad nor evil… Are you going, or not?

Pause.

VIRGÍNIA: *(Making an effort.)* I'm going, Ismael.

ISMAEL: Then, go. Quickly. I'll wait here.

VIRGÍNIA abandons the bedroom. She stops, at the top of the stairs. Her attitude expresses the most profound suffering. She goes down, slowly, as if fighting against herself. At the same time, THE AUNT and her COUSINS appear in the garden.

THE AUNT: Will he kill her?

COUSIN: Course he will!

CRAZED COUSIN: I won't leave here until it's over.

THE AUNT: We can't stay here. What if someone arrives?

COUSIN: But we can stay close by.

CRAZED COUSIN: I'd like to hear a shot, a scream…

COUSIN: Oh, I hope so!

THE AUNT: Let's wait near the fountain?

COUSIN: Excellent!

THE AUNT: From there, we can hear.

THE AUNT and COUSINS have barely left when ELIAS and VIRGÍNIA appear at the door to the living room. ELIAS has an idyllic expression, dream-like. They go in; VIRGÍNIA goes up with an air of fatigue as if the stairs were as difficult to climb as a steep mountain.

ELIAS: See what a good thing it is that I stayed? I knew for sure you'd come. I didn't even lie down. Just sat down and waited. But is he spending the night out – the whole night?

VIRGÍNIA: He sent word.

ELIAS: So I can stay till tomorrow? I can, can't I?

VIRGÍNIA: *(Hiding her anguish, badly.)* Careful with the steps.

ELIAS: You didn't answer me.

VIRGÍNIA: *(Briefly in transit.)* Yes, you can. The whole night, until morning.

ELIAS: You seem sort of – sad!

VIRGÍNIA: *(With great sadness.)* It's happiness!

VIRGÍNIA and ELIAS go up arm in arm and enter the bedroom.

ELIAS: Your must have a very fair skin!

VIRGÍNIA: *(With anguish.)* Very.

ISMAEL is immobile, in the middle of the bedroom, merely watching.

VIRGÍNIA: *(Sitting at the edge of the bed, with ELIAS.)* Sit here with me. *(Increasingly agitated.)* I can only think of our son. *(Looking at and caressing ELIAS's face.)* I imagine how he'll be, when he grows up… He'll be like you, exactly like you. He'll have your voice, the same mouth, your way of kissing, the innocent passion…

ELIAS: Love my son… as if he were me!

VIRGÍNIA: *(Holding on to ELIAS, forcefully.)* As if he were you! You could die, couldn't you? *(Looks at her husband.)* It's so easy to die! But remember these words: I know

222

I will love your son, not with a mother's love, but a woman's. *(Changes her tone, looking, terrified, at her husband, who remains impassive.)* No, Elias, no. I'm crazy! This is madness *(Always looking at her husband, lowers her voice.)*, a quiet frenzy, which makes me say mad words...

ELIAS: *(Also holds on to VIRGÍNIA, who now seems cold.)* I'm scared again...I feel death closing in... *(With more energy.)* Virgínia! You promised you'd love our son as if he were me!

VIRGÍNIA: *(Violent.)* Stop it! Don't say a thing! All of your words call for death!

ELIAS: *(As if possessed by fear.)* What are you hiding from me? By everything that's most sacred, don't lie. You're betraying me, wishing me dead... But I don't want to die, now that I've met you, now that you're mine and not that nigger's... *(Vehement.)* I don't want his hands on you, or his desire on you... And if you're his, if he makes you his, even once more – I'll curse you forever, in my name, in our son's name... *(Changes his tone, a sort of desperate tenderness.)* No! Forgive me... I'd never curse you...Not even if you gave yourself to him and to other men... To me, you'd never be a prostitute. And even if you were, I'd still love you, maybe even more...

VIRGÍNIA: *(Quick.)* Elias, you must tell me something. But don't lie. I want the truth.

ELIAS: I'll answer.

VIRGÍNIA: Am I the first woman you've known?

ELIAS: Yes.

VIRGÍNIA frees herself from ELIAS and retreats to the back of the bedroom. ELIAS pursues her and, unaware and unwillingly, walks towards ISMAEL. ISMAEL, very calmly, raises his gun and points it, not to the stomach, nor to the heart of his enemy, but at ELIAS's face. He fires. ELIAS falls, instantly dead. Down below, outside, THE AUNT and COUSINS reappear, very excited.

THE AUNT: What did I tell you?

COUSIN: She died.

COUSIN: Virgínia is dead.

THE AUNT: *(Emphatic.)* Praised be, Dear Lord, for avenging my daughter!

COUSIN: She had it coming!

COUSIN: *(In a lament.)* I fear him.

COUSIN: She looks silly!

THE AUNT: *(With tragic sweetness.)* Rest, dear daughter, now you can rest in your gloomy bed of darkness – Virgínia's dead...

ISMAEL remains immobile, with the gun in his hand. VIRGÍNIA, as if glued to the wall, looks from side to side.

END OF ACT 2

Act 3

SCENE 1

Same set as the first two acts: ISMAEL's house. Sixteen years have gone by and the sun never shone again. For ISMAEL and his family, daylight no longer exists. An endless night looms over the house now. It seems like a curse. Instead of a son, a daughter, ANA MARIA, was born. She is now fifteen years old. Extremely beautiful, she appears to live in a state of serene wonderment. VIRGÍNIA has aged but she's still a good-looking woman. ISMAEL, more taciturn than before, still wears his very starched white suit and his patent leather shoes. Nevertheless, his mood changes when speaking to ANA MARIA. The BLACK WOMEN remained onstage, commenting on facts, feelings and people.

The curtain opens and ANA MARIA appears – a beautiful adolescent – touching the objects in her room. She is obviously blind. ANA MARIA soon disappears.

BLACK WOMAN: Praised be, oh, God Almighty…

BLACK WOMAN: Fifteen years ago, a daughter was born…

BLACK WOMAN: A white one.

BLACK WOMAN: Not a boy, but a girl.

BLACK WOMAN: With her white skin!

BLACK WOMAN: She was born naked, and her father said immediately: "It's a girl."

BLACK WOMAN: Because she was born naked.

BLACK WOMEN: *(All in a chorus.)* – Virgin Mary… Holiest art thou…

BLACK WOMAN: For sixteen years there's been no sun in this house. For sixteen years it's been night.

BLACK WOMAN: The stars have fled.

BLACK WOMAN: The girl survived. Now, she's a woman.

BLACK WOMAN: Now, she's become a woman.

BLACK WOMAN: Oh, Dear Lord! Spare Ana Maria from the lust of men, the filth of drunkards… Spare her from lone men that, with their loneliness, lust even more!…

BLACK WOMAN: There haven't been anymore funerals.

BLACK WOMAN: No flowers.

BLACK WOMAN: No more funerals…

Their voices are lost in whispered prayers. A dialogue between ISMAEL and VIRGÍNIA.

VIRGÍNIA: Where was it?

ISMAEL: Near the fountain, I suppose.

VIRGÍNIA: So close by.

ISMAEL: No one came to help.

VIRGÍNIA: She must've been mad to walk alone, at night, in such a deserted area, that everyone knows is dangerous…

ISMAEL: *(With a certain surprise.)* Suddenly, she stopped shouting, as if she'd died…

VIRGÍNIA: *(In a shiver.)* Perhaps she did?

ISMAEL: *(With angst.)* I felt no pity…

VIRGÍNIA: *(Not paying attention to him.)* She shouted like I did, over there. *(Points to her maiden bed.)* It reminded me of myself, that night. You remember? When I heard the woman's cry for help, I guessed it right away; it was as if it was happening in front of me. *(Horrified, slowly.)* To be ravished like that, dear Lord!

ISMAEL: *(Slowly.)* All cries sound the same!

VIRGÍNIA: Why didn't you help her, Ismael?

Pause.

ISMAEL: *(With rancour.)* Because she was a stranger, a woman like any other *(Slowly.)* as all women are to me. All except one…

VIRGÍNIA: Who?

ISMAEL: You know who.

VIRGÍNIA: No, I don't.

ISMAEL: Ana Maria.

VIRGÍNIA: *(Suffering.)* Only Ana Maria?

ISMAEL: Only her.

VIRGÍNIA: Not me?

ISMAEL doesn't answer.

VIRGÍNIA: What if it was me?

ISMAEL: *(As if he just heard the question.)* What if it were you?

VIRGÍNIA: If it were me, and not some stranger, if it were me and not some woman you've never seen? Huh? You'd leaving me crying for help? You'd leave me crying forever?

ISMAEL: *(After a pause.)* I don't know…

VIRGÍNIA: *(With vehemence.)* You do know, yes, you do! *(Changing her tone, pleading.)* Tell me, Ismael. I must know for sure.

ISMAEL: If it was you, I'd let it happen. Did you or did you not belong to another man?

VIRGÍNIA: *(In a crescendo.)* Are you telling me that if I were in a deserted place, at night; and if a man…

ISMAEL: *(In a low voice, but still with passion.)* If you belonged to one man, you can belong to another, to many others *(Furious.)* to all men! I'd let you shout and I wouldn't lift a finger; I'd stay by my daughter's side, listening; she and I would just listen. Until your shouts ceased and nothing else could be heard.

VIRGÍNIA: Your daughter means everything to you. And I mean nothing?

ISMAEL: Nothing.

VIRGÍNIA: *(Violent.)* And why is it "your" daughter? You know you're not her father, her father's someone else. I can say – "my daughter" – not you.

ISMAEL: I'm not her father, but she thinks I am. *(In transit.)* She adores me. She's crazy about me!

VIRGÍNIA: Ana Maria must learn a few things, one of which is that you're a stranger, a man like all others; and that you are the one who killed her father…

ISMAEL: And who's going to tell her?

VIRGÍNIA: I will.

ISMAEL: *(Fed up.)* Go on. Tell her. Why don't you?

VIRGÍNIA: I'll also tell her that when she was born and you realised she was a girl… *(Changing her tone, remembering something far too painful.)* Do you remember, Ismael, do you remember what you did?

ISMAEL: No.

VIRGÍNIA: I know you didn't forget, and you never will. *(Face to face with him.)* Tell me what you did once Ana

Maria was born? You were watching over her cradle. For months and months, only the two of you in the room; you looking at her and she looking at you. For hours and hours. You wanted her to engrave it in her memory, your colour and the colour of your suit: you wanted that image burnt in her brain *(Sobbing laughter.)* the Black in all white. *(Raising her voice.)* You didn't speak, Ismael, so she wouldn't recognize your voice later on. Til one day, you took her away. Ana Maria was a year, or two, or even six months old, I don't know, I can't remember…You took her away and I thought you were going to drown her in the well; or worst, to bury her alive in the garden. *(Deeper in daze.)* I could never have guessed what you were doing to her – to a child, an innocent child – you'd poured acid over her eyes – acid! *(Nearly hysterical.)* Didn't you, Ismael? Or am I crazy, so crazy that I make up those stories? *(Pleading.)* Didn't you do that to my daughter, to Elias' daughter?

ISMAEL: I did.

VIRGÍNIA: *(Dazed, in a whisper.)* You did!

ISMAEL: *(With sinister humour.)* Wasn't her father blind?

VIRGÍNIA: *(Unsure.)* He was.

ISMAEL: *(With vehemence.)* Then why shouldn't the daughter also be, why? *(Changing his tone, more serene.)* I had hoped you'd have a son, a boy… I'd never imagined – neither had you – that she'd be a girl.

VIRGÍNIA: *(In free fall towards detachment.)* I was hoping for a son. Hoping for a boy!

ISMAEL: During those nine months, I felt it in your eyes, in your mouth – the desire, the hope, the want to have a son, not a daughter. Do you know what else you were thinking then?

VIRGÍNIA: *(Taken by despair.)* I'll tell you what I thought. I thought when he grew up...

ISMAEL: *(Completely taken as well, interrupting his wife.)* You'd love him, not as a mother, but as a woman, as a female in heat!

VIRGÍNIA: *(In the same tone.)* Yes; as a woman, or, even better as a female in heat! *(Changing her tone, slowly.)* – When Elias said, – "Love my son as if he were me" – I understood everything. I understood a white son would come to avenge me. *(Assuming a lower tone.)* To make you pay, you and all those niggers! *(Euphoric.)* After he'd grown up, he'd rest his head on my pillow, leaving his sweet scent in my pillowcase... *(Violent.)* He'd be a man and he'd be white!

ISMAEL: And blind!

VIRGÍNIA: *(Challenging.)* And blind, why not? It'd be better if he were blind, Ismael. If he couldn't see, he'd be totally mine, I'd take him for myself, and that would be it; I'd never let anyone – no woman – come between us. He and I would create such a small world, such a tight one, it'd be ours like a living room... No, not like a living room! Like a bedroom... *(Euphoric.)* Nothing beyond these walls, nothing beyond this view – our bedroom.

ISMAEL: *(In a savage joy.)* Not only that! Let me tell you what else you'd do. You'd lie, right?

VIRGÍNIA: *(Passionately.)* I would! I'd lie, all the time!

ISMAEL: To a blind person, who we raised since she was born, whom we've hidden and taken care of, it's better to lie – isn't it? We could even change the Ten Commandments.

VIRGÍNIA: *(Recovering her senses, cowardly.)* Why the Ten Commandments? Not the Ten Commandments. I fear God. God will punish me!

ISMAEL: Wait! *(Changing his tone, insidious and ignoble.)* You'd tell your son – oh, yes, you would – that one of the Ten Commandments says to love our mother above all things – as if she were the Virgin Mary! And you'd tell your blind son that you, with your own hands, you and no one else, created water, and fire and the fish. That's what you'd tell him, right? You'd tell him all women – not you, but all the others – were rotting like a piece of fruit that's gone bad – while you were the only one amongst them – the only pretty one, the only beautiful one, *(Laughing sordidly.)* the only one whose skin wasn't tainted... You'd say all that. You'd keep your son next to you, trapped with these lies and so many others; and you'd get away with it. *(Like a beast.)* Or wouldn't you? *(Laughing.)* Who knows if I didn't do that to your daughter?

VIRGÍNIA: *(Without hearing the last sentence.)* I'd convince my son – yes, from day one – that all other women were corrupt; I'd tell him that, instead of eyes, they had empty holes. *(With sobbing laughter.)* He'd believe me, believe everything I said! I could throw myself into the arms of every man, each and every one *(At the height of a hysterical fit of laughter.)* and my son would go on thinking that the others were corrupt, not me!

ISMAEL: *(Ecstatic.)* But, instead of a boy, who would be, for sure, a man by now – and white – Ana Maria was born!

VIRGÍNIA: *(Recovering her senses, dazed.)* Ana Maria was born!

ISMAEL: *(Laughing loudly, pointing at his wife.)* When you saw she was a girl – your eyes were filled with hatred. *(Stopping his own laughter abruptly.)* You hated your daughter, Virgínia. Admit it!

VIRGÍNIA: *(Suffering.)* At that moment, I hated her, yes. *(Ashamed of her feelings.)* At that moment, I hated her!

ISMAEL: *(Filling up the stage with his grave and melodic black voice.)* But I didn't. When I saw it was a girl, and not a boy, I said: "Oh, praised be the Lord! Thank God! I burned Ana Maria's eyes, but without malice – none at all! You thought I was cruel, but God, who is God, knows better. He knows I did this so she'd never know I was black. *(With sobbing laughter.)* And you know what I've been telling her? Since she was little? That other men – all the other men – are black, and that I – you see – I'm white, the only white man *(Violent.)* me and no one else. *(Lowers his voice.)* Do you see how this was a gift from God? It was a miracle, don't you see? I am white and the others, are not! She's been blind almost from birth but she hates blacks as if she knew the difference…

VIRGÍNIA: Ismael, she's my daughter.

ISMAEL: I know.

VIRGÍNIA: And not yours.

ISMAEL: But if it had been a son, you'd take care of him – he'd be yours, only yours, isn't that so?

VIRGÍNIA: But he'd be my son and Ana Maria isn't your daughter.

ISMAEL: *(Obstinate.)* A girl was born. I took her for myself. She's mine!

VIRGÍNIA: I won't stand for it! I won't allow it. She'll know you're black; that you killed her father; and that you put acid in her eyes… And what you did, right over there, when I wasn't even a woman yet, when I was just a child. She'll know I screamed just like that woman today!

ISMAEL: Go talk to Ana Maria.

VIRGÍNIA: But not with you here.

ISMAEL: With me present.

VIRGÍNIA: Why do you have to be there? Until today, I've never been alone with my daughter, not even once. You're always there, looking, listening. *(Accusing.)* You stole my daughter's love, you didn't let her like me – I know she must hate me, or she's afraid of me… *(Changing her tone, with fear in her heart.)* Did you tell her I killed your sons?

ISMAEL: Maybe.

VIRGÍNIA: *(Desperate.)* Yes, you told her. I can read it in your eyes. *(Poignant.)* And you didn't even tell her that I only did it because they were black, that they had to be killed one by one… *(Mystic.)* Never let a black child live… *(Changing her tone, pleading.)* Did you tell her that, did you tell her they were … coloured?

ISMAEL: I don't know.

VIRGÍNIA: Listen, you can come with me. But, at least, keep quiet so she won't know you're there. I don't want her to know you're there, that you're witness to our words, see?

ISMAEL: Only if you promise me something.

VIRGÍNIA: I promise.

ISMAEL: You can tell her whatever you want about me, except that I'm black. She wouldn't believe you anyway, but I don't want you to.

VIRGÍNIA: All right – I won't tell her that.

ISMAEL: Wait, I've changed my mind. Tell her I'm black. It's better that way…

At this moment, a noise is heard outside. The BLACK MEN appear. The same ones as in Act 1, inevitably. They are bare-chested, wearing straw hats, smoking cigars. They bring with them a bed sheet with a body in it, carrying it by the corners. One of the BLACK MEN shouts out – a shout as melodious as a song – calling ISMAEL.

BLACK MAN: Doctor Is-ma-el! Doctor Is-ma-el!

ISMAEL comes down with a lantern, as the night still weighs heavily upon his house. The lantern makes ISMAEL look like a ghost. Lights shine on the white bed sheet. The BLACK MEN speak with northern accents, at times resembling certain black men from Mississippi.

BLACK MAN: Are they up?

BLACK MAN: Or still sleeping?

BLACK MAN: Call them again.

BLACK MAN: I hear people coming.

ISMAEL appears holding the lantern.

BLACK MAN: How's it going, Doctor Ismael?

ISMAEL: Fine. What's this?

BLACK MAN: A cadaver.

ISMAEL: *(Bringing the lantern closer and shouting.)* Who?

BLACK MAN: Didn't you hear all that shouting?

BLACK MAN: Some woman?

BLACK MAN: A woman crying for help?

ISMAEL: I did.

BLACK MAN: This is her, right here.

ISMAEL: *(Terrified.)* Dead?

BLACK MAN: More than dead.

ISMAEL: *(Repeating himself, due to this fear.)* Dead!

BLACK MAN: *(Without hearing him.)* We don't know the bastard who'd done it.

BLACK MAN: I think I do.

BLACK MAN: The one what's got six fingers?

BLACK MAN: I figure that's right.

BLACK MAN: What you thinking?

BLACK MAN: Something tells me he's done it. *(To ISMAEL.)* Doctor, it was the black guy. The one who never looks you in the eye, who has one hand – or maybe both – with six fingers.

ISMAEL: *(As if afraid of asking the question.)* Is she young?

ISMAEL points to the bed sheet.

BLACK MAN: *(As if not having heard him.)* And she wasn't even worth it…

BLACK MAN: Downright ugly, Doctor.

BLACK MAN: Way over the hill. About forty something?

BLACK MAN: Man, she saw forty go by way back!

ISMAEL: *(With such tension the BLACK MEN would never comprehend, filling the stage with his baritone voice.)* Past forty? *(Fiercely joyful.)* And here I was thinking she'd be young, very young, an innocent girl, fifteen years old – and blind! Blind!

BLACK MAN: Well, if she was young like that, it'd be another story.

BLACK MAN: That would explain it.

BLACK MAN: Yeah, brother.

BLACK MAN: But this sorry one over here, not even if I was paid…

BLACK MAN: And the bastard, after doing what he did, killed the poor bitch. It ain't right.

BLACK MAN: It just ain't.

ISMAEL: *(Unexpectedly aggressive.)* What do you want from me, then?

BLACK MAN: *(Awkward.)* Maybe you could let us stay here 'til the car comes round.

ISMAEL: There's no room here. Where were you thinking?

BLACK MAN: We could go round back to the stable. Drop the body in a corner.

BLACK MAN: 'Til the car comes round to pick us up.

ISMAEL: All right, but move it! And don't make a sound!

At this moment, THE AUNT appears, dragging herself on stage.

THE AUNT: Ismael.

ISMAEL: *(Lifting the lantern.)* Who is it?

THE AUNT: It's me.

ISMAEL: After such a long time, you're back.

The lantern illuminates THE AUNT's face.

THE AUNT: Did you recognize the body?

ISMAEL: No.

THE AUNT: *(Bitterly.)* You didn't even want to look…
(Lowering her voice.) It was my daughter, the only one I had left. The others – one by one – died. *(Dazed.)* All virgins, except for this one. But not this one, *(With pride.)* thanks

to me. To me, Ismael. *(Excited.)* I knew the man slept near the fountain… Every night, I sent my daughter there for a walk… Then, today… Did you not hear the shouting? *(Dazed but without any regrets.)* I just think he didn't have to kill her, don't you agree, Ismael? What for? *(Changing her tone.)* He probably got frightened because of the shouting. *(As if justifying, not without something somewhat sweet.)* That's why he killed her – so she wouldn't cry anymore…

ISMAEL: Enough!

THE AUNT: I'm going after my daughter – I think the men went that way. But first, Ismael, I want your wife to hear my voice *(Advances towards the place where VIRGÍNIA is hiding; and, then, she shouts like someone possessed.).* Your daughter will die, Virgínia! *(With sweetness, without transition.)* But, don't worry – death becomes your daughter well. Little boys and young women should be dying every morning…

ISMAEL: *(Shouting.)* No, not Ana Maria! I don't want her to die!

THE AUNT: *(Still sweet, without noticing the interruption.)* Each time they die, they become more beautiful – their eyelashes long… *(Frantic once again.)* Your daughter will die – still a virgin!

ISMAEL: *(Retreating, terrified.)* No! No!

ISMAEL goes inside. Places himself next to VIRGÍNIA. THE AUNT moves forward and speaks as if she was seeing them.

THE AUNT: *(In a crescendo.)* As for you, Virgínia, damn you! May your love be a bed of flames and shouts; may your desire be a ever consuming fever; and may the fever set your hair on fire and devour you; and when you die, may no one bind together your dead feet! *(Pauses, with a full, grave voice.)* You be damned, on earth as you are in heaven.

THE AUNT disappears going in the direction where the four men went. She moves with slow and uncertain steps.

ISMAEL: You heard all that?

VIRGÍNIA: Everything... are you scared?

ISMAEL: *(Astonished.)* Scared of what?

VIRGÍNIA: For her.

ISMAEL: Ana Maria?

VIRGÍNIA: Yes. My daughter.

ISMAEL: *(With vehemence.)* Not yours. Mine. Only mine.

VIRGÍNIA: *(As if she were also scared.)* My aunt said she'd die a virgin. *(Changing her tone.)* But it's impossible to keep a woman that way...

ISMAEL: Do you still want to talk to your daughter?

VIRGÍNIA: You know I do.

ISMAEL: Alone?

VIRGÍNIA: Alone.

ISMAEL: *(Excited, once again.)* Then go. I won't go with you. Talk to her, but not for half an hour. Talk to her for three nights. Three nights, that's what it'll take to reach the point. *(Even more excited.)* A point where no desire can reach my daughter! *(Changing his tone.)* I mean, "your" daughter and the daughter of that brother of mine, Elias *(Lowers his voice.)* who I, myself, killed and buried in this house's garden... *(As if possessed.)* Tell your daughter anything you want; but make sure you tell her I'm black...

VIRGÍNIA: *(In a fury.)* I will!

ISMAEL: ...that I'm the only black in the world; tell her that, except for me, all men are white, including her father *(His voice changes, becomes hoarse.)*. And, after that, you can leave – I order you to leave this house, I don't want you anymore – I cast you out!

END OF SCENE 1

SCENE 2

When the curtain opens, ANA MARIA and VIRGÍNIA are in the middle of a heated discussion. Down below, stage front, there is a strange tomb, transparent, made of glass, a subtle reference to Snow White's coffin. ISMAEL is near the tub, as if saying a prayer.

VIRGÍNIA: *(As if in conclusion.)* And that's what happened, since he came into my life...

ANA MARIA: And he's not my father?

VIRGÍNIA: I swear he's not!

ANA MARIA: And you think I believe you?

VIRGÍNIA: *(Carried away.)* If you had known your father. He was so beautiful – I never saw such sweet lips! *(Passionate.)* He could take me, or any other woman, and there would be no sin – none at all! The body would be purer than before...

ANA MARIA: *(With a certain sweetness.)* For three nights, you've lied...

VIRGÍNIA: *(Astonished.)* Three nights? Already?

ANA MARIA: But it's not your fault – you're mad – I feel the madness in your words...

VIRGÍNIA: Was he the one who told you that? It was him, wasn't it? Did he say I'm mad?

ANA MARIA: *(Vehement.)* No, it wasn't him!

VIRGÍNIA: *(Sweet, persuasive.)* Admit it. Was it him?

ANA MARIA: Yes, it was him. But before that, a long time before my father told me…

VIRGÍNIA: *(Quick.)* He's not your father. Your father's dead and buried.

ANA MARIA: I don't believe this story about a father who died; and, even if I did, I don't accept it. A father is who we want him to be, who we chose, like a fiancé…

VIRGÍNIA: *(Desperate.)* No, Ana Maria, no!

ANA MARIA: It doesn't matter that, one day, you called in a blind man… Made this blind man come up the stairs and then get him into your bedroom… I chose another father… He is the chosen one… Fair, light… I feel him when he's coming, when he's near… I feel his presence like a heart beating within me, in this house…

VIRGÍNIA: And you don't even feel sorry for your real father! If you saw how he died! In my bedroom, Ana Maria, shot, not through the heart, not here *(Presses her hands against her stomach.)*, but in the face… *(Dazed.)* In the face!

ANA MARIA: You want me to cry over your lover? Why should I cry over your lover?

VIRGÍNIA: Over your father, my dear daughter. And there's something else I haven't told you.

ANA MARIA: Here comes another lie!

VIRGÍNIA: Ismael is black.

ANA MARIA: My father, black? *(Feral.)* No, not him. The others, yes. That's why he hides me here, why he protects me, why he won't let anyone talk to me except for you. Because everyone's black *(Repeats, astonished.)* everyone! Even in the book my father reads me...

VIRGÍNIA: In the book, too?

ANA MARIA: The characters are black.

VIRGÍNIA: And how about me?

ANA MARIA: You?

VIRGÍNIA: *(Feral.)* Am I black, too?

ANA MARIA: I don't know what you're like, what your hair is like, your face, your hands... He didn't tell me and I don't want to know...

VIRGÍNIA: Ana Maria, you have to listen to me, you have to believe me...

ANA MARIA: *(Fanatic.)* No!

VIRGÍNIA: *(Scared.)* The three nights are over. Soon it'll be too late. *(Passionate.)* I'm your mother. Whether you like it or not, I'm your mother – I gave you life; all mothers love their children...

ANA MARIA: Not you!

VIRGÍNIA: Yes, I do. Don't you see how I move my fingers through your hair?

VIRGÍNIA makes the corresponding gesture.

VIRGÍNIA: ... how I hold your head so you'll hear the beating of my heart...

ANA MARIA frees herself violently.

241

ANA MARIA: For three nights, you've tormented me!

VIRGÍNIA: It's impossible you don't feel the tenderness in my hands. This man will be your ruin, as he was mine, he'll be your undoing – I swear it – as God is my witness, it's not a lie!

ANA MARIA: You never liked me. When you show up, I feel the air isn't the same anymore, it changes; I feel the coldness of your heart. My father didn't have to tell me – I knew, on my own, since I was a child, that you're my enemy. You hate me; and it's not something new – you've hated me since I was born!

VIRGÍNIA: No!

ANA MARIA: When I was born, you wanted a boy, yes or no?

VIRGÍNIA: *(With passionate serenity.)* Ana Maria, you mean everything to me, everything. In my life, nothing else exists, only you exist. Do you know why, since you were born, I've never caressed you, never smiled at you, never said a loving word?

ANA MARIA: Because you can't stand me?

VIRGÍNIA: Because he wouldn't let me. Never – do you hear me? I couldn't hold your face, couldn't smell your hair or kiss you or smile at you. I couldn't be near you without his presence. There was never any intimacy between us, no abandon, no shared secrets. He wouldn't allow it. He'd say: – "No, no!" And, in this house, I always obeyed.

ANA MARIA: Except when you took a lover…

VIRGÍNIA becomes silent.

ANA MARIA: Cat got your tongue?

VIRGÍNIA: *(Lowering her head.)* Except when I took a lover.

ANA MARIA: Ah!

VIRGÍNIA: You see what it's like to be a mother? You tell
me so many harsh things, insult me, deny me your love.
And I don't get offended: I suffer but I don't wish your
unhappiness. *(Vehement.)* I'm here to save you. He lies…

ANA MARIA: *(Fanatic.)* I don't care!

VIRGÍNIA: … he lies when he says all men are black. That
they're mean. That they're worthless. If you only knew
how there are men who are handsome, and white, *(Carried
away.)* men whose caresses make us shout so loud! He
also lies when he says that this here, this bedroom, these
walls – that this is the whole world and everything else is
grim. *(Holding her daughter.)* Ana Maria, there're so many
things beyond your bedroom, beyond my bedroom, so
many things beyond these walls!

ANA MARIA: *(Poignant.)* Only my bedroom is real!

VIRGÍNIA: That's a lie! The sea – do you know about the sea?
Or didn't he ever mention the sea? And the boats? But
that's not all. The men are what count… *(Transfigured.)*
How beautiful they are; and sweeter than women… Look!
To caress a man's hair like this…

ANA MARIA: Like you did with your lover!

VIRGÍNIA: *(Without listening.)* To hold a man's face in your
hands – to feel it between your hands, a living face!

ANA MARIA: How do you know I never did that to my father?

VIRGÍNIA: *(Without paying attention.)* You have to know men,
Ana Maria, you have to love them; and, later on, you'd
choose one – forever… *(Sweet.)* We could go – the two
of us – to a place I know. A maid of mine told me about
it. She had a daughter who went there; and her daughter

wrote her saying wonderful things, so much so that she never came back. Men from all over the world, even Norway, go there! *(Charmed.)* Sailors, with blond, curly hair…

ANA MARIA: Are there many blacks?

VIRGÍNIA: Not a single one. Well, maybe one or two. Sometimes it's the man, some other times, the woman who chooses the partner. *(Persuasive, seductive.)* And it's not like here – or other places – where the woman – are you listening? – can only have one, they can have more than one…

ANA MARIA: Has she got many?

VIRGÍNIA: Very many! *(Thrilled.)* Let's go there, Ana Maria. Let's run away – the two of us – I'll guide you and stay by your side, always. I'll ask for fair men with hair so blond it's almost white, and blue eyes… I'll explain that you're blind but they won't even care… Later on, you can come back whenever you want to, if you want to, but I doubt you will… My maid's daughter didn't, neither will you…

ANA MARIA: What about you?

VIRGÍNIA: Me, too. Let's go, now that your father's busy, down there, doing God only knows what, for the past three nights. Afterwards, it'll be too late.

ANA MARIA: No.

VIRGÍNIA: *(Controlling herself.)* You don't want to? You don't trust me? *(Aggressive.)* I want to take you away from this place, from this bedroom that's as tight as a coffin… Staying here's death. You're dead.

ANA MARIA: I love my father…

VIRGÍNIA: But that's not the kind of love I'm talking about!

ANA MARIA: *(Suddenly like a beast.)* Oh, yes it is!

VIRGÍNIA: *(Dazed, in a whisper.)* No!

ANA MARIA: *(Passionate.)* Love just like in that place full of sailors... He's loved me like that – like a sailor, not black but white... *(Lowering her voice, passionate.)* A sailor with a tattoo on his arm, like the one in the book... the only white in the book... With a tattoo, I don't know if it was on his arm or on his chest... *(Challenging.)* Touch me, touch my face, and you'll know I've already been loved...

VIRGÍNIA: *(Dazed.)* When?

ANA MARIA: Does it matter when?

VIRGÍNIA: *(Grabbing her daughter, hoarse.)* You couldn't have done that. He's mine, not yours...

ANA MARIA: *(Elated.)* He's not yours, not anymore... Hasn't been for a long time, do you hear me? You want me to tell you since when? Since the day you gave yourself to another man, that wasn't him... Sixteen years ago... You died for him – as a woman – you died!

VIRGÍNIA: *(Dazed.)* I should've known you weren't pure anymore, that you stopped being pure... My aunt's curse was useless... You're not a girl, but a woman, like me...

ANA MARIA: Yes. A woman.

VIRGÍNIA: *(Changing her tone, vehement.)* But I lied when I said I loved you... When I said you were everything to me...

ANA MARIA: I knew it!

VIRGÍNIA: You were always my enemy.

ANA MARIA: Always.

VIRGÍNIA: *(To herself.)* Oh, when he told me it was a girl and not a boy! I saw I'd never have – in this house – the love of two men! For sixteen years, I've done nothing but hate you. Just now, when I was talking about a place full of sailors – you know what's my dream?

ANA MARIA: I can imagine.

VIRGÍNIA: Your ruin. I'd take you and leave you there, amongst those men – blind. Later, I'd tell Ismael: "She ran away with a man." And I'd lie: "A man with six fingers just like the one who attacked that woman." That was my wish – not your happiness.

ANA MARIA: I know.

VIRGÍNIA: I'm telling you this so you know I never wished you well.

ANA MARIA: Are you done?

VIRGÍNIA: Yes.

ANA MARIA: Then, get out of my bedroom!

VIRGÍNIA leaves the bedroom and runs, desperate, towards ISMAEL. The BLACK WOMEN, in a semicircle in the garden, speaking with their backs to the audience, as if making an appeal to the mysterious powers of destiny.

BLACK WOMAN: Have pity on the white girl!

BLACK WOMAN: Spare her from desire!

BLACK WOMAN: And from the sailors!

BLACK WOMAN: Spare Ana Maria from all men!

BLACK WOMAN: So she can die a virgin!

BLACK WOMAN: Kill Ana Maria before it's too late!

BLACK WOMAN: Before desire awakens in her flesh!

BLACK WOMAN: She might not even be a virgin anymore.

BLACK WOMAN: She'll have to let go of her virginity!

BLACK WOMAN: Most of all, save her from the man with six fingers!

BLACK WOMAN: So one day her body is buried, still pure.

BLACK WOMEN: *(All together, as if saying "Amen".)* Still pure...

VIRGÍNIA appears. She stops, dazed, in front of the mausoleum.

ISMAEL: The three nights are up. You will not stay another day in this house. I don't want you anymore, you're no longer my wife. But, before you leave, I want you to see something. Do you see?

VIRGÍNIA: *(In a very small voice.)* My daughter has also cast me out.

ISMAEL: *(With hesitance in his voice and real tension.)* Do you know who this is for?

VIRGÍNIA: Who?

ISMAEL: For me and for Ana Maria...

VIRGÍNIA: *(In a very small voice.)* Dead?

ISMAEL: *(Voice low and grave.)* Alive...

VIRGÍNIA: *(Shaking her head, terrorized.)* No, no.

ISMAEL: Ana Maria and not you...

VIRGÍNIA: *(With rancour.)* Her!

ISMAEL: Didn't I once say I needed to find a place to hide with you; a place where no one would enter, where no one could enter; and where the desire of these whites *(Seems to point at invisible whites.)* could not reach you? I told you, not just once, but many times.

VIRGÍNIA: A long time ago.

ISMAEL: *(More excited, pointing to the mausoleum.)* This is the place. *(Moving his hand over his wife's shoulder.)* This is it. But the one who's going in there with me, forever – isn't you.

VIRGÍNIA: It's my daughter.

ISMAEL: Your daughter, not mine, but yours. *(In a spasm of will power.)* I want only my desire to exist, and no other… *(With euphoria.)* Your daughter and your lover's daughter!

VIRGÍNIA: It shouldn't be Ana Maria…

ISMAEL: *(Repeating.)* Your daughter…

VIRGÍNIA: *(In a crescendo.)* No, Ismael! Let me go in there with you – me, not her! I'm your wife!

ISMAEL: *(Out of control.)* No, not you. *(Delirious, indicating Ana Maria's bedroom, with the joy of the feeble-minded.)* Her… She's my wife, her! *(Changing his tone, violent.)* You've always hated me!

VIRGÍNIA: That's a lie! I never hated you!

ISMAEL: Always!

VIRGÍNIA: I loved you, even while I pretended to hate you… And I never loved you so much, liked you so much as on that day… *(Suddenly insidious, passionate.)* Do you remember Ismael?

ISMAEL: *(With rancour.)* No!

VIRGÍNIA: *(With serene enchantment.)* The day my cousin hung herself? My aunt sent for you. And, before you could open the door, I, myself, turned off the lights – I did that – and waited… I knew what was going to happen, I swear I knew… When you came in, there was no light, but it was as if I could see your face, read the desire in your face… I imagined you'd kill me and I wanted that death, not a calm death, but one filled with shouts… To die shouting

248

like a woman in labour… When you came near me,
I smelled your sweat… *(Enamoured.)* You, black and me,
white… Black… *(Caresses ISMAEL's face, then his hands.)*
They seem like hands made of stone and they're alive…

ISMAEL: You've always hated my skin… You killed my sons
because they were black…

VIRGÍNIA: I hated your colour… I killed your sons… I
hated and adored you… *(Out of control.)* Or was it just
now, having spoken to my daughter… during these three
nights – have I realised I've always loved you? My God,
when was it?

ISMAEL: I know you lie… *(Violent.)* You've always lied!

VIRGÍNIA: I've lied a lot. I lied before, but not this time. Look
into my eyes. Right into my eyes. I didn't know I loved
you, but my flesh called out for you. Now I know! You've
cast me out, and I don't want to be free, don't want to
leave – ever… I'll stay here 'til I die, Ismael…

ISMAEL: Go!

VIRGÍNIA: *(Reliving the past.)* When you covered up my
mouth – that first night – you know what I remembered?
In spite of all my terror? *(As if under a spell.)* I remembered
four blacks I saw up North, when I was five years old –
carrying a piano in the middle of the street… They carried
the piano and sang… I still see and hear them, as if they
were right in front of me… I don't know why that image
should appear so alive for me! Now I know. *(Lowers her
voice, in the most absolute confidence.)* Today, I believe that
was my first desire, the very first.

ISMAEL: Is that what binds you to me? Just that?

VIRGÍNIA: But it's everything! It's so much! Don't you know
those black workmen were a sign? *(Lowers her voice, mystic.)*

A sign from God, announcing I'd belong to you? *(In transit.)* If you knew, that was the only thing that remained from my childhood, those men. I don't see anything else – no face, no towel, no vase, no embroidery. Just them! These black men who buried my sons, and also these black women – they won't leave me in peace. *(Changing her tone.)* Not my daughter, but me, I'm the only wife you have, your only wife!

ISMAEL: Don't you know it yet? Ana Maria didn't tell you?

VIRGÍNIA: Yes, she told me! *(Clinging to ISMAEL.)* But she's just a child, pure and innocent like her father… And she doesn't love you! She never saw the piano carriers!

ISMAEL: No? *(Elated.)* If you heard what she said to me – crazy things, as if I were God…

VIRGÍNIA: *(Scornful.)* And she thinks you're white, blond! *(Triumphant.)* If she knew you were black! *(Changing her tone.)* She loves you because she thinks you're the only white… She loves a man who's not you, who never existed… If she saw you like I do – if she knew you're the one who's black *(Bestial laughter.)* and the others aren't; if she saw your thick lips, just as they are, she'd abandon you for any man, even for that man with six fingers…

VIRGÍNIA clings even more to her husband, enveloping him.

VIRGÍNIA: But not me, no! I want you black, and if you knew how beautiful I find you, just like the piano carriers! Barefoot, singing!

ISMAEL: You're as sweet as a prostitute!

VIRGÍNIA: I am, aren't I?

ISMAEL: *(Passionate.)* But she isn't! *(With rancour.)* She gives herself in the same way as her real father – with such purity! *(Entranced.)* It wouldn't be like with you… She wouldn't have the fear you've always had... She wouldn't shout... She loves without suffering, without fear... And she doesn't know I'm black, *(With sobbing laughter.)* she doesn't know I'm "a hideous black" as I was once called... She only loves me because I lied – everything I told her were lies, all of it; none of it's true! *(As if possessed.)* It's not me she loves, but a bloody white man who's not even real!

VIRGÍNIA: Come with me, come!

ISMAEL: *(Dazed.)* But what about her? Don't you understand she won't let me? She'll always come between us?

VIRGÍNIA: I know what to do – so she'll be in peace... *(Resolute.)* Go get my daughter. Bring me my daughter. Tell her you're taking her for a walk. And, when she gets here, I want you to kiss her like I kissed your son before he died, in the tub...

ISMAEL goes off to get ANA MARIA. VIRGÍNIA, very dignified, very serene, opens the doors to the glass tomb. ISMAEL and ANA MARIA come back. ANA MARIA has an absolutely idyllic expression.

ANA MARIA: Is it night?

ISMAEL: *(Loving.)* It's always night.

ANA MARIA: Where are you taking me?

ISMAEL: I don't know yet.

ANA MARIA: Father, she told me about other men...

ISMAEL: Your mother?

ANA MARIA: She said they were beautiful; and that some had hair so blond it was white. But they can't be more beautiful than you... And they can't be white... Only you are white, isn't that so, Father? And even if they're beautiful – what does it matter? You're the only man who exists. *(With sudden passion.)* Why did you rip up

251

Mother's dresses one day and not mine? *(Sweet again.)* I'm as much a woman as she is, or do you think I'm a girl? *(Humble.)* But it's not important, you don't even have to answer… And don't think I dream about other men *(Spiteful.)* Father, I can't live knowing my mother's also alive… *(Lowers her voice.)* At night, she doesn't sleep; she keeps walking around the bedroom and thinking of you… I know it's you she thinks of. *(In fear.)* She must be wishing me dead. *(Pleading.)* Father, don't let that woman hurt me *(Changing her tone.)* and forgive me if I'm crazy! Forgive me!

ISMAEL: Go…

VIRGÍNIA points to the open doors. ISMAEL kisses ANA MARIA. ANA MARIA, as if foreseeing the disaster, is conducted by her pretend father into the mausoleum. ISMAEL doesn't accompany his daughter. VIRGÍNIA closes one door and ISMAEL, the other. ANA MARIA senses the danger.

ANA MARIA: Father?

ANA MARIA is now locked in. She cries for help, or rather, we suppose she does. It is evident that, from the outside, nothing can be heard. With closed fists, ANA MARIA hits the glass walls. VIRGÍNIA takes ISMAEL away.

VIRGÍNIA: She'll cry for a long time, but we won't hear her. Come. Our bedroom is as tight as this tomb as well. I'll wait for you there.

VIRGÍNIA goes ahead. Soon after, the BLACK WOMEN follow. VIRGÍNIA goes into the bedroom and lies on the bed. ISMAEL – already tormented by the rebirth of his desire – follows his wife. The BLACK WOMEN place themselves alongside the bed, in two tightly knit lines, blocking the audience's view. ISMAEL appears; overwhelmed, he pounces on her. The lights are dimming as the scene ends.

BLACK WOMAN: Oh, White Virgínia!

BLACK WOMAN: *(Quick.)* Mother without love!

BLACK WOMAN: Your hips are at rest!

BLACK WOMAN: Your womb now carries a new son!

BLACK WOMAN: He's not flesh yet, has no colour yet!

BLACK WOMAN: He is a future black angel who will die like the others!

BLACK WOMAN: Who you will kill with your own hands!

BLACK WOMAN: Oh Virgínia, Oh Ismael! *(In a contralto.)* Your love, your hatred have no end in this world!

BLACK WOMEN: *(Slow and grave.)* White Virgínia…

BLACK WOMEN: *(Grave and slow.)* Black Ismael…

VIRGÍNIA's maiden bed is lit up. It presents the same setting as the night when VIRGÍNIA was raped. After that, everything is dark except for the glass tomb. ANA MARIA's silhouette is seen in a frantic and useless effort to be free. Finally, tired of her own despair, she lets herself slide, in slow motion, down the glass wall. ANA MARIA stays down on her knees, her arms extended in a cross; she seems fixed in that position. It is the last image of the blind girl.

END OF ACT 3 AND FINAL ACT

WALTZ NO.6
A Play in Two Acts (1951)

By Nelson Rodrigues
Translated by Daniel Hahn

Characters

SONIA, *a girl murdered at the age of fifteen*

ACT 1

(A set without furniture. Only a white piano. Red curtains as backdrop. A teenage girl sitting at the piano, dressed as if for her first dance. A tortured expression on her face, rather like an antique mask. Hands resting on the keys. In the background, the noise of a bass drum, which accompanies all the action. When the curtain opens, the stage is in shadow, with just one single light falling on the girl's face. And then she plays a passage from Chopin's "Waltz no.6". Her face starts to express passion, almost a kind of amorous ecstasy. The music stops abruptly. The lights come up on the rest of the stage. The girl straightens up, without leaving her place. Terror.)

THE GIRL: *(Her voice getting increasingly loud, till she is shouting.)*

Sônia! . . . Sônia! . . . Sônia! . . .

(To herself.)

Who is Sônia? . . . And where is Sônia?

(Quick and fearful.)

Sônia is here, and there, and everywhere!

(She draws back.)

Sônia, always Sônia . . .

(Quiet.)

There's a face that's always with me . . . And a dress . . . And underwear . . .

(She looks all around, and then at the audience, with a sort of laugh.)

Yes, underwear.

(Suffering.)

Diaphanous, seamless . . .

(Afraid, crouching down at one of the edges of the stage.)

A dress that's pursuing me . . . Oh God, whose could it be?

(She runs, nimbly, all the way downstage. Striking a defiant pose.)

But I'm not crazy!

(Friendly now.)

That's obvious, of course! . . .

In fact, on the contrary, mad people have always scared me!

(Pleasantly, helpfully conveying information to the audience.)

In my family, we have never – thank God – had a single case of madness . . .

(She shouts, exultant.)

Oh no, no mad relatives for me!

(With no great excitement, humble and naïve.)

I just don't know what I'm doing here . . .

(She looks around her.)

Or what this place is . . .

(She draws back, amazed; she presses her face between her hands.)

There are people looking at me!

(She looks from side to side and up. Wailing more now.)

Oh God, why are there so many watching eyes in the world?

(No transition, frivolous and friendly.)

Later I'm going to remember everything I was, everything I am.

(As if giving a lecture.)

So then Dr Junqueira called my mum and said . . .

(She walks like one of those old veterans with a wooden leg, doing a doctor impression.)

(Aside.) In my mum's time people wore corsets, rose-coloured with whalebone . . .

(Frivolous.)

Mum's crying . . . Dad's next to her, he's so nervous!

(Terrified again.)

But what's happened, for goodness' sake?

(Frivolous.)

Dr Junqueira says . . .

(Imitating an old man.)

Mental imbalance – ha! ha! Mental imbalance!

(Dread again.)

About what? Whose mental imbalance? Not mine!

(Protesting.)

I don't want to be the first mad woman in my family!

(Fierce.)

I know why Dr Junqueira figured out I was crazy. *(Unsure.)* Who? Dr Junqueira?

(To the audience, suddenly gentle.)

Dr Junqueira, our doctor, remember?

(Petrified.)

I was always so afraid of him, Dr Junqueira!

(Quieter, imitating an old man.)

How old are you then, ha ha!

(Dread.)

No! No!

(Imitating an old man.)

Fourteen already, eh?

(Tensing up.)

Don't touch me!

(Resentful.)

He said I was crazy because I started seeing things . . .
And I was hearing voices . . .

Voices wandering through the air . . .

(Pointing.)

I was seeing hands, faces and feet floating in the air . . .

(She runs all the way downstage, almost happy, eager to share an entertaining confidence.)

One night, it actually got kind of interesting. I suddenly found, on the wall of my bedroom, there was a face, always the same one. A face that never went away!

(She laughs.)

I went to wake up my mum. Mum, come look, Mum!

(Imitating the mother.)

What is it, my dear? You're frightening me!

(Laughter, pointing.)

Over there, Mum!

Over where?

(With unhealthy irritation.)

Is it really possible you can't see it, mother?

(Slow and serious.)

But she couldn't see it. Nothing, at all . . . And then, my mum turned to me. What she wanted to do was shout. But why doesn't she shout? *(Exasperation.)* So shout, Mum, shout!

(Suddenly gentle.)

She drew back, like this. *(She shouts.)* Mother, where are you going?

Come back! A mist, a kind of cloud was enveloping my mum. *(She laughs, fiercely.)* She was struggling inside the mist!

(Quietly.)

I felt a pain sticking into my forehead!

(As her own chorus.)

Call for an ambulance!

Doctor!

Ambulance!

Dr Junqueira!

Holy Mother!

Dr Junqueira's on his way! He's coming! He's coming!

(To herself.)

I shouted.

(Quietly.)

My shouts spread everywhere. My shouts beat against the walls, the furniture, like blind birds.

(She starts running, going around in circles, like a child.)

There were people running inside the house.

(Chorus.)

A washbasin!

A washbasin, what for?

Of course! A washbasin!

(The maids' exhortation.)

Saint Jorge!

Saint Benedito!

Saint Onofre!

(Conveying information again.)

I could feel myself asleep . . . Fast asleep amid all the shouting . . .

(Shouting.)

So is this Dr Junqueira coming or not?

(A child again.)

I don't want Dr Junqueira! I'm not letting him look at my throat!

(Assuming a child-like attitude.)

I won't allow any man to see my tonsils!

(Quietly, fearful.)

Here comes Dr Junqueira . . . His footsteps on the sidewalk . . . Then in the living room . . . Now on the stairs . . .

(Shyly.)

He wants to see my tonsils!

(Conveying information.)

My mum grabs hold of Dr Junqueira. She's really having a fit now.

(Imitating the two of them.)

My daughter's dying, doctor!

Oh, do calm down!

Save my daughter! For God's sake, save her!

(No transition, laughing.)

Really quite something, that Dr Junqueira!

Such a funny one!

(Imitating.)

Is my daughter going to make it, doctor?

(Change of tone.)

And then Dr Junqueira . . .

(She pauses, uncertain; she comes all the way downstage.)

Does anyone here know Dr Junqueira? Because I – just imagine! – I still know his name, but I can't remember his face and . . .

(She holds her head in her hands.)

Maybe he's young?

(She sits at the top of the stairs that lead down to the audience.)

And that's why even I think I'm crazy sometimes . . .

(Wailing.)

Because things, people slip away from me, like snakes . . .

(Quietly.)

I know that, that night, Dr Junqueira came out in his pyjamas, with a rubber raincoat on top . . .

(She straightens up, pointing.)

But I can only see the pyjamas, and the coat, and nothing else . . .

(She comes down into the audience.)

Right now. You senhor, right there . . .

(She chooses a man in the audience.)

Yes, senhor, you! I see your jacket . . . And your shoes . . .

They're here . . .

(Laughing.)

I can touch them . . . But I can't see anything else . . .

(Annoyed.)

As if there weren't any feet in the shoes . . .

(Shouting.)

But you need to have a face!

(Talking to herself.)

I do know that people wear faces . . .

(She comes back up the stairs, doing the calculations.)

There are two sides to every profile, and . . .

(She turns, fierce, towards the audience, and challenges the same gentleman.)

So how come you senhor don't wear two faces?

(Laughing.)

Are we going to save the girl, doctor?

(Conveying information.)

Now the doctor's going to deliver the intramuscular injection, quite painless . . . In the gluteal region . . .

(Mimes the giving of the injection.)

Boom!

(To the audience.)

Sedol. The sedative we use here.

Fast-acting. Bullseye.

(Walking with her hypothetical wooden leg.)

The sick girl's going to sleep now.

(The mother, mellifluous.)

I do hope so, doctor!

(Imitating the old man.)

God is great, ha, ha, God is great!

(She imitates her father now, twisting one end of his moustache.)

She's going to be alone now! Everyone out of the bedroom! Right now.

(Change of tone.)

Sônia!

(Distress.)

It's the only woman's name I've kept. All the others have disappeared out of my life . . .

(Evocative.)

Sônia, a name I find beautiful, almost perfectly pure . . .

(Protesting.)

But not me, Sônia, you don't fool me!

(She looks all around her, terrified.)

I know you're home, you're somewhere in the house . . . Maybe in my own bedroom . . .

(She runs over to the piano and plays "Waltz no.6", desperately.)

I've got it!

(Downstage now.)

I bet Dr Junqueira's an old man. One of those nice little old men, who wear a waistcoat. Who use a pince-nez. And who have asthma!

(Pleasant.)

Oh, and who only take care of women, that wicked old man! Young women, ladies or little girls!

(She laughs.)

On the tram, he pays for the tickets of little ones he's never met before. Even schoolgirls – can you imagine!

(A different tone.)

They all left the room . . . My dad, he already knows . . .

(She twists her moustache.)

All I remember about my dad – it's funny – is his moustache . . . Well, Mum's crying now, poor thing! Dad's ended up having to tell her off!

(Twisting her moustache.)

You're making a scene! Such a scene!

What the hell are you playing at!

(Her mother, mellifluous.)

But she's my daughter!

(With a conclusive sob.)

A little girl with such lovely manners!

(Twisting her moustache.)

So anyway, doctor . . .

(Wooden leg.)

It's a serious case!

How so?

You're frightening us!

Such a devil!

What are you insinuating?

(Wooden leg.)

I think, that is, it seems to me . . . Though of course I could be wrong . . .

And what else?

(To the audience.)

It was her age!

It was what?

Her age!

By Jove!

Well, will you look at that!

That's a good one!

Doctor, please tell us the truth!

(Wooden leg.)

The girl is fourteen years old.

(The mother.)

Fifteen.

(Wooden leg.)

Or fifteen.

(The mother, perking up.)

But what's that got to do with anything? Is it a crime? Isn't a girl allowed to be fifteen years old?

(Father.)

Do go on, doctor.

(Wooden leg.)

It's the passage . . . The transition . . .

(Mother.)

I haven't the faintest idea what you're talking about!

(Wooden leg.)

Your daughter was a little girl. She has become a woman . . .

(In a caricatured crescendo.)

And then came the shock! The earthquake!

(Mother.)

Her age! I think you've figured it out, doctor!

(Happy.)

My daughter has changed a lot, doctor! You have no idea!

(She runs to the piano. She plays a passage from "Waltz no.6".)

It really was! A huge earthquake. And that's why, sometimes, I have certain peculiarities and I see certain things . . .

(Pained.)

I changed so much!

(A sudden euphoria.)

Before, I was a little girl . . .

(She runs all around the stage, stumbling, like a mad Ophelia.)

And I felt happy. Whereas now . . .

(Unsure.)

What was it my mum said?

(Mother.)

What Paulo did to my daughter is just not done!

(A sophisticated cry.)

It wasn't acceptable!

(Amazed.)

Paulo . . . Oh God, Paulo!

(Wooden leg.)

Her getting upset did contribute to it, too!

(Amazed, again.)

Upset, me?

(Frivolous.)

But I wasn't upset at all! If you don't count meaningless bits of silliness . . .

(A different tone.)

Yes, I did get upset, I remember now . . . It was a Sunday . . . I was all ready to go to Mass, when it started raining . . .

(Mother, mellifluous.)

My child!

Yes?

(Mother.)

You can't go in this weather. No – oh, do try to understand, I'm just not letting you!

(Whimpering.)

In that case, I'm going to be committing a sin. The priest said not going to Mass is a sin! . . .

(With dramatic dignity.)

Yes, it was raining . . . And when it rains on churches, the angels trickle down the walls . . .

(Frivolous.)

That was why I got upset . . .

(Unsure.)

Some other time I can remember getting upset . . . No,
that's the only one I can remember.

(No transition, tensing up.)

If Dr Junqueira wanted to pay for my tram ticket, I
wouldn't let him!

(Evocative.)

But Paulo . . . That's a sweet name . . . And affectionate . . .
Was he my cousin? Or maybe even my boyfriend?

(She lowers her head, bashful.)

Or fiancé?

(Afraid.)

No, no!

(Sweetly.)

If I had a boyfriend – or a fiancé – he'd be here, with me,
holding my hand . . .

(Shouting.)

Me, a bride?

(She questions the audience.)

But whose?

(Pained.)

Tell me!

(Questioning a woman in the audience.)

Do I have the face, the hands, the eyes of a bride?

(She arranges her hair.)

Is there a crown of flowers on me that I can't see? In my hair?

(Total despair.)

A crown of flowers tormenting my forehead?

(Contained despair.)

But in that case, I'd have to be somebody's bride!

(Laughs.)

And what if I'm nobody's bride?

(Desperate.)

Paulo and Sônia . . . I want to remember them both . . . And . . .

(Shocked.)

Oh, Dr Junqueira paying for a schoolgirl's ticket!

(She sits at the piano and starts the "Waltz no.6". Then a short piece from the "Wedding March".)

Paulo's just a name . . .

(She straightens up and mimes as if grabbing a name out of the air.)

. . . a name suspended in the air, which I could catch hold of as if it was in a brief flight.

(She catches hold of the flight.)

But a name that's empty, ownerless.

(She falls to her knees.)

Protect me, my beloved Saint Teresa!

(Crying.)

I can't remember anything, nothing except the names . . .

(To herself.)

That's why a lot of people are afraid of me . . . And
nobody ever contradicts me . . . Because I'm in a world .
. . Yes, in a world where the only thing left of people are
their names . . . Everywhere . . .

(She points in every direction.)

Names, everywhere . . . Running down the table legs . . .
Getting caught in your hair . . .

(Fierce.)

I'm bumping into them, tripping over them, for God's
sake!

(And she does indeed seem to bump and trip over names.)

And who knows, whether . . .

(She looks from side to side.)

Paulo might even be right here, beside me . . .

(Wild.)

Laughing at me . . .

(Incoherent.)

No, Paulo, no!

(Voluptuous.)

Embracing me!

(A pretend embrace. Euphoria.)

Or maybe even kissing me?

(Mellifluous.)

It actually surprises me, Paulo, that that's what you think of me!

What – me?

Oh, but you don't know me!

But look: I've never been up to Quinta da Boa Vista. The others used to go, they invited me – but no chance!

(Bitter.)

Don't come here, Paulo!

(She retreats, panting.)

Get away from me, damn you!

(Serious and slow.)

Whoever you are, I hate you!

(She approaches the audience.)

I hate a Paulo I don't know, who I've never seen before . . .

But . . .

(She faces up to somebody in the audience.)

If I don't know Paulo, he could be one of you! . . .

(She laughs, hums to herself.)

Maybe one of you is Paulo . . .

(Afraid.)

But I can't see your face . . . Or anybody else's face here . . .

(Shouts.)

And what about each of you?

(She scans the audience, examining each face in turn.)

Are you certain of your own existence?

(Shouts.)

Answer me!

(Quietly, with a laugh that is muffled, happy and cruel.)

Or are you a vision of mine, you and that chair you're sitting on?

(She runs staggering up to the stage. She sits at the piano. She starts to play "Waltz no.6".)

No!

(Desperate.)

I don't want that piece of music anymore! Any piece but that!

(She sings to herself.)

A-tisket a-tasket

A green and yellow basket

I wrote a letter to my mum

And on the way I dropped it,

I dropped it, I dropped it,

A little boy he picked it up etc. etc. etc.

(She speaks the "etc. etc. etc.".)

I'm going to play that one, it's more beautiful.

(She sings.)

A-tisket a-tasket . . .

(But without wanting to, she plays "Waltz no. 6".)

That's not it!

(Her singing is insistent.)

A little boy he . . .

(And what comes out of the piano, again, is the "Waltz".)

That damn Waltz!

(She holds her head in her hands.)

That "thing" is the only thing my fingers know how to play!

(Desperate.)

A waltz that made me dream about Paulo and Sônia . . .

(Sleepwalking.)

A translucent Sônia and a threadbare Paulo . . .

(Covering her face and laughing.)

Dr Junqueira's crazy about "Waltz no. 6"!

(In the character of an old man.)

Oh, play it, girl, for the love of God, play that waltz!

(She comes all the way downstage.)

Paulo, I hate you, and why, Paulo?

(A plea.)

What have you done to me, to my face and my fifteen years?

(Fierce.)

If I could stick my nails into the soft flesh of your neck!

(Pleading.)

At least tell me, what am I to you?

Your bride?

Cousin?

Sister-in-law?

(Exasperated.)

What am I to you?

(Triumphant.)

Wait, wait!

(She runs over to the piano, and plays "Waltz no.6".)

I'm starting to remember! Bit by bit . . .

(To the audience.)

Paulo is growing like a frightened lily . . .

(With one of her hands she draws the slow growth of the symbolic lily.)

I can see his forehead, his eyebrows, his eyes, the pure contours of his lips!

(Stopping short.)

But your face is mutilated!

(Wailing.)

You're missing several features!

(Fascinated.)

Now I can see you with your body nearly complete . . .

(Unsure.)

"Nearly", because yes, I remember everything . . .

(Pleading.)

I only can't remember your shoes. What colour were they, what style?

(Looking down, ashamed.)

And since I can't remember your shoes, the picture of you that appears in my memory is barefoot.

(A plea.)

Why don't you put some shoes on, Paulo?

(With no transition.)

I bet Sônia's around there somewhere.

(Gentle.)

But Paulo, I do remember you and me. And nothing else. And yet two people can't exist without any facts.

(In happy amazement.)

Facts! Yes, that's it! That's just it!

(Excited, to the audience.)

Facts . . . I knew I was missing something. It was them, the facts!

(Frantic.)

What happened between us, Paulo? Something's got to have happened!

(Pleading.)

What did you do, Paulo?

(Delighted and sensual.)

Did you kiss me, darling, was that it?

(Fierce.)

Or did you betray me?

(Developing this theory further.)

And what if it was with Sônia?

(At the piano now she plays a violent chord.)

The only person I didn't want it to be with was Sônia!

(Frivolous and irresponsible.)

And if you've kissed me already, what would that kiss be today but a lost sensation?

(Desperate.)

And yet, the thing is . . . You did something, you did, something I don't remember, a thing, I don't know, that keeps you and me apart and . . .

(A dynamic chorus.)

She's very sweet!

A good little girl.

Well brought up.

Indeed she is.

(Violent.)

I am, aren't I?

(Smooth and perverse.)

But nobody knows how desperate I am.

(Fierce.)

To hit you!

To strangle you, Paulo!

(Mellifluous.)

Maybe you're as sweet as a cousin who was brought up with us, but . . .

(Slowly.)

The dagger, that my dad gave me . . . The silver one.

(Quick and fierce.)

I'd drive this dagger into you!

(Smoothing down her dress, delighted.)

You know, Paulo?

I was hiding my hatred, disguising it day and night.

(Cordial and prosaic.)

Although I did have real bad insomnia.

(Intense.)

Insomnia that was studded with hatred!

(She runs over to the piano. "Waltz no.6". Amazed.)

But they've taken my dagger . . .

(Frivolous.)

What? Oh yes, of course! My silver dagger . . . Penetrating so smoothly, almost painless . . .

(Sweetly.)

And that day, you leaned over, Paulo . . .

(She looks up, her lips part slightly.)

. . . for a quick kiss.

(Amazed.)

But Paulo! You didn't kiss me!

(In a whisper.)

No, not me . . .

(Wailing.)

You kissed somebody who wasn't me, and I'm the one who's your girlfriend or bride!

(She draws back, terrified and pointing.)

The woman you'd kissed, she still had her mouth partly open . . .

I saw it in the mirror, I saw it all!

(Unsure.)

But who was it, Paulo? Who was it?

(With a wild shout.)

Sônia! You kissed Sônia!

She runs to the piano, and passionately plays the "Waltz no.6", while at the same time sobbing, her face turned towards the audience.

END OF ACT 1

ACT 2

(The same setting. Behind the scenes, the bass drum, with its insistent accompaniment. The little girl is no longer at the piano. In the middle of the stage, she is on her enchanted journey into the past. She is now a child immersed in a children's game.)

This little piggy went to market,

This little piggy stayed home,

This little piggy had roast beef,

This little piggy had none . . .

(A very emphatic mistake in her grammar.)

This little piggy "haves" none!

(A parody of a delirious childish laugh. She is transformed, and wails.)

Oh God, I don't know!

That's it – I know! It went like this.

(She sits at the piano. A short passage from "Waltz no.6".)

I was playing the waltz, at somebody's request.

(To the audience.)

That was it, right?

Then that somebody came over really slowly, from behind me . . .

(Strikes a blow on the piano.)

And, oh God, what else? What else?

(Quivering.)

There was nobody else in the room. Just the two of us . . .

(A blow on the piano.)

But then I had a bad premonition . . . I stopped playing . . .
The person asked: KEEP PLAYING! KEEP PLAYING!

(She plays and stops.)

They shouted: MORE! MORE! MORE! DON'T EVER STOP!

(Plays and stops.)

And then . . .

(To the audience.)

What happened then?

(Astonished.)

The memories are coming back to me in pieces . . . Just a
moment ago, I was a little girl . . .

*(She transforms into a little girl. She runs, all over the stage,
stumbling.)*

Oh my darling, oh my darling, oh my darling Clementine
. . .

(She kneels down to peer into the water of an imaginary river.)

I see scraps of memory, floating in a river,

(She points at the floor.)

In a river that might not exist . . .

(She laughs, happy.)

Gestures and facts passing by on the current . . .

*(With the tips of her fingers she pulls something out of the invisible
water, something that in theory is dripping.)*

This is a very old fact.

(Pointing into the air.)

I also see pieces of myself, scattered all over . . .

(Outraged.)

Oh God, what was my face really like, and my hair, and each one of my features?

(To a woman in the audience.)

You see, senhora, I've lost my face somewhere.

(Fierce.)

But I'm not leaving here till I know who I am and what I'm like.

(She attempts a return to childhood.)

Oh my darling, oh my darling . . .

(She stops, then insists.)

Oh my darling, Clementine . . .

Oh,

(She stops again.)

I think I'm a little girl!

(Unsure.)

No, no . . .

(She arrives downstage.)

Oh, my darling . . . I think I'm a woman . . .

(Striking a pose.)

. . . smoking with an amber cigarette-holder . . .

(In a crescendo of distress.)

Or otherwise a fat lady who has kidney troubles, and liver troubles, and complains of heartburn!

(A change of tone.)

Tell me, senhora, do mirrors exist, or did they?

Or otherwise do you know the translucent water of a river?

Yes, a river, where my face can lie down amid the waters?

(She runs to the piano.)

This music, you hear it?

("Waltz no.6".)

Sônia absolutely adored it!

The piece of music Sônia was always playing!

(Playing a wild chord.)

But I don't hate Paulo!

(Another blow.)

Did I say I hated him?

Oh no, never!

It was all just a misunderstanding!

(Irresponsible.)

Actually, I really like him!

I totally worship him!

(Scandalised chorus.)

What does she mean worship?

Oh, for crying out loud!

After what he did!

He kissed another girl!

Just think!

(Wild.)

Yes, I do hate, but it's Sônia!

(She shakes her finger threateningly.)

Oh, if it was up to me!

Because you should know how bad-tempered I am!

(She puts on a Northern voice.)

I was born up in Recife, the Capunga neighbourhood!

(Swaying, vulgar.)

And don't even think about it!

(Pained.)

You should know I love Paulo!

(Compassionate.)

He's so handsome that if I could . . .

(With a more intense sweetness.)

. . . I'd be constantly lighting candles in front of him.

(Troubled and sinister.)

But Sônia won't leave me alone. She's spying on me!

(Looking from side to side.)

This very moment . . .

(Lowers her voice.)

I feel Sônia's eyes inside of me . . .

(She grabs hold of threads, which seem to be encircling her legs.)

Sônia at this very moment is . . .

(A sobbing laugh.)

. . . wrapped around my legs, like a thousand-coiled serpent!

(A plea.)

You, Paulo! I'm begging you!

(Crying.)

Mon chéri! Chéri!

(She freezes.)

Who?

Sônia!

Well, imagine that!

(Contemptuously.)

Just imagine, Sônia!

(Fierce.)

So fake, she's so totally fake!

(Quickly.)

Those eyes, that smile, the colour of those eyes!

(Jubilant.)

Everything about Sônia is good-for-nothing, I swear!

(She runs all the way downstage.)

I even learned about an affair . . . I don't know if
somebody told me or I saw it myself . . .

(Fierce.)

I saw it myself!

With these eyes that the earth will gobble up!

(Greedy chorus.)

You saw it, did you?

Tell us!

Oh, do tell us!

(Various tones of voice and caricatures of supplication.)

But it's a total secret, OK?

(Deliberately slow.)

So, Sônia . . .

(Frivolous.)

. . . is having an affair . . .

(She drops the bombshell.)

. . . WITH A MARRIED MAN!

(Pause.)

So what do you think?

(Scandalised whispering.)

What?

What about Sônia?

Blessed Virgin!

Mother of God!

What blasphemy!

(Confirming the fact, fiercely.)

That's right, a married man! Real married! And is that right? Well, of course not, obviously, you've never seen such a thing! Just imagine!

(Vain.)

Oh, not me, God help me! A married man, he's dead to me, dead and buried!

(A sudden anguish.)

Oh, Paulo!

(Incoherent.)

Besides, I wouldn't find a married man handsome!

Married men aren't handsome.

(With unintentional sweetness.)

And he wouldn't have sweet lips for kissing,

(Unsure.)

Or a blue shadow of a beard!

(Vehemently.)

I'd rather die!

(Solemnly.)

No married man has ever brushed against my body with even the hint of a desire!

(Transforming herself into the mother of the family.)

But why doesn't Sônia go out with a boy her age?

That's totally natural, isn't it?

(Sarcastic.)

Oh, no! No chance!

(Cruelly.)

She'd prefer somebody's husband!

(Conveying information.)

She can't stand young lads!

(Contemptuously.)

She only thinks and dreams . . .

(Covering her face, ashamed.)

. . . about grown men!

(With no transition, she starts to play hopscotch.)

Interesting!

(Evocative.)

Until the other day . . . The other day just in a manner of speaking . . . It was like a year ago . . .

(She laughs, happily.)

. . . Sônia was still playing hopscotch. How brilliant!

(She stops.)

Oh . . . My darling . . .

Darling . . .

Clementine . . .

Oh . . .

(Slow and suspicious.)

Oh.

(Frivolous and nimble, she starts to play hopscotch.)

Sônia with socks on her feet . . . And her hair tumbling over the silence of her shoulder blades . . .

(Cordial.)

Sônia was a little girl, still so little, that we even used to take a bath together, the two of us . . .

(Still friendly.)

Perfectly.

And the towel was really fluffy.

I liked seeing the drops, thousands, yes, millions of drops on Sônia's back, on her arms.

Every gesture . . .

(She laughs, delighted.)

. . . was a chaos of drops.

(Laughter stops.)

But I only like boyfriends my own age.

Or just a little older, no more than that.

(Terror.)

But all of a sudden, the little girl . . .

(She stops.)

What's happened to the little girl?

(Doing a maternal impression.)

Well, Dr Junqueira? Huh? What happened to her?

(Clears her throat, walks with a stiff leg.)

Nothing, nothing. No big deal.

(Distressed mother.)

But Sônia's been so sad.

She cries for no reason . . .

Or she laughs too much!

(Lowers her voice.)

She ended up being embarrassed by everything.

Everything, doctor!

It's really too much!

(Clears her throat.)

Her age, madam, her age. The transition . . .

Her age?

(Conveying information.)

Sônia was between fourteen and fifteen years old.

Fourteen.

Or fifteen.

She started being embarrassed by everything. By her own feet. Her heart would start racing if she saw her own feet,

(Sweetly.)

cold and naked, with no socks or shoes.

(Modest.)

Oh God, bare feet!

(Excited.)

There's more, there's more!

(She comes all the way downstage to make this new revelation.)

She was embarrassed by the furniture.

I mean furniture that was uncovered, without a throw or a tablecloth on it. In other words, naked furniture.

(Affected.)

Such nonsense!

(No transition – a shout.)

And what about me?

Everyone just talks about Sônia! Even I only think about her myself!

But now I'm only going to talk about me. And about Paulo, too.

(Wailing.)

Oh, Paulo! I still don't know who you are.

Maybe my cousin, my fiancé or my brother-in-law, but I know there are those "other people" between us . . .

(With loathing.)

Those "other people" always exist, they're everywhere . . . But, no . . .

(Quietly.)

The person keeping me apart from you must be Sônia . . .

(In a rage.)

I know she thinks about you,

and closes her eyes.

And locks herself in her room.

To think about you.

Even when she's dead, she'll think about you.

(She runs over to the piano. "Waltz no. 6".)

But I've got my silver dagger.

(Out of her mind, she grasps the invisible dagger.)

And if only I could stab a name, stick a dagger into that name . . . then watch it dying at my feet.

(Vehemently.)

If only I could kill the name of Sônia!

(Astonished.)

But they've stolen my silver dagger.

(Sudden fear.)

No chance! I would never kill anybody. Not even a name, I swear!

(Shouting.)

There's no murderer in me!

(Quiet.)

Besides, a dead person contaminates everything with its death, everything, the table and the dahlia.

(To the audience.)

I would never kill. Now, Sônia's a different matter!

(Confiding.)

She's capable of anything!

(Shouting.)

But they only praise Sônia. And not me.

Sônia's this, Sônia's that.

(Caricatured impression.)

Sônia has a gift for music,

piano-playing,

embroidery.

(A parody of the doctor.)

Sônia needs an operation on her tonsils.

(Contemptuous.)

I need one, too, for crying out loud!

I also want to take my tonsils out!

And I can play "Waltz no.6" perfectly.

(She runs over to the piano and gives the keyboard a violent blow.)

Sônia has wished somebody dead.

Who?

Him, obviously. But who is this him?

He must be a married man . . . Or otherwise Paulo!

(She runs all the way downstage.)

Yes, she wished Paulo dead. She imagined Paulo dead.

(In a whisper.)

She dreamed about a wake that was all in white, for some reason.

(She dances and hops about, foot to foot.)

Sônia dances, Sônia sings!

(She stops.)

She would even dance at Paulo's wake.

(Slowly.)

And you never know, while she's dancing she might trip on a votive candle . . .

(Cordial, friendly, worldly.)

But there's always coffees served at a wake.

The distribution and noise of cups and saucers.

More sugar, senhora?

(Furious.)

Hypocrite! Liar!

(Friendly.)

Oh, I do know how to do a lot of things.

I do recitations.

I know, oh, so many cake recipes.

(Happy.)

And one time, I darned a pair of dad's trousers so well it didn't even show.

(Chorus.)

She would never wish anybody dead.

Not even Sônia?

Maybe Sônia.

A great idea, Sônia dying.

(Slow and serious.)

But Sônia isn't going to die.

(Jubilant.)

Oh yes, she's got to die!

I'll make my vow!

(Shouting.)

Did somebody scream?

No.

Yes, they did! It was a scream, wasn't it? . . .

(Terrified.)

A scream like one I know. But it can't be …

(Still afraid.)

It was just a coincidence.

(Unsure.)

Funny, sounded so much like my own screaming.

(Imitating the whispering of a group of old gossips.)

What was that? What was that?

A girl.

Somebody's killed a girl.

Where?

A girl.

Really young.

(Like an old witch.)

She wasn't the first to die.

(Slowly.)

A married man killed her!

(Shock and euphoria.)

Married?

Another woman's husband?

(Chorus.)

Yes, married!

In church and everything.

With kids.

He had such a lovely wife!

(A witch.)

They're saying …

(She runs, desperately, round in a circle.)

They're saying what? I want to know what they're saying!
I need to know!

(Whispering.)

Apparently, the victim . . .

(Shouting.)

Not the victim! Her name! I want her name!

(She reaches the front of the stage and appeals to the audience.)

Does anybody know her name? If you do, say it, for the love of God. That's all I want, just the name!

(Crying.)

And what's a name, anyway?

(A different tone.)

So they're saying the victim was playing a piece of music . . .

(She sits down, fiercely, at the piano.)

This one?

("Waltz no.6".)

It is, isn't it?

(More whispering.)

And so then the murderer came up, real slow . . . From behind . . .

(Eagerly.)

What else? For the love of God, what else?

(Sinister.)

There was nobody else in the room.

Just those two people.

Yes, just those two.

The victim was going off to her first dance . . . She was wearing a white dress, with silvery sequins, a veil over her shoulders . . . And it sounds as though she had a bad premonition, because . . .

(Shouting.)

Go on!

(Quietly.)

Because she stopped the music . . .

I know, I know!

Then the murderer asked her . . .

(She runs over to the piano.)

More, more!

("Waltz no.6".)

Don't ever stop!

(Another bit of the music.)

Ever, ever!

(Frenzied.)

Louder!

(The piano nearly collapses.)

And the victim kept playing. She was never going to stop, and then . . .

(Pause. She leaves the piano.)

The murderer plunged the silver dagger into the girl's back.

Even though she was wounded, the victim wanted to go on playing and . . .

(Two more chords.)

She screamed?

She screamed.

I know.

But she never set much store by death because she kept on playing more . . . And yet her head slumped onto the keyboard . . .

(A blow on the keyboard.)

When people arrived, Sônia was already dead.

(Screaming.)

SONIA!

(Quietly.)

Sônia, did they say Sônia?

(Whispering.)

Sônia, yes – of course.

That girl.

A girl who played so well.

And spoke French.

Quite naturally.

Studied at the best schools.

(Mellifluous.)

She wouldn't hurt a fly!

(Calm and cruel.)

She died. Finally, she died. But I'm not satisfied.

Not satisfied at all. On the contrary . . .

(She looks from side to side.)

Her funeral must have been very beautiful.

And she must have been too, because dead women are always appealing.

(Affected.)

I say this because good manners require it.

(Evidently hypocritical.)

A dead virgin amid the flames.

(Fierce, no transition.)

Let go of my legs, Sônia.

(Slowly.)

You're already dead.

Your eyes are blind inside me.

Damn you!

(A mellifluous aside, to the audience.)

It's not nice to speak ill of the dead.

(Fierce.)

And yeah, your dress, your dress with the silvery sequins isn't pursuing me anymore!

(Downstage.)

You hid your nastiness from everyone! Nobody knew your face.

(Stiffly.)

You wore a face that was sweet and noble but which wasn't yours.

(Quieter.)

Only death saw your real, final face.

(Wild.)

You would have danced, wouldn't you?

You would have danced, if Paulo died? Well, I'm going to dance too!

(She runs across the stage and stops to mimic the old gossips.)

Did you see the killer?

Who?

The killer!

Can't believe it!

Totally senile!

A trained doctor!

So competent!

(A mocking commentary.)

Old men today are the worst!

(Calling the others.)

Let's go have a peek, shall we?

(Cruel.)

There she is, lying there, the little girl who deceived everyone.

(As if praying.)

She looked like a young saint, white and spotless, so fragile and so refined.

(Gossip.)

She was too good for this world!

(Religious.)

Go!

Now Paulo has been purged of you.

And I don't want anybody to see you anymore.

Not even the flowers along the way.

I hope your dead girl's profile passes among the blind lilies!

(A stronger curse.)

And that wherever you are, you'll hate your agonising earthly form.

(Chorus of old gossips.)

Her father's totally lost it!

What a nightmare!

And her mother?

Her mother's just great. She's had fifteen fits!

(A drunk, with typical hiccups.)

Do you know what really got me?

(Greedily.)

What was it? What was it?

(Drunk.)

It's that, even though she was wounded, even with the dagger buried in her back . . .

(Hiccup.)

. . . the victim still wanted to keep on playing.

Wow, that's real dedication!

(Old gossip, mellifluous.)

At times like these, I really feel for those who are left behind!

And I feel for the one who's died.

(Affected.)

But there's no comparison.

Right?

Of course! Because the person left behind cries . . .

And the one who's dead?

The dead one doesn't even know they've died!

(Sônia runs over to the piano. "Waltz no.6". And she shouts within the music.)

Ever! Ever!

END OF ACT 2 AND FINAL ACT

FORGIVE ME FOR YOUR BETRAYAL

A tragedy of manners
in three acts (1957)

By Nelson Rodrigues
Translated by Susannah Finzi

Characters

NAIR
GLORINHA
POLA NEGRI
MADAME LUBA
DEPUTY JUBILEU DE ALMEIDA
DOCTOR
NURSE
UNCLE RAUL
GILBERTO
AUNT ODETE
CECI
CRISTINA
JUDITE
MOTHER
BROTHERS

Act 1

NAIR and GLORINHA are at Madame Luba's door. They are dressed in school uniform; short skirts, hair in ponytails, satchels under their arms. GLORINHA hesitates, NAIR is insistent.

NAIR: Are you coming or not?

GLORINHA: I'm scared!

NAIR: Scared of who? Scared of what?

GLORINHA: *(Sighing.)* Something might go wrong.

NAIR: Don't start that. What could possibly go wrong?

GLORINHA: I know! *(A change of tone.)* Suppose my uncle finds out?

NAIR: Look, wasn't it you who asked me to bring you along in the first place?

GLORINHA: I did ask you, but … it's a big deal. You don't know my uncle.

NAIR: I do. All too well!

GLORINHA: I doubt it! I didn't tell you …

NAIR: He's a pain!

GLORINHA: I told you, the other day just because I was half an hour late – not even that, maybe fifteen minutes – he gave me a real belting. He said next time he'll kill me. He'll really kill me!

NAIR: It's just talk! Just talk!

GLORINHA: It's true! I really have to watch it!

NAIR: But he isn't going to know! How will he find out? *(Lowers her voice.)* Just this once, OK?

GLORINHA: *(Tempted.)* I really want to, I promise!

NAIR: OK. This is what you do. You come in just for a moment. I introduce you to Madame Luba, She's from Lithuania but she's really nice.

GLORINHA: And then what?

NAIR: You say it's a pity but you can't for this that or the other reason – make it up. And then we leave. But if you don't come in, the one who gets it will be me because I promised, I swore I'd bring you!

GLORINHA: I'll go, but just so you know, I'm not staying!

NAIR: You don't know what you want, girl.

NAIR and GLORINHA are in Madame Luba's room. On stage, POLA NEGRI, a typical pimp. His frenetic volubility is ceaseless. He tousles his hair, sprawls, yawns, stretches out his legs and arms.

POLA NEGRI: Hello there!

NAIR: *(To GLORINHA.)* This is Pola Negri. He's a nice guy! A real number!

GLORINHA: *(Surprised.)* It's a pleasure to meet you.

POLA NEGRI: *(To NAIR.)* Is this the one? *(Walks around the startled GLORINHA.)*

NAIR: What do you think?

POLA NEGRI: Very nice!

NAIR: Really?

POLA NEGRI: *(Nudging NAIR.)* Madame will be over the moon. *(Without a break, to GLORINHA.)* Dress size 42.

GLORINHA: *(Intimidated.)* Yes. That's right.

POLA NEGRI: *(To NAIR.)* I'm the best!

NAIR: I've got more curves!

POLA NEGRI: Age seventeen. More or less.

NAIR: Close!

GLORINHA: Sixteen.

POLA NEGRI: Better and better. What's great is sixteen, fifteen, fourteen … *(Without a break to GLORINHA.)* Nervous?

GLORINHA: *(Beside herself.)* A bit.

NAIR: She's a bundle of nerves.

POLA NEGRI: *(Optimistic.)* She'll get over it.

NAIR: It's a habit.

GLORINHA: *(To POLA NEGRI.)* It's just that we're in a hurry … Are you staying? I've got to go, Nair!

NAIR: *(With authority.)* Hang on a minute! First talk to Madame Luba!

GLORINHA: My uncle will kill me!

POLA NEGRI: Look, here comes Madame!

MADAME LUBA is an immense woman who moans as she walks, dragging her slippers, giving an impression of sordid neglect.

MADAME LUBA: *(Mellifluous.)* How are you Nair? How are you getting on? *(She speaks to NAIR but doesn't take her eyes off GLORINHA.)*

NAIR: Very well. And you Madame?

MADAME LUBA: *(With a strong accent.)* I'm always fine. Never so much as a toothache ...

NAIR: I brought her ...

MADAM LUBA: Oh, yes, your schoolfriend Glorinha!

GLORINHA: *(Enthusiastically.)* I'm overcome Madame!

NAIR: *(Almost at the same time.)* She can't make up her mind!

MADAME LUBA: *(To GLORINHA.)* Don't worry about little things. Chairs, Pola Negri! Why don't you sit down? We don't stand on ceremony in my house. Biscuits Pola Negri! Licorzinho! *(To GLORINHA.)* I could be your mother!

GLORINHA: I need to go Madame! They're waiting for me ... Nair told me, thank you so much, but I can't. I'm sorry ...

NAIR: *(To MADAME LUBA.)* First she wants to, then she doesn't! *(To GLORINHA.)* I've had enough of you!

MADAME LUBA: I understand, but she doesn't need to be nervous. We're not talking about a seven-headed monster here ... drink your licorzinho. I don't force people ... In my house everything is spontaneous ...

GLORINHA: *(Puts down her glass.)* So I'll go then, OK?

MADAME LUBA: *(Rising.)* Just a moment!

GLORINHA: *(Worried.)* Imagine if my uncle knew I was cutting class!

MADAME LUBA: Cutting class isn't important ...

GLORINHA: I can't, Madame!

MADAME LUBA: *(Raising her voice with unexpected authority.)* Sit down! You're just a chit of a girl and I wasn't born yesterday.

GLORINHA: *(An outburst.)* Suppose the police come … and they take everyone away and my uncle comes looking for me around here? … Madame, my uncle will beat me to death, I swear! *(Collapses sobbing.)*

POLA NEGRI: The police don't poke their noses in here.

MADAME LUBA: I've got the police eating out of my hand! I take precautions! Pola Negri, tell her how smart I am!

GLORINA cries.

NAIR: *(Furious.)* You idiot, at least listen!

GLORINHA: *(To NAIR, suddenly.)* You'll pay for this!

POLA NEGRI: *(Posturing with huge gestures and 1001 inflexions.)* The business is a hundred percent. Pay attention and you'll see. Madame Luba planned this right. In the first place, the only people who come here are Deputies, in other words … customers with immunity. I ask you, are the police going to arrest a Deputy? On what authority? And besides, this isn't a whorehouse. We only work with girls of fifteen, sixteen … down to fourteen. From good families!

MADAME LUBA: You see?

POLA NEGRI: *(Insolent.)* You, for example. Girls like you!

GLORINHA: Me?

POLA NEGRI: You're from a good family aren't you?

GLORINHA: Yes, I am.

POLA NEGRI: Right! You get the deal. You're just the ticket. For example, if by chance the police came, imagine the scandal? Everybody would know that there's a place operating this way, don't you see? A house of young ladies, with pupils from the best private schools on offer,

the finest flowers, seventeen years old or less, daughters
of the most fabulous families ... and they come here for
money ... *(Hoots with laughter.)* They're paid! They're
paid!

NAIR: Do you get it?

POLA NEGRI: And they're paid by whom? By some small
fry? By Their Excellencies themselves! All this in the very
Capital of the Teofilist Republic! So I'm telling you and
Nair knows it very well; Madame uses her head! In this
place we're drowning in immunities!

MADAME LUBA: I have a highly-developed intellect!

NAIR: I'll tell you something else I never said; from our
school alone ten girls or so have been here. Maybe more.
Cross my heart and hope to die. I swear, at least ten!

GLORINHA: *(More self-assured and more furtive.)* Madame,
I understand, but this is how it is for me: I live like a
prisoner. Because my uncle ...

NAIR: *(Violent.)* What kind of game are you playing?

GLORINHA: What kind of game?

NAIR: Yes, a game missy! *(To MADAME.)* Madame, Glorinha is
two-faced! *(To GLORINHA.)* And that party we were at, we
two, yes!

GLORINHA: What party! When?

NAIR: At carnival, this last one! *(To MADAME.)* Madame, a
group of us went to this guys' apartment. And there,
you know how it is; we were drinking, generally letting
our hair down. Glorinha was in a strapless dress with
nothing on underneath. *(To GLORINHA.)* Some joker came
up behind her and pulled the zip all the way down. *(To
MADAME.)* She was stark naked Madame!

GLORINHA: *(Impassioned.)* I was drunk, Madame! I'd smoked so much pot, I don't even remember!

NAIR: And you have the guts to talk about modesty!

GLORINHA: I was only kissed!

NAIR: You're shameless!

GLORINHA: You're the one who's masquerading!

MADAME LUBA: Let's not waste time. The girl's right – a kiss isn't exactly sinful. There's no danger; just a little kiss, just for fun … you can get married later on with a wreath and a veil. Nothing's going to happen …

POLA NEGRI: *(To MADAME.)* His Excellency has an appointment. He's asking what's going on.

MADAME LUBA: Nearly ready. We won't be long. *(To NAIR.)* Let's settle this. I'm not getting my hands dirty.

NAIR: *(Resolute.)* Leave it with me, Madame. *(Face to face with GLORINHA.)* Let's fix this. Look; you said you wanted to come, we agreed everything and at the last minute you back out. It's a bit late for that.

GLORINHA: I changed my mind.

NAIR: Tough luck. Look: there's a Deputy here, a pervert, he's crazy about you.

GLORINHA: *(Astonished.)* Does he know me?

NAIR: He knows you.

POLA NEGRI: *(In GLORINHA's ear.)* And he's generous!

GLORINHA: He knows me from where?

NAIR: He's seen you lots of times. He can get you a big job in one of those Institutes. He got one for Ivonete. He'll get one for you too, no problem.

GLORINHA: Let's see … so what's his name?

NAIR: Doctor Jubileu de Almeida.

GLORINHA: *(Recoiling in panic.)* Him? The one who moved into my street? A neighbour?

NAIR: *(Emphatic.)* Yes. That's him.

GLORINHA: *(Desperate.)* Are you crazy? Have you been drinking? *(Gritting her teeth.)* No neighbours, no family. Never!

NAIR: It's a bit late, because the guy's been here waiting for you for an hour.

POLA NEGRI: You silly girl, he'll get you a great job at some Institute or other!

GLORINHA: *(Furious.)* No neighbours!

MADAME LUBA: *(With sudden violence, she thunders, filling the stage with her voice. Her anger is real.)* Don't you start shouting. In my house I'm the only one who shouts! When I was your age, back in Lithuania, I had your small waist, I had your body. I was alive! I wanted to know what a caress was! But you don't want the thrill of it. You have no life, girl. *(Abrupt, brutal.)* Call this girl's uncle! Call the uncle! Get me the phone!

GLORINHA: No!

NAIR: I'm going to phone him!

GLORINHA: *(Pleading.)* You're my friend, Nair!

POLA NEGRI: Do you agree or not?

NAIR: Yes or no?

GLORINHA: *(Sobbing.)* What do I have to do? I don't know what I have to do!

NAIR: *(Persuasive.)* Easy as pie! It's no big deal. It's nothing. I don't even pay attention. *(Vague.)* You just have to be friendly with the guy. That's all. I promise you nothing will happen. He's so old he can't keep it up any more.

MADAME LUBA: Take the girl to the bedroom, Pola Negri!

DEPUTY JUBILEU DE ALMEIDA: I'm here. *(He's just appeared at the door. He's old. Very old.) (Paternal.)* You can leave the girl, Pola Negri!

MADAME LUBA: She's a very clever girl, Deputy!

POLA NEGRI: Yes, very!

DEPUTY JUBILEU DE ALMEIDA: *(Approaches. Leans towards GLORINHA.)* Look at me, like that. Dry those tears and let's talk. You can use my handkerchief. It's clean. *(Hands GLORINHA his hankercheif.) (To MADAME.)* You know that Glorinha and I – her name is Glorinha isn't it? We're neighbours, Madame?

MADAME LUBA: Really, I had no idea!

DEPUTY JUBILEU DE ALMEIDA: Yes, we are. And now, if you please, I'd like to be alone with her. *(To GLORINHA.)* Do you trust me?

GLORINHA: *(Blowing her nose.)* Sort of.

The others exit.

DEPUTY JUBILEU DE ALMEIDA: But you'll promise me something. You won't cry any more. Do you promise?

GLORINHA: I promise.

DEPUTY JUBILEU DE ALMEIDA: That's how I like it. And another thing: is your mama still alive?

GLORINHA: She died.

DEPUTY JUBILEU DE ALMEIDA: *(Controlling himself.)* See, I won't do anything to you? I'm your admirer, but here we are, talking like normal people. Your mother died and … do you have a father?

GLORINHA: *(Without listening, tense.)* My mother killed herself!

DEPUTY JUBILEU DE ALMEIDA: Fancy that!

GLORINHA: I was two years old. My father went mad with grief and my uncle took charge of me.

DEPUTY JUBILEU DE ALMEIDA: *(Running his hand through GLORINHA's hair.) (Beginning to pant.)* Ever since I moved here, I've seen you every day. Your little body that … and perfect skin, not a single blemish. *(Trembling.)* You know, young girls have a special scent of their own. *(Changes tone.)* Are you saying you didn't even know your mother *(Exultant and unable to control his own words.)* But there must be pictures, memories. *(Grabs hold of GLORINHA.)*

GLORINHA: You're hurting me!

There's not the slightest connection between what DOCTOR JUBILEU says and what DOCTOR JUBILEU does.

DEPUTY JUBILEU DE ALMEIDA: *(Breathless.)* Do you know how to type? I can arrange you a job, we can overstate your age, I swear it, I'll arrange it, I really can arrange it. Look, don't take any notice of what I say, don't … *(Suddenly he begins to roar like one possessed. Out of his mind.)* The two modalities of electricity we can observe in bodies correspond to the two kinds of electrical charge found in the atom. *(Changes tone, in a sobbing appeal.)* Don't move: stay just like that!

GLORINHA: *(Shoves him away violently.)* Get me out of here! This man is crazy!

DEPUTY JUBILEU DE ALMEIDA: *(Falls to his knees and crawling, with sweat pouring off him, pursues her.)* Don't interrupt me, don't interrupt me!

GLORINHA: *(Infuriated.)* You're a crazy old man! *(Jumping on chairs, tables.)*

DEPUTY JUBILEU DE ALMEIDA: *(With a huge moan.)* I can't be interrupted!

GLORINHA: *(Shouting.)* I don't want to. I said I don't want to!

DEPUTY JUBILEU DE ALMEIDA: *(Breathless.)* Why?

GLORINHA: *(Behind the furniture.)* I have to go!

DEPUTY JUBILEU DE ALMEIDA: *(Almost weeping.)* But that isn't the point! Let's do this: – just ten more minutes, or five. Five, OK? *(A huge moan.)* Five, my little girl, five! I'll give you everything … everything. *(GLORINHA is trapped against the wall, unable to escape.)* Are you angry with me? I didn't do anything to you. What did I do?

GLORINHA: Nothing. But if my uncle knew I came here, that I'm here now …

DEPUTY JUBILEU DE ALMEIDA: Be a good girl, my dear! *(Holds her by her arms. Roars convulsively.)* We can see that the nucleus of the atom, the nucleus of the atom, aye, aye, aye! The nucleus of the atom…is made up of protons … the nucleus of the atom, the nucleus of the atom OH, the nucleus of the atom … is made up of protons …the nucleus of the atom …

GLORINHA extricates herself with a ferocious shove. The Doctor pursues her, shakily, in his frantic appeals.

GLORINHA: You're filthy! You're indecent!

DEPUTY JUBILEU DE ALMEIDA: Listen! I'll talk to you from over there, I won't go near you, I swear! I won't touch you! I know what's upsetting you; it's those things I say, isn't it?

GLORINHA: *(Sobbing.)* I want to get out of here!

DEPUTY JUBILEU DE ALMEIDA: Listen! I was talking about a simple point of physics, do you understand? I have to be able to spell out a simple point of physics or I'm not a man, I'm nothing! In my house I can't do this … *(Breathless.)* A point of physics … but if you don't want to hear it you just cover your ears. *(He wants to get close to GLORINHA but she threatens him.)*

GLORINHA: Don't come any closer or I'll scream!

DEPUTY JUBILEU DE ALMEIDA: *(Furious. He moves towards the door.) (Shouts.)* Pola Negri! Pola Negri!

POLA NEGRI: *(Running in.)* You called, Excellency?

DEPUTY JUBILEU DE ALMEIDA: *(Frantic.)* Come here Pola Negri. What kind of a deal is this?

POLA NEGRI: What happened?

DEPUTY JUBILEU DE ALMEIDA: This girl, if she's here in this place, it's because she's depraved, she's corrupted … *(Changes his tone.) (Sobbing, stretching out his wrinkled hands.)* … but she doesn't want anything to do with me, Pola Negri. *(Aggressive again.)* Perhaps she thinks I'm some kind of nobody! Tell her who I am!

POLA NEGRI: But she knows who you are Excellency!

DEPUTY JUBILEU DE ALMEIDA: *(Without listening.)* Tell her the newspapers write about me as a monument to morality! Tell her I'm a university professor!

POLA NEGRI: I'll see to her, right away. *(Moves towards GLORINHA, who recoils.)*

GLORINHA: *(Furious, to POLA NEGRI.)* You're not man enough!

POLA NEGRI: You little bitch!

DEPUTY JUBILEU DE ALMEIDA: *(Begging.)* Get hold of her, Pola Negri, get hold of her!

POLA NEGRI: *(Springs and grabs GLORINHA and holds from behind with her arms behind her back, GLORINHA is helpless.)* Right, Excellency.

GLORINHA: *(Mad with fury.)* I'll spit in your face!

DEPUTY JUBILEU DE ALMEIDA: *(From several metres distance.)* *(Stutters.)* Do you like me, my little angel?

GLORINHA: *(Frantic.)* You make me sick!

POLA NEGRI: She likes you Excellency! She really does!

DEPUTY JUBILEU DE ALMEIDA: *(Delirious.)* Does she like me, Pola Negri, does she really like me? *(Suddenly, he starts to scream.)* The nucleus is surrounded by free electrons! *(Sobs.)* Electrons, the atom, the atom! *(Begs POLA NEGRI.)* Keep on saying she likes me, Pola Negri, don't stop, don't stop!

POLA NEGRI: *(Mechanically.)* She likes you, she loves you, she adores you, yes, she likes you very much!

DEPUTY JUBILEU DE ALMEIDA: *(At his peak.)* An atom can lose or gain electrons on its periphery and these operations destroy the equilibrium between the charges of the protons and those of the peripheral electrons …

DOCTOR JUBILEU falls on his knees. He has reached orgasm. On his knees, he hides his face with both hands and moans continuously, like the mooing of a cow. Synchronised with him, POLA NEGRI pronounces the words.

POLA NEGRI: She likes you, most certainly, she likes you, she adores you, she loves you, she adores you!

DEPUTY JUBILEU DE ALMEIDA: *(Between sobs.)* Ah, if my wife saw me here, aye, aye, aye, if my wife saw me here, aye aye aye, if she saw me! And my wife is the grand-daughter of a baron! My wife!

POLA NEGRI: Go on, Excellency!

DEPUTY JUBILEU DE ALMEIDA: That's enough, Pola Negri, that's enough!

POLA NEGRI: I'll let this cry baby go then!

She shoves GLORINHA aside. DOCTOR JUBILEU gets up, helped by POLA NEGRI. GLORINHA, freed from POLA NEGRI, collapses on a chair in tears. NAIR and MADAME LUBA enter. NAIR runs to GLORINHA and MADAME LUBA to the Deputy.

NAIR: *(To GLORINHA.)* See how easy it was?

MADAME LUBA: *(To POLA NEGRI.)* Get the Deputy's heart medicine!

GLORINHA: *(Still sobbing.)* I was so scared!

NAIR: It's a piece of cake!

MADAME LUBA: *(Mellifluous.)* Are you tired, Doctor?

DEPUTY JUBILEU DE ALMEIDA: *(Falling to pieces.)* I'm not as young as I used to be! *(Takes the medicine POLA NEGRI gives him.)*

NAIR: At last – now you know it's not a beast with seven heads?

GLORINHA: I'm a bit dizzy!

NAIR: They're talking about you!

GLORINHA: I think I made an idiot of myself!

MADAME LUBA and DOCTOR JUBILEU who were whispering, now speak more audibly.

MADAME LUBA: Do you think the girl is worth it?

DEPUTY JUBILEU DE ALMEIDA: A little colourless, a little insipid. *(Lowers his voice, to MADAME, near the door.)* She interrupts a lot. And at my age, Madame, I can't be interrupted. *(Emphatic.)* I mustn't be interrupted. It's just a matter of training, perhaps adaption, who knows? *(Lecherous.)* But interesting!

NAIR: *(Whispers to GLORINHA.)* This is the real deal, five hundred a time!

DEPUTY JUBILEU DE ALMEIDA: *(To MADAME.)* Get her to come tomorrow, eleven in the morning … and I'm going … I need to go … *(Exits.)*

GLORINHA: *(To MADAME, still very nervous.)* I'm so sorry, Madame! Imagine, I was so scared, wasn't I, Pola Negri? I even called him names, Madame!

MADAME LUBA: The Deputy didn't come to any harm! *(A change of tone, to NAIR.)* You're not coming tomorrow because of that business you have to do. *(To GLORINHA, with unexpected authority.)* But you come! Here – at eleven o'clock!

GLORINHA: *(In a panic.)* Me?

NAIR: Skip school and come!

MADAME LUBA: *(Shouts, possessed.)* Listen girl, I won't have disobedience in my house! In my house, I'm in charge! *(Louder, to GLORINHA.)* Either you come tomorrow or you'll get a cancer of the tongue! You can go now!

POLA NEGRI: Eleven o'clock on the dot!

MADAME LUBA: You'll get your money tomorrow. I pay tomorrow.

GLORINHA: *(Running.)* Madame, I'll do my very best!

MADAME LUBA: Remember I cursed you!

They exit, one after the other, as if they were being thrown out. POLA NEGRI and MADAME LUBA remain on stage.

POLA NEGRI: Be careful Madame, they're a pair of real trouble makers!

MADAME LUBA: Oh, there's no danger of trouble there! Anyone who crosses me, pays! Don't let's talk about such boring things, Pola Negri! Let's talk about lovely things … For the last two weeks I dreamt every single day of a little carousel horse. I lie down, I close my eyes and hey presto! I'm asleep with carousel horses … I don't want any noise. Take the phone off the hook!

Madame Luba's room is in darknesses. NAIR and GLORINHA again.

GLORINHA: I still have to think if I want to do it or not! If it wasn't for my uncle, to hell with him! OK, I'm off now!

NAIR: Wait!

GLORINHA: What is it?

NAIR: *(Grasps GLORINHA's arm.)* I've got something to tell you. A real bombshell!

GLORINHA: For me?

NAIR: It'll knock you for six when you hear it. Ready!

GLORINHA: Go on then!

NAIR: I'm pregnant!

GLORINHA: *(Emphatic.)* You're kidding!

NAIR: Word of honour and may God strike me down if I'm lying!

GLORINHA: Does your family know?

NAIR: Not likely!

GLORINHA: Suppose it's a false alarm?

NAIR: If only! I did all the tests and there's no way out. I really am.

GLORINHA: *(Fascinated.)* So you really took a risk! But it doesn't show, you can't see anything.

NAIR: It's only two months. Our maid gets rid of one every month. She told me a whole load of things to do. I did them and …

GLORINHA: Nothing worked?

NAIR: Nothing at all.

GLORINHA: Are you going to get rid of it?

NAIR: It depends.

GLORINHA: How do you mean it depends?

NAIR: It depends on you.

GLORINHA: Why me?

NAIR: Let's sit here.

They sit. NAIR takes GLORINHA's hands between her own.

GLORINHA: Go on then.

NAIR: Didn't you always say you thought your mother's death was a beautiful thing? Didn't you?

GLORINHA: I did.

NAIR: At school you were always bragging that she didn't die of illness, or old age or an accident. And you wanted to die like her; young, pretty, drinking poison. I'm not lying am I? Go on, tell me!

GLORINHA: Yes, that's right.

NAIR: *(Carried away.)* Would you have the courage?

GLORINHA: For what?

NAIR: *(Impatient.)* To die like your mother? *(Puts her hand on her breast.)* With me, by my side, the two of us in each other's arms?

GLORINHA: *(Shocked.)* Die with you?

NAIR: *(Impassioned.)* Don't you think a suicide pact would be fantastic? It would be amazing, just amazing! *(Low and ardent.)* I'd die right now, this very minute if … *(Tense with fear.)* Because I don't want to die alone, never! *(With a strangled voice.)* What makes death so frightening is that everyone dies alone, that's it isn't it? That's it! We need someone to die with us, anyone! I swear I wouldn't be afraid of dying at all if you died with me!

GLORINHA: *(Furious protest.)* No!

NAIR: *(Almost crying.)* I wouldn't need to get rid of the baby, I wouldn't need to abort it. *(Lowers her voice alluringly.)* I've imagined the whole thing, like this: we'll go to a cinema and in the middle of the film, we'll swallow the poison, both of us at the same time. And when the lights go up, there we'll be, dead. It'll be a film with Gregory Peck …

GLORINHA: Gregory Peck? That's just great!

NAIR: *(A wholehearted appeal.)* Do you want to? Didn't your mother kill herself?

GLORINHA: *(Numb with fear.)* I'm scared!

NAIR: Everything scares you!

GLORINHA: *(Trembling.)* Everything! I wanted to go to Madame Luba's and I told you: I even took a bubble bath, sprayed myself all over with perfume, got all fixed up and when the moment came I made a fool of myself ... And when I'm dating – I'm scared all over again ... *(Grimacing tearfully.)* Scared of I don't know what...

NAIR: Of your uncle, of course!

GLORINHA: *(Miserable.)* Of my uncle? Sure, of my uncle!

NAIR: That's right isn't it?

GLORINHA: I'm more scared of my uncle than I am of dying ... *(Clings onto NAIR.)* It's him that stops me dying with you in the cinema ... at Madame Luba's I was thinking of him all the time ...

NAIR: *(Furious.)* If I was you, because of your uncle, I'd sleep with my bedroom door locked!

GLORINHA: *(Terrified.)* I have to go!

NAIR: *(Angry, fearful.)* Don't go back! Stay with me. Come to the doctor's with me!

GLORINHA: What about the time?

NAIR: It's early!

GLORINHA: It's late. Anyway, I can't stand the sight of blood!

NAIR: *(Desperate.)* So you think I'm going alone to that doctor? I'm scared of pain and I could die couldn't I? *(Impatient.)* They said the danger is a perforation. That's what's dangerous. Oh my God. *(Fierce.)* I asked you to die with me and you didn't want to! *(Begging.)* At least do this one thing, it costs you nothing. I want someone with me, someone holding my hand. And if I die, I want you to kiss me, at least that: I want to be kissed, an innocent kiss, but a real one!

GLORINHA: *(After a pause, suddenly sweet.)* I'll go with you! I'll take you!

Fade to the consulting room of the "maker of angels" – the abortionist. Seated figures of young black girls who appear to be domestic servants.

NURSE: *(As if in a barber's shop.)* First!

GLORINHA: It's you!

NAIR: *(Surprised.)* Already?

GLORINHA: *(Nudging her.)* Off you go!

NAIR: *(Pleading.)* Come with me! *(They are facing the NURSE.)*

NURSE: Is it you or her?

GLORINHA: It's her!

NAIR: *(Distressed.)* From Madame Luba's.

NURSE: Ah, yes. Pola Negri phoned. *(To GLORINHA.)* And who are you?

GLORINHA: Her friend.

NAIR: I'm terribly nervous. I want my friend to be with me …

NURSE: Over there, sweetheart.

NAIR: *(Turning.)* Will it hurt?

NURSE: Not much.

NAIR: *(Fervently.)* I hope you're right!

The DOCTOR appears, eating a tangerine and spitting out the pips.

DOCTOR: In you go!

NURSE: *(To the DOCTOR.)* From Madame Luba's …

NAIR: *(To GLORINHA.)* Pray for me!

DOCTOR: Are there a lot of them in the waiting room?

NURSE: *(To NAIR.)* This way, my angel *(To the DOCTOR.)* Enough. Ten or so.

Darkness. On the stage only the four faces are illuminated; the DOCTOR, the NURSE, GLORINHA and NAIR.

DOCTOR: *(To GLORINHA.)* Does the sight of blood upset you?

GLORINHA: A bit.

DOCTOR: It's not a good idea to watch. It's better you leave.

NAIR: *(Pleading.)* She won't look, Doctor!

GLORINHA: I'll look the other way.

NAIR: *(Tearful.)* I don't want to see my blood!

DOCTOR: *(To the NURSE.)* Get the next one in!

NAIR: *(Screaming.)* No Doctor, no!

DOCTOR: *(Irritated.)* Look, my girl, you may have the endurance of a saint, but Madame didn't authorize anaesthesia! Take a handkerchief and stuff it between your teeth so you don't yell. *(To GLORINHA.)* Give her a handkerchief!

NAIR: I can't take any more!

GLORINHA: *(Gives NAIR a handkerchief. In a low voice in NAIR's ear.)* Bite it!

DOCTOR: Quiet!

GLORINHA: *(Crying.)* Don't cry sweetheart!

NURSE: *(Who had left the room, returns.)* We're running out of water!

DOCTOR: *(Throwing down his surgical instrument.)* I don't believe it!

NURSE: Shall I send the others away?

DOCTOR: *(Explosive.)* Do you think I can work without water?

The NURSE exits. The DOCTOR returns to his job.

GLORINHA: *(Impassioned.)* Is it dangerous?

DOCTOR: Don't you start! What are you doing here anyway? Go on, get out, get out!

GLORINHA: *(Retreating.)* I'll go, yes, I'll go … in fact the way things are … Goodbye Nair …

NAIR: *(Half delirious.)* No! No! Come back Glorinha, come back … I don't want to be alone …

DOCTOR: *(To GLORINHA.)* Come here *(Half supplicating, half threatening.)* Not a word about this out there! I'm a responsible man, I'm a doctor, and at the end of the day it's totally unjust if I suffer because of you girls and your peccadillos! Go, get out of here, and not a peep of this to anyone!

The lighting dims. GLORINHA retreats to the door, still facing NAIR.)

GLORINHA: *(Before exiting and with a certain fascination.)* So much blood!

NAIR: *(Delirious.)* Glorinha, I can't see you *(Confused and in agony.)* Who will kiss me if I die – when I die?

DOCTOR: *(Shouts.)* Stop talking about death!

NAIR: *(Delirious.)* Back home, I want them to go on thinking I'm a virgin …

DOCTOR: *(Beside himself.)* Either you shut up or I'll slap your face!

NURSE: *(Low voiced.)* Shall I call an ambulance?

DOCTOR: *(Surprised.)* What kind of a joke is that?

NURSE: I think we should.

DOCTOR: *(Shouts.)* Have you been drinking?

NURSE: *(Violent.)* Don't shout!

DOCTOR: Call an ambulance. Brilliant! *(Furious.)* Great, my name all over the papers! And I have to show up at the police station!

NURSE: *(Resentful.)* You're in a really bad mood today!

DOCTOR: Hold your tongue! I've told you I won't have informality during working hours. Here I'm addressed as doctor, do you understand? Get off my back!

NURSE: If you're not satisfied, you can fire me! *(Insolent.)* And if she dies?

NAIR: Die with me, Glorinha ...

DOCTOR: *(Breathless.)* All people talk about around here is death. *(To NAIR, hysterical.)* You can't die in my operating room! *(To NURSE.)* Can you believe it! I get it in the neck because of some little slut! *(Appealing.)* If there's a scandal, how can I face my father-in-law, the one who makes out he's Mr Morally Upstanding?

NAIR: I don't want to die alone ... save me, doctor!

DOCTOR: This little idiot never stops wingeing. *(To NURSE.)* Get some gauze, stop this bleeding with gauze! And listen. If you grass on me, I'll tell them you're a common-as-dirt maker of angels, I'll say you've killed lots of girls. I've got your number, and don't you forget it!

NAIR: *(With a great moan.)* Glorinha will pay me ...

With the enormity of the situation, the DOCTOR speaks with an intense calm, a passionate serenity.

DOCTOR: Gauze isn't going to solve this, and neither is an ambulance, nothing's going to do it!

NAIR: I can't take any more, Glorinha ... let's die ... the two of us ... Glorinha ...

DOCTOR: *(An explosion of shouting.)* This has never happened to me before, never! I don't know how this happened! *(To NURSE.)* Pray, go on, pray, and least you can pray!

The NURSE falls to her knees, her hands clasped at her breast.

DOCTOR: *(Shouting.)* You're not praying?

NURSE: I'm praying!

DOCTOR: *(Furious.)* Don't just pray for yourself! Pray for me as well! I want to hear! Go on! Louder! Pray, you cretin!

The NURSE rises and starts to sing a spiritual chant. The DOCTOR sobs.

END OF ACT 1

Act 2

Uncle Raul's house. On stage is AUNT ODETE, UNCLE RAUL's wife, a silent inscrutable lady. From time to time she pronounces a short phrase which is always the same. She lives on an endless journey, walking through the rooms of the house and she never sits down.

AUNT ODETE: It's time for the homeopathy!

AUNT ODETE moves on ... GLORINHA enters, in a khaki-coloured uniform ready to go to school. She drinks the remains of a milky coffee from a large cup. CRISTINA and CECI, her two school friends, appear at the door.

CECI: *(From the door.)* Glorinha!

GLORINHA: Hi! Come in!

CECI: What about your uncle?

GLORINHA: He isn't here. You can come in. Come in!

CECI: Did you know?

GLORINHA: What?

CRISTINA: You don't know?

GLORINHA: My head's all over the place today.

CECI: Nair's vanished!

GLORINA: *(Aghast.)* Nair?

CRISTINA: She disappeared and get this: she didn't sleep at home!

GLORINHA: My God!

CECI: *(Excited.)* Yesterday she wasn't in school, she played hooky and just disappeared!

CRISTINA: Tricky, my friend, very tricky!

GLORINHA: What about her father?

CECI: Her father! He must be climbing up the walls!

GLORINHA: But not coming home at night. That really is the end!

CRISTINA: They've called the hospitals, the police, the morgue, the whole works!

CECI: It's even on the radio!

CRISTINA: Perhaps she ran off with some guy!

CECI: It could be a real disaster, like suicide, couldn't it?

CRISTINA: Listen, Glorinha, were you at school yesterday?

GLORINHA: *(Numb.)* Me?

CRISTINA: Well were you?

GLORINHA: Why?

CRISTINA: I don't remember seeing you!

CECI: *(Deliberate.)* Or don't you trust us?

GLORINHA: I skipped class, but look: my uncle absolutely mustn't know. Right Cristina! And you!

CECI: Right. OK!

GLORINHA: Anyway, today there's something I have to do. At eleven o'clock, a place I have to be … and what a place! But I'm not going, no way!

CRISTINA: Look at the time!

GLORINHA: Oh, let's get out of here before my uncle shows up. *(She picks up satchels, books, files.)* Can you believe it: he didn't come home last night, for the first time! He never did that before!

CECI: He's running about with some woman or other!

GLORINHA: Right! But my uncle doesn't do that stuff! He's not like other men that way!

CECI: Don't tell me he doesn't like women?

GLORINHA: He doesn't give a toss about them.

CRISTINA: A sham?

GLORINHA: *(She's made her preparations to leave the house. In frivolous haste, she kisses her aunt on the face.)* See you later, auntie, see you later!

AUNT ODETE: *(Slow and sweet.)* It's time for the homeopathy!

CECI: *(Hesitates. In spite of everything, she is fascinated by ODETE's insanity. With a certain respect.)* It's like a magic spell: "It's time for the homeopathy!"

In spite of her school slang, CECI is both fascinated and afraid. The others are already on their way out.

CRISTINA: Come!

CECI: *(Almost sweet.)* Did she have a stroke? It's so sad she doesn't sit down. She never stops!

All three go to the door, at the precise moment that UNCLE RAUL enters in the opposite direction. GLORINHA stops, together with the others.

GLORINHA: Ah, Uncle!

UNCLE RAUL: *(Sober but implacable.)* Go back inside.

GLORINHA: *(Tense.)* Why?

UNCLE RAUL: You're staying here.

GLORINHA: *(Whispers.)* I'm not going to school?

UNCLE RAUL: I'm telling you: you're staying here!

GLORINHA: But I've got an exam today!

UNCLE RAUL: And you're not going, my girl. *(To the others.)* And you two – scram!

CRISTINA: *(In a panic.)* Good-bye, then!

CECI: See you soon.

The two girls pass by him, heads down, as if they were running away.

UNCLE RAUL: *(Controlled anger.)* Put your satchel on the table. Now, stand still, like that, because I want to look at you, you with your sixteen years.

GLORINHA: But Uncle, if I don't go to school today I'll get a zero.

UNCLE RAUL: Before I forget, you're going to tell me: were you in class yesterday? I could ask the school themselves but I'd prefer to hear it from you. Were you?

GLORINHA: *(Surprised.)* I was.

UNCLE RAUL: And you swear by what or by whom? Do you swear on the soul of your mother that you were in school yesterday?

GLORINHA: On the soul of my mother?

UNCLE RAUL: *(With a certain vehemence.)* Yes, on the soul of your mother! She died when you were two years old, you didn't know her, but do you love her, or are you afraid of her? *(Lovingly, low voiced.)* Tell me. That mother of yours you didn't know, do you love her very much?

GLORINHA: *(Sadly.)* Very much.

UNCLE RAUL: And you swear on the soul of your mother? That you weren't playing truant?

GLORINHA: *(Slowly.)* I can swear.

UNCLE RAUL: Wait! Don't swear yet, because it's about her, about your mother, that we're going to talk right now. *(Changes tone.)* What do you know about your mother?

GLORINHA: You told me she was beautiful …

UNCLE RAUL: Yes. Beautiful. And what else?

GLORINHA: You also told me she was a saint.

UNCLE RAUL: *(Excited.)* Exactly. A saint. A saint who at twenty-two years old killed herself, I mean, swallowed poison. Very good. And suppose I told you that I lied? *(Eager.)* You'd want to know who your mother really was, the way she really was, wouldn't you? And you'd want to know why she killed herself? Wouldn't you?

GLORINHA: *(Fervently.)* Yes, I would!

UNCLE RAUL: How old are you? Sixteen?

GLORINHA moves away from him slowly. Like a sleepwalker, she places herself in the plane of the past.

UNCLE RAUL: When you were two years old, and your parents had been married about three years, maybe less, I got a phone call. By the way – there was a rumour around at that time that your father and your mother used to fight a lot.

On the plane of the past, GILBERTO, Glorinha's father, has just appeared. JUDITE undoes her ponytail.

UNCLE RAUL: Your father had a very violent temper. Judite was exactly like you … same height, same look, same eyes, even the way you walk …

Pause while the scene being described is acted out. The husband and wife are alive and moving. GILBERTO approaches JUDITE.

GILBERTO: Let me give you one of those really loud kisses, in your ear.

JUDITE: *(Electrified.)* I'll scream!

GILBERTO: Just the one.

JUDITE: *(Struggles in GILBERTO's arms, shrieking and laughing.)* Not in my ear. No!

GILBERTO: *(Delighted, desiring.)* Why not?

JUDITE: *(Laughing and breathless.)* When you talk like that I come out in goose bumps all over! Don't fool around like that! *(Suddenly GILBERTO grabs her again. She protests and her voice is shrill.)* I'll make a row! *(GILBERTO kisses her on the ear – roaring with laughter.)* No, Gilberto. No! *(She's kissed on the ear again.)*

GILBERTO: Did you like it?

JUDITE: *(A sob.)* It's delicious! It's too delicious!

GILBERTO: *(Entranced.)* My little hysteric!

JUDITE: *(A voluptuous appeal.)* Don't call me that!

GILBERTO: *(Delighted astonished.)* Hey, are you going to be frigid?

JUDITE: God forbid!

GILBERTO: *(Grits his teeth.)* I really like you being like this: a bit hysterical!

JUDTIE: *(Laughing.)* I'm normal, do you hear, you bad boy?

GILBERTO: *(Laughing.)* Normal but difficult!

JUDITE: Come here. Now it's my turn: you're going to let me give you a bite.

GILERTO: That's not fair.

JUDITE: *(Eager.)* A bite. Here! *(Sticks out her lower lip.)*

GILBERTO: No, madame! Why is it that you women like to bite?

JUDITE: *(Eager.)* I'll be really soft!

GILBERTO: Better safe than sorry!

On the plane of the past JUDITE is immobile. GILBERTO exits.

UNCLE RAUL: *(Exasperated.)* On the contrary, they were the happiest couple in the family and furthermore, the only thing they thought about was sex! *(A change of tone, breathless.)* And then one day, I get a call in my office.

JUDITE: Hallo! Hallo! Who's speaking? Please … I would like to speak to Raul. Is he there? Please tell him it's his sister-in-law, Judite, yes, Judite. Of course. *(She speaks while she looks behind her, terrified. At the opposite side of the stage, also in the plane of the past, is RAUL.)*

UNCLE RAUL: Hallo! Raul!

JUDITE: *(Sobbing.)* It's me!

UNCLE RAUL: Ah, Judite, how are you?

JUDITE: *(Beside herself.)* I can't talk Raul. Grab a taxi and come here, quickly.

UNCLE RAUL: Has something happened?

JUDITE: I can't talk now. My life's in danger Raul! You may not get here in time! Hurry, hurry! *(Rings off.)*

GILBERTO: *(Appears in the doorway, in time to hear JUDITE's last words. With a triumphant exclamation.)* At last!

JUDITE: *(Steps back and knocks over a chair.)* What is it?

GILBERTO: Do you deny it?

JUDITE: *(With a tearful face.)* What?

GILBERTO: Are you denying that was your lover?

JUDITE: *(Sobbing.)* Of course I am!

GILBERTO: *(Grabs her by both arms. Speaks almost mouth to mouth.)* So who was it then?

JUDITE: A wrong number.

GILBERTO: You're a liar!

JUDITE: *(Frees herself violently – shouting.)* I don't have a lover!

GILBERTO: *(With evil humour.)* Tell me: it was that guy on the beach who was leering at you? Or the one from the yacht club? Tell me! Or that one in the queue at the cinema?

JUDITE: I'm not telling you!

GILBERTO: It's the third time I've caught you on the phone. The excuse is always the same. Wrong number. *(Emphasising each word.)* The excuse of the adulterer! *(Frantic.)* I want to know who it was and right now, this minute, you're going to give me a name!

JUDITE: I lied!

GILBERTO: You admit it?

JUDITE: *(Sobs.)* It wasn't a wrong number!

GILBERTO: OK. The name.

JUDITE: Raul.

GILBERTO: *(Stupefied.)* Who?

JUDITE: *(Violent.)* Raul, yes, Raul! I was talking to Raul!

GILBERTO: *(Slowly.)* My brother. Not your lover! Was it him who called you?

JUDITE: I called him. It was me!

GILBERTO: *(Surprised.)* But why? What for?

JUDITE: *(Hanging her head.)* I'm not going to say.

GILBERTO: Tell me or I'll tear you to pieces!

JUDITE: *(Between sobs.)* I was talking to Raul because…

GILBERTO: Go on!

JUDITE: Because I can't stand any more and wanted to know if he would talk to you … because Raul is the only person in the world you respect, so maybe he can save me, who knows?

GILBERTO: *(Almost crying.)* You called him? He's coming here?

JUDITE: Yes.

GILBERTO: Now?

JUDITE: He's on the way.

GILBERTO: *(Desperate, seizes her.)* And did you tell him anything? Did you tell him?

JUDITE: No.

GLBERTO: *(Pleading.)* Nothing, Nothing at all?

JUDITE: *(Shouting.)* Nothing!

GILBERTO: *(Distorted by rage, he speaks face to face with his wife.)* You're not going to tell him anything. Or rather, you will tell him, but you'll tell him everything the other way around. Tell him nothing happened and we're the happiest of people, we're like two lovebirds.

JUDITE: I have to lie?

GILBERTO: So now you've got scruples, you squalid creature? *(He stands in front of his wife with his back to the door. He doesn't see RAUL appear.)*

JUDITE: *(A sigh of relief.)* He's here.

GILBERTO: *(Turns slowly. Insincere, unsettled.)* Hello there!

UNCLE RAUL: How are you Judite?

JUDITE: *(With painful cordiality.)* Not bad, not bad. How are you, OK?

UNCLE RAUL: *(Sombre.)* Just about managing.

GILBERTO: *(His hand on RAUL's back. With a coarse laugh.)* Can you believe this; sometimes when I'm at work I suddenly have a terrible desire for Judite! I have to fly home. And another thing; the real honeymoon goes on and on …

UNCLE RAUL: *(Looking from one to the other.)* What happened here?

GILBERTO: Happened? Nothing. Nothing happened. Why?

UNCLE RAUL: You Judite, you're very silent, you don't say anything?

JUDITE: *(Confused and desperate.)* Me? I've not been very well and …

UNCLE: Is that all?

JUDITE: *(Anxious.)* As far as I know, that's all.

UNCLE RAUL: If that's it, then there's something I need to say. I have a fault which maybe isn't really a fault. I am very frank, very direct. Sometimes I'm lacking in tact, that's the word for it, tact. And I'll be frank one more time, I'll be direct; either you or Judite owe me an explanation. One of you does.

GILBERTO: I don't know what you're talking about.

UNCLE RAUL: You will. The fact is I was in my office and I got a phone call. I came running and now you tell me it isn't anything. I'm not naïve you know!

GILBERTO: Who called you?

JUDITE: It was me, Gilberto. You weren't here, and suddenly I began to feel bad, my heart was beating so fast and I couldn't breathe properly. *(To RAUL.)* I get so nervous these days, so nervous. *(To GILBERTO.)* Luckily I'm better now and you showed up …

UNCLE RAUL: So it was just a scare?

JUDITE: *(Sadly.)* Thank God, yes it was.

UNCLE RAUL: That's good. In that case I'll go.

JUDITE: *(Desperate.)* No!

GILBERTO: Judite!

UNCLE RAUL: What are you hiding? Tell me. You can say it!

GLBERTO: *(Mellifluous and calming.)* Tell Raul you're not hiding anything. Tell him!

JUDITE: *(Sobbing.)* I swear I'm not hiding anything. I swear it!

UNCLE RAUL: Or you don't trust me!

GLBERTO: *(A sudden explosion.)* You don't even know how to lie! *(To RAUL, impatient.)* Raul, I didn't want you to know

343

so I told Judite to lie to you. But a hysteric can't control themselves. *(To JUDITE.)* Now I'm the one ordering you, I'm ordering you to tell him everything.

UNCLE RAUL: You're fighting?

JUDITE: *(Desperate.)* I'm not going to accuse my husband!

GILBERTO: *(Violent.)* But if you don't accuse me, I'll accuse you! *(Triumphant, he paces from one side to the other, possessed.)* Raul can you see this woman? I gave her a slap with the back of my hand on her mouth and here, on her ear! So she falls over a chair and I swear, Raul – I'd like to kill her!

UNCLE RAUL: *(Stupefied, to his sister-in-law.)* So he hit you?

JUDITE: *(Biting her lips.)* I don't know.

GILBERTO: *(With tremendous excitement.)* Right. You know my wife's version of events. Now you can hear mine. A man who hits his wife, he has his reasons too.

JUDITE: *(Furious.)* It's a lie.

UNCLE RAUL: What are your reasons?

GILBERTO: Just the one. She betrays me. Isn't that enough?

JUDITE: *(Possessed.)* If I ever betray my husband, may my daughter die a leper! *(Grabbing her brother-in-law.)* I'll tell you what happened and what didn't happen and nothing more. Raul, on my word of honour: one day I was taking a bath, and he knocked on the door and I didn't want to open it. Because of that, he hit me, and he called me all kinds of horrible names!

GILBERTO: *(Triumphant, to his brother.)* Look, she's shameless! Women are like that, they love revealing intimate sexual details!

UNCLE RAUL: You've got no other proof, besides a bath?

GILBERTO: *(Frantic.)* You think that's not much? You don't see it's a symptom? A symptom Raul? *(Anxious to convince him.)* Listen. Before that, my wife wasn't ashamed around me, never, never, never! We were crazy about each other! When we got married, on the very next day she took a bath with me Raul. We took a bath together!

JUDITE: *(A furious protest.)* Enough!

GILBERTO: *(To JUDITE.)* You started this. Now I'm going to the finish it. *(To RAUL.)* For two whole years, every single day, the bath we had together was sacred! And then, suddenly, Raul, suddenly she's ashamed in front of me, all bashful! Puts a stop to our bath together – the bath that had been going on for two years that she wanted in the first place, Raul, she herself demanded it! *(Violent.)* What does this mean? It's obvious: when a wife starts being ashamed in front of her husband it's because she's got someone else, because she's fixed herself up with a lover. Isn't that so?

UNCLE RAUL: Your reasoning is monstrous!

GILBERTO: Exactly. And it's correct. *(Beside himself.)* I married a slut!

JUDITE: *(Crazed.)* And I married scum!

UNCLE RAUL: Gilberto, I think you're outrageous!

GILBERTO: *(Surprised.)* No, Raul!

UNCLE RAUL: *(To JUDITE.)* You're absolutely right, Judite. If I was a witness in court, or for the police, or wherever, I would be on your side and against my brother. We must act right now; after he hit you and you called your own husband scum, it's obvious, there can't be anything more between you. Nothing! This has to be resolved now. Go and get your daughter and let's leave together.

JUDITE: *(Tense.)* Where to?

UNCLE RAUL: Your parent's house.

JUDITE: Leave and not come back?

UNCLE RAUL: Obviously you won't come back!

JUDITE: *(Withdraws.)* I don't want to!

UNCLE RAUL: You don't want to come with me?

JUDITE: I'm staying!

UNCLE RAUL: *(Exasperated.)* But wasn't it you that called him scum?

JUDITE: My place is here!

UNCLE RAUL: *(Contains his anger.)* One last question: I want to know if you still love this man, the man who called you a slut? I want to know if you still love him.

JUDITE: *(Hysterical.)* I love him! I love him! *(Collapses in tears. At the same time, GILBERTO shouts triumphantly.)*

GILBERTO: *(Grabs hold of his brother.)* See? *(Eager.)* That bath was a symptom wasn't it? I slapped her face and I hit her on the ear, but she's staying. And she stays because she's betrayed me! She stays because she's an adulteress! She has no courage, not even the courage to leave. *(Sobbing laughter.)* She doesn't even cry, Raul! She took a beating without a cry! An innocent woman would scream!

JUDITE: *(Crazed.)* I scream, I really do. *(Screams.)* I'm innocent!

UNCLE RAUL: *(Without anger. Disgusted.)* You two deserve each other!

JUDITE: *(Desperate.)* But if I go with you, he'll put someone else in my place …

UNCLE RAUL: *(He has had enough.)* In that case, there's nothing more I can do here and …

GILBERTO: *(Throws himself on his brother appealing.)* Don't go Raul! Not yet!

UNCLE RAUL: *(Sober and unbending.)* You're despicable!

GILBERTO: *(Reaching tense hands towards his brother.)* Suppose I told you I'm sick? *(He grabs onto his brother.)* Raul, I can't be left alone because I swear, I'm capable of killing my wife and killing myself. *(With a crazed smile.)* Just now I had the feeling that the furniture in the house, the tables are coming to strangle me *(Presses his head.)* And my head? It's full of obscenities! I open my eyes and I see my wife's lovers. *(Points to the walls.)* Her lovers getting in here like water through the cracks in the walls … and when you came, I thought you wanted my wife as well, that perhaps you found her lovely, lovely, lovely. *(A fierce appeal.)* I want to be locked up, Raul!

UNCLE RAUL: *(Astonished.)* Calm down. I've got a doctor. He's well-known. I'll speak to him tomorrow.

GILBERTO: I can't wait! Tomorrow will be too late! Do you know where there's an asylum?

UNCLE RAUL: What for?

GILBERTO: *(In floods of tears.)* Raul, take me, right now, in a taxi Raul, to an asylum. Right now.

UNCLE RAUL: *(Conciliatory.)* Wouldn't something like … psychoanalysis be a better idea?

GILBERTO: No, Raul! I want a place where I can scream, where I'm physically held down! Not a psychoanalyst.

Sedatives, I want sedatives! Or, I know, malaria! I don't believe in psychoanalysis but I believe in fever! I want a fever to burn up my brain and most of all I don't want to think. *(Increasingly fanatical.)* I don't want to, I don't want to, I don't want to! *(Ends sobbing.)*

UNCLE RAUL: I'll call a doctor. He'll come here.

GILBERTO: I'm not waiting another minute. Let's go now!

UNCLE RAUL: I'll take you.

JUDITE: Just a moment Raul. I want to kiss my husband.

GILBERTO: *(Retreats, in a violent crisis, shouting.)* No! Your kiss is full of your lover's saliva!

UNCLE RAUL and GILBERTO exit. Darkness on the plane of memory. On the plane of present reality, UNCLE RAUL appears.

UNCLE RAUL: *(Informative.)* We got a taxi on the corner. On the way, he was shouting …

On the plane of memory, GILBERTO moans, his tense hands outstretched.

GILBERTO: I hate my wife and I hate my daughter because she's the daughter of my wife!

GILBERTO is immobile on the plane of memory. UNCLE RAUL alone in present-day reality.

UNCLE RAUL: So your father went into the Gavea asylum in the clothes he stood in …

GILBERTO speaks in the plane of memory.

GILBERTO: *(Tense.)* Tell them I don't want to see anyone! Not my mother, nor my wife, nor my brother, nor my friends. If I come back, I shall come back a different man. I don't want to be what I am any more. *(Furious.)* I want to be able to be crazy in peace and by myself!

Lights down on the plane of memory. UNCLE RAUL in the present.

UNCLE RAUL: He spent seven months there. We phoned them for updates. No one visited him. Not ever. There wasn't a man on earth more alone than him. And then one day, I phoned them ...

JUDITE is on the plane of memory, with the gestures of someone doing their make-up.

UNCLE RAUL: ... and they told me "he's just left". But it's not possible! How did he leave? Was he discharged? That suddenly, and without warning? Ah! He wanted it to be a surprise? I see ... a surprise.

Behind JUDITE, without her noticing, GILBERTO has appeared.

GILBERTO: *(With controlled passion.)* You beauty!

JUDITE: *(Turning rapidly in a panic.)* Gilberto!

GILBERTO: My darling!

JUDITE: *(Withdrawing.)* Why didn't you tell me you were coming?

GILBERTO: *(Advancing.)* What about my kiss? *(Grabs JUDITE.)*

JUDITE: *(Turning her face away.)* Mind my make-up!

GILBERTO: *(Still controlled.)* How lovely you smell!

JUDITE: *(Impatient, speaking low.)* Let's talk.

GILBERTO: First the kiss!

JUDITE: On my cheek!

GILBERTO: *(Beside himself.)* On your mouth, lovely and wet. On your mouth, I want your mouth, this mouth, come!

JUDITE: I have to go out!

GILBERTO: *(Without anger and almost amazed.)* Go out? What about me? I'm back. Don't you realize, I've come back? That this is my resurrection? *(Eager.)* Remember when I used to ask you to put your tongue in my mouth *(In her ear.)* I want to drink from your mouth, come!

JUDITE: *(Brusquely.)* Wait a moment!

GILBERTO: Wait?

JUDITE: You didn't tell me and I've got a commitment. Patience, my dear!

GILBERTO: But Judite! Don't you see there can't be any commitment as important as my resurrection? Or are you afraid of me? I'm fine. I was discharged, I had malaria. Judite!

JUDITE: *(Slow and insincere.)* Unfortunately I just can't miss it!

GILBERTO: Who is it with?

JUDITE: *(Vacillating.)* With someone.

GILBERTO: Are they more important than me? More important than our love? Look, phone, and say I've come back, it's easy!

JUDITE: It isn't a person.

GILBERTO: What?

JUDITE: *(More informative.)* It's a pledge.

GILBERTO: About me?

JUDITE: About you.

GILBERTO: *(Crescendo.)* For my recovery? For my return?

JUDITE: But of course.

GILBERTO: *(Delighted.)* You missed me that much. Oh darling! *(Grasps his wife in his arms.)* Forgive me for insisting! Don't think I'm angry or irritated. I'll never be irritated again I promise you! Now give me a kiss and go, yes, go! Kiss me!

JUDITE: Afterwards, and anyway I'm already late, really late. Bye! Bye!

GILBERTO: I'll be waiting for you!

JUDITE is at a little distance moving towards the door.

GILBERTO: I'll kiss you all over from head to toe!

JUDITE: *(With fake voluptuosity.)* Don't tease me! *(She withdraws. Her husband calls to her for the last time.)*

GILBERTO: One more thing!

JUDITE: *(From the door.)* What?

GILBERTO: *(Humble.)* God bless you!

JUDITE: *(Frivolous.)* Amen! *(She exits.)*

GILBERTO picks up a pink slip from on top of a chair. He rubs it across his face and puts it back on the chair. UNCLE RAUL enters.

UNCLE RAUL: What was that? *(They embrace with great warmth.)*

GILBERTO: And mama? And everyone else? How are they?

UNCLE: Your face is really different!

GILBERTO: The face is the least of it. It's my soul that's different. I swear to you, I'm changed. Profoundly changed. *(Distressed.)* And do you know why we go crazy? Because we don't love.

UNCLE RAUL: Do you mean to say the malaria fixed it?

GILBERTO: You can talk about my illness as much as you like, I'll even be amused. Yes, the malaria of course, yes, but it wasn't only the malaria; most of all it was the will to live and to love.

UNCLE RAUL: *(Looking around.)* Where's your wife?

GILBERTO: She went out a moment ago, this instant.

UNCLE RAUL: What? Today, when you just came back?

GILBERTO: It was such a coincidence: I arrived just as Judite was going out to fulfil a pledge, a pledge for my sake, obviously. I'm telling you: women are fabulous. This thing about the pledge is a perfect example. We men don't make them. *(Euphoric.)* Men are animals, we really are.

UNCLE RAUL: Right, I'll be on my way. I have some business to finish. It's complicated. I'll come by tomorrow.

GILBERTO: *(Moved.)* Come. And bring everyone with you.

Darkness. The opposite side of the stage is lit. UNCLE RAUL's whole family appear; MOTHER, dressed in black and wearing a hat, BROTHERS. UNCLE RAUL moves to the plane of reality and speaks. The others remain in profile, immobile and very formal.

UNCLE RAUL: The next morning we took two taxis and we all went to Gilberto's house.

Lights on GILBERTO and JUDITE. He is naked from the waist upwards, with his face covered in soap and is shaving. JUDITE is beside him wearing a kimono.

GILBERTO: We're a bit short of soft drinks.

JUDITE: And Coca Cola. *(Takes a note. GILBERTO stops shaving for a moment.)*

GILBERTO: I've been meaning to tell you … in the hospital, after the malaria, this is what I thought: we get things so wrong in many respects. Do you want an example? We don't make a big deal about a kiss on the mouth. And in fact, see if I'm right … *(With real tenderness.)* the real deflowering is the first kiss on the mouth.

JUDITE: Good Lord! … *(Light hearted again.)* How many sandwiches?

GILBERTO: Maybe eighty or so?

JUDITE: Is that enough?

GILBERTO: It's plenty.

JUDITE: What else do we need?

GILBERTO: More pickles.

JUDITE: And I better add cookies!

UNCLE RAUL: *(Calls.)* Anyone at home? *(Speaking from the floor below.)*

JUDITE: Raul!

GILBERTO: *(Approaching the imaginary stairway.)* Come on up Raul!

UNCLE RAUL: I've got everyone with me!

GILBERTO: Mama, what a surprise!

JUDITE: We were expecting you a bit later.

GILBERTO: *(Euphoric.)* It's an invasion!

MOTHER: *(Brusquely to JUDITE.)* Don't kiss me, I've got a cold.

VOICES: But you've put on weight! You've got some colour! You look really well!

GILBERTO: Look, we're going to have something to eat later!

JUDITE: Do you want to take off your hat, Dona Nieta?

MOTHER: *(Formal.)* I'm fine like this. *(To UNCLE RAUL.)* Tell him, Raul!

UNCLE RAUL: Right. Gilberto, there's something we want to talk to you about.

GILBERTO: To me? Sure. Has something happened?

MOTHER: It's a private matter, son.

JUDITE: Can't I hear it too?

UNCLE RAUL: No, you can't. It's a matter between Gilberto and ourselves. No one else.

JUDITE: I understand. Excuse me. *(Exits.)*

GILBERTO: *(Disconcerted.)* Come here, Judite. *(JUDITE doesn't notice.)* Why can't she hear it?

UNCLE RAUL: Let's go through there!

They gather at the other edge of the stage. They sit on small benches. UNCLE RAUL and GILBERTO stand.

GILBERTO: *(With uneasy delight.)* All this mystery!

UNCLE RAUL: Gilberto, what brings us here is the following.

GILBERTO: One moment. I'll go and put on some clothes … I'll be back in a moment … *(Exits.)*

The others whisper amongst themselves.

UNCLE RAUL: *(Low voiced.)* Look at the way he is, his reactions, look at them! And then tell me I'm not right!

FIRST BROTHER: What I sense in him is a sick kind of goodness, isn't it!

SECOND BROTHER: That malaria therapy is so out of date!

GILBERTO with JUDITE.

JUDITE: Did you see how your family's behaving?

GILBERTO: I did and that's why I'm here. Look, don't worry about them, angel, don't worry. What matters is that I love you. I love you more than ever! *(Uncertain.)* I just think you're a little different, I don't know. Or is that just an impression?

JUDITE: *(Painful.)* It's just an impression.

During the conversation, GILBERTO changes his shirt.

GILBERTO: *(Anxious.)* Last night, I didn't feel you really abandoned yourself; you're still resisting, Judite, as if you doubted me. I kissed you on the ear and you reacted like you did before and … *(With false euphoria.)* In any case I thought you were gorgeous … right, I better go. They're waiting for me. *(Makes a kissing gesture.)* A kiss on that lovely little mouth.

JUDITE: You too.

GILBERTO is with the family. Silence between them.

GILBERTO: This is feeling like a court room!

MOTHER: Who knows?

UNCLE RAUL: *(To the others.)* I'm asking you, please don't interrupt me. *(To GILBERTO.)* Very early this morning, I brought the family together to tell them what I'm about to tell you. As a matter of fact, the real interested party is you. It's this; when you were in the hospital, I started to notice a number of things that displeased me. Finally, a month ago, this is what I did. I paid an ex-detective, a friend of mine, to follow her *(Raising his voice.)* to follow Judite!

GILBERTO: Why Judite? What was the point?

UNCLE RAUL: We'll get to that. The guy pulled out all the stops: He spied through keyholes, listened at doors, hid behind wardrobes. After twenty days he came to see me. Gilberto, my hunch was right. I've got it all here with me right now; name, address, telephone number and even some of those dirty little secrets.

GILBERTO: But what's this about? Whose name? What address?

UNCLE RAUL: *(Fierce.)* The lover's, don't you see? The lover's!

MOTHER: Your wife's lover!

FIRST BROTHER: Lower your voice!

GILBERTO: Are you talking about Judite?

UNCLE RAUL: I'm telling you, his name, his profession, his age. Don't you want it?

GILBERTO: It's a lie!

FIRST BROTHER: Don't shout. She'll hear you!

MOTHER: Just listen to the rest of it!

UNCLE RAUL: Even yesterday, the very day you came back, she had the effrontery to leave you here and under what pretext? Of a pledge? The pledge was the lover, the lover who was waiting for her. *(Change of tone, breathless.)* What day was it yesterday? It was Friday. Right. Friday is one of the three days of the week she always meets her lover.

GILBERTO: Have you finished?

UNCLE RAUL: Why?

GILBERTO: There's something I want you to tell me. What's this to you? Is she my wife or is she your wife? And why do you hate it so much when the person who's betrayed is me, not you?

MOTHER: Do you believe it or not?

GILBERTO: *(A strangled scream.)* No!

UNCLE RAUL: *(Possessed.)* Do you deny the evidence? Do you refuse to look at the facts? Are you ignoring proof?

GILBERTO: I refuse! I don't believe in proofs, I don't believe in facts. I believe in a human being, naked and alone.

UNCLE RAUL: She's an adulteress.

GILBERTO: An adulteress is purer because she's saved from the desire that festers within her.

UNCLE RAUL: *(To the others.)* Do you see what I mean? *(To GILBERTO.)* Is this your cure? Is this the result of your malaria therapy?

GILBERTO: *(Vehement.)* Listen! I haven't finished!

UNCLE RAUL: *(Mocking.)* Let's hear it! Let's hear it!

GILBERTO: In the asylum I was thinking: we should love everything and everyone. We should be brothers even to the furniture, brothers to the simplest cupboard! I left that place loving everything so much more! There are so many things we fail to love, so many things we forget to love. But I get back here and what do I find? Nobody loves anybody, nobody knows how to love anybody. Betrayal becomes a necessity. It's the yearning for an impossible love. *(Grabs his brother.)* Everything is about the lack of love; from breast cancer to a simple eczema, it's love that's not fulfilled!

SECOND BROTHER: Great!

FIRST BROTHER: What a load of rubbish!

UNCLE RAUL: *(Contained.)* And finally, what's your conclusion?

MOTHER: *(To herself.)* My son doesn't know what he's saying …

GILBERTO: Judite isn't the one at fault! And if she betrayed me, the fault is mine, I'm the one to blame for being betrayed! I'm the bastard.

UNCLE RAUL: *(Grabs GILBERTO in his arms and shakes him.)* Your "cure" is a nonsense. Your generosity is sick! In fact, you're completely insane!

GILBERTO: *(Withdrawing.)* What do you want from me?

UNCLE RAUL: Teach your wife a lesson?

MOTHER: A real humiliation!

FIRST BROTHER: Mark her face!

GILBERTO: Do I have to punish her myself? In front of you all? *(With sudden triumph.)* Judite! Judite! *(To the others.)* You'll see! You'll be there! *(Shouts.)* Judite! Judite!

JUDITE: *(Appears in a panic.)* What is it, God in heaven?

General silence. And beside himself, GILBERTO falls at her feet.

GILBERTO: *(Sobbing helplessly.)* Forgive me for your betrayal!

JUDITE: *(Extricating herself in fierce revulsion.) (Stands up.)* You're insane!

GILBERTO: *(Ignoring her.)* Forgive me!

JUDITE: *(To the family.)* He's not himself! I haven't betrayed anyone!

UNCLE RAUL: *(To the agitated family.)* Don't interfere! Don't say anything! *(To his sister-in-law, both loving and vile.)* You can speak, Judite! You agree with us don't you? You also think that your husband has had, shall we call it, a relapse?

GILBERTO: Don't answer him, Judite!

JUDITE: But it's obvious he's changed. And then he says "Forgive me for your betrayal". It makes no sense.

UNCLE RAUL: I think he should be committed, don't you agree Judite? Tell that to your mother-in-law and your brothers-in-law, tell them Judite!

JUDITE: *(Tense with a certain shame.)* He should be committed!

UNCLE RAUL: *(Quick and violent.)* Help me!

GILBERTO: What's this?

GILBERTO is secured, first by UNCLE RAUL and then by the others. The sick man kicks and sobs.

MOTHER: Careful, don't hurt my son!

GILBERTO: To love is to be faithful to those who betray us!

UNCLE RAUL: *(Breathless.)* Exactly! You can't be on your own! *(To the others.)* Put him in a taxi and take him back to the asylum, right now!

GILBERTO: *(Shouts.)* You don't abandon an adultereress!

MOTHER: *(Crying.)* You will be alright, Gilberto!

GILBERTO and the others exit. RAUL, DONA NIETA and JUDITE remain.

JUDITE: I can't understand why the doctors discharged him!

UNCLE RAUL: *(He has his back to her.)* Judite, please, can you bring me a glass of water?

JUDITE: Mineral or tap water?

UNCLE RAUL: Tap water. A half glass will do.

JUDITE exits.

MOTHER: *(With hatred, following JUDITE with her eyes.)* How
    clean she is, how fragrant! Can you imagine it, she told me
    herself she washes her intimate parts three times a day!
    I doubt if that much care for her personal hygiene was for
    her husband!

UNCLE RAUL: *(Irritated.)* Mama, that's not the problem. I'll
    solve it all, leave it to me. Go outside for a moment, wait
    outside, please Mama?

MOTHER: Humiliate her, rattle her, but no violence. No
    violence. No hitting.

*Exits. JUDITE reappears with a glass of water. UNCLE RAUL
    takes the glass.*

JUDITE: This has ruined my day.

UNCLE RAUL: Thank you Judite. It's ruined your day, I can
    believe that. First I'm going to add this here … *(He adds a
    powder to the water.)* a committed husband is very relaxing
    … *(Sober and unshakeable.)* Now, drink it!

JUDITE: *(Withdrawing.)* For me?

UNCLE RAUL: Sure!

JUDITE: *(Her hands behind her back.)* What is it?

UNCLE RAUL: *(Still contained.)* Guess!

JUDITE: *(A tearful grimace.)* A remedy?

UNCLE RAUL: Poison.

JUDITE: *(A strangled voice.)* Have you gone crazy?

UNCLE RAUL: I'm taking the place of my brother. He's the one who's crazy.

JUDITE: I deny it. And you're not my husband!

UNCLE RAUL: I'll tell you a detail, just one detail, and you'll see it's useless to lie. *(With a strangled laugh.)* Isn't it true that your lover likes you to talk dirty? *(Triumphant.)* And I'm not telling you how I know this, no I'm not! Maybe spying through the keyhole, or listening behind doors! *(Stops his vile laughter.)* Now before you die, confess that you have a lover!

JUDITE: *(A sobbing laugh.)* A lover? Just the one? You know about the one and not about the others? *(Violent and tough.)* Look, go and tell your mother and your brothers and your aunts – I went with many men, many, many men. *(Suddenly serious and tender.)* I've had sex in exchange for a "good morning" greeting! And another thing you don't know; I adore young boys – boys young enough to have pimples!

UNCLE RAUL: *(With a sob.)* Either you kill yourself or I'll kill you! Drink it!

JUDITE: *(A change of tone, her voice breaking in sobs.)* I regret my husband, but I don't regret my lovers! *(Takes the glass and raises it to her lips, slowly.) (Hoarsely.)* My daughter!

JUDITE drinks the contents in one. Then she drops the glass which splinters on the floor. She falls on her knees, with her guts on fire and with a huge deep groan. She is still writhing in agony when the exhausted UNCLE RAUL goes to meet his MOTHER.

MOTHER: Did she get a good reprimand?

UNCLE RAUL: *(Exhausted with hatred and almost sweet.)* She won't betray anyone ever again …

END OF ACT 2

Act 3

UNCLE RAUL has just recounted the story of Judite to GLORINHA. AUNT ODETE passes by, and for a moment stops to pronounce her usual words.

AUNT ODETE: It's time for the homeopathy! *(She continues walking, and after her exit, her shadow is cast at the back of the stage.)*

UNCLE RAUL: *(To GLORINHA.)* So, I said "She won't betray anyone ever again"!

GLORINHA: She died? Mama died?

UNCLE RAUL: She died.

GLORINHA: Then it wasn't suicide?

UNCLE RAUL: I killed her! It was me! And look: no one knows, no one! Even my mother and my brothers still think it was suicide! *(Low voiced, with a small vile laugh.)* *(Louder.)* But the murderer is here and it's me, I'm the murderer! *(Breathless.)* I was one of her pallbearers, I went to the cemetery and at her graveside I left a spoonful of petals on top of her coffin. You see?

Pause.

GLORINHA: What?

UNCLE RAUL: You don't have anything to say?

GLORINHA: *(Sobs.)* Nothing!

UNCLE RAUL: *(Clutches GLORINHA, shaking her and shouting.)* But I'm the murderer! *(Lowering his voice.)* Do you really have nothing to say to the man who murdered your own mother!

GLORINHA: Nothing! *(Turns her face away.)*

UNCLE RAUL: And you turn your face away!

GLORINHA: *(A brusque complaint.)* You're hurting me!

UNCLE RAUL: *(Commanding.)* Look this way when you speak to me!

GLORINHA: I'm looking!

UNCLE RAUL: *(Violent.)* Tell me what you feel for me, right now? And what you felt before? And what you've always felt, tell me?

GLORINHA: I don't know.

UNCLE RAUL: You do know! You hate me! Is it hatred? I want to know: Do you hate me? *(Pause.)* Or is it fear? Yes, of course, always ...

GLORINHA: Respect.

UNCLE RAUL: *(Loud.)* Liar!

GLORINHA: *(Sobbing.)* I swear it!

UNCLE RAUL: *(Surprised.)* Not love, not hate, not respect: just fear? Now it will always be fear! *(With dull desperation.)* Even if you don't respond, if you don't say anything, you must want to know why I told you all this, why I told you the whole story! Yes, you bitch, I didn't tell my mother anything, I didn't tell my brothers, nobody, but I told you! *(Violent.)* And why? *(With a half smile softly.)* I'll tell you why. *(Astonished.)* Not love, not hate, not respect: just fear! I'll tell you in a moment ... but first: have you seen Nair?

GLORINHA: *(Tense.)* Nair?

UNCLE RAUL: *(With false naturalness.)* Yes, exactly, Nair, the one who used to come here, and who then stopped coming, Nair, exactly. Have you seen her?

GLORINHA: Why?

UNCLE RAUL: *(Shouts.)* Have you seen her?

GLORINHA: No.

UNCLE RAUL: Not even yesterday?

GLORINHA: I don't see her any more!

UNCLE RAUL: *(Firing the questions.)* Weren't you friends?

GLORINHA: Not really.

UNCLE RAUL: Or you were?

GLORINHA: On the contrary.

UNCLE RAUL: *(Brusquely.)* She died.

GLORINHA: *(Surprised.)* Who died?

UNCLE RAUL: *(Triumphant.)* Nair, the very same, the one who came here, the one who stopped coming here, she died. Satisfied?

GLORINHA: *(Desperate.)* It's impossible!

UNCLE RAUL: *(Change of tone.)* Yesterday I was here at home, and everything was fine, when the phone rang. I answered it. It was someone who I never saw in my life and was calling me to come urgently. I went and do you know what? It was a gynaecologist who knows you.

GLORINHA: Knows me?

UNCLE RAUL: Yes, you!

GLORINHA: But what's his name?

UNCLE RAUL: You've never been to a gynaecologist?

GLORINHA: *(With wild fear.)* Never!

UNCLE RAUL: *(A vile laugh.)* What an innocent! *(Changes to a violent tone.)* Why are you lying?

GLORINHA: Word of honour, uncle!

UNCLE RAUL: *(Breathless.)* It doesn't matter that you're lying. You've been lying since you were two years old. And I'll tell you something else, mark my words; *(A new laugh.)* you have to lie, now you can lie, lie, go on!

GLORINHA: And if I swear to tell the truth?

UNCLE RAUL: *(Beside himself, screaming at his niece.)* I'm ordering you to lie!

GLORINHA: *(Sobbing.)* I didn't lie!

UNCLE RAUL: Oh no? The doctor described you in great detail …

GLORINHA: *(Interrupting.)* It was just a guess! Believe me! It was a guess!

UNCLE RAUL: *(Breathless.)* A guess … the miserable creature was beating his head against the walls and wanted me to spit in his face … but Nair … Nair told me everything before she died, you shameless creature!

GLORINHA: Nair did that?

UNCLE RAUL: She told me as she lay dying!

GLORINHA: *(Violent.)* Uncle, it's a lie, you mustn't believe it! Nair's rotten, she was always rotten! It's false uncle! It's false! She has no shame at all and I can prove it! She was angry, she hated me, because she wanted to die together with me and I refused, that's how it was!

UNCLE RAUL: You talk like that about a friend who's just died?

365

GLORINHA: She wasn't my friend!

UNCLE RAUL: *(With pained astonished.)* If you could have seen how she was bleeding!

GLORINHA: She wanted to take me to places that only gentlemen go!

UNCLE RAUL: *(Grabs GLORINHA. Decisive.)* Come here and tell me!

GLORINHA: They even offered me money, uncle!

UNCLE RAUL: Tell me, look at me, like that: Nair was shameless. What about you?

GLORINHA: Me?

UNCLE RAUL: Did you have any decency – ever? When was it?

GLORINHA: I am a decent person!

UNCLE RAUL: So explain to me: that time at carnival when I was away, did you or did you not go …

GLORINHA: No!

UNCLE RAUL: It was in the apartment of some degenerate, you with a costume over your bare skin? You smoked pot all night and then they took off your costume, or am I lying? I want the truth and you're going to tell me the truth! Tell me!

GLORINHA: Nair was lying!

UNCLE RAUL: Didn't you go to one of those houses, one of those places just for Deputies? A house full of girls of good families? *(With a horrible sweetness.)* Weren't you there, with a Deputy? No one lies at the moment of their death and you're saying Nair lied?

GLORINHA: She lied!

UNCLE RAUL: Or are you the liar?

GLORINHA: It's her!

UNCLE RAUL: And there's another thing: Why do you say so very little, because you hardly talk at all, and you just say "yes" and "no", and you play act and you bite your lips?

GLORINHA: *(Beside herself.)* I don't know!

UNCLE RAUL: Because you never talk, I'm curious about you, about your soul, about everything that you don't say, about everything that you don't admit to. *(Exasperated, turning in the direction of AUNT ODETE.)* Because I'm sick of silence, I'm sick of things which are not said. It's not just you, it's also my wife.

AUNT ODETE: *(With solemn tenderness.)* It's time for the homeopathy.

UNCLE RAUL: She doesn't speak, or rather she repeats a sentence again and again. She lives, she survives because of a single sentence. *(With deep suffering.)* But maybe she's as false as you, in her crazy silence! Perhaps she hates me just like you hate me! And all I want to know is what she doesn't say, what she doesn't admit to! *(Suddenly, he begins to laugh, crescendo. Cuts the laugh.) (No longer excited.)* I spent a sleepless night, watching that bleeding. I'm tired and thirsty! *(Slowly, without taking his eyes off her.)* Go and get me a glass of water. *(Pause.)* Didn't you hear me? I'm thirsty. Go and get me a glass of water.

GLORINHA: *(Withdrawing.)* No.

UNCLE RAUL: *(Affectionate and vile.)* Are you afraid? What are you afraid of?

GLORINHA: *(Crying.)* I didn't do anything, uncle!

UNCLE RAUL: But if you're afraid, why don't you scream?

GLORINHA: Because I don't want to?

UNCLE RAUL: Or why don't you run away?

GLORINHA: *(Sobbing.)* I don't know.

UNCLE RAUL: But I know. You don't run and you don't scream because you belong to me. But I'm warning you: If you run or you scream, I've got a gun and I'll kill you with one shot, just try it! *(Laughs.)* Now you know why I told you the story of your mother? *(They are speaking close together, face to face.)* *(Low.)* Because you two are as alike as two peas and your fate, Gloria, is the same as hers!

GLORINHA: *(Low voiced.)* I don't want to die!

UNCLE RAUL: *(Triumphant.)* And everyone will say it was suicide!

GLORINHA: *(Sobbing.)* I want to live! *(Falls to the feet of her uncle, clutching his legs.)* Forgive me uncle!

UNCLE RAUL: *(Indifferent and ironic.)* For what? Forgive you for what, if you don't admit to anything? If you deny everything? Get up! *(Helps GLORINHA to her feet.)* So you want to live and you'll do anything to live?

GLORINHA: *(Fiercely.)* Anything!

UNCLE RAUL: Listen! There's only one way you can save yourself!

GLORINHA: *(Fiercely.)* Anything!

UNCLE RAUL: Just wait a moment! This is my offer: I'll let you live if you tell me everything. I want to know who you are. I always believed you to be one thing but now I see you were another. Do you know how I thought of you? A girl innocent of sex, exactly that, a girl innocent of sex. I never thought that, at sixteen years old, you ever felt any desire, not ever. And suddenly someone tells me you're hiding a monstrous perversity. I want to know if it's one thing or the other. I know nothing about you, nothing about your soul. On the other hand, I know what Nair told me. Now I want your own confession. And if you tell me everything, absolutely everything, I'll spare your life. Do you accept that?

GLORINHA: I accept.

UNCLE RAUL: Let's begin: you hate me?

GLORINHA: *(Vacillating.)* No.

UNCLE RAUL: *(Exasperated.)* You don't hate your mother's murderer?

GLORINHA: *(Beside herself.)* No!

UNCLE RAUL: *(Possessed.)* You're a liar!

GLORINHA: *(Exploding.)* All right. I hate you, I hate you!

UNCLE RAUL: Fine. You hate me ...

GLORINHA: I hate you.

UNCLE RAUL: *(Breathless.)* That's not enough. I want to feel the spontaneity you never had. You're still inhibited – you're ruled by fear, by fear. Tell me: to save your life, would you insult me?

GLORINHA: Insult you?

UNCLE RAUL: Yes, me!

GLORINHA: But why?

UNCLE RAUL: Because of the following: If you insult me, you're being spontaneous. What I need most is spontaneity... go on, insult me!

GLORINHA: But I don't know how, Uncle!

UNCLE RAUL: *(Infuriated.)* How come you don't know? Of course you know! Have you never heard a dirty word? You never said a dirty word?

GLORINHA: No.

UNCLE RAUL: *(Violent.)* Would you rather die? Because I'll kill you, Gloria, like I killed your mother, your shameless mother! *(Almost sweet.)* Come, I'll teach you. For example, call me a bastard. Come on, say it, a bastard!

GLORINHA: *(Lethargic.)* I don't have the courage!

UNCLE RAUL: *(Exasperated.)* I'm ordering you to say it!

GLORINHA: *(Crying.)* Not that, Uncle!

UNCLE RAUL: *(Furious.)* So you're not saying it? You don't want to say it? *(Suddenly starts hitting her.) GLORINHA, under the blows, retreats in a circle.*

GLORINHA: *(Sobbing.)* For the love of God, uncle!

UNCLE RAUL: Are you going to say it or not?

GLORINHA: I'll say it. *(Uncle and niece are face to face.)*

UNCLE RAUL: I'm waiting.

GLORINHA: *(Low voiced.)* Bastard ...

UNCLE RAUL: Louder!

GLORINHA: Bastard!

UNCLE RAUL: Shout!

> *GLORINHA (Shouting.) Bastard! (Falls to her knees, sobbing.)*

UNCLE RAUL: *(Breathless and placated.)* Very good: you just called the uncle who, until a moment ago was sacred, your sacred uncle, your esteemed uncle, the uncle who was more than a father to you, almost a God ... you've just called him a bastard. *(He lifts her face towards him.)* And now you can tell me everything, Gloria. Is it true what Nair told me?

GLORINHA: *(Sobs.)* I feel so sorry for Nair!

UNCLE RAUL: Nair doesn't matter! *(Shouting.)* Why are you crying? Dry your tears, come on, dry them! *(Enraged.)* I want you candid, really candid, and vulgar, above all vulgar! No girl-of-good-family attitudes! *(GLORINHA has already dried her tears.)* Yesterday, were you or were you not in that house of girls?

GLORINHA: Yes, I was.

UNCLE RAUL: Right. Pay attention, it's important – what happened between you and the Deputy? Tell me the truth, Gloria, don't hide anything from me, absolutely nothing. When you two were alone in the bedroom ...

GLORINHA: It was a living room.

UNCLE RAUL: Or the living room. But ... why a living room? Was it in front of everyone?

GLORINHA: There was no one there, just we two.

UNCLE RAUL: And what did he do to you? Did he embrace you? Did he kiss you?

GLORINHA: He didn't touch me!

UNCLE RAUL: How come he didn't touch you?

GLORINHA: He stood away from me and he shouted, but he never came near me!

UNCLE RAUL: *(With indignity, disbelief.)* You didn't even take your clothes off? You weren't naked? Naked?

GLORINHA: He was old. He was gaga ...

UNCLE RAUL: *(Shouting.)* That's enough! *(Grabs her.)* Do you think I believe you? You've already deceived me so many times and now that's it! All you do is lie!

GLORINHA: OK. I lied, yes, it was a lie...I

UNCLE RAUL: Go on!

GLORINHA: I took off my clothes and he wasn't gaga at all ... he must be about your age ...

UNCLE RAUL: *(With a tearful grimace.)* My age?

GLORINHA: About forty-eight, maybe.

UNCLE RAUL: *(Passes his hands through her hair.) (With a strangled sob.)* When I remember seeing you just born, and I held you in my arms, I took care of you! *(Change of tone.)* But if he was about my age ...

GLORINHA: Just like you!

UNCLE RAUL: Like me?

GLORINHA: Like you. *(Speaking low. Caresses the top of her uncle's head.)* He just has more grey hairs. You have almost no grey hairs. Just one or two.

UNCLE RAUL: *(Surprised.)* Not that old guy, our neighbour? Nair told me it was him.

GLORINHA: I thought so much about you, so much!

UNCLE RAUL: *(Beside himself, withdraws, shakily, from his neice. Speaks with his back to her.)* Did he pay you? Did you take his money?

GLORINHA: *(Ignoring him and speaking low.)* They said they'd pay me today and he wants me to go back at eleven o'clock.

UNCLE RAUL: *(Turns around, amazed and throws himself towards his niece. Desperate.)* He wants you to go back, and what about you? *(Change of tone.)* Now tell me, if I didn't know anything about this, would you go back? Or if I spared you your life, would you go back there secretly?

GLORINHA: *(Vacillating.)* No.

UNCLE RAUL: Liar! I want the truth! Your life depends on the truth! Tell me!

GLORINHA: You really want to know?

UNCLE RAUL: Everything.

GLORINHA: *(Violent.)* Right. Now that I know, I'd go back there, today at eleven o'clock and every day after that. To get back at you, sir.

UNCLE RAUL: For the moment you can drop the "sir".

GLORINHA: *(Energised.)* To get back at you. To get back at the others, all of them. My uncles, my grandmother. And as for you, you disgust me.

UNCLE RAUL: *(Sardonic.)* I disgust you, that's perfect, and what more?

GLORINHA: *(Exhausted.)* That's all.

UNCLE RAUL: *(Triumphant.)* Is that it then? You don't need to say any more. You've said everything, everything I wanted to know, everything! *(Starts to laugh, in a crescendo. GLORINHA withdraws, horrified.)*

GLORINHA: But it was you who told me to say everything!

UNCLE RAUL: And now you can call me "sir" again!

GLORINHA: I'll call you that, yes. *(Shouting.)* You promised, sir! *(UNCLE RAUL reaches for the glass of water.)* *(GLORINHA is*

373

frantic.) And I lied! I lied! The Deputy was old, yes he was, and gaga! I didn't take off my clothes! He didn't touch me, he didn't lay a finger on me!

UNCLE RAUL: *(Putting a powder in the glass.)* Do I disgust you that much?

GLORINHA: Not you sir! The Deputy disgusts me, Pola Negri disgusts me, Madame Lula disgusts me, but not you sir, no Uncle, I swear, I like you very much!

UNCLE RAUL: *(Handing her the glass.)* Drink it.

GLORINHA: *(Her hands behind her back.)* I won't go back there, never! I only went yesterday because Nair put the idea into my head that I had to!

UNCLE RAUL: *(Gentle and insidious.)* Really!

GLORINHA: *(Fascinated.)* *(Takes the glass.)* And if I don't drink it?

UNCLE RAUL: Either you'll take your own life or I'll kill you!

GLORINHA: *(Slowly.)* If I have to die, I want a kiss! A kiss!

UNCLE RAUL: You hate me and I hate you!

GLORINHA: *(Approaching her uncle.)* I want to be kissed before I die!

UNCLE RAUL: Don't you hate me?

GLORINHA: When I was with the Deputy I thought only of you sir ... now kiss me ... *(UNCLE RAUL touches his lips to GLORINHA's forehead.)* On the mouth!

UNCLE RAUL: *(A strangled sob.)* I already kissed you!

GLORINHA: I want it on my mouth. *(Turns and puts the glass on a piece of furniture. Comes back and approaches her uncle.)* First put your arms around me!

UNCLE RAUL: *(Magnetised, he obeys and embraces his niece.)* You
   devil! *(There is a frustrated kiss.) (UNCLE RAUL is impatient.)*
   Don't close your mouth. Kiss me with your mouth open.
   But you know that. I know you know how to kiss, this isn't
   the first time … kiss me like you kissed the others …

Another kiss, with desperate love.

GLORINHA: And now sir has kissed me, forgive me, uncle!

UNCLE RAUL: Forgive you?

GLORINHA: *(Sobbing.)* I want to live!

UNCLE RAUL: *(Savage.)* That kiss was a lie, another lie, do
   you only know how to lie? You just kissed me to save your
   life? Was it fear?

GLORINHA: *(Desperate.)* It was LOVE!

UNCLE RAUL: Or was it hate?

GLORINHA: I love you.

UNCLE RAUL: *(With a tearful grimace.)* Me?

GLORINHA: Always.

*For a moment, UNCLE RAUL puts a hand behind his niece's head
and looks into her face. Then he pushes her away.*

UNCLE RAUL: That was your last lie on this earth!

GLORINHA: *(Clings to her uncle.)* Can I make my last wish on
   this earth?

UNCLE RAUL: Tell me.

GLORINHA: Now I have to die, I don't want to die alone like
   Nair. *(Low and supplicating.)* Die with me uncle, together
   with me! *(Sobbing.)* I swear that with you I wouldn't be
   afraid of dying!

UNCLE RAUL: We two together? Die together?

GLORINHA: It would be so beautiful! And I know you love me! You do don't you?

UNCLE RAUL: First tell me: did you take off your clothes for the Deputy?

GLORINHA: No, uncle!

UNCLE RAUL: *(With an immense sob.)* If that was a lie, I still love you, I love you, I love you, I love you!

From time to time AUNT ODETE passes across the stage. When she is absent, her shadow, enlarged, is projected at the back of the stage pacing from one side to the other.

UNCLE RAUL: Now we're going to die, Gloria, we can say everything; we don't need to hide, we don't need to be silent, we can do all the shouting we like, all of it. *(Violent, indicating the shadow of AUNT ODETE.)* The one who doesn't speak is her over there, in her crazy silence. Speak, Gloria! Because we can speak!

GLORINHA: *(Gritting her teeth.)* You're old!

UNCLE RAUL: *(Astonished.)* What else?

GLORINHA: You're gaga!

UNCLE RAUL: *(With dumb suffering.)* Go on …

GLORINHA: *(Laughing in crescendo. Peals of laughter, mocking her uncle.)* You look like the Deputy!

UNCLE RAUL: *(Desperate.)* I do?

GLORINHA: You do!

UNCLE RAUL: *(Grabs his niece by the wrist.)* I'll smash your face!

GLORINHA: BASTARD!

UNCLE RAUL: *(Releasing her.)* But I never did anything to you, nothing, nothing at all! Listen Gloria, before you die, listen! I told you the story of your mother, but I didn't tell you that I loved her, that I had always loved her. Even now, at this very moment, it's her I love. *(Shouting.)* My sister-in-law, she rejected me and I killed her. I killed her because she rejected me. *(Grabs GLORINHA again – with an immense sob.)* JUDITE!

GLORINHA: I'm not Judite!

UNCLE RAUL: *(Astonished.)* So who are you?

GLORINHA: Gloria!

UNCLE RAUL: *(Disconsolate.)* You're Gloria? You're not Judite?

GLORINHA: Judite is dead!

UNCLE RAUL: *(Ignoring her, delirious.)* Judite, when I made you drink the poison you fell on your knees with your belly on fire, and I held you by your hair, like this Judite! *(He grabs GLORINHA by her hair.)* I saw what was going to die was a body that had been kissed by so many others, but never kissed by me! In your agony you were mine, my darling! For the first time, you were mine! Your lips were closed to my kiss … but not even your husband, not even your lovers, no one kissed you at the moment of your death, only me!

GLORINHA: Murderer!

UNCLE RAUL: *(A sobbing laugh.)* I never knew if your cry was agony or lust, Judite …

GLORINHA: *(Exasperated.)* I'm Glorinha!

UNCLE RAUL: Judite, you were possessed by so many, but I was the only one who loved you! *(He speaks face to face with GLORINHA.)*

GLORINHA: *(Violent.)* Enough about my mother!

UNCLE RAUL: *(Returning, slowly, to reality.)* Your mother ... *(Pause.) (In tears.)* It's nearly time for you to be at the house of the young ladies. *(Shakily he goes to get the glass.)*

GLORINHA: You're walking like the Deputy!

UNCLE RAUL: *(Taking the glass with his back to her.)* Go on, insult me! *(Pushing the glass towards her with a trembling hand.)*

GLORINHA: You're trembling like the Deputy. *(UNCLE RAUL approaches, still trembling.)*

UNCLE RAUL: It's time, Glorinha!

GLORINHA: So I'm not Judite any more?

UNCLE RAUL: *(Indicates the glass on top of the furniture.) (Older than ever.)* Take it, Glorinha ... let's drink ... from the same glass ... but before dying ... tell me ... did you take your clothes off for the Deputy?

GLORINHA: *(Holds the glass.)* DRINK IT!

UNCLE RAUL: Do you love me?

GLORINHA: I love you!

UNCLE RAUL: I raised you for myself. Day and night, I raised you for myself! Now die with the thought that I raised you for myself!

They raise the glass to their lips, at the same time. UNCLE RAUL drinks the contents in one. GLORINHA still has not drunk. UNCLE RAUL falls to his knees, sobbing.

UNCLE RAUL: *(Appealing.)* Drink! DIE WITH ME! *(A huge groan.)*

In her fury, GLORINHA empties the contents of the glass over his face.

UNCLE RAUL: JUDITE!

Beside herself, GLORINHA runs to the phone. UNCLE RAUL is still moving.

GLORINHA: *(Dials in desperation.)* Pola Negri! It's me, Pola Negri! Glorinha! I'm fine thank you. Look – I'll be there soon, tell Madame and the Deputy I'm on my way. My uncle … don't worry … he agrees … so everything's all just great. Bye.

UNCLE RAUL is in agony. He manages to get up, with the last of his strength. But then rolls onto the steps. GLORINHA runs, opens the door and disappears. AUNT ODETE, who was passing, stops. She walks slowly towards her dead husband. Sits on the step and places UNCLE RAUL's head on her lap.

AUNT ODETE: *(With sweet nostalgia.)* My love!

END OF ACT 3 AND FINAL ACT

SEVEN LITTLE KITTIES

Divine Comedy in Three Acts
& Four Scenes

By Nelson Rodrigues (1958)
Translated by Almiro Andrade

Characters

BIBELOT

AURORA

DONA ARACY (GORDA[1])

DÉBORA

SEU[2] NORONHA

ARLETE

HILDA

SILENE (MANINHA)

SEU SAUL

DR. PORTELA

DR. BORDALO

---

1 'Gorda' means 'Fat' in Portuguese. It does not carry the tenderness present in its English counterpart 'fatty', yet it does bear the nickname-quality of the adjective.

2 'Seu' is a Brazilian corruption of the Portuguese honorific title 'Senhor'; it means 'Mister'. However, the title 'Seu' is usually followed by the person's given name, not their family name. 'Dona' is the feminine version of 'Seu'.

Act 1

AURORA had met BIBELOT the day before. He was wearing white and, by the way, his starched and pressed suit, fresh from the cleaners, had really left an impression on her. He is a tall young man, perhaps twenty-five or pushing thirty years old, wide shoulders, a well trimmed cheeky little moustache, lips made for kissing and eyes of a violent and unexpected blue. He was wearing a thin, transparent shirt, the first button undone, through which you could see a religious medal featuring one of those saints. During the play, BIBELOT kisses the little medal constantly. They met while standing on the pavement by the bus stop, waiting for their bus. They both live in Grajaú, which is a coincidence that has made things a lot easier. And, when the bus arrived, it was so full, they both travelled standing next to each other, holding on to the metal handles. Later, as they said their goodbyes, a date was set for the following day. Now, they're meeting for the second time. AURORA left work at five sharp. She met him on the agreed spot and, wearing white once again, BIBELOT appears and bows.

BIBELOT: *(Low and insidious.)* Very nice!

AURORA: Do you think so?

BIBELOT: You're a vision in blue!

AURORA: *(With a hard-to-contain happiness.)* Merci!

BIBELOT: So what's the deal?

AURORA: We wait for the bus!

BIBELOT: Could we do something else?

AURORA: Such as?

BIBELOT: What if – instead of a bus – we took the streetcar.

AURORA: *(Tempted.)* The streetcar?

BIBELOT: This way we could sit down, have a little chat, and then some!

AURORA: *(Responding with the most delicious rustle.)* I'm in!

BIBELOT: *(Happy.)* Then, what are we waiting for?!

AURORA: Before I forget, there's something I've been meaning to ask you since yesterday – Why do they call you Bibelot?

BIBELOT: *(With amusement.)* Well, it's because…

AURORA: *(Not knowing what to say.)* It's just such a funny nickname, I don't know!

BIBELOT: *(Hesitates, clears his throat, then laughs.)* It's simple – they call me Bibelot because some of them believe I'm lucky when it comes to women.

AURORA: *(Delighted.)* I like your honesty, and your gumption!

They both take a few steps forward. BIBELOT stops suddenly.

BIBELOT: Wait!

AURORA: What?

BIBELOT: Just had another idea!

AURORA: The clock's ticking!

BIBELOT: It's still early.

AURORA: What's the plan?

BIBELOT: First, tell me: are you brave enough?

AURORA: Brave enough for what?

BIBELOT: *(Clearing his throat.)* Brave enough to let me take you somewhere, to this place…

AURORA: *(Faster than him.)* Hands off!

BIBELOT: Are you?

AURORA: Where to?

BIBELOT: Right there.

AURORA: That depends.

BIBELOT: It'll be great!

AURORA: Where is this place?

BIBELOT: Copacabana.

AURORA: *(In panic at the distance.)* Too far!

BIBELOT: Not if we take a taxi. And, look: there's a record player, I'll put on some music, and we can enjoy it together.

AURORA: *(With sweet irony.)* That's all?

BIBELOT: *(Somewhat uncertain.)* I'll get to kiss you a bit and that's all.

AURORA: Just kissing, that's all?

BIBELOT: Sure!

AURORA: *(Sighs.)* Men!

BIBELOT: *(Eager.)* I swear! The apartment isn't mine. It belongs to a friend who's out of town. He gave me the key and, besides the key, there's a deadbolt, we can lock it from the inside and there'll be nothing to worry about, silly! What's more, the building's entirely residential, very discrete!

AURORA: *(Sweet and sad.)* What do you take me for?

BIBELOT: *(Slightly confused.)* Take you for? *(Incisive.)* I'll take you wherever you want, for crying out loud!

AURORA: *(Also incisive.)* Liar! You've just met me yesterday, waiting for my bus, just saw me for the first time. And I don't even know you. Do I? Come on, tell me! Do I?!

BIBELOT: So you don't know me, Aurora?

AURORA: I don't even know where you work!

BIBELOT: Don't sweat it. I can tell you my life story. Look: I was in the police force for a while but they kicked me out.

AURORA: Why?

BIBELOT: I shot a fella. You know how it goes; he tried to get clever.

AURORA: Did he die?

BIBELOT: The fella? *(Making a gesture as if washing his hands off.)* Your guess is as good as mine. I couldn't care less.

AURORA: So what do you do now?

BIBELOT: Nothing really, just waiting to see where the tide takes me.

AURORA: *(Shooting, at point-blank.)* Are you married?

BIBELOT: *(With a slight hesitation.)* Yes.

AURORA: I knew it!

BIBELOT: Why?

AURORA: When I fancy a bloke, he's always married!

BIBELOT: Well, but you see, my wife had to go under the knife, had her uterus, her ovaries, all lady bits taken out and…

AURORA: She doesn't feel pleasure anymore?

BIBELOT: Exactly, she's not a woman anymore. So upsetting! *(Changing his tone.)* Now, how about us? Shall we?

AURORA: *(Raising her head to look at him, harder expression in her face.)* Not me! No way!

BIBELOT: *(Excited.)* We'll be there for half an hour, tops!

AURORA: *(Resentful.)* You're trying your luck, love!

BIBELOT: *(Astonished.)* Am I?

AURORA: You're too keen to get me to this apartment! You didn't even try to romance me!

BIBELOT: Listen, Aurora!

AURORA: *(Vehement.)* If by any chance, a long shot, I went to this apartment with you.

Let's suppose I did. How about my father?

BIBELOT: *(Impetuous.)* You got me all wrong! You didn't understand my plan!

AURORA: Oh, believe me, I did. Now, tell me: how about my father?

BIBELOT: What about him?

AURORA: *(Emphatic.)* My father's a changed man. Way back, he wouldn't give a toss. But once he found out about this Theophilist religion. I think that's what they call it: Theophilist. He's always on our case! And now, he's a psychic!

BIBELOT: A psychic?

AURORA: *(With certain pride.)* Yes, a psychic! He hears voices, sees moving shadows in the hall. It's a gift and a curse! Look: Do you really want to know who my father is? Let me tell you something that'll knock your socks off! After he got religious, *(Emphasising it, strongly.)* he doesn't let us bring toilet paper into the house, he thinks toilet paper is a luxury, a blasphemy, or whatever. I don't know!

BIBELOT: I mean, what a scabby horrible creep!

AURORA: Father?

BIBELOT: I'm gobsmacked…

AURORA: *(Continuing her previous sentence.)* I've never seen anyone like my father! And, when he's at the Council, he really means business!

BIBELOT: What Council?

AURORA: The Council of Representatives, at Parliament.

BIBELOT: *(With renewed interest.)* What does he do there?

AURORA: *(Slightly hesitant.)* He works there.

BIBELOT: *(Excited.)* Wait a minute: if your father works at Parliament, maybe he's got some say… Who knows, maybe he could get me back into the force. Is he well connected in there?

AURORA: *(Bewildered.)* Well.

BIBELOT: Is he?

AURORA: *(Blushing.)* He's a clerk.

BIBELOT: *(Disappointed.)* I see… *(Changing his tone.)* So, you're not coming to the apartment, right?

AURORA: I'm not.

BIBELOT: Pity.

BIBELOT waves goodbye with his fingers and moves a few steps away from her.

AURORA: *(Agitated.)* Where are you going?

BIBELOT: See ya.

AURORA: Come here.

BIBELOT: Look, babes, I don't go against anyone's will. It's not in my nature. If you want to come with me, great. If not, I couldn't give a toss. Arrivederci!

BIBELOT begins to walk away again. AURORA, eager, grabs him by the arm.

AURORA: Listen: what if I told you I've changed my mind?

BIBELOT: Sure thing!

AURORA: *(In a sudden burst of desire.)* What if I say I really like you?

BIBELOT: Yeah, right.

AURORA: *(Drastically changed.)* You know you look really good in a white suit? I saw you yesterday wearing your white suit, and now today. Is it the same suit?

BIBELOT: *(In his vanity.)* No way! It's a different one! I only wear white! I have ten of this same suit at home. Come rain or sunshine, I'll be wearing a fresh one every day!

AURORA: *(Fascinated.)* That's great!

BIBELOT: *(Adamant.)* Let's get things straight here! Are you coming or what?

AURORA: Hear me out: I've just remembered there's a late session today at the Council and father won't be back till late. My availability is a bit more flexible.

BIBELOT: Hallelujah, it was about time!

AURORA: But, hold your horses! *(Changing her tone.)* Do you have any money?

BIBELOT: What do you mean, money?

AURORA: Do you?

BIBELOT: *(Uncertain.)* Some.

AURORA: How much, more or less?

BIBELOT: *(Not comprehending.)* Wait, what is the hold-up, now?

AURORA: *(Happy.)* There's no hold-up. Just me, being me; whimsical, get it? When I make up my mind about a fella, you know: I'll do anything. And you've got me all worked up, I don't know if it's you, the white suit, I don't know. I know I'm going with you and that's that!

BIBELOT: Now the hold-up is going to be finding us a taxi this late!

AURORA: But you do have at least five hundred cruzeiros, don't you?

BIBELOT freezes. He looks askance at the girl. He's visibly confused.

BIBELOT: Five hundred cruzeiros?

AURORA: Look, love, I usually charge between fifteen hundred to two thousand, sometimes three thousand. The room sets me back five hundred, but since you have the apartment, *(Pause.)* five hundred will cover it, alright?

BIBELOT: Come here: look me in the eye.

AURORA: Alright.

BIBELOT: Tell me: are you really expecting for me to give you money?

AURORA: *(Lascivious.)* Five hundred and you can call the taxi!

BIBELOT: *(Protesting.)* Are you drunk?

AURORA: *(Eaten by desire.)* I can't do it for any less than that!

BIBELOT: Not even a schilling!

AURORA: *(Nearly crying.)* Listen, I do like you and on top of that: a white suit, fresh from the cleaner's gets my motors running, drives me up the wall! But I do need the five hundred. I really need it, do you hear me? *(Pleading.)* I have expenses and I promised Mother. Cross my heart: the money's not for me!

BIBELOT: Babe, I've never paid for it and I never will!

AURORA, who was holding on to BIBELOT, lets go of him, in clear female spite.

AURORA: I see. They're the ones who pay you!

BIBELOT: *(Brutal.)* That's true!

AURORA: You have that pimp look!

BIBELOT: So what?

AURORA is overwhelmed by her desire. She lunges on towards BIBELOT, once again.

AURORA: The thing is you have this hold on me, I like it!

BIBELOT: So, come with me.

BIBELOT pulls the girl towards him.

BIBELOT: There's a free taxi right there. Let's catch it!

BIBELOT pulls AURORA, both running. Two chairs facing the audience represent the taxi.

AURORA: *(Sitting down.)* But it's not going to be free, love!

BIBELOT stretches his legs, euphoric. Every now and then, they act as if the taxi is moving: they control their chairs as if the taxi was making turns or going fast on zigzags.

BIBELOT: *(To the invisible driver.)* Barata Ribeiro street, mate. *(To AURORA, happy.)* Ah, I feel like I always end up with the dollymops!

AURORA: *(Insulted.)* What!? I'm no dollymop, mate.

BIBELOT: *(Euphoric with the taxi's movement.)* Tough!

AURORA: Why tough?

BIBELOT: *(Happy.)* Because, I only truly like those really nasty ones, you know!? For instance, I've met a really nice girl. Great body, what a body! What's more, she was seventeen, tops.

AURORA: A virgin?

BIBELOT: Used to be. You know how it is: she went to the apartment with me, we started fooling around and I always close the deal. But she was such a sweet girl, that it got me thinking: what a bummer! Family girls, I don't know, they put me off!

AURORA: Promise you don't like this girl? Promise me!

BIBELOT: *(Falling on top of AURORA as if the taxi had made a sharp curve.)* Delicious curves... *(Changing his tone.)* Do I like her? Who cares! But the bird adores me, puts me in a pedestal!

AURORA: *(Jealous.)* Promise, swear to God you don't like her! Look at me – Swear to God!

BIBELOT: *(Teasing.)* Swear to God?... I don't believe in that kind of thing, I mean... *(Holds on to his medal, hanging from his neck.)* I only believe in this one here...

BIBELOT kisses his medal.

AURORA: Then swear by that one hanging from your neck!

BIBELOT: No, not a chance I'm swearing on it! But I give you my word: I prefer the ones like you, with these whorish ways.

AURORA: Excuse me! What do you take me for!? I can make a life like this, but I don't go with just anyone. Only with fellas I know or who I'm formally introduced to. I live with my parents and I have them to answer to. I have a job in the Council and my mother knows about what I do, but my father doesn't; he has no idea.

BIBELOT: *(Pulling her towards him.)* Must be tough being this delicious!

AURORA: *(Nagging.)* Be quiet! *(Changing tone.)* And look: I have to be very discreet, keep an incredibly low profile. I can't do this every day. Two or three time a week, perhaps, between five and eight. What you don't know, what you can't even imagine, is why I do what I do.

BIBELOT: Come here!

BIBELOT kisses her neck, suddenly. AURORA is electrified by her own lust.

AURORA: *(In her frenzy.)* No, not my neck or I get all worked up, look… I'm shivering… *(Nagging, lowering her tone.)* No, not here! We're not alone… *(Changing tone.)* Let me tell you: my life could be stuff of novels! Listen. There are five of us at home, five sisters in total. Between the youngest and the one before her, there was a ten-year gap. The four oldest ones never got married. Only Maninha's left. She's just turned sixteen and goes to the best school around here. We want – not just want, it's our goal – that she gets

393

married in a church with a proper white wedding dress, a veil, the works. We save every penny for her.

BIBELOT: *(In a sort of sleazy laugh.)* These days no one cares about being a virgin!

AURORA: You might not care but we do, what are you on about!? *(Changing her tone.)* But I'll tell you one thing: Maninha's wedding is going to be out of this world. It'll put to shame all those rich names out there, do you hear me? I don't mind getting paid for it, but the money goes straight towards her trousseau… All I spend is the salary I get from my day job.

BIBELOT straightens himself up in the imaginary car.

BIBELOT: We're almost there!

AURORA: *(Lickerish, holding on to his arm.)* The money's not for me: it's for Maninha's trousseau!

BIBELOT: *(Not listening, pointing out.)* That building. There, second floor!

AURORA: Every day, I have to take home a set amount!

BIBELOT: *(To the driver.)* You can stop right there. *(To AURORA, like a brute.)* Pay the man!

AURORA: *(Shocked.)* Me?

BIBELOT: I'm broke!

BIBELOT gets out of the taxi.

AURORA: You get back here!

Stupefied, AURORA looks inside her purse. She stutters as she asks the question.

AURORA: How much? Ninety-three?

AURORA hands over crumpled bills to the imaginary driver. Desperate, she gets out of the car. BIBELOT is waiting for her at the door of the building.

AURORA: *(Ironic.)* How nice of you!

BIBELOT: I haven't got a penny!

AURORA: *(Full of wrath.)* Yeah right!

BIBELOT pulls AURORA by the arm.

BIBELOT: Let's go in!

AURORA: *(Full of resentment.)* I bet you treat that young one like a princess!

They go inside and stop at the foot of imaginary stairs.

BIBELOT: *(Eager.)* Come, give me a kiss!

AURORA, scared, looks around.

AURORA: Here?

BIBELOT: There's no one around!

AURORA: *(Taken already by her desire.)* Okay, but hurry!

They kiss, right there, in a desperate kind of love. AURORA sobs, in her female fascination.

AURORA: You're an animal!

BIBELOT: *(Impatiently, full of desire.)* Let's take the stairs. It's only two floors.

BIBELOT pulls her by the hand. AURORA still resists.

AURORA: *(Pleading.)* The five hundred for the trousseau!

BIBELOT: *(Brutal.)* Don't start with that again!

AURORA: *(Desperate.)* At least the taxi, ninety-three cruzeiros!

BIBELOT: Enough chit chat! Come here!

AURORA lets herself be taken over by her powerful desire. She follows BIBELOT. They walk in circles around the stage as if they were going up two flights of stairs, then go into the apartment.

AURORA: *(Lustful.)* Do you bring the girl here, too?

BIBELOT: *(Elated and brutal.)* Right on that bed!

The brief and desperate ballet of their love-making begins. Symbolically, they undress each other, tearing off their imaginary clothes. BIBELOT, in theory, takes off his jacket and shirt, picks up a real gun and, panting, empties it, removing all its bullets.

AURORA: *(Undoing her bra.)* What's that?

BIBELOT: *(Panting and laughing.)* I was told a whore was going to shoot me. *(Ferocious and triumphant.)* So, if you want to kill me, shoot, go on, shoot me with an empty gun!

BIBELOT laughs like an animal, throwing the gun down and putting the bullets on a piece of furniture. For all intents and purposes, they have taken off all of their clothes; they should be completely naked.

AURORA: *(Showing off her naked body.)* How about it? Am I a match for your girl? *(As if hallucinating, cracking her teeth with desire.)* Come, come here, you animal!

BIBELOT kisses his medal. And then, out of sight, they perform their barbarian desire. Suddenly, AURORA starts laughing with horrendous hysteria; screeches and shrills.

AURORA: *(Delirious.)* Talk dirty to me! Call me a whore! Slap me right across the face!

END OF SCENE 1

SCENE 2

SEU NORONHA's house – AURORA's father – on a street that crosses 28 de Setembro's Boulevard. DÉBORA, one of SEU NORONHA's and DONA ARACY's daughters, is coming in. DONA ARACY is drying a dish at the door to the kitchen.

DÉBORA: *(Looking around.)* Is father home yet?

DONA ARACY: There's a late session tonight!

DÉBORA: Oh, that's right! Today there's a… *(Changing her tone.)* Mother, please, come here! I can't face it!

DONA ARACY: What is it you can't face, girl!?

DÉBORA: Eek! First, let me sit down!

DÉBORA sits down. Then, takes off her shoes. She groans; and starts to massage her feet.

DÉBORA: *(Sighing.)* I have to get my toenails done. *(Without pausing.)* You won't believe it: guess where I just came from?

DONA ARACY: Where from?

DÉBORA: From Seu Saul's shop! I went there to make a phone call. I was on the phone, my back to the shop floor. All of a sudden, someone comes from behind me and pushes a rolled up piece of paper into my hand. I jumped out of my skin and turned around. At first, I thought; I don't even know what I thought. It was Seu Saul!

DONA ARACY: Seu Saul loves playing practical jokes!

DÉBORA: But I haven't finished: he knew he'd scared me, and you know what he said to me? He said, in his weird accent: "Lovely girl, no need to have fear. Old people no have sex!"

DONA ARACY: *(Incisive.)* Old people have bad kinks!

DÉBORA: *(Winking at her mother.)* Don't I know it! *(Changing her tone.)* So then, an…

SEU NORONHA, head of the family, comes in, wearing his working suit from the Council.

DONA ARACY: Look at that! It's your father!

DÉBORA: *(Turning around.)* Your blessings, father!

SEU NORONHA: *(Abbreviating.)* Bless'ya!

DONA ARACY: Wasn't there a late session?

SEU NORONHA: *(Taking off his jacket.)* A member of Parliament died. *(Walking around, back and forth.)* Gorda, go fetch me the paper.

DONA ARACY: *(To her daughter.)* Go fetch your father the paper.

SEU NORONHA: *(Anguished.)* It must have been something I ate…

DÉBORA fetches the paper and her father grabs it from her. SEU NORONHA goes into the house, offstage.

DONA ARACY: *(To DÉBORA.)* Tell me the rest of the story.

DÉBORA: *(Massaging one of her feet.)* My feet are really rough! *(Changing her tone.)* As I was saying… Then, I looked at the piece of paper and I was gobsmacked: it was a cheque, mother, a cheque!

DONA ARACY: He gave it to you?

DÉBORA: To me.

DONA ARACY: How much?

DÉBORA: Guess!

DONA ARACY: How am I supposed to guess?!

DÉBORA: *(Triumphant.)* Ten thousand cruzeiros, mother, out of nowhere!

DONA ARACY: That's what I don't really get. What is he after? Yes, he must be after something, but what?

DÉBORA: I haven't got a clue what he's after! He even said to me when I left: "Friendship worth more than sex"!

DONA ARACY: *(Taking the cheque and reading it.)* It's a cashier's cheque, brilliant! Ten thousand! Tomorrow, I'll put it in the box, for your little sister's trousseau!

And, out of nowhere, SEU NORONHA bursts into the living room, shouting from the top of his lungs. One of his suspenders has fallen to his waist but, infuriated, he pulls it back up.

SEU NORONHA: Gorda!

DONA ARACY: What's happening now!?

SEU NORONHA: So what do you think that is, in there!?

DONA ARACY: *(Not understanding the reason behind his violence.)* Hold on, pap!

SEU NORONHA: Go to the bathroom! Go on, go! It's the final straw!

DONA ARACY: Is it clogged up again?

SEU NORONHA: Clogged up? *(Changing his tone and, in his wrath, walks around, back and forth.)* I get home, with my usual bad stomach, go to my bathroom and I'm met by walls covered with filthy words, obscene drawings!

DONA ARACY: Where?

SEU NORONHA: In the bathroom! *(Panting.)* To see that, in my own house!

DONA ARACY: *(Disconcerted.)* Let me have a look!

SEU NORONHA: You stay right here! You have no business going there! What I want to know is who did this!

DONA ARACY: Why should I know?

SEU NORONHA: *(Threatening.)* Oh, you don't know, then?

DONA ARACY: *(Responding in kind.)* You and your horrible suspicions!

SEU NORONHA stops and faces his wife. He lands his hand gently on her face.

SEU NORONHA: Truly hurtful is a hand slapping your face!

DÉBORA: Father, you're going too far!

DONA ARACY: *(Retreating.)* Not even my own father has ever hit me!

SEU NORONHA: *(Opening his arms to heaven.)* Is this a home?

DONA ARACY: Why should a husband be the one to lay a hand on me?

SEU NORONHA: Shut up, Gorda!

DÉBORA: *(Conciliatory.)* Father, you're making a mountain out of a molehill!

SEU NORONHA: Where are the girls?

DÉBORA: I'm here, Daddy!

SEU NORONHA: The others! I want the others! All of them!

DONA ARACY: *(To DÉBORA.)* Go call your sisters! *(Talking to herself.)* I've never been hit!

DÉBORA: *(Screeching.)* Arlete! Hilda!

SEU NORONHA: *(To himself.)* This is the final straw! And Gorda here tells me she's got nothing to do with this mess!

ARLETE appears. She's wearing a bra and a petticoat. HILDA appears behind her. There's foam under her arms, as she is shaving it with a razor. SEU NORONHA has his back to his daughters and doesn't see them approaching.

ARLETE: What's going on?

DÉBORA: Father's calling you!

ARLETE: Did you call us, father?

SEU NORONHA turns around and sees his daughter in her underwear.

SEU NORONHA: *(In his heinous sarcasm.)* Is this how I raised you both?

ARLETE: *(Grinding her teeth.)* Not pussyfooting around, are you, father?

SEU NORONHA: What do you think you're wearing?

ARLETE: *(Insolent.)* I'm in my own house!

SEU NORONHA: *(In a crescendo.)* How dare you address your father like that, naked?

ARLETE: I'm not naked!

SEU NORONHA: Yes, you are, young lady! Go put on some clothes, I'm not telling you again!

ARLETE: Pfff, at the beach I can wear a bikini!

HILDA: Don't you push Father too far!

ARLETE: *(Mocking.)* Look at miss boot-licking!

HILDA approaches. ARLETE picks up a blouse and starts putting it on.

401

SEU NORONHA: Aurora is missing!

DONA ARACY: She's still not home.

SEU NORONHA: Great, she's still not home! She gets home whenever she likes; she couldn't care less, doesn't give a toss!

ARLETE: Besides, Aurora's way past the age and… Father, can you tell us what you want, I'm going to the cinema and I really don't want to be late!

SEU NORONHA: *(Changing his tone.)* Well. Before I begin, let's get something straight. Here's the deal: just now, I threatened your mother, physically. Débora saw it. Pff, I don't think I have the right to threaten anyone physically. Whoever threatens anyone physically is disgraced in the eyes of The Lord. Therefore, I, before you all, ask Gorda to forgive me. *(Turns to his wife.)* Gorda, forgive me!

DONA ARACY: *(Making a point.)* You offend me and now you're sorry?

SEU NORONHA: *(Triumphant.)* You see? You can't be nice to a woman. *(To DONA ARACY.)* Gorda doesn't accept my apology! I've done my bit! *(Changing his tone.)* Let's get to the point, then. Something happened in this house, that wasn't supposed to happen. Débora knows what it is. You two don't but you will in just a minute. I'll question you, one at a time. I want the truth and the guilty party will confess to everything! *(To ARLETE.)* You, first!

ARLETE: *(In her subtle mockery.)* But of course.

SEU NORONHA: *(Changing his tone, lowering it, almost sweet.)* I want to know, and you will tell me, who's writing dirty words in the bathroom!

ARLETE: God knows!

SEU NORONHA: *(Point-blank.)* Perhaps it was you!

ARLETE: Father! Are you being serious!?

SEU NORONHA: *(Yelling.)* Answer me!

ARLETE: *(Looking at the ceiling.)* I already have!

SEU NORONHA: *(Brutal.)* What an innocent soul! *(Changing his tone, looks around.)* So, who was it?

ARLETE: No one!

SEU NORONHA: *(Hysterically.)* It had to be one of you! One of my daughters! *(Suddenly staring at his wife.)* Or else, it was you, Gorda!

DONA ARACY: Excuse me!

SEU NORONHA: *(Almost pleading, to DÉBORA.)* Was it you?

DÉBORA: Father, don't put me in the mix!

SEU NORONHA: *(To HILDA.)* You're probably another innocent…

HILDA: I've got nothing to do with this.

SEU NORONHA: *(More exasperated.)* I need to know who was the last person in the bathroom! *(To his wife.)* Who was it?

DONA ARACY: You.

SEU NORONHA: Are you insane?

DONA ARACY: Papa, didn't you come from there just now, weren't you just there?

SEU NORONHA: Don't get funny with me, Mama! I asked you who went there before me!

ARLETE: Me.

SEU NORONHA stops and faces ARLETE.

SEU NORONHA: *(Ever-knowing.)* You! *(Slow.)* Yes, you, out of everyone in here, you have the dirtiest mouth; you're the only one who doesn't respect my authority... *(Digging his fingers into her arm.)* What were you doing in the bathroom?

ARLETE: *(Direct and triumphant.)* Pissing!

SEU NORONHA: Little bitch!

SEU NORONHA raises his hand as if to slap ARLETE, but stops halfway through it. His hand is mid-air.

ARLETE: *(Defiant.)* Go ahead – hit me!

SEU NORONHA: *(Panting.)* I shouldn't. I don't have the right to... I have to control myself...

And, suddenly, SEU NORONHA gives in to his impulse. He hits his daughter violently. ARLETE staggers away.

HILDA: *(In a hysterical plea.)* Father!

Soon, ARLETE raises her hardened face.

ARLETE: *(As if spitting.)* You're nothing but a stupid clerk!

SEU NORONHA: *(Astonished.)* Say that again!

ARLETE: *(Trembling.)* Stupid clerk!

SEU NORONHA hits her again.

ARLETE: *(Emphasising each syllable.)* Stupid clerk, yes, stupid clerk! I said stupid clerk!

SEU NORONHA raises his hand for another slap. Once again, his hand stops mid-air. HILDA runs and grabs her father's hand, while sobbing.

HILDA: Father, I feel for you, I really do, oh father! *(She lets go of SEU NORONHA; turns to ARLETE, and shouts.)* Don't call Father a stupid clerk!

SEU NORONHA: *(To himself.)* Stupid clerk. *(Panting.)* Of course no one's going to confess to anything.

DÉBORA: Father, you're overreacting!

SEU NORONHA starts to get worked up once more.

SEU NORONHA: Me, overreacting? Me of all people? *(In a triumphant shout.)* The exact opposite: I'm under-reacting! I've been indifferent! If I was as worked up as you say, I'd be trashing the house, I'd have already burned the whole house down.

HILDA: *(Lowering her tone of voice.)* Lower your voice, father!

SEU NORONHA: *(Not paying attention to her.)* I'm up to here with you all telling me I am overreacting! My daughters leave the bathroom wrapped in towels! Change their clothes with their doors open! More often than not, I see them walking around naked. Am I lying?

ARLETE: *(Avenged.)* I've already called my father a stupid clerk, now I'm going to the cinema.

ARLETE makes a happy goodbye gesture.

ARLETE: So, if you'll excuse me.

SEU NORONHA: *(Beast-like.)* No! *(Pleading.)* Come here, Arlete!

ARLETE: *(Stopping.)* Father, after Maninha gets married, I have some stuff to get off my chest! I'll tell you the truth!

SEU NORONHA: *(Trembling.)* Listen, Arlete: what I did was wrong, but matter of fact is… It's true, I've been working too hard, I've been on edge and, sometimes, it might sound funny but I can't control myself… Arlete, I beg of you: sit down for a minute. Sit down, my dear. I need all my daughters – and Gorda – to listen to me. What I

405

have to say has to do with the whole family. *(Calm and plaintively, he begins to speak.)* I had five daughters. See if you follow my reasoning: four didn't get married.

ARLETE: So, what else is new?

SEU NORONHA: *(Not paying attention to her.)* Any whore can get married. Tolentino's daughter, our neighbour. Didn't she get married? She used to be seen rubbing herself against anyone with a dick and isn't she married now? In the church, all in white, a veil, the works. Now, she's even got herself lovers, the harlot! *(Triumphant.)* But she's married now, and that's the point! Really married! And my daughters are not! *(Furious.)* Why not?

DÉBORA: I'm a fatalist, father!

HILDA: We just have no luck with it!

SEU NORONHA: It's not a matter of luck! Luck's got nothing to do with it! *(In a strangled voice, slowly.)* There's someone amongst us! Someone leading my daughters astray!

DONA ARACY: Who?

SEU NORONHA: *(Exasperated.)* Someone who won't let my daughters get married!

DONA ARACY: Say the name!

SEU NORONHA: *(Furious.)* The name doesn't matter! Nor does the looks! *(Staring at his daughters' and wife's faces, one by one; making a fist.)* I don't believe in names, nor in looks! *(With sudden inspiration.)* This someone could even be *(Prompt and triumphant.)* Seu Saul!

DÉBORA: How come Seu Saul?

DONA ARACY: He's such a nice man!

SEU NORONHA: *(In an uproar.)* The name they are known by on Earth, the look they assume here on Earth, those mean nothing!

ARLETE: At this rate, I'm not going to the bloody cinema anymore...

SEU NORONHA: *(Not paying attention to her.)* Now, here's the point I'm trying to make. I've always felt you girls were tainted and, finally, yesterday, I found out the reason why you're all lost causes! That is, I heard it from someone unimpeachable, a sure thing! The one who told me all those things *(Emphatic.)* never lies!

DONA ARACY: And who's that?

SEU NORONHA: *(Triumphant.)* Dr. Barbosa Coutinho! *(Takes a deep breath.)* Dr. Barbosa Coutinho, who died in 1872, is a being of light! He was Dom Pedro the Second's doctor and you don't know the best part: Dom Pedro the Second's famous words don't belong to Dom Pedro himself. Dr. Barbosa Coutinho wrote most of them. Dom Pedro the Second just signed them. *(Triumphant.)* Get it?

ARLETE makes a gesture indicating her father is mad.

SEU NORONHA: Hear me out! *(Changing his tone.)* I've always felt there was someone after my family, day and night. Someone leading our virgin girls astray! And, like I was saying, yesterday, Dr. Barbosa Coutinho confirmed that this someone really does exist. Someone who changes his name and looks. It could be a dashing young man, or even an old one, like Seu Saul.

ARLETE: Pff, father, you really buy into all this nonsense!

SEU NORONHA: There's just one thing I want to tell you, Arlete: do you know why you're so disobedient with me? Because you're a psychic who still hasn't developed your abilities. *(Emphatic.)* Embrace them, Arlete, or you'll have a tragic end. And that's enough, do you hear me? Enough! *(Changing his tone.)* So, then, Dr. Barbosa Coutinho told me to look into the old mirror. *(Panting.)* So I did. I looked into the big mirror and I saw a pair of eyes, you see, two eyes, one that blinks as normal and the other one that doesn't, bigger and wide open. *(In sudden violence.)* What's worse is that only the bigger one cries. The normal one doesn't.

ARLETE: Jesus, Mary, Joseph! Touch wood!

DONA ARACY: So what's his name?

SEU NORONHA: *(Furious.)* Gorda, don't you understand, Gorda?! On Earth, we use a name that's not ours, not the real one, a false name! *(Welling up.)* This someone, who cries from only one eye, knows we still have a virgin in this house!

DÉBORA: Maninha...

ARLETE: Touch wood!

SEU NORONHA: *(Almost crying.)* Silene, so young, so virgin! *(Changing his tone.)* But I swear! I won't die before taking Silene down the aisle by the arm, wearing a white dress, a veil, the works!

DONA ARACY: With God's grace!

SEU NORONHA: *(Stretches his hands out, curling his fingers, toward his daughters.)* We must save my little virgin. She hasn't even fully developed yet!

ARLETE: *(Furious.)* Oh, don't start with that again, father!

SEU NORONHA: *(Not paying attention to her.)* And you all have a task, to lure the man who cries from only one eye here to this house. His name doesn't matter. He'll betray himself with the one tear. All that matters is the tear.

ARLETE: Even I've got goose bumps after this one!

SEU NORONHA: I warned you all and you'd better warn Aurora. I saw it in the old mirror, I saw it, I swear! And Dr. Barbosa Coutinho never lies!

SEU NORONHA takes out a small, silver dagger. He raises the dagger, in cruel joy.

SEU NORONHA: My silver dagger!

SEU NORONHA plunges the dagger in the table next to him. He turns towards his daughters.

SEU NORONHA: *(Desperate.)* The eye that cries must bleed, the eye that cries a single tear!

SEU SAUL enters. He is an old gringo, red faced and freckled, with thinning blond hair. He has a noticeable accent.

SEU SAUL: Excuse me.

DONA ARACY: Oh, come on in, Seu Saul!

SEU NORONHA: Come on in. *(With noticeable irony.)* Your ears must be burning.

SEU SAUL: Good evening.

SEU NORONHA: *(Sarcastic.)* I was just talking about you!

DONA ARACY: *(To HILDA.)* Go get Seu Saul a chair.

SEU NORONHA: Please, take a seat, Mr. Saul.

SEU SAUL: Oh, I no stay. *(To HILDA.)* Thanks you. *(To SEU NORONHA.)* I come by only to give you message from your daughter's school.

SEU NORONHA: Silene's school?

SEU SAUL: They call me in shop and say to you she's coming home today.

SEU NORONHA: My daughter? Why today? Is she sick?

SEU SAUL: They just say not to be surprised. The school bus brings your daughter.

SEU NORONHA: But I don't understand!

ARLETE: *(To the others.)* What must have happened?

DONA ARACY: What can it be… out of nowhere!

SEU SAUL: Well, excuse me! I go now.

SEU NORONHA: Gorda, walk Seu Saul to the door. *(Holding his head with both hands.)* – This is all so odd!

DONA ARACY: *(To SEU SAUL.)* Thank you, and don't be a stranger.

SEU SAUL: *(To everyone.)* Good night.

SEU NORONHA: *(Pacing back and forth.)* I have a bad feeling about this!

AURORA enters. ARLETE runs to meet her.

ARLETE: Maninha's coming home!

AURORA: Liar!

DÉBORA: She is!

AURORA: When?

ARLETE: Right now!

AURORA: But that's wonderful!

Suddenly, SEU NORONHA runs towards his wife. He shouts at the top of his lungs.

SEU NORONHA: I almost forgot, Gorda! Chop chop! Go in the bathroom, right now, and wipe off all those dirty words, those curses and filthy drawings, hurry up, Gorda!

END OF ACT 1

Act 2

SCENE 1

Same set: SEU NORONHA's house.

DÉBORA: *(Running.)* She's here!

DONA ARACY: Shite!

> *They all run around, bumping into each other. At some point they all converge outside the front door. Only SEU NORONHA remains, for a moment, in the middle of the living room, eyes shut, his hand wide open up across his chest.*

SEU NORONHA: *(As if in prayer, lower voice.)* Oh, Silene!

> *Suddenly, amongst her mother's and sisters' loud chatter, SILENE enters. She's a cute little girl, a tad cloying, who seems to be about fifteen or sixteen years old. She wears a school uniform. She has a kind of convalescent frailty, and speaks with a whiney voice, typical of a very spoiled child. Behind them, sporting a walking stick, enters a very solemn and severe bald man; DR. PORTELA. DONA ARACY accompanies him.*

SILENE: Father!

SEU NORONHA: My baby girl!

DONA ARACY: Please, do us the honour of joining us, Dr. Portela!

DR. PORTELA: *(Clearing his throat.)* Excuse me.

> *Father and daughter embrace. DONA ARACY brings in the guest.*

DONA ARACY: *(To ARLETE.)* Bring a chair for Dr. Portela.

DR. PORTELA: Oh, you really shouldn't bother!

> *ARLETE brings the chair. DR. PORTELA sits down.*

412

DR. PORTELA: Thank you.

HILDA: *(Eager.)* What was this about?

AURORA: It's all so sudden!

DONA ARACY: *(To DR. PORTELA.)* If you excuse me for a moment, Dr. Portela!

DONA ARACY joins her daughters.

SEU NORONHA: *(Eager.)* How's your appetite?

SILENE: *(Languorous.)* Same as usual.

SEU NORONHA: *(Quieter.)* Got rid of the worms?

SILENE: *(With a smirk full of disgust.)* I don't like needles!

ARLETE: *(Telling her sister off, sweetly.)* You're so stubborn, Maninha!

SEU NORONHA: *(To those seating either side of him.)* Leave her alone! Don't give her a hard time!

DONA ARACY: *(To her husband, under her breath.)* Don't forget Dr. Portela!

SEU NORONHA lunges at DR. PORTELA, his most honourable guest.

SEU NORONHA: Dr. Portela, my apologies!

DR. PORTELA: *(Standing up.)* No problem whatsoever!

SEU NORONHA: Are you well, Doctor? Please, no need to stand up for me! Sit!

DR. PORTELA: I'm well, coping with the heat! How about you, sir?

SEU NORONHA: *(In a happy sigh.)* I don't know where to turn for this. It's such a surprise…. *(Looks at all his daughters gathered.)* And, besides, Silene's so frail health-wise; she

413

has this worm thing going on, you may find it hard to believe, sir, but she hardly eats, only nibbles a bit.

DONA ARACY: Would you like some coffee, Dr. Portela?

DR. PORTELA: *(With gusto.)* A coffee would do me perfect, thank you.

DONA ARACY: Do you take it leaded?

DR. PORTELA: Leaded and strong.

DONA ARACY: Great! I'll go get you some!

DONA ARACY exits. The sisters are cackling with laughter, except SILENE who seems distant and sad.

ARLETE: Did you hear who finally got a boyfriend?

HILDA: As if!

SILENE: Who?

ARLETE: Celeste!

SILENE: That scrawny little one?

ARLETE: And he looks just like that actor, Victor Mature!

SEU NORONHA looks back and forth, between DR. PORTELA and his daughters.

DR. PORTELA: So, Seu Noronha; may we have a chat?

SEU NORONHA: But of course! I'm here for you, sir!

And, out of nowhere, SILENE shouts at the top of her lungs.

SILENE: Don't believe a word he says, father!

She points at DR. PORTELA.

AURORA: *(In panic.)* What's the matter, Maninha?

414

HILDA: Don't you speak to the doctor that way!

DR. PORTELA: It's all right. No need to upset yourselves. I understand!

SEU NORONHA: Young lady, where are your manners? *(To DR. PORTELA.)* She's never acted up like this before, Dr. Portela.

DR. PORTELA: *(With an air of superiority.)* She's nervous, it's totally natural!

SILENE: I didn't do any of it, father!

SEU NORONHA: Silene! Young lady, you'll apologise to Dr. Portela!

DR. PORTELA: *(Generous.)* There's no need! What for?

SEU NORONHA: *(To SILENE.)* Shame on you, Silene, shame! *(To DR. PORTELA.)* I'm deeply sorry, doctor!

DR. PORTELA: Oh, it was nothing, really.

SEU NORONHA: *(To his daughters.)* Take Silene in… *(To SILENE.)* I'll have a word with you later, young lady… *(To DR. PORTELA.)* She's a handful! But you were about to say something, sir, just before we were rudely interrupted…

DR. PORTELA: Seu Noronha, you must be gobsmacked. For sure! Your daughter is back so suddenly, in the middle of the week and…

SEU NORONHA: I must admit I am, indeed, slightly surprised, it's only natural…

DR. PORTELA: Let me explain.

SEU NORONHA: Wait a second! *(Once again frightened.)* She's not sick, is she?

DR. PORTELA: *(Hesitating.)* Well...

SEU NORONHA: Is she? Sick?

DR. PORTELA: *(More incisive.)* No, not physically speaking.

SEU NORONHA: I don't understand.

DR. PORTELA: Here's the deal: I'm here because, as advisor to the school board, I'm considered in their highest esteem and they trust me... So, here I am. But, believe me, this is a very unsavoury visit.

SEU NORONHA: You're scaring me, doctor!

DR. PORTELA: Your wife's coming.

DONA ARACY enters carrying a tray with two small cups of coffee. First, she offers a cup to her guest.

DONA ARACY: I hope it's the way you like it.

DR. PORTELA: Thank you.

DONA ARACY: I just don't know if I've put enough sugar.

SEU NORONHA picks up a cup and spills most of the coffee in the saucer.

SEU NORONHA: Now leave us a moment.

DR. PORTELA: Sugar's fine, Dona Aracy.

DONA ARACY: Well then, I'll leave you two to talk.

SEU NORONHA drinks the coffee spilled on the saucer.

SEU NORONHA: Go on, Dr. Portela...

DR. PORTELA: *(More emphatic and pedantic.)* Seu Noronha, this is why I brought your daughter home: It happened yesterday at school, something very unfortunate, something truly despairing, Seu Noronha.

SEU NORONHA: But... what's that got to do with my daughter?

DR. PORTELA stands up and walks back and forth whilst speaking. Every once in a while, he gets carried away by his speech.

DR. PORTELA: *(Emphatic and pedantic.)* Something, Seu Noronha, which did not bode well at all, with horrible repercussions. There were even some girls who fainted. One of the girl's father was at school today and threatened to take his daughter out of our school. *(Changing his tone, clearing his throat.)* Seu Noronha, there was a female cat at our school. In fact, this cat wasn't even ours. She belonged to our neighbours. *(In a sudden heatwave.)* A very pretty kitty, very pretty.

SEU NORONHA: *(Impatient.)* Yeah right, go on!

DR. PORTELA: *(Carrying a certain voluptuousness.)* She had a very soft fur, silky, like an Angora and, you know what: perhaps she was an Angora. On the other hand, I'm not so sure because, as far as I know, Angoras have two kitties in a litter, tops. So she'd come all the away across the fence from our neighbour's – and she was very meek, really mild – all the way down to our patio. *(Lowering his voice, to SEU NORONHA.)* And guess who, amongst our eight hundred students, most took a liking to the pet? *(With a triumphant cruel sense of satisfaction.)* Your daughter!

SEU NORONHA: Silene?

DR. PORTELA: *(Satisfied.)* Precisely. Silene used to put the cat on her lap, gave her milk from a saucer and, once or twice, she even did something forbidden in our school: she slept with the cat! There would've been havoc in her dormitory each morning, once the other girls realised what was going on. We looked the other way; after all, it was just a minor transgression. So then, one day, we noticed the cat was carrying kitties. Are you paying attention, Seu Noronha?

SEU NORONHA: Go on.

DR. PORTELA: *(In a crescendo.)* Then yesterday, during recess and in the presence of all the students – the cat was murdered, beaten to death!

SEU NORONHA: *(Frightened.)* By whom? Who killed the cat?

DR. PORTELA: Beaten to death, Seu Noronha! In front of seven, eight or nine-year old girls! *(With a triumphant challenge.)* What do you say to that, Seu Noronha?

SEU NORONHA: But who killed it?

DR. PORTELA: *(Changing his tone.)* Seu Noronha, have you ever seen a cat give birth?

SEU NORONHA: *(Disconcerted.)* Never.

DR. PORTELA: Actually, that's not the real question here. Have you ever seen a dead cat give birth?

SEU NORONHA: Also no.

DR. PORTELA: *(Triumphant.)* Well, I have, with these very eyes! And that's what happened to that cat. Yes, sir! She was dead and, are you paying attention: the kitties, all bundled up in their dead mother's womb, were born one by one, all before the students and teachers. We tried to hide it from the younger students, but it was impossible. There were too many of them! Just imagine it: a dead mother and this sudden gush of life! Seven little kitties, in total.

SEU NORONHA: All alive?

DR. PORTELA: All full of life!

SEU NORONHA: But who killed the cat, after all?

DR. PORTELA: *(Lowering his voice, sharp.)* Your daughter?!

SEU NORONHA: *(Also lowering his voice, astonished.)* Say again!

DR. PORTELA: Your daughter, Silene!

SEU NORONHA: *(Hoarse with despair.)* My daughter? Are you trying to tell me, doctor, that my daughter...

DR. PORTELA: *(Peremptory and crude.)* Exactly! She has the manners, the emotions, the thoughts of a little girl and, yet, she killed! All that puerility is just a front, Seu Noronha, it's a front!

SEU NORONHA: *(Out of control.)* Do you realise the weight of your words, Dr. Portela?

DR. PORTELA: *(Dismissive and mocking.)* I know quite a bit about psychology!

SEU NORONHA: But you don't know my daughter! If you knew her like I do – because I know my daughter, Dr. Portela, I can read my daughter's soul... If you knew Silene, you'd never say something like that, I bet you!

DR. PORTELA: Your daughter needs serious psychological treatment!

SEU NORONHA: *(Stunned.)* What treatment? She'll miss school! *(Changing his tone.)* What if my daughter didn't do it?

DR. PORTELA: There were witnesses, Seu Noronha, myself included! I was the one who held her back, who dragged her away when she also tried to kill the little kitties! You must take your daughter to a psychiatrist!

SEU NORONHA: *(Astonished.)* Psychiatrist?

DR. PORTELA: *(With satisfaction.)* As soon as possible!

SEU NORONHA: *(Squeezing his head with both hands.)* To take Silene to a doctor for crazy people, what for? When we have a doctor, here in the neighbourhood, he's a GP, but good, very good – called Dr. Bordalo! He even performs childbirths, free of charge!

DR. PORTELA: She needs a psychiatrist, Seu Noronha!

SEU NORONHA: What about school? She can't miss school!

DR. PORTELA: *(With extremely superficial sympathy.)* Seu Noronha, it seems you still haven't really grasped the problem…

SEU NORONHA: What do you mean?

DR. PORTELA: *(Unyielding.)* Your daughter's not to return to our school!

SEU NORONHA: *(Repeating, in shock.)* Not to return… *(Slow.)* You're telling me my daughter's been expelled?

DR. PORTELA: You make of it what you will.

SEU NORONHA: *(Desperate.)* All because of a stupid pregnant cat? *(Furious.)* Answer me, Dr. Portela! Because of a stupid pregnant cat?!

DR. PORTELA: You're missing the point, Seu Noronha!

SEU NORONHA: I'm going to the papers! I'll destroy your school's reputation!

DR. PORTELA: I have to disagree with you there, Seu Noronha! You say, a stupid pregnant cat, right. Then what's next? *(Firm.)* Listens carefully, Seu Noronha: picture a woman. I do understand abortion, I understand it's a woman's right, or even a woman's duty to have an abortion. I see the logic behind a single mother wanting

420

to get rid of an unwanted child. There's the obvious moral obligation for her to go to her GP and say: "How do I go at it, doctor"? It's still cruel, I do agree. *(Acting more and more frantic.)* You must understand: There are a set of social conventions, scruples, morals one must navigate... *(Shouts.)* However, a cat, a pet, a creature that acts on instinct, pure instinct, who doesn't know right from wrong, a cat must not be murdered! It's monstrous. I apologise but, it's beyond vile!

SEU NORONHA: *(Imploring.)* But there must be a solution for all this!

DR. PORTELA: Take her to a psychiatrist! Let's not waste any more time. Take her to a psychiatrist!

SEU NORONHA: *(Humble.)* If we did that, would the school take my daughter back?

DR. PORTELA: Look, Seu Noronha: an educational centre has certain responsibilities, real ones. What would the other parents say? Your daughter's rage is an illness. She can't be left alone with the other girls. My most sincere apologies, but your daughter cannot go back.

SEU NORONHA: *(In a controlled fury.)* Is this your final word?

DR. PORTELA: Yes. There was a meeting at school and the decision was unanimous. On that note, Seu Noronha, I should be going.

SEU NORONHA: *(In full wrath.)* Wait a second!

DR. PORTELA: *(Looking at his watch.)* I'm sorry, I have an appointment.

SEU NORONHA: *(Threatening.)* Oh, but you'll wait, right here! My daughter came home calling you a liar. *(Panting.)* We have to get to the bottom of this.

DR. PORTELA: Do you think I am lying?

SEU NORONHA: I'll believe you, once my daughter confesses… *(Shouting.)* Gorda! Gorda!

DONA ARACY: Did you call for me?

SEU NORONHA: Bring Silene and the others. All of them, bring in all of them! *(To DR. PORTELA, as DONA ARACY exits to bid his orders.)* Let's see who's the liar! *(To his daughters, entering the room.)* Come and hear what Dr. Portela has told me!

DONA ARACY: What did he say?

SEU NORONHA: *(To the older daughters.)* Lock the doors! All the doors!

DR. PORTELA: *(Looking around, scared.)* What's going on here?

AURORA: Father, calm down, please!

SEU NORONHA: Lock everything!

DR. PORTELA: But this is violent, an assault on my rights!

SEU NORONHA: *(Shouting.)* A cat was killed at the school and they're accusing Silene!

DR. PORTELA: This is what happened! These are the facts!

SEU NORONHA: And, to top it all off, they are expelling Silene!

DONA ARACY: You mad, mad man!

DR. PORTELA: *(Out of control.)* But, Dona Aracy, I saw it, eight hundred children saw it!

SEU NORONHA: Yes, the whole world saw it but us, yet here, we only believe Silene. *(To his wife and daughters.)* Isn't that so, Gorda?

DONA ARACY: Obviously!

SEU NORONHA: Come here, baby girl. Look him in the eye. Tell him, go on: was it you?

SILENE: *(Savage.)* Liar!

DR. PORTELA: There were witnesses! Witnesses! *(To SILENE.)* Silene, wasn't it you, Silene? Can you swear it wasn't you?

SILENE: *(Brutal.)* I swear!

ARLETE: What a horrible man!

SEU NORONHA: *(Triumphant.)* Enough, girls! *(To DR. PORTELA, in his face, making him retreat.)* You've lied, Dr. Portela... You're a liar...

DR. PORTELA: I have not lied, I swear!

ARLETE: Let's take him down!

DR. PORTELA finds himself surrounded by the girls. ARLETE picks up a small statue.

SEU NORONHA: *(To his daughters.)* Back off, all of you! *(Takes out the silver dagger and exposes it to the guest.)* Do you see this? This silver dagger? If you say another word, I'll stab you right in the stomach, you scum!

SEU NORONHA touches DR. PORTELA's stomach with the tip of his dagger.

DR. PORTELA: *(Almost voiceless.)* For the love of God!

SEU NORONHA: If you talked about any of my other daughters, any of them, I wouldn't say a thing. Right now, if you were to call, or actually called any of these *(Points at the older daughters.)* or even Gorda bad names; called them sluts. I'd wash my hands of it... But you've insulted the only one that cannot be tarnished... You can't even begin to understand how pure my daughter is. Or do you think my daughter's like your wife? *(Grinding his teeth.)* Don't you move or I'll stab you right here! *(Changing his tone.)* Your wife wears those tight dresses. You can even see the outline of her underwear. *(Proud, pointing at SILENE.)* Not my daughter! She barely has any hips, or breasts; her breasts are only now starting to bloom, just now! For us, Silene is pure, or can't you see she's still pure just for us? *(At the top of his voice.)* Speak!

DR. PORTELA: *(With a strangled voice.)* Forgive me!

ARLETE: He's a coward!

SEU NORONHA: Maybe you humiliated my daughter because you found out I'm just an assistant clerk? *(With sobbing laughter.)* When I enrolled Silene at your school, I introduced myself as an employee of the Council at the Parliament, but I am just an assistant clerk! *(Lower voice, in his face.)* Now, call me a stupid clerk, go on, call me a stupid clerk!

DR. PORTELA: Why?

SEU NORONHA: Because I want you to!

DR. PORTELA: Stupid clerk.

SEU NORONHA: Stupid clerk... Now, cry!

DR. PORTELA: But why?

SEU NORONHA: *(At the top of his voice.)* Cry!

DR. PORTELA: *(Gasping for air.)* I can't!

Nonetheless, DR. PORTELA cries. The tears flow copiously.

SEU NORONHA: *(Frustrated.)* You don't cry the cry I'm looking for. *(Changing his tone, to SILENE.)* Come here, baby girl!

SILENE: *(Moaning.)* I'm tired!

SEU NORONHA: *(In his wrath.)* Slap him right across his face!

SILENE: *(Stepping back, scared.)* But why, father?

SEU NORONHA: This bastard insulted you, humiliated you! Slap him! *(To DR. PORTELA.)* You'll take it and won't say a word, or else!

AURORA: *(To SILENE, opening her hand.)* Hit him with your palm wide open, like this!

SILENE: *(Stepping back, terrified.)* I can't.

SEU NORONHA: Silene, I'm the one telling you to do it, baby girl!

Suddenly, SILENE freezes. She looks at her parents and sisters, in an outburst.

SILENE: *(Brutal.)* Do you want to know the truth? *(Grinding her teeth, as if hallucinating.)* I did it, so there!

SEU NORONHA: *(In the midst of his pain and suffering.)* You, baby girl?

SILENE: *(As if holding a long stick, about to strike it down.)* I killed it like this!

DR. PORTELA: *(To everybody.)* I witnessed it. She beat the poor cat's head to shreds!

SEU NORONHA lets the dagger drop on the floor. He walks toward SILENE, stumbling.

SEU NORONHA: But why, baby girl, why?

SILENE: *(Closing her eyes, hands pressed together in her chest, as if praying.)* I don't know.

SEU NORONHA grabs SILENE by the arms. He cries.

425

SEU NORONHA: Tell me. Why?

SILENE: *(In her trance.)* Repulsion!

SEU NORONHA: Why repulsion?

SILENE: *(With an evil ritual.)* Loathing!

AURORA: *(Astonished.)* But why, loathing a pet that'd never hurt you? A pet, Maninha?

SILENE: *(Exploding.)* Repulsive cat!

SILENE wipes her mouth with her hand, almost squeezing it with pure disgust.

DR. PORTELA: *(Now back to normal and satisfied.)* You see? *(Triumphant.)* It's a mental health issue, clear as day!

DR. PORTELA picks up his hat and walking stick.

DR. PORTELA: *(Superior.)* And one more thing, Seu Noronha. In fact, when you, sir, enrolled your daughter at our school, you told me you were not only an employee at Parliament, but a head of department, if I remember it well. But I was there last week and you can't believe how surprised I was to see you, in a clerk's uniform, serving coffee to the members of Parliament! You didn't see me and I found it quite funny, actually. Who would've thought, a stupid clerk, Seu Noronha? Well, I believe you now owe me an apology…

ARLETE: *(Interfering.)* Apologise? How dare you!? *(Manly, to DR. PORTELA.)* Listen: who are you calling a stupid clerk, you little shit? *(Poking his chest. DR. PORTELA steps back.)* And what about your wife? With those tight dresses, showing off her big arse? You scum!

DR. PORTELA: I didn't mean anything by it! *(Stuttering.)* Well, I'll be going. Good night.

DR. PORTELA exits. SEU NORONHA holds SILENE tightly against his chest.

SEU NORONHA: *(Kissing her forehead.)* No school will ever be good enough for you! They all envy you, how pure you are! The human race is a disgrace! Girls aren't girls anymore, they're little females in heat, nothing else. Only you are my baby girl, only you! *(Sobs.)*

END OF SCENE 1

SCENE 2

SILENE's bedroom. She was lying on her bed, but quickly gets up. DR. BORDALO, the family doctor, having just examined the girl, finds it odd to see the girl is now crying.

DR. BORDALO: *(With happy tenderness.)* Why are you crying?

SILENE: *(Sniffling.)* It's embarrassing.

DR. BORDALO: *(With amused surprise.)* In front of me? Do I embarrass you? How silly! My dear, I was there when you were born, I delivered all your sisters, all of them and, to me, you'll always be babies.

SILENE: I know, doctor, but...

DR. BORDALO: Look at me!

DR. BORDALO holds SILENE's chin.

DR. BORDALO: You are no longer embarrassed, right?

SILENE: *(Enthralled.)* Right.

DR. BORDALO: See?

SILENE: So doctor, what's wrong with me?

DR. BORDALO: With you? Nothing really. Now, be a good girl and go fetch me your father.

SILENE walks toward the door, but the doctor stops her.

DR. BORDALO: *(Amused.)* My dear, you'd better put on your knickers!

SILENE: *(Freezes.)* How silly of me!

Behind DR. BORDALO, SILENE puts on an imaginary piece of underwear.

SILENE: Knickered up, doctor!

DR. BORDALO: Now, you can go.

SILENE exits. SEU NORONHA and DONA ARACY enter, right after.

SEU NORONHA: *(Eager.)* What about Silene, doctor?

DR. BORDALO: *(To DONA ARACY.)* If you could leave us alone, Dona Aracy. I want to speak to your husband first. I'll call you straight away.

SEU NORONHA: Go on, Gorda. Leave.

DONA ARACY exits.

SEU NORONHA: *(Eager.)* Is everything okay, Doctor?

DR. BORDALO: Close the door.

SEU NORONHA obeys. DR. BORDALO, still standing up, points him towards the bed.

DR. BORDALO: Have a seat.

SEU NORONHA: *(Trembling.)* It's not leukaemia, is it?

DR. BORDALO: *(Surprised and amused.)* Why leukaemia?

SEU NORONHA: Just a guess, Doctor, a dream I had!

DR. BORDALO: Knock on wood. Nothing like that, not at all.

SEU NORONHA: *(Euphoric, rubs his hands together.)* Thank God! What a relief, Doctor! *(Changing his tone.)* But the worms she's had for a while now, they also concern me...

DR. BORDALO: *(Not pay attention to him.)* Noronha, I know you really love Silene.

SEU NORONHA: Silene's everything to me!

DR. BORDALO: And, you're obviously an understanding father!

SEU NORONHA: *(With trembling tenderness.)* Silene walks all over me!

Unwavering, DR. BORDALO sits next to SEU NORONHA in bed.

DR. BORDALO: Noronha, let's talk, the two of us, man to man!

SEU NORONHA: Doctor, are you hiding something from me?

DR. BORDALO: Here it is: I tried to get Silene to spill the beans, but she denies it.

SEU NORONHA: Denies what?

DR. BORDALO: She denies it but I don't blame her. It's in a woman's nature to say no at first. But, after all, does Silene have a boyfriend or not?

SEU NORONHA: Of course not!

DR. BORDALO: Never had one?

SEU NORONHA: Never! I can assure you of that, cross my heart!

DR. BORDALO: But Silene has a boyfriend now. That's for sure!

SEU NORONHA: *(Astonished.)* A boyfriend?

DR. BORDALO: Oh, yes, she does!

SEU NORONHA: Impossible! She can't have a boyfriend, doctor. A girl who lives in a boarding school, never out by herself! Well that's not really true: She's left school once a month. That's all. She'd spend a day at home and return the following day. Here and back, always with a chaperone. How can she have a boyfriend?

DR. BORDALO: *(Getting up and placing a hand on SEU NORONHA's shoulder.)* So, who's the father?

SEU NORONHA: *(In a painful disbelief.)* The father?

DR. BORDALO: Come on, Noronha. Let's set the record straight, now. When I examined Silene, I thought; after all you've called me… But you don't know, you don't suspect a thing, do you?

SEU NORONHA: *(Astonished.)* Carry on.

DR. BORDALO: *(Slowly, and sorry for him.)* Your daughter's almost entering her second trimester. *(An astonishing pause.)*

SEU NORONHA: You mean to say that Silene.

DR. BORDALO: *(Slowly.)* Is pregnant.

SEU NORONHA grabs hold of DR. BORDALO's arms, in a desperate appeal.

SEU NORONHA: That can't be true! *(Panting.)* She doesn't have the hips; she's too narrow! Tell me, doctor, tell me it's not true!

DR. BORDALO: First of all, you are all looking at Silene with love goggles. Her dimensions are perfectly normal. As far as for the pregnancy, that's no lie. It's a sure thing.

I examined her myself. Sure thing. Now, find the man who's responsible and get him to marry her.

SEU NORONHA: You're telling me Silene isn't a virgin? No longer a virgin?

DR. BORDALO: Noronha, don't get all worked up. You're making a mountain out of a molehill. *(Caring and persuasive.)* Nowadays, virginity isn't important anymore. And, after all, a woman's honour doesn't lie in a membrane. Virginity is just a thin membrane.

SEU NORONHA: *(Outraged.)* You have a daughter, Dr. Bordalo. Same age as mine. Single. I want to know if your daughter's virginity is also just a thin membrane?

DR. BORDALO: Let's be practical. You must find the father.

SEU NORONHA: *(With a strangled voice.)* Doctor, you know nothing of purity, of innocence... Have you ever been to a church and seen the virgin in a stained glass panel? Listen: in the afternoon, the sunshine hits the church... And the light shines through the virgin... *(Points at the ceiling, as if pointing at an invisible sun.)* This is Silene for us – a virgin who allows the light to shine through her... *(With tearful expression.)* And, by adoring my daughter as much as I do, I became aware that she's the most pure girl amongst all the girls in the world, she's the only true virgin... But, now you tell me she is pregnant...

DR. BORDALO: Unfortunately, she is.

SEU NORONHA: *(In a sob.)* The shameless whore!

SEU NORONHA stumbles towards the door. DR. BORDALO holds him by the arm. SEU NORONHA turns around, bewildered.

DR. BORDALO: *(With strength.)* Come back here!

SEU NORONHA: *(Hoarse.)* What?

DR. BORDALO: *(Always strong.)* You won't do anything stupid. Remember, a father's duty is to protect and forgive, no matter what.

SEU NORONHA: *(Sarcastic.)* Thank you for the preaching.

DR. BORDALO: I'm not preaching. You have to find the father. Make her give you a name. In fact, I'll talk to the boy. Do you want me to fetch Silene? Don't you think it's better for us to talk here? I do. Should I call her?

SEU NORONHA: Call her. Better yet, not here – in the living room. It has to be in front of the whole family. *(Stumbling.)* Come on, Doctor, come with me.

DR. BORDALO accompanies SEU NORONHA, who's in frenzy. They meet the family in the living room.

SEU NORONHA: *(With DR. BORDALO.)* Gorda, come here!

DR. BORDALO: Calm down, Noronha, take it easy!

DONA ARACY: It's nothing serious, is it?

SEU NORONHA: *(To the older daughters.)* You, too... *(Face distorted by anger, pointing at SILENE; she's a few feet away from him, and immediately hugs AURORA.)* Do you all want to know why she killed the pregnant cat? Do you?

DR. BORDALO: *(Lower voice, reproaching him.)* No need to humiliate her!

SEU NORONHA: *(Loud, with sobbing laughter.)* She's also pregnant!

AURORA: *(Grabbing SILENE by the arms.)* Maninha!

ARLETE: *(To SILENE.)* Who was it?

HILDA: *(In a sob.)* Our Maninha has been tarnished!

Despair. Madness. It's almost like someone has just died. SILENE steps back, both hands covering her stomach, in an aggressive panic.

SILENE: It's all a lie!

DR. BORDALO: *(To each one in the room.)* Calm down! Calm down! Let's put our heads together here! Noronha is now going to talk to Silene, and Silene will tell him who it was or who it wasn't. I've even offered to talk to the boy. I'll talk to the boy, and that'll be it!

SEU NORONHA: *(Shouting.)* Everybody, shut up! *(Lower voice, panting, to SILENE.)* Come here. Tell me – who's your boyfriend?

SILENE: *(Holding back.)* I don't have a boyfriend.

SEU NORONHA: A lover, then?

SILENE: *(Gasping.)* No.

SEU NORONHA: *(In a tamed wrath.)* Who's the father of your child?

SILENE: No one.

SEU NORONHA: *(With a dark sense of humor.)* So, you're still a virgin?

SILENE: *(Sobbing.)* I am, father!

SEU NORONHA: *(To DR. BORDALO.)* See how she lies, doctor? *(Brutal, to SILENE, with heinous humor.)* Since you're not pregnant, I can kick you in the stomach!

SILENE: No one's going to harm my baby!

SEU NORONHA: *(With a sordid chuckle.)* So, you are carrying… *(Furious.)* Where did you get this baby? Was it at school? Tell me! During class? On the school bus?

DR. BORDALO pushes SEU NORONHA away, grabbing SILENE by the arms.

DR. BORDALO: Talk to me, Silene! We just want to know who he is, then we can talk to the boy and he can marry you!

SILENE: He's married! *(Brutal.)* He's married, he lives with his wife, he loves his wife; *(Sobbing.)* now, for God's sake, leave me alone!

DONA ARACY: *(Sobbing.)* They're all rubbish! They're all worthless!

DÉBORA: *(Full of wrath, amidst her tears.) (To SILENE.)* For your information: because of you, I had to fix women with creepy old men, and gave all the money to Mum for your trousseau!

ARLETE: Enough talking! *(To DONA ARACY.)* Mother, you'll give us back this money for Maninha, and we'll share between ourselves; each of us will keep their part!

HILDA: I want my part right now, so I can finally leave this house!

SEU NORONHA: And go where?

HILDA: To Santos!

SEU NORONHA: What the hell is in Santos?

HILDA: That's none of your business, father! *(Changing her tone.)* Oh, you know what, fuck it! I'm going to Santos because a friend of mine made in a month, just in a single month, one hundred and seventy grand. But now that I know Maninha is just like us, or maybe even worse...

SEU NORONHA: *(Shouting.)* She's worse!

ARLETE: That's right. I'm not staying here anymore! I'm not staying here a minute more!

SEU NORONHA: *(In another sudden shout.)* Wait! I've just had another idea! Nobody has to go anywhere! You too, Dr. Bordalo, come closer!

DR. BORDALO: But there's no reason for all this! No reason at all!

SEU NORONHA: *(Frantic.)* Listen to my idea. *(Lowering his voice, insidious, ignoble.)* I'm not going back to work, not now, not ever; and do you know why? Why should I? I'm staying home because instead earning what you've earned out there, you'll earn it all here, right here!

DR. BORDALO: *(To all of them.)* This man is mad!

SEU NORONHA: *(Brutally confrontational.)* Why mad? Go ahead, tell me!

DR. BORDALO: You're proposing to open a brothel using your own daughters!

SEU NORONHA, out of control, grabs DR. BORDALO by the arms, with desperate energy.

SEU NORONHA: Why the hell not? Look: I won't be serving coffee or water any longer to those members of Parliament! *(To his daughters.)* You can quit your jobs, too. *(To DR. BORDALO, with a sordid chuckle.)* My daughters' jobs are a mere front! *(Stopping his chuckle.)* I just had another idea *(Face to face with the doctor.)*: do you want in? Do you want to be our first?

DR. BORDALO: *(Stepping back.)* What are you insinuating, exactly?

SEU NORONHA: I know you like to play saint: you deliver those nigger's babies for free, you don't charge for your consultations, but I insist *(Points to his daughters.)* choose: any of them, the choice is yours!

435

SEU NORONHA grabs his youngest daughter, SILENE.

AURORA: *(Screaming.)* No, father!

SEU NORONHA throws SILENE on the floor, by DR. BORDALO's feet.

SILENE: *(Pleading, both hands cover her belly.)* I don't want to!

DR. BORDALO: *(Helping her up.)* Stand up!

SEU NORONHA: *(Possessed, to SILENE.)* Either you go with him, or I'll stomp this baby out of you! *(To the others.)* Since she already gave herself to one, she can give it to anyone!

AURORA: *(Hysterically.)* I'll go in Maninha's place!

SEU NORONHA: I want Silene to do it!

DR. BORDALO: *(Losing his mind, to all the others.)* What about the rest of you? Won't you say anything? No reaction? Nothing? Not even you, her mother? *(Shouting.)* Why don't you all just run? Run away! Leave this house! *(Pointing at SEU NORONHA.)* That man is mad! *(To the older daughters.)* You can all come to my house! You can stay there until…

SEU NORONHA: *(Triumphant.)* See? *(Pointing to AURORA.)* Only this stupid one tried to protest. The others just watch and say nothing… The door's wide open and they choose to stay!

DR. BORDALO: *(Furious.)* You all must have souls and… *(Freezes, realising.)* Do you even have souls? *(As if thinking out loud.)* But if you don't run, it's because you're all slaves, slaves to one another…

SEU NORONHA: *(Elated.)* They'll never be free of me and I'll never be free of them! *(To SILENE.)* Are you going with the good doctor or not?

AURORA: *(Sobbing.)* No, not Maninha, father!

SILENE: *(To AURORA.)* Thank you, Aurora… *(In a trance, to her father.)* I'll go.

SEU NORONHA: *(To SILENE.)* Go ahead and wait in the bedroom!

SILENE looks at their faces, they're all in shock. She walks towards her bedroom, slowly.

SEU NORONHA: *(With a heinous laugh.) (To DONA ARACY.)* Gorda, we're slaves; you're my slave and I'm yours, according to the doctor, am I right? *(To DR. BORDALO, changing his tone.)* My daughter's waiting for you, Doctor; in there!

DR. BORDALO: *(Almost crying.)* I have no idea why I shouldn't just shoot you, you bastard!

SEU NORONHA: *(In a false and mocking astonishment.)* A bastard, who, me? *(Incisive.)* Not only me! We're all bastards in here! *(Laughing heavily.)* You're also a bastard, doctor! You as well! *(Serious and violent again.)* Do you know why this family hasn't just gone rotten out in the street yet? *(With a sob.)* Because there was a virgin amongst us! You don't understand, no one understands it but Silene made a virgin of us all, an angel of us all, and a good girl of all of them! *(Brutal.)* But since now Silene is in that bedroom, waiting on you – *(Desperate laughter.)* we can finally start to truly rot and stink… Do you want to see something? I'll show you. *(To the women.)* Who wrote dirty words in the bathroom? *(Triumphant.)* You can confess now, we've already began to rot. *(To the doctor.)* Pay attention, doctor! *(To the women.)* Who was it?

DONA ARACY: I did it.

SEU NORONHA: *(Radiant.)* Gorda!

DONA ARACY: *(Almost crying.)* I did.

SEU NORONHA: *(Euphoric, to the DOCTOR.)* She's got varicose veins and a sour sweat! *(To his wife.)* But, why Gorda? Why did you draw all that filth on the bathroom walls?

DONA ARACY: *(Confused and crying.)* I don't know…Maybe because I almost never go to the movies or to the theatre; I'm so alone! And also because *(More aggressive.)* I don't have a husband! *(To SEU NORONHA.)* How long has it been since you made me feel like a woman? *(To the DOCTOR.)* I don't even remember anymore! *(With a kind of dignity.)* So, I'd go to the bathroom, draw all that filth and wipe it off afterwards. Yesterday, I just forgot to wipe it and…

SEU NORONHA: *(To his daughters.)* What about you all? Speak! *(To HILDA.)* You!

HILDA: *(Exalted.)* I saw Arlete kissing a woman on the lips!

ARLETE: *(Violent.)* Yes, I kissed a woman!

HILDA: Shameless!

ARLETE: *(In a sudden wrath.)* Men disgust me! The most repulsive thing I can think of is men's dirty underwear!

SEU NORONHA: *(To AURORA.)* Don't you have anything to say?

AURORA: I'll stay by Maninha's side until I die.

SEU NORONHA: *(Grabbing hold of the DOCTOR.)* See, Doctor? You don't have any reason to be ashamed here, none at all! Ashamed? Ashamed of what, why and of whom?

DR. BORDALO: *(Grinding his teeth.)* What the hell am I still doing here?

SEU NORONHA: I offer you a girl who's the closest thing to a virgin and you refuse her? Wow!

DR. BORDALO: *(Towards the bedroom, with mortal anguish and somewhat delirious.)* Silene... I have a daughter your age... and, if I ever touched you, *(Caressing the air.)* I'd never be able to kiss my daughter again, never again... You're so beautiful *(Shouting.)* Silene! Silene! Your name's a dahlia!

SEU SAUL just appears at the front door. He stops himself, in silence.

SEU NORONHA: *(Furious.)* Do you want her or not?

DR. BORDALO: *(Once again, shouting.)* I don't want her!

SEU SAUL: *(Entering.)* I want!

SEU NORONHA: Come on in, Seu Saul, come in! So, then, do you want her?

SEU SAUL: I hear everything from open door... I know everything... I want her!

SEU NORONHA: *(Panting.)* That's the room over there, Seu Saul! Right over there!

SEU SAUL: Excuse me!

SEU SAUL walks towards the bedroom. Everyone follows him with their eyes. He goes in and closes the door.

SILENE: *(In panic.)* No! Not you, Seu Saul! I'm here for the doctor!

SEU SAUL: Oh, no be afraid... I am not abuse you... Just calm, calm for Saul...

SILENE: *(Crying.)* Just don't hurt my baby!

SEU SAUL: I have wound from war, from First World War...

SILENE: You do?

SEU SAUL: A grenade explode next to me, in Germany, and a piece of shrapnel kill my wish to... I'm good man, I no want sex... all I want is hold your little hand, like this.

SILENE: Thank you, so much...

SEU SAUL: After, we leave room and fool the father. Oh, we are lucky no one knows of war wound!

Outside, DR. BORDALO, who was pacing back and forth, as if possessed by something, stops.

DR. BORDALO: *(Furious.)* I'm next!

SEU NORONHA: Changed your mind!

DR. BORDALO: *(Not paying attention to him.)* What I really feel like doing is throwing that dirty old man out of there! *(Somewhat delirious.)* Silene, oh, Silene! *(Whispering.)* She's my daughter's age!

SEU SAUL leaves the bedroom, speaking to SILENE, who's still inside.

SEU SAUL: Bye-bye.

DR. BORDALO: Now, it's my turn... But before I go in; I want one of you... *(Chooses AURORA.)* You, Aurora, for the love of God, Aurora! *(Stretching his hands, clenching his fingers, towards AURORA.)* Before I go, I want you to spit on my face!

AURORA moves away from her sisters. She approaches the doctor slowly, dignified and noble. SEU SAUL is also standing there, still. AURORA spits on DR. BORDALO's face.

DR. BORDALO: Thank you, oh, thank you! *(Letting out a heinous shout.)* Silene! Silene!

DR. BORDALO stumbles towards her bedroom.

SEU NORONHA: Go, you bastard! *(Changing his tone, picking up his dagger.)* This dagger is still longing for that single tear!

END OF ACT 2

Act 3

The third act begins with a seance at SEU NORONHA's house. Those present are: SEU NORONHA – the old man, DONA ARACY, all of their daughters except for SILENE, who's in her bedroom. HILDA is the psychic. She's just been channeling their recently deceased cousin, Alípio. HILDA walks around the stage with wide and manly steps; she pants and snorts; she lets out heinous shouts; all in a masculine voice.

DONA ARACY: Ask her if and when this man is coming here.

SEU NORONHA: *(Lowering his voice, to his wife.)* Did she have to be possessed by cousin Alípio. The man couldn't stand me… *(Changing his tone, humble.)* Brother of light, is he on his way here?

HILDA performs tremendously complex caprioles.

HILDA: You shameless old rag! You want to kill a man!

ARLETE: Cousin Alípio couldn't care less about us!

SEU NORONHA: *(To ARLETE.)* Stay out of it!

Once in a while, as HILDA is being possessed by a primal spirit, she has to be subdued.

DONA ARACY: *(After an especially complex capriole.)* Hold her down! Hold her down!

HILDA, subdued, flounces out in vain.

HILDA: *(With her masculine voice, panting.)* You dirty old killer!

SEU NORONHA: *(Humble.)* Brother of light, this man has soiled my reputation! He dishonoured my daughters!

HILDA: Your daughters are shameless whores! They get on with all kinds of men!

SEU NORONHA: *(Eager.)* But this man cries from only one eye!

HILDA: You are tainted!

SEU NORONHA: Does this man shed a single tear?

HILDA: Watch it or you'll be the one to be killed!

SEU NORONHA: How will I know it's him? Or who he is? Is he Jewish? What is he like?

HILDA: The man cries, when he cums; he dies, when he cries!

SEU NORONHA: *(Repeating, in angst.)* He cries when he cums, he dies when he cries… *(In a plea.)* But is he coming here? When?

HILDA: The man dressed as a virgin!

SEU NORONHA: Dressed as a virgin!

HILDA: Bury him in the garden, the man and his tear! You should all help carry the body… *(To SEU NORONHA.)* And you, you bury the knife in his heart!

SEU NORONHA: But I wanted to stab the man in the eye with the single tear.

HILDA: Let the man sleep and bury the knife in his heart!

SEU NORONHA is slowly taking out the silver dagger. HILDA snaps out of her trance state with tremendous spasms.

AURORA: Was that it?

SEU NORONHA: What did I tell you? Sure thing!

AURORA: There are some things I just can't accept!

SEU NORONHA: Are you still questioning me?

AURORA: Father, cousin Alípio is the same spirit who, just the other day, tried to pass that lie as gospel!

SEU NORONHA: How stupid are you!? *(Addressing the others, all of them.)* You all saw! *(Grabs his wife.)* You were a witness, Gorda!

DONA ARACY: I didn't really quite get it!

SEU NORONHA: *(Shaking her into sense.)* Listen: Dr. Barbosa Coutinho had already warned me and cousin Alípio has only confirmed the whole thing – the man who only cries from one eye destroyed my family! Now, do you still question me?

AURORA: Father, you don't even know what I was going to say!

DONA ARACY: Let Aurora speak!

AURORA: *(In a sulky sigh.)* Pff, hilarious!

ARLETE: Say it, Aurora!

AURORA: *(Vehement.)* Father, can you let me give you my honest opinion? My take on this?

SEU NORONHA: Here we go again!

AURORA: Ha, hilarious! We can talk about all the men in the world here, all except for one!

SEU NORONHA: *(Sarcastic.)* Who?

AURORA: Come on!

SEU NORONHA: Spill!

AURORA: *(Sharp and violent.)* The bloody son of a gun who did what he did to Maninha…

SEU NORONHA: So what?

AURORA: So, he's the worst of them all! *(To the others.)* I know, the exact same thing has happened to each one of us. But we're whores, we've always been whores, it's in our blood. I remember when I started, for example, I did – when I was eight, but that's not the point I'm trying to make... This could never have happened to Maninha, never! *(Covers her face with one hand and sobs.)* It's like I said, when push comes to shove, it's not that beast we hate. If I, even just a woman like me, ah, if I got my hands on that one! *(To SEU NORONHA, violent.)* You're wrong, father!

SEU NORONHA: Are you trying to teach me the ropes? Me?

AURORA: *(To the others.)* Don't you all agree with me?

ARLETE: Kind of.

AURORA: *(Violent.)* Do you or don't you!?

DÉBORA: I do.

SEU NORONHA: *(Somewhat puzzled.)* Carry on.

AURORA: That fella should be shot in the mouth!

SEU NORONHA: *(With sobbing laughter.)* A shot? Why? *(Stops laughing.)* No shots, you stupid bitch! *(Showing her the dagger.)* This is much better: it doesn't make any noise, it goes in smoothly, so smoothly you can hardly feel it...

AURORA: Look, if Father doesn't want to, if you're scared, I'll finish him off for you!

SEU NORONHA: *(Sarcastic.)* I'm looking for the single tear, the tear is all I care about... But, what would you do to him? Tell me.

AURORA: I'd kill him, that's all! Kill him!

SEU NORONHA: *(Crushingly spiteful.)* You?

AURORA: Or someone would do it for me.

SEU NORONHA: *(Alarmed.)* Who?

AURORA: *(Hesitant and slow.)* A boy I met.

SEU NORONHA: *(Still alarmed.)* Tell me: can you trust him?

AURORA: Of course! He's my boyfriend. He has killed before and if I were to ask him; all I have to do is ask, I'm sure, well, almost sure, that...

ARLETE: Do you want to know my take on it?

AURORA: Sure.

ARLETE: Don't bring more people into this. Strangers.

DONA ARACY: I agree with Arlete.

AURORA: *(Determined.)* Mother, I'd walk through fire for him.

SEU NORONHA: What's his name?

AURORA: *(Hesitating.)* His name?... Bibelot.

DONA ARACY: What kind of name is Bibelot?

AURORA: It's a nickname.

SEU NORONHA paces back and forth.

SEU NORONHA: *(To himself.)* Bibelot... I was starting to forget to hate the man who tainted Silene... *(Grabbing AURORA by the arm.)* Can I meet this Bibelot?

AURORA: He's on his way here.

SEU NORONHA: When?

AURORA: He's supposed to stop by today. We're going to the cinema.

DONA ARACY: What if he's arrested and spills the beans about us?

AURORA: He likes me, mother!

SEU NORONHA: *(To DONA ARACY.)* Stay out of it, Gorda! You're always meddling, when it's none of your business! *(To AURORA.)* I need to see the fella, look at him; I need to go with my gut!

DÉBORA: Well, look who's here!

SEU SAUL has just popped up at the door, panting and wiping up his sweaty forehead.

SEU SAUL: You hear news?

SEU NORONHA: What news?

SEU SAUL: Oh, you not know man hung himself with electric iron cord?

DÉBORA: Spill it!

SEU SAUL: *(Filling the stage with his voice.)* Dr. Bordalo!

ARLETE: He killed himself?

SEU SAUL: *(In a solemn voice, heavy and prophetic.)* Dr. Bordalo now hang from the top of door, with black tongue, cheeks like that, like a carnival mask!

AURORA lunges, enraged, on top of SEU SAUL.

AURORA: *(Hoarse with rage.)* Liar!

SEU SAUL: *(Still rotund.)* I swear!

AURORA: *(Flipping back in a sob.)* You're a bald faced liar!

DONA ARACY: *(Crying.)* He killed himself for no reason!

SEU SAUL: *(Emphatic.)* Dr. Bordalo have reason! Very good reason!

SEU NORONHA: *(Threatening.)* Then you tell us the reason!

SEU SAUL: I know, and you all know reason too!

SEU NORONHA: Are you trying my patience, gringo?

SEU SAUL: *(Opens his arms.)* Dr. Bordalo leave note, short note, which I read: "I don't want my daughter to kiss me in my coffin!"

SEU NORONHA: *(In his stifled desperation.)* He doesn't want his daughter to kiss him but he can kiss mine, the hypocrite!

HILDA: *(Sobbing.)* Don't speak ill of the dead, Father!

SEU NORONHA: *(To SEU SAUL.)* How about you, gringo? Why don't you kill yourself, too?

SEU SAUL: *(Puffing out his chest, triumphantly.)* I have wound from war, the Kaiser Wilhelm war, from First World War!

SEU NORONHA: Make yourself scarce!

SEU SAUL: *(Stepping back, still facing the family.)* Your daughters will destroy you!

SEU NORONHA: *(Shouting.)* This is my country and I'm not a stupid clerk anymore! Fuck off back to your country! I'm not a stupid clerk!

SEU SAUL freezes at the door.

SEU SAUL: *(Going out of sight.)* Your daughters will destroy you!

SEU NORONHA: *(Addressing his daughters, who are crying.)* What are you crying for? For whom?

HILDA: *(Crying.)* He was a saint!

SEU NORONHA: *(In a brutal fit of laughter.)* Him, a saint? *(Lowers his voice, triumphant, in HILDA's face.)* A saint just because he'd help those niggers who have all those babies, free of charge! *(Grabs HILDA, with the assurance of zealous*

447

fanatic.) It was all a disguise! *(To all of them.)* A saint who had his way with my daughter, almost in front of my very eyes.

HILDA: You told him to!

SEU NORONHA: *(Huffing, puffing and panting as trying to speak.)* I told him to and he didn't hesitate to have his way with her. And called her a dahlia. And she didn't even cry, if she had at least cried for help, but she didn't! Now, the cheap bastard refuses his daughter's kiss!

SEU NORONHA stumbles around, in circles.

SEU NORONHA: This bloody gringo comes into my home and tells me my daughters are going to destroy me! *(To all of them.)* But, when I die, I want each of my daughters to give me a kiss and *(In a sobbing fit of laughter.)* I even want you to give me a kiss, Gorda!

DONA ARACY: *(Crying.)* Hallelujah!

SEU NORONHA: *(Sharp.)* Go fetch me this Bibelot fella!

AURORA: First, Maninha has to tell us who it was. She still hasn't told us!

SEU NORONHA: I'll slap some sense into her and she'll tell me!

AURORA: Calm yourself down, father, calm down! This is what we need to do, listen: I know how to talk to her, let me do it and she'll tell me who it was or who it wasn't! Isn't it better this way?

SEU NORONHA: Get that name out of her!

AURORA: *(Already on her way.)* When I'm through, I'll call you.

AURORA makes her way towards SILENE's bedroom.

SEU NORONHA: *(To the others.)* No one can make me believe Seu Saul isn't the man who cries from only one eye!

SILENE's bedroom. AURORA sits next to her sister in bed.

AURORA: Look at me.

SILENE: *(Already cornered.)* I'm looking.

AURORA: Who is he?

SILENE: He?

AURORA: The one who did this.

SILENE: *(With very obvious dissimulation.)* He is out of town!

AURORA: Where is he?

SILENE: He went on a trip.

AURORA takes SILENE's hands, holding them between her own hands.

AURORA: Listen: do you trust me?

SILENE: *(Always nervous.)* Why?

AURORA: *(Sharper.)* Do you trust me or not?

SILENE: *(In fear.)* I do.

AURORA: Then, tell me everything!

SILENE: It's not like that.

AURORA: *(Furious.)* Than tell me how it is! Why is not like that? Tell me! I want to know! And if I catch you lying to me, I'll wash my hands of you and look at me: after what happened, who is your only friend in this house, the only one who stood up for you? Me, right? The others are up to here with you, if you don't believe me, Father has his belt ready!

SILENE: *(Starts crying.)* I know you like me, I do, I'd never deny that!

AURORA: Then tell me: are you ready to answer all of my questions?

SILENE: I am.

AURORA: Name

SILENE: *(Scared, once again.)* His name?

SILENE gets up and walks away, as if trying to hide.

SILENE: But why do you want to know his name?

AURORA: Are you serious!?

SILENE: *(Pressing and squeezing both hands together.)* If he's been married, can't he marry again? What difference does a name make? *(As if thinking out loud.)* Then I tell you his name, I'm a minor, you'll go to the police and it will be a whole scandal!

AURORA: *(At the brink of losing her patience.)* My gut is telling me to slap your face, hard!

SILENE: *(Also aggressive.)* Why do you all want to know his name?

AURORA: You stupid girl, try to put this through you thick head: you're a minor and he's an adult, that's it!

SILENE: *(Slowly, trying to picture a thousand different scenarios.)* Suppose I tell you his name, what would you all do?

AURORA: *(Chipper.)* It's like this: I had a fling.

SILENE: *(Without understanding.)* What's a fling?

AURORA: Pff, can you be any thicker!? *(Changing her tone.)* It's a kind of boyfriend. I have a boyfriend who won't think

twice about beating or even killing the man. No big deal
for him!

SILENE: *(Gradually realising the gravity of the threat.)* So, you'd
have someone beat up my...

AURORA: *(Violent.)* Beat him up? As if! We'd shoot him in the
eye! Bullet through the skull!

SILENE: *(In her astonishment.)* Kill him?

AURORA: Your fella will eat a bullet and never know what's
hit him!

SILENE: *(In her brutal desperation.)* He's not to blame! It's all
my fault!

AURORA: He took advantage of you, a little girl, a mere child!
He's a dirty bastard!

SILENE: *(Sobbing.)* No! No!

*Out of her mind, SILENE clings on to AURORA and slides down her
sister's body. She's down on her knees, holding on to her sister's legs.*

AURORA: *(Stunned, with an intolerable sense of pity.)* What are
you doing? Maninha, get up!

SILENE stands up. In a sudden burst of energy, she grabs her sister.

SILENE: Aurora, the one who's talking to you right now is not
your baby sister anymore. I'm no longer a little girl. I'm
a woman like you, more than all of you, perhaps because
I'm pregnant, praise the Lord! *(Changing her tone.)* What
I really need to hear from you is: do you really have a
boyfriend. Do you like him?

AURORA: Why?

SILENE: Do you?

AURORA: I do.

SILENE: Is it love?

AURORA: *(Aching.)* Beyond love.

SILENE: *(Violent.)* The same way you love your fella, so do I! He's no bastard! He didn't want anything to do with me because I'm a minor, but I insisted, I was the one who wanted to have the baby!

AURORA: But he turned you into a disgraced woman!

SILENE: On the contrary! I'm not disgraced! Are you disgraced?

AURORA: *(Astonished.)* Me?

SILENE: It's so good to love someone!

AURORA: *(Bursting into tears.)* I'm so happy! Oh, I am! So much!

SILENE: *(Euphoric.)* Me too! You can't be against me! *(Changing her tone.)* Let me tell you: he's different from all the others! He's such a good man that, can you imagine… *(Holding her sister's hands.)* His wife is sick and he, believe me, he bathes her every day, so patient! Can you imagine, she only weighs about five stone? The poor thing. She's just skin and bones!

There's a knock on the door. The others speak from outside the room.

ARLETE: Are you going to open this door or what?

AURORA: *(Grinding her teeth.)* What a pain! *(To ARLETE, raising her voice.)* Almost done!

DONA ARACY: Hurry up in there!

AURORA: When I'm done, I'll call you! *(To SILENE.)* But, listen – what I don't understand, what no one here understands is how, locked up in a boarding school like you were, you got out and had this happened to you! Where did you meet this fella? Or did you know him from before?

SILENE: I didn't know him from anywhere.

AURORA: Does he work at your school?

SILENE: Swear you won't tell?

AURORA: I swear!

SILENE: He lives near my school.

AURORA: Go on.

SILENE: Father cannot hear any of this! God forbid! *(Changing her tone.)* He lives right next to my school. The back of my school faces right into his house. He used to stroll by on the pavement in front of the school and, this once, he looked right at me. I looked back at him, and, picture it; it was that kind of look, you know? It gave me shivers! And his mouth just makes you want to kiss him!

AURORA: Handsome?

SILENE: Gorgeous! You know who he looks like? That fella, what's his name? You know the one I'm talking about.

AURORA: Which one?

SILENE: I can't remember a thing these days! Lana Turner's gangster? The one Lana Turner's daughter kills in the film! Strampagato, no: Stompanato! I saw this magazine, and there was his picture. The spitting image, you should see!

AURORA: And where would you two be together?

SILENE: That school is a right mess. We used to talk over the wall; it was kind of a short one. But you don't know the best part: the cat belonged to him.

AURORA: What cat?

SILENE: The one I killed. Then, one day, I jumped over the wall and…

AURORA: That's too risky!

SILENE: We went to his maid's room. It was her day off. His wife doesn't get out of bed. She is always upstairs, with a deaf aunt of hers. Now I'll tell you something, you won't believe me!

AURORA: Tell me everything!

SILENE: *(Triumphant.)* I asked him for a child! I did! He didn't want one; he said "It's not worth it" but I'm stubborn and, in the end… I am the one to blame! *(Severe and mature.)* And I don't regret it!

AURORA: That's simply stupid!

SILENE: I said he was different from everyone else because he has the most handsome, the most gorgeous tear I've ever seen!

AURORA: *(Astonished.)* Did he cry in front of you!?

SILENE: *(In her puerile irresponsible joy.)* Well, cry is not really the right word for it. He didn't actually cry. He was kissing me in the bedroom, and we kissed, and we kissed; out of nowhere, he got really bad hiccups, and once he managed to stop and turned to his side… I only caught a quick glimpse of his eyes and I saw a single tear right here, off his eyelash…

AURORA: *(Stunned.)* A single tear?

SILENE: *(Once again, joyfully irresponsible.)* A single tear, hanging, off his eyelash…

AURORA: *(Vehement.)* Does he really mean the world to you?

SILENE: *(Violent.)* The world!

AURORA: Then, I'm going to save this young man, I have to! *(Grabbing her sister.)* Does he really only cry from one eye?

SILENE: *(Again, in pure delight.)* And, you know, when he walked by, all the girls at school would say: "Here comes the man dressed as a virgin"!

AURORA: *(Stupefied.)* Say that again!

SILENE: Dressed as a virgin.

AURORA: Tell me, this is important; why "dressed as a virgin"?

SILENE: Because he only wears white, he's always wearing a white suit!

AURORA: *(In her pain and suffering.)* He wears white, all white, and cries from only one eye!

SILENE: *(In sudden sorrow.)* There's only one thing that makes me sad: he's married and, obviously, he can't spend the night with me, not even a single night with me. That'd be so nice! *(With angst.)* But in this sense, you're luckier because... Obviously, your boyfriend is single, he'll marry you, for sure!

AURORA: *(Taciturn.)* Who's to say?

SILENE: *(Even more anguished.)* And he'll be spending his nights next to you, that's brilliant! *(Changing her tone.)* And, last time, we went to this apartment in Copacabana and... he's got this medal of a saint in a chain hanging off his neck...

AURORA: *(In an explosion.)* Stop.

SILENE: *(Astonished.)* Why?

AURORA: *(In her controlled fury.)* I know all I need to know. I don't need to know of anything else!

SILENE: But I didn't tell you his name. Come on!

AURORA: No one cares about his name!

AURORA walks toward the door.

SILENE: *(Not fully comprehending her sister.)* He's got such a weird nickname!

AURORA: I don't want to hear it, no names, no nicknames!

SILENE: *(Stunned.)* But I trust you!

AURORA: Forget about it! Listen: don't leave your bedroom, stop talking, don't say anything. I'll take care of it all. I'll go there, make something up; tell them he went on a trip…

SILENE: *(Humble and pleading.)* Aurora, you're an angel! And, listen: you'll be my baby's godmother, I won't take "no" for an answer!

AURORA leaves the bedroom; enters the living room.

SEU NORONHA: What's what?

AURORA: She told me everything.

SEU NORONHA: So, who is it?

AURORA: Father, let me handle this one. Don't try to butt in, any of you. When the time's right, I'll tell you everything.

DÉBORA comes from the front door.

DÉBORA: *(Cheerful.)* There you are, Aurora! There's a fella looking for you!

AURORA: Young or old one?

DÉBORA: He's wearing white!

AURORA: Bibelot! *(To SEU NORONHA.)* Father, it all depends on this chat I'm going to have with Bibelot! I have so much to tell you! *(To DÉBORA.)* Tell him to come in!

DÉBORA: *(Before leaving.)* He's a hunk!

DÉBORA exits.

AURORA: I'll introduce him to you and, then, you all leave, do you hear me, Father?

BIBELOT enters.

DÉBORA: Right this way.

BIBELOT: Afternoon!

SEU NORONHA: *(Effusive.)* Do us the honour, young man! Come on in!

AURORA: *(To BIBELOT.)* Everything okay?

BIBELOT: Super!

AURORA: *(Introducing.)* Father, here's that friend of mine.

SEU NORONHA: We need a chair for our guest!

BIBELOT: *(To HILDA, who brings the chair.)* Thanks.

AURORA: *(In a general introduction.)* Those are my sisters. *(Remembering DONA ARACY.)* Have you met my mother?

BIBELOT, who was already sitting down, stands up to greet the lady of the house.

BIBELOT: Pleased to make your acquaintance, madam!

DONA ARACY: Sit yourself back down!

SEU NORONHA: I was just telling them, before our honourable guest graced us just now, about something very interesting that happened to me. Today, it happened today. I've been an employee of the Council, at Parliament, for the past twenty-five years. And, today, I realised I'd just had it. I'd had it, and I went down there to hand in my resignation. And I told the vice-chair: "Anyone with daughters as beautiful as mine has no business being a stupid clerk"! Oh, had he said one little peep, I would've beat him to a pulp; to hell with his status! Because I don't have to take shit from anyone!

DONA ARACY: Do you think that was smart? After twenty-five years of service and all?

BIBELOT: Well...

SEU NORONHA: Nobody asked for your opinion, Gorda! *(To BIBELOT.)* Well, gentleman, mi casa su casa, make yourself at home and... We're going in for a moment... If you'd excuse us.

BIBELOT: Pleasure to meet you all.

They all leave, except BIBELOT and AURORA.

BIBELOT: We can't go to the cinema!

AURORA: That's great!

BIBELOT: Why?

AURORA: I'd rather stay here with you, just the two of us, alone.

BIBELOT: I can't.

AURORA: *(In her feminine daintiness.)* Not even if I ask you nicely?

BIBELOT: *(With sombre sadness.)* She's dying.

AURORA: Who?

BIBELOT stands up. With his back to AURORA, in a neutral tone of voice, informative, he reports.

BIBELOT: Yesterday, she started feeling sick and I called an ambulance. She went into A&E and straight into surgery.

AURORA: *(Curious.)* Your wife?

BIBELOT: *(Not paying attention to her.)* A surgery to treat an ulcer, they said. *(With a cigarette between his fingers.)* The doctor opened her belly and closed it straight away.

AURORA: Why?

BIBELOT: *(Almost sweet.)* All rotten inside.

AURORA: So, they didn't operate on her?

BIBELOT: It wasn't a simple ulcer.

AURORA: What was it?

BIBELOT: Cancer! Where's the ashtray?

AURORA: Right here.

BIBELOT extinguishes his cigarette in the ashtray; then sits down.

BIBELOT: *(In a non-violent fury.)* They had her drinking those little cups of milk. *(Changes his tone.)* These doctors are all stupid! Treating cancer with just milk and porridge!

AURORA: *(Too happy to disguise.)* Is she that sick?

BIBELOT: There's no hope for her.

AURORA: *(Transfigured with hope.)* Are you saying...

BIBELOT: She may not make it through the night. *(With a more delicate tenderness.)* She looks like a poor little skull and... always on morphine... and sores on each cheek because of all the injections...

AURORA sits at BIBELOT's feet, resting her head on his knees.

AURORA: *(In a restrained happiness.)* You'll be single.

BIBELOT: A widower.

AURORA: A widower, right.

BIBELOT: But not for long.

AURORA: *(Slowly and amazed.)* What?

BIBELOT: *(Already yawning.)* Didn't I tell you I needed to have a woman at home and another one on the side?

AURORA: You did!

BIBELOT: One of these days, I'll have to get married again, for sure!

AURORA clings on to him.

AURORA: *(Passionately humble.)* Tell me you love me!

BIBELOT: *(Amused.)* Is this a joke?

AURORA: *(Pleading.)* Is it so difficult for you to say you love me?

BIBELOT: *(From the depths of his fatigue.)* Not today, babe!

AURORA: *(Poignant.)* It has to be today! *(With a growing desperation.)* Do you love me?

BIBELOT: *(Standing up.)* I gotta go.

AURORA: *(From violent to humble.)* Don't go yet!

BIBELOT: I'm tired. For the past two nights, I haven't had even a nap, enough now!

AURORA: *(Pleading.)* Sit down for a moment, just for a second.

BIBELOT sits down. Until the end of this scene, he'll yawn a lot.

AURORA: My love, listen; I have a reason and look: it's a very good reason to ask you... I ask for so little, just a word, just a single little word, it won't cost you a thing... Tell me you love me, that'll be enough... *(Lower voice, in angst.)* Perhaps certain developments won't have to result in tragedy... *(More aching.)* Till this day, no man has ever come up to me and said: "I love you"!

BIBELOT: *(Yawns.)* I'm so sleepy!

AURORA: *(Standing up.)* *(In her controlled fury.)* So you won't say it, then?

BIBELOT: *(Explosive.)* Aurora! Stop messing with me!

And, once again, AURORA's anger turns into humble suffering.

AURORA: Okay. Then, I'll ask you another question. *(Caressing his face and hair.)* Can you answer this one? Will you?

BIBELOT: What's the question?

AURORA: *(Trying to seduce him.)* Tell me what you think: do you think I am, perhaps, I'd be able to become wife material?

BIBELOT: *(Astonished.)* Wife material?

AURORA: *(Trembling, not knowing what to say.)* Yes, a homemaker?

BIBELOT: *(In a devilish tone.)* I want you on the streets, I like it!

AURORA: *(Recoils, her voice is barely a whisper.)* Shut up! Don't say another word!

(In BIBELOT's face.) If there were ever a moment when you shouldn't insult me, it would be this one, right now!

BIBELOT: But, Aurora: take a look at yourself! Go on, over there, in the mirror! Go ahead!

AURORA: *(Furious.)* You're still humiliating me!?

BIBELOT: But it's true! *(Spanks her butt, loudly.)* This is bound to make me a lot of money!

Out of control, AURORA grabs him by the collar of his jacket.

AURORA: Listen to me, you pimp!

BIBELOT pushes her away violently.

BIBELOT: Talk all you want, but don't lay your hands on me again like this! I'll beat you so hard, you'll lose all your teeth!

AURORA: *(Controlled and gasping.)* Just one more question. Since I'm not wife material...

BIBELOT: *(Shocked and amused.)* What are you saying? Did you want to be my wife? *(Explosive.)* Hold your horses! This is not the time for stupid jokes!

AURORA: *(Hysterically.)* Stop insulting me!

BIBELOT: Fine. Ask your question.

AURORA: *(Still crying.)* Well. It's like this: since I'm not, obviously, wife material, have you chosen someone else, yet?

BIBELOT: *(Slightly disgusted.)* My little skull-wife hasn't even died yet! She's still in a hospital bed!

AURORA: *(Determined.)* Answer me!

BIBELOT: Okay, I've chosen someone, satisfied?

AURORA: Who is she?

BIBELOT: Is that any of your business?

AURORA: Of course it is!

BIBELOT: *(Tapping ash from another cigarette.)* Bring the ashtray here.

AURORA puts the ashtray next to him.

BIBELOT: *(Ironic.)* What was it you asked?

AURORA: Do you think you're funny!? *(Furious.)* I asked who'll be your new wife!

BIBELOT: The girl, the one I told you about, the seventeen year-old!

AURORA: *(Out of control.)* Why, with so many women, so many girls, you had to choose, dear Lord! *(New tone.)* I kind of knew it! I was sure of it!

BIBELOT: The funny thing is, as soon as the doctor said "cancer", I thought of that girl!

AURORA: Great. That's really fantastic! She stays at home and I'm your nasty side piece, selling myself! *(With violence.)* Do you not fear my love will turn into hate?

BIBELOT stands up.

BIBELOT: I'm going, I can barely keep my eyes open.

AURORA: *(Changing immediately, seductive.)* Come take a nap with me!

BIBELOT: Here?

AURORA: *(Pleading.)* In my bedroom.

BIBELOT: What about your father?

AURORA: Things around here aren't the same anymore. Father doesn't really care about anything anymore. I'll explain later. Come!

BIBELOT: *(Stopping, with a sudden sharp pain.)* But my little skull's in the hospital, dying!

AURORA: Just for half an hour, forty minutes, tops.

BIBELOT: But you must remember to wake me up!

They walk toward the bedroom. BIBELOT pulls out his gun and empties it.

AURORA: You scared?

BIBELOT: If your love turns to hate, you might betray me… *(Gives her the gun, after putting the bullets in his pocket.)* Do you want to kill me? Go ahead!

AURORA takes the gun from BIBELOT.

BIBELOT: *(Forcing his laughter.)* Shoot, go on, right here! Through the heart!

BIBELOT opens up his shirt slightly. AURORA pulls the trigger several times. BIBELOT rips off his shirt. Before he lies down, he kisses the medal of his saint.

BIBELOT: Call me in an hour. Now, give me a kiss.

AURORA kisses him. She looks at her lover's face. Then, without making a sound, she leaves the bedroom, going to meet her family in the living room.

AURORA: *(Gasping for air.)* Do you want the man who disgraced Maninha? The man who cries from only one eye? Do you?

SEU NORONHA: Oh, yes!

SEU NORONHA pulls out the dagger, in a vengeful impulse.

AURORA: He's in my room!

SEU NORONHA: But, who is he?

AURORA: Bibelot. He's sleeping in my bed. Go on.

SEU NORONHA charges into her bedroom.

AURORA: *(To the others.)* Let's go.

DONA ARACY: *(To one of them.)* Don't make a sound.

They all follow the patriarch into the bedroom. For a moment, SEU NORONHA looks at the sleeping young man. He raises his dagger and sinks it, all the way in, into BIBELOT's heart. BIBELOT jerks out of bed and lets out a strangled howling. Then, he finally tumbles, gasping in his agony. AURORA drops to her knees.

AURORA: *(With a deep moan.)* My love, forgive me for hating you!

ARLETE moves forward.

ARLETE: *(Eager.)* I want to see the single tear of death!

DÉBORA: He died!

ARLETE holds the young man's face.

ARLETE: *(Astonished.)* But he's crying from both eyes! *(Hysterical.)* There are two tears!

HILDA: *(Also hysterical.)* Father! He's not the man who cries from only one eye!

ARLETE: *(In a crescendo, to her father.)* Murderer!

The daughters all advance towards their father, who retreats.

SEU NORONHA: *(Already cornered by fear.)* But he deserved to die, he turned Silene into a prostitute!

ARLETE: *(Hysterical.)* You liar! You're the one who turned her into a prostitute!

SEU NORONHA: I swear I didn't!

ARLETE: *(Grabbing him.)* You sent in Seu Saul and, then, the doctor! *(To the others.)* All of you! Listen up! Something I've never told you, something I hid even from myself. *(Violent, to her father.)* Old man! You set me up with one of the members of Parliament!

SEU NORONHA: *(Desperate.)* Don't believe her!

ARLETE: The man told me: "Your father sent me".

SEU NORONHA: *(Pleading, to DONA ARACY.)* Gorda, my daughters want to destroy me!

DONA ARACY: *(Out of control.)* Stop calling me Gorda! I don't want to be called Gorda!

ARLETE: *(Shouting.)* Answer me: was it you who sent those old men after the others?

DÉBORA: Is this true, Father?

ARLETE: Spill it out, old man!

SEU NORONHA: *(Terrorised.)* I can explain!

ARLETE: *(Blind with hate.)* Speak!

SEU NORONHA: *(Out of breath.)* I only did it because... And all of you prostituted yourselves to give Silene the wedding of an angel... *(Suddenly brutal.)* besides all that, you *(Looks at ARLETE and then to the others.)* she kisses women on the lips!

ARLETE: I kiss women on the lips so I can feel less like a prostitute!

SEU NORONHA: *(Again cowardly.)* Forgive me!

ARLETE: *(Violent.)* Old man! You turned your daughters into prostitutes and you don't even cry? Won't you cry for us, or for yourself? Cry, old man!

SEU NORONHA: I am crying.

ARLETE: *(Holding her father's face between her hands.)* Let me see your tear… *(Slowly, stunned.)* One tear, one single tear… *(With a triumphant yell.)* Old man! You're the demon who cries from only one eye! Give me the dagger, old man! That dagger! Give it to me!

ARLETE takes the dagger from him. The others grab hold of the old man.

ARLETE: *(Brutal, raising the dagger.)* The dagger in the eye of the tear!

HILDA: *(Shouting from the top of her lungs.)* Let go of my father! You murderers!

And, suddenly, HILDA falls back into her trance. She's possessed once again by cousin Alípio.

HILDA: *(With the man's voice.)* Kill him, yes, kill the old shameless bastard! Kill and bury the old man and the tear in the back garden! Old shameless bastard!

END OF ACT 3 AND FINAL ACT

ALL NUDITY WILL BE PUNISHED
An obsession in three acts (1965)

By Nelson Rodrigues
Translated by Susannah Finzi

Characters

HERCULANO

NAZARÉ

PATRÍCIO

AUNT NO. 1

AUNT NO. 2

AUNT NO. 3

GENI

ODÉSIO

SERGINHO

DOCTOR

PRIEST

POLICE CAPTAIN

Act 1

HERCULANO arrives home. He is pleasantly tired.

HERCULANO: *(Shouting.)* Geni! Geni!

The black maid enters.

NAZARÉ: You're early, Doctor Herculano?

HERCULANO: Nazaré, where's Madame Geni?

NAZARÉ: She went out.

HERCULANO: But I told her! I phoned from the airport and told her she could start dinner.

NAZARÉ: I know.

HERCULANO: Where did she go?

NAZARÉ: She didn't say.

HERCULANO: *(Half surprised, half amused.)* You're joking!

NAZARÉ: She told me to give you this.

At the same time, NAZARÉ takes a packet from the table.

HERCULANO: *(To NAZARÉ.)* I'm devilish hungry! Are you serious! What's that?

NAZARÉ: Here.

HERCULANO: *(Takes the packet.)* Did she leave any kind of message?

NAZARÉ: Not with me.

HERCULANO, intrigued, opens the packet.

HERCULANO: A tape! *(Not understanding.)* That's great!

NAZARÉ: Madam Geni said you should be sure to listen to the recording.

HERCULANO: What recording? Ah, the tape! *(Change of tone.)* Nazaré, you can stop kidding now. She's here isn't she?

NAZARÉ: I'm not kidding.

HERCULANO: *(An outburst.)* Geni! Geni!

NAZARÉ: *(Laughing.)* I swear it!

HERCULANO: Go and get the cassette player. Go on. It's some kind of clue. Go and get it.

NAZARÉ obeys.

HERCULANO: Now I remember. Give me that. Geni told me on the phone she had a surprise for me. I don't know what it could be. A surprise.

While he speaks, HERCULANO, amused and unhurried, sets up the cassette player.

HERCULANO: *(Examining the machine.)* She's here, of course. I'll bet my shirt on it. She's making a monkey of me. What are you laughing at?

NAZARÉ: I'm laughing because you don't believe me, Doctor Herculano. She went out!

The tape is ready. HERCULANO presses the button for the first time. Sounds of the tape rewinding. He stops it and turns to NAZARÉ.

HERCULANO: Go and make me a quick coffee.

NAZARÉ: A black coffee?

HERCULANO: Really black.

NAZARÉ: What about your stomach?

HERCULANO: *(Pausing the machine.)* Yes, yes, I know. Those doctors are idiots! *(Change of tone.)* It's better. A little. It's the same. Go on, get me the coffee.

NAZARÉ exits. Alone, HERCULANO whistles to himself and gets ready to hear the recording. The stage is dark. In the darkness the voice of GENI can be heard.

GENI: Herculano, the person talking to you is dead. I'm dead. I killed myself.

At the same time as GENI speaks, part of the stage is lit. PATRÍCIO and the AUNTS appear. While GENI is speaking, they are immobile and mute.

GENI: Herculano, listen to this right to the end. You think you know everything. But you know so little! *(With triumphant cruelty.) (Violent.)* There is something you don't know, something you don't even suspect, but something you're going to know now, you're going to hear it from me and it will be all of it. I'm telling you this for you and for myself. *(Distressed.) (Resentful and in earnest.)* Listen. One night in your house …

PATRÍCIO reads the newspaper. The AUNTS start to speak.

AUNT NO 1: Quick, call Padre Nicolau!

PATRÍCIO: It's a bit late for that!

AUNT NO 2: Priests don't keep a diary!

AUNT NO 1: Go!

PATRÍCIO: A man can't even read the paper around here.

AUNT NO. 3: Would you rather your brother died?

PATRÍCIO: A priest isn't a doctor!

AUNT NO. 1: What Herculano has isn't an illness, it's grief.

AUNT NO. 3: We've had enough death in this family!

PATRÍCIO: But Auntie! Don't you find it rather beautiful that a widower kills himself? A widower who misses his dead wife so much that he puts a bullet through his own head?

AUNT NO. 3: Don't you start with your mockery!

AUNT NO 2: Herculano is the head of the family. He can't die.

PATRÍCIO: I'll go and get Padre Nicolau!

AUNT NO. 1: You say you're going but you just sit there!

AUNT NO. 2: You don't love Herculano!

AUNT NO. 3: You hate your brother!

PATRÍCIO puts down the newspaper and turns.

PATRÍCIO: *(Clearly ironic.)* Do you think there's no reason I hate him? What did he ever do for me! When I was going bankrupt he was the only person who could have stopped it, with one gesture, one word. *(Assertive.)* But he didn't do a thing. He didn't say a word. And I was ruined! *(Breathless.)* But that's water under the bridge!

AUNT NO. 1: Are you going or not?

PATRÍCIO: I'm going. *(Brusquely.)* Money for the taxi.

AUNT NO. 1: *(Takes a note from her inside her blouse.)* Take it, but hurry!

PATRÍCIO: Bye, Bye!

AUNT NO. 3: Hurry!

PATRÍCIO exits, and a moment later, returns.

PATRÍCIO: I've got a brilliant idea! I've remembered a woman who'll save Herculano far more quickly than the Padre. A woman who …

AUNT NO. 1: *(Quickly.)* A spiritualist?

PATRÍCIO: *(Disconcerted.)* A spiritualist? *(Shifty.)* I won't go into details. But it might be the answer.

AUNT NO. 3: *(Furious.)* We want Padre Nicolau.

The stage is dark. Light in Geni's room. PATRÍCIO enters. A rumpled bed. Cushions on the floor.

PATRÍCIO: Geni, can I use your phone for a moment!

GENI: Will you be quick?

PATRÍCIO: *(Dialling.)* Just a minute.

GENI: I'm waiting for a trunk call.

PATRÍCIO: *(To GENI.)* I'm phoning home. *(Speaks to the person who answers his call.)* Hullo? Auntie? It's me. Look. I went by Padre Nicolau's, but can you hear me? He can't come. He's got an asthma attack. Asthma Auntie. A really bad attack. But listen, listen. I'm at the house of that lady. Yes, exactly. I'll speak to her. Yes. Ciao.

GENI: What lady is that?

PATRÍCIO: You, of course. Who else would it be? The perfect lady.

GENI: Me?

PATRÍCIO: *(Humming the bolero.)* Yes, a lady, they're calling you a lady! *(Without a break.)* Geni, I need a favour, a favour from a mother to her favourite little cherub!

GENI: I'm not doing any more kinky stuff, not at any price!

PATRÍCIO: It's nothing like that. This is serious business!

GENI: Pick up that cushion.

(PATRÍCIO obeys.)

PATRÍCIO: This is the deal.

GENI: *(Interrupting.)* Do you know how much you owe me?

PATRÍCIO: I'll pay you, don't worry. I'll pay you.

GENI: You really will pay me, because I'm broke, and you know how it is.

PATRÍCIO: But listen. It's my brother.

GENI: The big shot?

PATRÍCIO: Herculano.

GENI: The one whose wife died?

PATRÍCIO: Right. He's a widower.

GENI: Wow. He's the best catch in Brazil. There's money there. Tell me something: is it true his wife died of ... ?

PATRÍCIO: Cancer. Breast cancer. *(Without a break.)* Where's the ashtray?

GENI: *(Fetches an ashtray.)* Here. Put it there. *(Change of tone. With new interest.)* Breast cancer is a terrible thing!

PATRÍCIO: It's a killer!

GENI: *(Half showing-off but with a certain sweetness.)* It's better when you don't know. But I've got this intuition. I'm going to die of breast cancer.

PATRÍCIO: That's a ridiculous idea!

GENI: *(Intense.)* I'm not joking! *(Impetuous.)* I had an aunt. A spinster. She was pretty. I don't know why she never married. And she died. She lost one breast, then the other. It was me who looked after her. I remember the day she called me and she said "Geni, come here. Take a look."

And she took out her breast and showed me. I saw the lesion. That was it.

PATRÍCIO: This is a really tedious subject!

GENI: *(With a certain piety.)* I'm a fatalist! *(Change of tone.)* But was she pretty, the one who died, your brother's wife?

PATRÍCIO: My sister-in-law? Ugly as sin!

GENI: Did she have nice breasts?

PATRÍCIO: I doubt it.

GENI: Do you want to know something? The most difficult is when it's really lovely breasts. *(Sadly.)* And what about mine? *(Change of tone.)* The one thing I do have is lovely breasts.

PATRÍCIO: You're making this up!

GENI: *(Dreamily.)* I know one day I shall find one. *(She opens her blouse and takes hold of her breast.)* A lesion like the one my aunt had.

PATRÍCIO: Geni! Don't talk like that. It's bad luck.

GENI: I'll talk that way if I want.

PATRÍCIO: Where was I? Ah, my sister-in-law was ugly as a mule. But I've noticed ugly people can get lucky. She was the only woman – the only one! – that my brother ever knew. Knew in the carnal sense, that is.

GENI: Not even before?

PATRÍCIO: The only one until now! I never saw anyone else like him. He never got drunk. Well, only once, just the once, he almost, almost …

GENI: Whoever marries him will get lucky. Your sister-in-law died and then what did he do?

PATRÍCIO: You'll never guess!

GENI: Look out for the ashtray!

PATRÍCIO: So there's my brother, more of a widower with every day that passes. He sent all his suits to be dyed black. He's the only man in full mourning in the whole country.

GENI: And then what?

PATRÍCIO: My aunts are in a panic. My family is almost all aunts. An aunt for every occasion. And they're afraid that all of a sudden my brother will shoot himself in the head. They told me to call Padre Nicolau who's got asthma. So for a joke, I said I knew a lady who, etc. etc.

GENI: But wasn't his wife so boring?

PATRÍCIO: But this just proves how boring she was! *(Change of tone.)* Herculano mustn't die. Every last dollar I spend depends on him. He reminds me of it all the time but he comes up with the goods. *(Appealing.)* Geni, you're going to save my arse.

GENI: How am I going to save your arse?

PATRÍCIO: I'm the cynic in the family and cynics are the ones who can see the obvious. A woman is the only salvation for Herculano. Sex! *(Triumphant.)* There's nothing more obvious than that!

GENI: It's daft idea! Someone as loaded as him won't be short of women.

PATRÍCIO: Are you dumb! I'm not talking about any woman. Do you want to know something? Out of every thousand women, only one of them isn't, sexually speaking, simply tedious. Nine hundred and ninety nine of them are utterly boring.

GENI: Are you saying I'm not boring?

PATRÍCIO: *(Delirious.)* Not in bed you're not! *(Change of tone.)* I'm a genius. For Herculano, who's actually a semi-virgin – we need a really great whore! Like you! *(Radiant.)* Aren't I a genius?

GENI: How old is your brother?

PATRÍCIO: Forty-two.

GENI: Is he – worn out?

PATRÍCIO: Worn out? Didn't I tell you he's a semi-virgin? He doesn't know a thing. Geni, you can teach him the works! The full works! My job is to bring him here. I don't know how, or even if it's possible, but it has to be here. The place has to be pretty run down …

GENI: What do I get out of this?

PATRÍCIO: Don't worry about a thing! I promise you … but look. Give me that photo. The one of you naked. That one.

GENI: Why?

PATRÍCIO: Because … I'll leave it lying around. As if by chance.

GENI takes the photo.

GENI: It's my only copy.

PATRÍCIO: *(Looks at the photo and holds onto it.)* I'll give it back. I just want to see his reaction.

GENI: Just a minute. Is your brother as tight-fisted as you are?

PATRÍCIO: I'm not tight-fisted. I'm the one who's short of money in the family. I lost everything, I was bankrupt.

But look, if Herculano does come, little by little you'll be able to buy your way out of here.

GENI: Let me tell you the way it is.

PATRÍCIO: Don't be so mercenary, Geni.

GENI: No sir! I don't do charity! *(Change of tone.)* I'm telling you I'm buying an apartment. Off plan. There'll be readjustments, the usual crap. And do you know when they start? I have to come up with the money next week. The guy said he won't wait a single minute for it.

PATRÍCIO: *(Shouting.)* Geni, my brother is totally chaste and a chaste man is a pervert. This photo's a dead cert.

The stage darkens. The recorded voice of GENI is heard.

GENI: Herculano, with you I was under a spell from the first moment. I admit it. Perhaps because there was a dead woman. A dead woman between us. And the lesion on my breast. I'm not like the others. I don't understand myself at all. When I was six or seven years old I saw a horse, a race horse. And I thought no one could ever be as naked as a horse like that.

One side of the stage is lit. The three aunts are listening at the door.

AUNT NO. 3: Oh my God! Two chimes, it's half past the hour!

AUNT NO. 1: *(To the eldest aunt.)* Go and look! Go on!

AUNT NO. 2: I'm afraid!

AUNT NO. 3: Well!

AUNT NO. 1: *(At the same time.)* Afraid of what!

AUNT NO. 2: *(In a panic.)* I'm afraid of Patrício. *(Changes her manner.)* I dreamt that Patrício murdered Herculano. It was a dream I had.

AUNT NO. 1: You and your dreams! *(Furious.)* You have to stop dreaming!

AUNT NO. 2: *(Like a person mentally challenged.)* It wasn't a dream, it was a nightmare!

AUNT NO. 1: *(Energetic.)* Look here. Pay attention. Patrício wouldn't have the courage to raise a finger against Herculano. Patrício just acts the fool. It's Herculano who puts the food in his mouth!

AUNT NO. 2: I don't want to dream any more. In my dreams the only thing I see is dying relatives, and Herculano who dies as well.

AUNT NO. 1: *(Not listening to her.)* Patrício is bringing some whisky. He said it gives you courage.

The stage is lit. PATRÍCIO and HERCULANO are on the scene. HERCULANO with a half-grown beard, his eyes glittering. PATRÍCIO carries a bottle of whisky.

PATRÍCIO: Are you going?

HERCULANO: *(Distracted.)* Where?

PATRÍCIO: There?

HERCULANO: *(Furious.)* To that Geni?

PATRÍCIO: She's a great girl.

HERCULANO: Patrício! If you weren't my brother I'd bust your face!

PATRÍCIO: You're not making sense. Listen, Herculano.

HERCULANO: *(Shouts.)* Get out of here!

PATRÍCIO: Herculano.

HERCULANO: *(A strangulated voice.)* You – you have the nerve to invite me to go to a whorehouse!

PATRÍCIO: It's not a whorehouse. It's a rendez-vous in a salon. Geni isn't what you think.

HERCULANO: She's a prostitute!

PATRÍCIO: Let's not make a beast with seven heads out of this. She isn't a bit like the others.

HERCULANO: *(Desperate.)* A tramp is a tramp!

PATRÍCIO: She finished high school. With Geni, you can have a real conversation. She's warm-hearted, do you understand? And I'll tell you something else. I've never met a woman who's more sympathetic.

HERCULANO: *(Feverish.)* And why is she there?

PATRÍCIO: I don't know. Bad luck.

HERCULANO: *(Triumphant.)* See! Some are born poets, or Jews, or firemen – and some are born whores!

PATRÍCIO: That idea doesn't hold water.

HERCULANO: And another thing.

PATRÍCIO: Geni …

HERCULANO: *(Brusquely.)* What's this to you? You want to take me there in exchange for what? Tell me!

PATRÍCIO: I'm doing something for you, I want to help you.

HERCULANO: *(Shouts.)* You're a cynic!

PATRÍCIO: *(Persuasive.)* I don't get anything out of this. Do you really think I do?

HERCULANO: What can a whore do for me?

PATRÍCIO: It's simple. It's so simple! She can give you *(Lively.)* a smile, a kind word, a gesture, that's it, right, human contact. Herculano, you're in the pit of misery. It's unmanly. Right now you're suffering, OK. And then what? It's ridiculous and it leads nowhere.

HERCULANO: *(Taciturn.)* I'm not suffering that much. I should suffer more.

PATRÍCIO: Do you really want to die?

HERCULANO: *(Triumphant.)* Now you've said it. Die. The only reason I don't put a bullet through my brain is because of my son. That's the only reason. *(Begins to cry.)* I should have been buried along with my wife.

PATRÍCIO: Don't you see this state of inertia is degrading?

HERCULANO: *(Hot-headed.)* What do you mean by degrading? You who …

HERCULANO grabs PATRÍCIO by the collar of his jacket.

PATRÍCIO: Look! Do something! At least have a drink! Come on, drink!

HERCULANO: *(Surprised.)* Is that why you brought the bottle?

PATRÍCIO: *(Exultant.)* Have a drink! You smell bad, you're falling apart!

HERCULANO: *(A crescendo.)* Drink? You want me to drink? You know I can't touch alcohol? I only had a drink once, that one time. And you know how I finished up. *(Grabs his brother by the collar of his jacket.)* Once I'm drunk, I could commit murder, I could commit incest. Now tell me to my face – tell me if you love me!

The two brothers are face to face.

PATRÍCIO: I'm trying to save you.

HERCULANO: Or is it hatred?

PATRÍCIO: It's pity.

HERCULANO: It's hatred! Of me! Hatred of our aunts, of our entire family. Hatred! Hatred!

PATRÍCIO: I'll leave the bottle here.

HERCULANO: Take it away.

PATRÍCIO: One moment.

HERCULANO: Take it.

PATRÍCIO: Calm down. I brought a photo. A portrait of Geni. So you'll recognise her. Look. Here it is on the table. Have a look. Geni finished high school. See you later.

PATRÍCIO pauses by the door.

PATRÍCIO: *(Quietly.)* Herculano, look at the photo and get yourself plastered.

Lights on GENI. She's outside her room, filing her fingernails.

GENI: Odésio! Odésio!

An effeminate waiter appears.

ODÉSIO: What is it, darling!

GENI: *(Hesitating.)* Look Odésio. Come here.

ODÉSIO: Did your little friend wake up?

GENI: *(Ignoring him.)* Go get me a sandwich!

ODÉSIO: Can't I take a look at your little friend?

GENI: *(Shouting, faking anger.)* No you can't, you're shameless! Go and get me a sandwich or else. Go on.

ODÉSIO: *(Cynical.)* The water's shut off.

GENI: A sandwich with ... cheese ... no. Make it salami.

ODÉSIO doesn't move, peeking at her "little friend". GENI explodes.

ODÉSIO: I'm going! Who said I wasn't going? I'm going!

ODÉSIO takes a couple of steps, stops and turns.

ODÉSIO: You, with that guy, you're wearing yourself out. You shouldn't be yelling like that.

GENI: Odésio, I swear – I'll belt you one!

ODÉSIO: *(Offended.)* You're not my father, you can't hit me. Not even my father, not even my own father did that. You can call me names but you can't hit me! OK?

GENI goes back into the room, now lit. HERCULANO wakes up in GENI's bed. He looks around him, horrified. He turns this way and that. He's covered up to his waist with a sheet.

HERCULANO: *(Surprised.)* Who are you?

GENI: Feeling better sweetheart?

HERCULANO: What is this place?

GENI: You're at Laura's.

HERCULANO: I mean ... *(Desperate.)* how did I get here?

GENI: Don't you remember?

HERCULANO: And you are ...?

GENI: Geni!

HERCULANO: *(At his wit's end.)* The very one.

GENI: Do you want a sandwich?

HERCULANO: *(Furious.)* So it was my brother. That piece of scum Patrício.

485

GENI: You came by yourself. You were drunk, and alone.

HERCULANO: That's a lie!

GENI: I had to take three showers. Three times you threw up all over me.

HERCULANO: *(Desperate.)* I've never ever been to a whorehouse. And if I'm here now it's because of my brother, that bastard. My brother, my brother. *(Looks under the sheet and sees that he's naked.)* Where are my pants?

GENI: A bit of civility please. I'm not here … for what you think.

HERCULANO: My pants, now!

GENI: You're a lout!

GENI takes the pants which are lying on the floor.

GENI: Here you are!

HERCULANO: It's the last straw!

GENI: Look at you now. *(Contemptuous.)* You arrived here crying. Crying!

HERCULANO: Crying? Me?

GENI: Yes, you! I was in here with a customer and you were out there at the door crying!

HERCULANO: I've never touched a prostitute. Never in my whole life.

GENI: I know your sort!

HERCULANO: You're loathsome!

GENI: *(Furious.)* Who's the one who's loathsome?

HERCULANO: You, you tramp!

Unaware of what he's doing, HERCULANO goes down on all fours on the bed.

GENI: Don't humiliate me or I'll …

HERCULANO: *(Brusquely.)* No one is humiliating you! You're already at the bottom of the heap! You're a urinal! A public urinal!

GENI: Right. Listen. You told me that your wife didn't anywhere get close to my technique. That's what you said. You shouted "My wife was boring!"

HERCULANO: *(Appalled.)* No. No! She was a saint! A saint! If you say that again I'll kill you!

GENI laughs; once again, HERCULANO is on all fours.

GENI: *(Pointing at him.)* That's how you came in here. On all fours. *(GENI laughs louder.)* Like a dog!

HERCULANO: Don't laugh! Stop laughing!

GENI: Your wife had varicose veins!

HERCULANO: *(Stupefied.)* How do you know that?

GENI: She had varicose veins didn't she?

HERCULANO: *(Crying.)* No! No!

GENI: She did! *(With peals of laughter.)* Oh yes, my God! You told me! It was you who told me. And your wife's varicose veins, you thought they were repulsive!

HERCULANO: *(Shouting.)* Stop it!

HERCULANO is still on all fours.

GENI: *(In angry defiance.)* And was she bow-legged? Huh, your bitch? *(Still with peals of laughter.)* Christ, I can't take this any more! *(A new impulse.)* And she took a sponge bath, a sitz bath, before she went to bed! She did this with her hand in the water. *(She imitates the gesture.)*

HERCULANO: *(Crying.)* I didn't say anything like that! It's a lie.

GENI: I haven't laughed so much in all my life!

HERCULANO: *(Breathless.)* Look here, you.

GENI: *(Breathless.)* Tell me.

HERCULANO: If I talked about my wife, my wife who is dead, if I insulted her and if I did mention the sponge bath … *(Stronger.)* You don't understand; purity is so depressing – a sponge bath is such a sad thing! *(Change of tone and angry again.)*

GENI: And I've got a pain right here from laughing!

HERCULANO: But if I really said all that, then I should be crawling around the room on all fours. I'm a dog. I've got a beard like a dog. *(HERCULANO passes the back of his hand over his mouth.)*

GENI: *(Suddenly sad.)* Your wife had a lesion on her breast didn't she?

HERCULANO: Did I tell you that too?

GENI: *(Distracted.)* I've been worried about it since I was a girl. I'm going to die of breast cancer too. It's a kind of intuition, you see.

At this moment, the waiter knocks at the door.

HERCULANO: *(In a panic.)* Who's that?

ODÉSIO: Your sandwich, Geni.

GENI: *(To HERCULANO.)* Stay there.

GENI goes to get the sandwich.

ODÉSIO: *(With a tray.)* Listen, there's no water.

GENI: You already told me that. Bring some bottled water. Bottled water.

GENI returns.

GENI: I'm crazy about salami.

HERCULANO: *(Intense.)* Don't you understand? A woman who dies of cancer of the breast – it's sacred. The most sacred thing there is.

GENI: *(Offering the sandwich.)* Do you want a bite?

HERCULANO: No.

GENI: Try it. Take a bite here.

HERCULANO sinks his teeth into the sandwich.

GENI: Are you afraid I'm going to ruin your reputation?

HERCULANO: *(In a panic.)* If you were to tell anyone, if you said that I ... that I ... *(Change of tone.)* I have a son. Eighteen years old. A boy who never, never ... When his mother died he wanted to kill himself, he wanted to cut his wrists. And he won't even hear of sex. Not even within marriage. He won't even hear of it. On the day she was buried, at her funeral – when we came back from the cemetery – he shut himself in with me in the bedroom. He tried to make me promise I would never have another woman. Not within marriage, or even outside it.

GENI: Did you promise?

HERCULANO: I did. Because I could. Because I was glad to fulfil that promise.

GENI: *(Begins to laugh.)* You're telling me this now? Here?

HERCULANO: *(Surprised and without seeing the absurdity.)* Why are you laughing?

GENI: It's obvious! Do you know how long you've been here? Seventy-two hours.

HERCULANO: What day is it today?

GENI: You asked for a drink, and then another, and then another. And you stayed.

HERCULANO: *(Desperate.)* I don't even drink! *(Change of tone.)* My son must never know, never, never, never! If he knew, he'd kill himself in front of my very eyes! *(Change of tone.)* Those seventy-two hours didn't happen. It's as if I'd been dead. Dead for seventy-two hours!

Unaware of what he is doing, HERCULANO goes down on all fours.

HERCULANO: What did I do?

GENI: You told me to talk dirty!

HERCULANO: *(Stupified.)* But I hate the very idea of a woman talking dirty!

GENI: And you told me that your wife never said an ugly word, not even merda!

HERCULANO: *(Furious.)* No, not my wife, nor my son. My son, when he was asking me to never betray my wife, never – he suddenly began to throw up.

GENI: Why?

HERCULANO: He's sickened by it. Sickened by sex. It disgusts him. *(Change of tone and grabs GENI in his arms.)* Come here now. You forbidden fruit.

GENI: Don't crowd me. You're hurting.

HERCULANO: In the name of my wife, touching is forbidden. *(Releases GENI and changes tone, beginning to cry.)* For me she has no face, no name, no expression. She's just a lesion, and it's almost beautiful. On her breast.

GENI: Shall we make some more sweet love?

HERCULANO: *(Disgusted.)* That's all you think about!

GENI: I like it with you! I really liked it! Not like with the others. Come.

HERCULANO: *(Contemptuous.)* I'm not drunk any more. Get away from me!

GENI: *(With a sudden cruel laugh.)* Do you have to be drunk to be a man?

HERCULANO: You don't understand a thing! *(Desperate.)* Listen, you have your destiny, my son has another and there's that lesion. I'm just a drunk who passed through your life and disappeared.

Lights down. In the darkness, HERCULANO exits. GENI's voice.

GENI: Herculano, You didn't show up for a whole week. There wasn't a sign of you. Every night I dreamt about the lesion. And in the dream there was always my spinster aunt or your wife. Both of them showed me their breasts. Nothing from you. It was your brother who kept saying: "He'll come back! He'll come back!" Until one day …

In the middle of her speech the scene above is lit. GENI is there. When the tape is finished playing, the phone rings and GENI answers.

GENI: *(In a neutral tone.)* Hallo! *(Pause. She changes her tone.)* At last! You just disappeared!

Light on HERCULANO at the other phone. He appears uncertain, as if his shame would betray him.

491

HERCULANO: I shouldn't even be phoning you. I just wanted to tell you.

GENI: Herculano, wait a moment.

HERCULANO: I'm in a hurry.

GENI: Wait a moment.

HERCULANO: I'm in a hurry.

GENI: I'm just going to get a cigarette.

GENI leaves the phone and fetches a cigarette. Returns to the phone.

GENI: Right. *(Change of tone.)* You didn't even want to know if I'm alive or dead?

HERCULANO: *(Bitter.)* I've been busy and besides …

GENI: So? After that night, are you still a virgin, or …

HERCULANO: Watch what you say, Geni.

GENI: *(Eager.)* Why don't you come by my place?

HERCULANO: *(Panic stricken. A change of tone.)* That was the first and the last time! I'm serious, Geni!

GENI: Didn't you like it?

HERCULANO: *(Assertive.)* Geni! I'm phoning to ask you something. Just one thing! *(Pause.)* How can you bear to live that kind of life?

GENI: *(Surprised and uncertain.)* How? It's a very long story. I'll tell you one day. I promise.

HERCULANO: *(Livelier.)* Geni, when we talked, that time. When I was referring to that kind of life, there's an expression I used.

GENI: A urinal.

HERCULANO: *(Rapid and unhappy.)* You don't have to repeat the word. Do you understand? I shouldn't have compared a human being to … *(Intensely.)* But you aren't like that. You can't be that.

GENI: *(Uninterested in his sermon, coquettish.)* You don't want to see me?

HERCULANO: *(Grief stricken.)* What I tell you goes in one ear and out of the other! You never listen.

GENI: *(Imploring.)* Are you coming?

HERCULANO: To your place?

GENI: *(Impatient.)* Look. I'm waiting for a client, but I'll cancel. It's more comfortable here.

HERCULANO: *(Desperate.)* Geni, I've only been there once, because I was drunk. You know very well, Geni! I'll never set foot in there again – never!

GENI: Never again?

HERCULANO: It's that thing I told you about my son. Any kind of sex is finished for me. I'm telling you this – heart to heart.

GENI: *(Desirous.)* OK. But do you know how many times we made love in those two nights?

PATRÍCIO enters.

PATRÍCIO: Hello there!

GENI indicates he shouldn't make a sound.

PATRÍCIO: *(Quietly.)* Herculano?

GENI: *(Feverish.)* Twelve times.

GENI takes another cigarette.

GENI: When you left, I had a real pain in my ovaries. Do you know, I had to go to the doctor? I went to the doctor …

HERCULANO: *(Concealing his emotion.)* Geni, we can't have this kind of conversation!

PATRÍCIO takes the lighter and lights GENI's cigarette.

GENI: I need to see you, I really do! There's a reason, my love. I didn't want to tell you. It's this. It's showed up on my breast. Are you listening to me?

HERCULANO: I'm listening.

GENI: There's a lesion on my breast. Just like my aunt had. It's like a little tattoo. I want you to look at it. Because of your wife's case, you understand. I'm afraid it might be that.

HERCULANO: It could be just a rash.

GENI: I'm frightened! Really frightened!

HERCULANO: You ought to go to the doctor.

GENI: I'm not going to the doctor. I want you to see it. *(Impulsively.)* There's something I didn't tell you, something no one else knows. Do you want to know why I have this idea? That I'm going to die like my aunt and your wife? They think I'm crazy but I'm not.

Lights down. In the darkness, HERCULANO exits.

It was my mother. I was twelve years old. One day she sent me to buy something or other, I can't remember what. And I took a long time. And when I got home my mother shouted at me: "You'll die of breast cancer!" My own mother said that. And you wonder how I came to end up here. Most women were young girls once. Not me. I can say with my hand on my heart I was never really a young girl.

PATRÍCIO: *(Amused.)* Don't be such a fake, Geni!

494

GENI: *(Ignoring him.)* Now you know everything. You know my mother cursed me, so don't you get it? Don't you get it? Even when I say I have a lesion on my breast? *(With sudden anger.)* If you were here I'd whack you in the face with my shoe!

GENI puts the phone down violently. Then collapses in tears.

PATRÍCIO: Was it him or you who phoned first?

GENI: *(Impetuous.)* Don't you start!

PATRÍCIO: Tell me!

GENI: It was him, of course!

PATRÍCIO: *(Amazed.)* He's on the hook! I knew it, I knew it! It's the perversity of the chaste. Listen.

GENI: *(Desperate and crying.)* Patrício, It's me that's hooked, it's me!

PATRÍCIO: It's him that's hooked on you. This is what you're going to do.

GENI: *(Furious.)* Stop joking! *(Change of tone.)* What you have to do is pay what you owe me, instead of hanging around here.

PATRÍCIO: If you don't want to listen to me, I'll leave and fuck you and Herculano and the whole world!

GENI: You're just irritating.

PATRÍCIO: Pay attention. When Herculano shows up …

GENI: *(Interrupting, violently.)* He won't come! He said he's not coming, the bastard!

PATRÍCIO: Calm down! He'll come! What do you bet that he comes? How much?

GENI: But he's just told me, right now, on the phone, this minute …

PATRÍCIO: So!

GENI: … that he never, never would! That's what he said!

PATRÍCIO: *(Seizing her.)* Geni.

GENI: *(Crying.)* I don't know why I was born!

PATRÍCIO: *(Shouting.)* Listen!

GENI: Life is shit.

PATRÍCIO: Listen to me. I know my kind of people. We're so pure. Well, not all of us. I'm not. *(With a half sobbing laugh.)* But I would have been, if there hadn't been that thing, that thing that happened to me. For Herculano, and my spinster aunts, there was never any funny business. *(Change of tone.)* Do you know what it was?

GENI: Sometimes you scare me!

PATRÍCIO: *(Upset.)* Me? Scare you?

GENI: *(Impatient.)* Patrício, sometimes I think you're not quite normal.

They are both standing. GENI moves away from PATRÍCIO who is serious, almost threatening. Changes his tone.

PATRÍCIO: Let me tell you. That would be great. When I was ten or eleven years old, I don't remember. Eleven. Our house was next to a field. One day, a she-goat appeared.

GENI: A she-goat?

PATRÍCIO: It belonged to some dumb guy or other. Anyhow, I spent the whole day in that field. *(With great intensity.)* And one of my aunts looked over the wall and saw me.

(He begins to laugh painfully.) She saw me, naked, with the goat.

GENI: I don't understand.

PATRÍCIO: You're so stupid! The goat was my very first sex! *(With a more vulgar laugh.)* The first sex I had was with a she-goat.

GENI: *(Without the slightest shock.)* Kids are so shameless!

PATRÍCIO: *(With a certain desperation.)* I wasn't the only one. There were other boys as well.

GENI: *(Detached.)* Do you think Herculano is coming?

PATRÍCIO is no longer talking as if to himself.

PATRÍCIO: *(Increasing desperation.)* So my aunt grabbed me. The other aunts grabbed me. And my punishment was to kneel for an hour on top of the corn stack. I was just a small boy and they treated me like an outcast, as if I was some kind of leper.

PATRÍCIO comes to himself.

PATRÍCIO: *(A change of tone. Triumphant.)* That's how we are. Me, Herculano, and my aunts.

GENI: And now?

PATRÍCIO: This is what you do when he shows up – and he will for sure. Chaste people have no resistance. Take me for an idiot if you like – but when he shows up you don't let him in. Give him the cold shoulder.

GENI: Stop joking. I like him.

PATRÍCIO: You're so stupid.

GENI: Your brother is a real man. Not like those guys who … He's macho.

PATRÍCIO: You're so stupid! Use your head. You're a whore. Don't you get it. *(Points to his head.)* Herculano is a guy who never, ever … Once a month, when his wife was alive, he played daddies and mummies with the lights out. He's the religious type.

GENI: But I'm crazy about him!

PATRÍCIO: I know. I know. *(More lively.)* That's exactly why you have to play it cool. If not, he'll dump you. Can't you see that?

GENI: I've just realized you sicken me. You sicken me! Don't give me any more of your advice.

PATRÍCIO: *(Shouting.)* If you say so. If you say so. *(Change of tone.)* You only touch me if you marry me! Only if you marry me. That's what you say to that idiot Herculano. *(Starts crying.)* Only if you marry me!

Lights out. We hear the recorded voice of GENI. The scene is lit again. She is alone and immobile.

GENI: But you came, Herculano. You came and I sent you away. I told them to say I was with a client. But what I really wanted was to bite you, scratch you, kiss you all over your body. That night, I was capable of … who knows? And there I was with a client, and you outside, going crazy.

HERCULANO enters. He appears desperate.

GENI: *(Insincere.)* Hello!

HERCULANO: You called. I came because you called and …

GENI, frivolous, takes a cigarette.

GENI: Light it.

HERCULANO: I don't smoke. But look, Geni …

GENI fetches the match.

HERCULANO: Are you going to listen to me?

GENI: *(Lighting the cigarette.)* I'm listening.

HERCULANO: I came out of friendship. I'd do the same for a
stranger. The possibility of cancer is serious, it isn't a joke.

GENI: *(Acting natural.)* I'll call the boy. What will you have?
I'm so hungry!

HERCULANO: I know you're going to make me regret
I came. *(Impulsive.)* You sent someone to tell me you were
with a client! You made me wait for hours. Who do you
think I am?

GENI: *(Explodes.)* Listen. You think that with a whore it's
just a matter of showing up and we're all yours? The kid
who was with me – it was his first time. It took a while.
Tough luck!

HERCULANO: *(Astonished.)* His first time! My God! She said
"first time"! *(Change of tone.)* Let's not waste time. Show
me. Show it to me.

GENI: *(Low-voiced and lascivious.)* Show you what?

HERCULANO: Didn't you tell me that …

GENI: But you're not a doctor.

HERCULANO: Are you joking?

GENI: Aren't my breasts pretty?

Pause.

HERCULANO: You think I …

GENI: *(Defiantly, shows him both breasts.)* Look here! If there's anything pretty about me it's my breasts!

HERCULANO: You have to know that what happened between us isn't going to happen again. Not ever. Show me the lesion.

GENI: I lied! I haven't got one. Look. You can look.

HERCULANO: I'm leaving.

GENI: You don't want to do anything with me?

HERCULANO: Are you still asking?

GENI: I'm asking.

HERCULANO grabs her by the arms.

HERCULANO: *(Almost crying.)* From now on, no son of a bitch will lay a hand on you! I won't allow it!

GENI: *(Marvelling.)* You're talking dirty!

HERCULANO: I'm not talking dirty!

GENI: *(With passionate humility.)* Can I do something?

HERCULANO: Do what?

GENI: Will you let me?

Suddenly, GENI falls to her knees and kisses HERCULANO's shoes.

HERCULANO: *(Desperate.)* What's this? Don't do that!

GENI: *(Still on her knees.)* Do you like it?

HERCULANO: It's ridiculous! Get up! Get up!

GENI: *(Softly.)* Sleep with me?

HERCULANO: We're not going through that again.

GENI: My darling!

HERCULANO: Geni, listen. Let me speak Yes? Let me speak. I came here for one reason only. Between us, there's no sex and there never can be. Understood?

GENI: *(Violent.)* So why would you want to take me away from here?

HERCULANO: Compassion!

GENI: *(Begins to cry.)* To hell with compassion! *(A change of tone. Passionately.)* I'm far better than most of them. I don't go with just anyone.

HERCULANO: *(Intensely.)* Geni, I'll get you a job!

GENI: *(Furious.)* I'm not looking for a job! *(Soft again.)* Sleep with me! Sleep with me! I don't know how to sleep alone! I'm scared. Did you know I'm scared of spiders?

HERCULANO: I'll give you money and you can …

GENI: *(Furious.)* If you don't want anything to do with me, what's this mania for telling me what to do. The guy I had before you also wanted to know how I came to live like this. What a load of shit!

HERCULANO: I pity your soul.

HERCULANO remains for a moment, with his back turned to GENI. She comes up behind him, sexy, pleading.

GENI: Shall we make some sweet love? Then you can go and I'll sleep with a new girl who's just arrived. Shall we make love?

GENI holds HERCULANO like a bitch in heat.

Just this once and never again!

HERCULANO: *(Held from behind and with a strangled voice.)* It will be the last time. And don't even say the name of my wife.

HERCULANO turns to GENI. They kiss furiously. Impatiently he starts to undo his tie and his shirt. And the same moment, GENI changes. She withdraws.

GENI: *(Furious.)* Why are you taking off your clothes? Don't do that! Get out! I'm anyone's, but not yours. You can only touch me if you marry me. You can only touch me if you marry me!

GENI cackles with laughter like a witch.

END OF ACT 1

Act 2

HERCULANO is in his bedroom, dressing. He is seated on the bed putting talc on his feet. SERGINHO enters. He stops and watches his father, who hasn't noticed him. HERCULANO is whistling.

SERGINHO: Father.

HERCULANO, with a start, turns.

HERCULANO: Ah! Serginho! When did you get here?

HERCULANO gets up to kiss him. SERGINHO withdraws.

SERGINHO: No.

HERCULANO: Are you refusing to kiss me?

SERGINHO: Where's your mourning suit? *(Triumphant.)* I reject it. I'm rejecting your kiss. *(Change of tone.)* Why did give up your mourning suit, father?

HERCULANO: Why are you calling me "father" instead of "papa"?

SERGINHO: And your mourning suit?

HERCULANO: Let's talk calmly son. I didn't give up my mourning suit. *(Chooses his words carefully.)* In fact, in fact people don't dress in mourning clothes any longer.

SERGINHO: *(Contained.)* People don't do that any longer. *(Impulsively.)* If people don't do that any longer, does that mean you've forgotten mamma? Forgotten her?

HERCULANO: Never! Come here and sit down, son!

SERGINHO: I'm fine like this.

HERCULANO: You know very well son, your mother was the love of my life?

SERGINHO: *(Brusquely.)* How long is it since you went to the cemetery?

HERCULANO: *(Disconcerted.)* I do go! Of course I go! I was there just the other day!

SERGINHO: Do you go every day, like me? When I'm here, I never miss a day!

HERCULANO: Son, I'd like to explain everything. I don't want ... for instance the mourning clothes. I never go out without a black tie.

SERGINHO: *(Desperate.)* Is that it? *(Almost crying.)* Mamma dies. And you put on a black tie. Right. I think a family in full mourning is a beautiful thing.

HERCULANO changes his tone. He wants to appear grave.

HERCULANO: Son, we need to have a serious conversation. Man to man. You're an adult, Serginho. You can't behave like a ...

SERGINHO: Like a what?

HERCULANO: There's a thing called common sense.

SERGINHO: *(Interrupting.)* Will you answer one question, father?

HERCULANO: *(Appealing.)* Don't call me "father"!

SERGINHO: Do you still love mamma?

HERCULANO: You're talking as if your mother was still alive!

SERGINHO: *(Furious.)* For me, she is! *(Beside himself.)* I go to the cemetery and I talk to her tombstone. Mamma hears me. She doesn't respond, but she hears me! And at night she comes into my room.

HERCULANO: Son, your nerves are all over the place, do you understand?

SERGINHO: *(Coming to his senses.)* You don't say if you still love my mother?

HERCULANO: *(Explicit and strong.)* I hold onto the memory of your mother.

SERGINHO: *(Hysterical.)* Memory, memory, is that all you can say? Papa, I came here to ask you a question, just one question. *(Change of tone. Passionate.)* Would you kill yourself for mamma?

HERCULANO: I'm a catholic.

SERGINHO: *(Desperate.)* That's not an answer!

HERCULANO leaves SERGINHO and moves to a new light focus, where the AUNTS are, all in mourning.

HERCULANO: *(To the AUNTS.)* What have you done to my son?

AUNT No.1: It's your fault.

HERCULANO: The boy doesn't live a normal life! He doesn't even have a girlfriend!

AUNT NO. 2: *(Disgusted.)* You only think about sex!

HERCULANO: My son condemns me because I put talcum powder on my feet. As if it was obscene to put talc on your feet.

AUNT NO. 3: That's right! That's right!

HERCULANO: You've got to convince him that my wife is dead.

AUNT NO. 1: Don't say that word! Your son doesn't want his mother to be dead.

HERCULANO moves to the area of light where SERGINHO is. He changes his attitude and his tone.

HERCULANO: Son, all families have their dead.

SERGINHO: It isn't that! *(Beside himself.)* You know very well what I'm saying, father, and you're pretending you don't. *(Assertive.)* When mamma died, you wanted to kill yourself, so they even hid your revolver. *(Softer, almost whispering.)* I really thought that you would kill yourself.

HERCULANO: *(Bitter.)* I don't believe it, I can't believe it. You wanted me dead, you actually wanted your own father dead?

SERGINHO: *(Breathless.)* I haven't finished yet.

HERCULANO: Tell me.

SERGINHO: *(Almost sweet.)* So I thought; my father will kill himself and I'll kill myself. One night, I came to the door of your room. I came to ask you to die with me. We two together. Mamma wanted me to die and she wanted you to die too. *(An outburst.)* But you didn't kill yourself.

HERCULANO moves to the lighted area where the AUNTS are.

HERCULANO: *(In anger.)* Now I'm having to beg for forgiveness that I'm still alive!

AUNT NO. 1: *(Hysterically.)* You always wanted to live! Always!

AUNT NO. 2: You did want to kill yourself. I stopped you. *(Crying.)* I almost regret I did that.

HERCULANO: The boy talks to a tombstone. This is beyond belief. Do you want my son to go crazy?

AUNT NO. 2: People who forget go crazy! You've forgotten. So you're crazy.

HERCULANO goes to meet his son.

HERCULANO: I pray! I prayed! I believe in prayer!

SERGINHO falls to his knees in front of his father.

HERCULANO: Get up, Serginho. Don't do that!

SERGINHO hits the floor with his fist. Suddenly, he grabs his father's legs.

SERGINHO: You're going to repeat that oath, yes, that one. Swear, swear to me you'll never marry again!

HERCULANO: *(Frightened.)* I'll swear whatever you want!

SERGINHO: No, it's not about what I want, Papa, the one who has to want it is you.

HERCULANO: Get up Serginho! Serginho!

SERGINHO: *(Crying.)* You didn't swear!

HERCULANO: I swear!

SERGINHO: Swear you'll never have another woman, even if you never marry?

HERCULANO: Listen, son.

SERGINHO: *(Fanatical.)* I want to hear you swear!

HERCULANO: Listen Serginho. Sex can be a noble thing, it can be beautiful.

SERGINHO: You never used to talk like that!

HERCULANO lifts SERGINHO to his feet.

HERCULANO: Look at me Serginho. Look at me.

SERGINHO: *(A gentle sob.)* You've changed!

HERCULANO: *(Sweet.)* You had a mother and I had a mother. Neither you nor I ...

SERGINHO: *(Desperate.)* Don't say it! Don't say it!

HERCULANO: You have to hear it all. Neither you nor I can hate sex. When sex is about love ...

In a ferocious outburst SERGINHO lunges towards his father.

SERGINHO: I wish I'd never been born! I'd rather my mother had died a virgin, like my aunts who are still virgins.

HERCULANO: Calm down, son. Don't be angry. Don't cry Serginho!

SERGINHO: *(Like one possessed.)* I need to cry! I need to shout!

HERCULANO: *(Also exulting.)* Then cry! Shout all you like!

SERGINHO begins to shout. His father, seated on the bed, covers his face with his hands and cries too. Lights down on HERCULANO and SERGINHO. Transition to GENI who is speaking on a public phone in the street, desperate.

GENI: Did that son of a bitch phone? I can't hear you. Talk louder. What? Louder. He didn't phone! Right! He'll pay me, he'll pay me. I'll destroy that guy!

GENI rings off, opens her umbrella. HERCULANO arrives.

GENI: Well, this is just great!

HERCULANO: *(Eager.)* I'm sorry my angel!

GENI: You left me here for forty minutes in the rain!

HERCULANO: *(Flustered.)* Let's get out of here, let's go.

GENI: Where's your car?

HERCULANO: I left it there on the other side. I came on foot so I wouldn't be noticed.

GENI: You're afraid of everything.

HERCULANO: *(Sweet.)* We mustn't be seen together.

GENI: *(Furious.)* Right. Because I'm just a tramp!

HERCULANO: It isn't that. There's a café over there.

GENI: This is the last straw!

HERCULANO: *(Begging.)* Let's go. Come.

GENI: There's a lot of men in there and nowhere to sit.

HERCULANO: *(Looking around.)* There isn't even a taxi!

GENI: What took you so long?

HERCULANO: Imagine it! My son showed up just as I was leaving.

GENI: *(Sardonic.)* I knew it!

HERCULANO: That's right. I had to stay behind. *(Lively.)* It's such a tragedy!

GENI: Your son's an idiot!

HERCULANO: *(Sweet.)* Don't talk like that!

GENI: Why not? I'll talk like that if I want!

HERCULANO: You don't know Serginho. He's a good boy, he's emotional. He has a heart of gold.

GENI: I don't care for your aunts either.

HERCULANO: You don't know my aunts! They're saintly!

GENI: *(Affected.)* So I'm the one who isn't good enough, right!

509

HERCULANO: *(Begging.)* Ah, if you knew the conversation I just had with my son! It was horrible!

GENI: It's your fault! You give him too much rope. My father, when he was alive … What do you think? He used to hit me. He used hit me right in the face!

HERCULANO: I'm against hitting, I always was. Close your umbrella angel, it's stopped raining.

GENI: *(Change of tone.)* Right. So why did you call me?

HERCULANO: *(Sweet and patient.)* I wanted to see you.

GENI: *(Vulgar.)* Ah, right! Here we go! *(Change of tone. Violent.)* You make a whole drama on the phone, I don't know this, I don't know that etc. This is after a whole month. Twenty-eight days. Twenty-eight days! Without a peep out of you. Today you phone. You say you need to have a serious conversation. You said a serious conversation with me. And here I am. What's the deal? Let's hear it.

HERCULANO: My darling, you didn't understand me.

GENI: *(Triumphant.)* Understand you! *(Change of tone. Assertive.)* Talk like a man! You're not going to fool me!

HERCULANO: Don't talk like that Geni!

GENI: I don't have any other way of talking. And listen. Why do I have to be all polite, when I'm not even good enough to sit my arse in your car?

HERCULANO: *(Desperate.)* I told you! It's to do with the family. Everyone in the world knows my car.

GENI: So?

HERCULANO: Let's talk. *(Looks around.)* If only a lousy taxi would come by.

GENI: Don't push me, Herculano! Talk right here. Right now. OK!

HERCULANO: *(Serious.)* A question. Do you love me? Do you really love me?

GENI: *(Astonished.)* What kind of joke is that?

HERCULANO: Geni, it's not a joke. Will you answer me?

GENI: You dumb fool! *(Changes tone through gritted teeth.)* I only have to look at you – and when you show up you just being there is enough – I get all wet!

HERCULANO: *(Really shocked.)* Geni my darling, why do you have to be so direct?

GENI: *(Desperate with desire.)* You men are such idiots! What do you think a woman is? A woman can be serious, that's for sure. But she can also have the hots for someone. *(Change of tone.)* See my hands, how icy cold they are. See! *(Breathless.)* Freezing!

HERCULANO: *(Bitter.)* That's not what love is!

GENI: *(Furious.)* Then can you tell me what it is?

HERCULANO: Some things a woman doesn't say, some things she shouldn't say. She can imply them. Imply them. But she shouldn't say them. In a woman, delicacy is everything.

GENI: *(Containing her anger.)* These days any woman can say motherfucker if she feels like it. Sometimes, just sometimes, you make me want to … I don't know. Make me want to slap your face, I swear. I suspect you'd like it. There are men who do.

HERCULANO: That's such a vulgar way to talk!

GENI: *(Indignantly.)* And to top it all, you mess me up! I'm leaving!

GENI tries to leave. HERCULANO throws himself at her.

HERCULANO: Come here!

GENI: Get your hands off me!

HERCULANO: *(Impulsively.)* Geni, I didn't tell you the most important thing.

GENI turns to him passionately.

GENI: *(Eagerly.)* So what about you? Do you love me?

HERCULANO: *(Vacillating.)* It's like this. I haven't known you very long. What I mean is, what's missing between us is a certain kind of familiarity.

GENI: *(Furious.)* What can possibly be missing between us when we've already done it all every which way?

HERCULANO: That's not what I'm talking about, Geni.

GENI: Sometimes you really behave like a faggot.

HERCULANO: *(Assertive.)* Look here. I can't love you, really love you, truly love you – while you still live this kind of life. Don't you understand me? Will you give it up, now, all of it? *(Repeats.)* Now, this minute? Leave all of it, all of it! Don't even go back for your clothes! Are you brave enough for that?

GENI: *(Intense.)* And you'll marry me?

HERCULANO: *(Quick and intense.)* You haven't answered!

GENI: Neither have you!

HERCULANO: I asked first.

GENI: *(Begins to cry.)* OK. I won't go back there again. Never. Isn't that what you want? I'll leave everything, clothes, everything.

HERCULANO: Shoes, everything!

GENI: Fine.

HERCULANO: *(Excited.)* The clothes don't matter. I'll give you plenty more. Money, thank God, isn't a problem. You can buy a whole wardrobe.

GENI: *(Eager, humble.)* And you, will you marry me?

For a few moments, suspense. Lights out on GENI and HERCULANO. Lights up on one of the AUNTS. HERCULANO appears.

HERCULANO: Won't you embrace me?

AUNT: *(Taciturn.)* I'll embrace you.

HERCULANO: Are we going to have that coffee?

AUNT: *(With a hoarse voice.)* What are you up to, son?

HERCULANO: *(With a false laugh.)* Up to – what do you mean? Nothing, why do you ask?

AUNT: *(Mournful.)* I've known you for a long time! I've known you since you were a small boy. I know when you're lying! And you're lying!

HERCULANO: *(Perturbed.)* I don't understand Auntie! You called me, and I came. I ask for a coffee and you start interrogating me?

AUNT: Is that why your face is turning red?

HERCULANO: Absolutely!

AUNT: *(Mournful.)* It's bright red, yes it is! You upset me, Herculano! Or have you forgotten you have a son?

513

HERCULANO: But what have I done? At least tell me that.

AUNT: Look! Look at me!

HERCULANO: Right!

AUNT: No! Don't look away. *(Rapid and desperate.)* They told your son you spent three days and three nights in a whorehouse!

HERCULANO: *(Desperate.)* But it's not true! It's absolutely not true! All my friends know I have an absolute horror of prostitution. I've never been to a whorehouse. I only went once. When I was single. I was just a boy. I went in and then I left straight away. Never again. Do you understand! Quite apart from that … I simply don't consider a prostitute is a woman. She isn't a woman!

AUNT: *(Slow and prophetic.)* Whatever happens to your son, whatever happens to your son, it's on your head!

HERCULANO: *(Furious.)* If only I knew – and I think I know. If I find out who it is – I'll kill him! I'll kill him!

Lights down on the two of them. Spotlight on PATRÍCIO. HERCULANO enters, and quickly grabs his brother by the lapels of his jacket.

HERCULANO: *(Almost crying.)* You bastard! So it was you!

PATRÍCIO: *(Without reacting and with desperate cynicism.)* You insult me because you give me money! You insult me because you pay me!

PATRÍCIO's laugh is almost a sob.

HERCULANO: You told my son.

PATRÍCIO: You can hit me if you like, go on, hit me! Because I need some money. *(Speaks without a break, eagerly, breathless.)* Herculano, I bought a second hand car, an old tin can of a car. I signed some papers that the owner OK'd. The one who's going to pay for it is you!

HERCULANO: You won't get a cent from me. You can walk! Now listen!

PATRÍCIO: *(Interrupting noisily.)* I didn't say anything! I swear, do you want me to swear? It wasn't me! *(Lowering his voice, impatient, imploring.)* I'm telling you the truth, the real truth! Think if our aunts, instead of sending your clothes to the laundry, think if they had a close look at your underwear!

HERCULANO: You're crazy!

PATRÍCIO: I'll die a leper if I'm lying! *(Exultant.)* And they can see, from your pants, that you're a man, that lust is dripping out of you! *(In a wild explosion.)* You're a man, a real man!

HERCULANO: Patrício, busting your face will get me nowhere!

PATRÍCIO: *(Sobbing with laughter.)* It's almost comic isn't it? A man accused by his underpants!

HERCULANO: I'll see you die of hunger!

HERCULANO leaves the lighted area. PATRÍCIO remains, shouting.

PATRÍCIO: *(Shouting.)* Herculano! To be human is to be crazy! No one sees it and the soothsayers are the only people who see the obvious!

GENI appears in the spotlight. HERCULANO enters.

GENI: *(Repeats her words with the same expression.)* And you, will you marry me?

HERCULANO: *(Serious, moved.)* That's exactly what I wanted to talk about. For that whole month.

GENI: *(Sweet.)* Twenty-two days.

HERCULANO: Yes. I thought about it a lot. I really thought hard. But there's a problem. My aunts won't …

GENI: I bet it's your son!

HERCULANO: Yes, my son. The devil of it is my son. Serginho scares me.

GENI: But he's a child! A boy! Herculano!

HERCULANO: You don't understand. No one understands. *(Lively.)* I'm afraid that boy will … Geni, between each one of us and madness there's the finest of lines. I don't want my son to go mad! I don't want him to suffer.

GENI: *(Not listening, irritated.)* So your son mustn't suffer. What about me? So it's alright if I suffer. Don't you think about me? Don't I exist?

HERCULANO: I'm not finished yet. *(Change of tone.)* I had an idea. An idea. I'll send Serginho on a trip.

GENI: *(Impatient.)* A long way away?

HERCULANO: Yes. First Europe. Then the United States. We have relatives in Portugal.

GENI: That's a fantastic idea! *(Repeats, transformed.)* Fantastic!

HERCULANO: With Serginho far away in some country place in Portugal, things will be simpler. I'll have more freedom to act, to be myself!

GENI places her hand on her stomach.

GENI: I feel icy inside. Here. It's the emotion.

GENI clings voluptuously to HERCULANO.

HERCULANO: *(Hesitant.)* Calm yourself, Geni!

GENI: *(Appealing.)* Let's make some madness? Now?

HERCULANO: No, Geni. It was you who were so certain when you said – only if you marry me, only if you marry me.

GENI: Listen. We're going to get married then? Come on! In your car!

HERCULANO: Are you crazy?

GENI: *(Hotheaded.)* Over there then. Look, there. It's dark. There's no one around. Let's do it standing up!

HERCULANO: *(Strong.)* Look, Geni! Listen! Will you listen to me?

GENI: *(Frustrated.)* OK, I'll just go and satisfy myself!

HERCULANO quickly grabs her and shakes her.

HERCULANO: *(Desperate.)* Don't talk like that! I don't want you to talk like that ever again. That Geni's finished. Gone. I'm a practising catholic. I only believe in sex within marriage.

GENI: *(Appealing.)* Just this time, just the once!

HERCULANO: Sweetheart, be reasonable! You're going to have a wedding night, as if I was deflowering you. And there's something else. I have a house outside the city. Right out in the suburbs. It's furnished, everything's there. The family that lived in it have just left. We can get a taxi. I'll leave you there. But, you already know – I'll be back, but not to sleep there. Only when you're my wife. You'll stay there and you won't go out, you won't go out!

Darkness on the stage. Light on the family DOCTOR. HERCULANO is beside him.

HERCULANO: Doctor, I need a favour from you, a big favour!

DOCTOR: Do you smoke?

HERCULANO: *(Impatient.)* I gave up. But give me one. I'll have it. *(Takes the cigarette.)* I'll smoke just the one.

The DOCTOR lights his client's cigarette and then his own.

HERCULANO: Thank you.

DOCTOR: What's the problem?

HERCULANO: It's the same. I only have the one problem. It's my son. You examined Serginho.

DOCTOR: Very superficially. The boy didn't take his clothes off. There wasn't half a …

HERCULANO: *(Bitter.)* The only people he isn't shy with are his aunts. Do you know that until now it's always one of the aunts who bathes Serginho, with the others helping?

DOCTOR: But here he wouldn't even take his shirt off. But in any case, we did talk.

HERCULANO: *(Impulsive.)* What was your impression?

DOCTOR: The worst possible!

HERCULANO: You're scaring me!

DOCTOR: Herculano, in this boy's life everything is all wrong!

HERCULANO: Are you saying he's been spoilt?

DOCTOR: He's a boy of seventeen, isn't he?

HERCULANO: He's eighteen.

DOCTOR: Eighteen. He's a man Herculano. These days a fourteen year old fights and kills. Serginho's a grown up. Does he have a girlfriend? No, he doesn't.

HERCULANO: Not that I know of.

DOCTOR: *(Affirming.)* No! And he never has had one. He told me. And another thing, he knows nothing about sex. He doesn't even masturbate. Do you want to raise a monster? Is that it? Quite simply, this boy needs to live! He can't become like his aunts!

HERCULANO: *(Seizing the suggestion.)* Now you've said it! You're absolutely right, doctor. It's the aunts! Serginho needs to be taken away from his aunts! Are you with me?

DOCTOR: I think so! Absolutely!

HERCULANO: *(Avid.)* So what do you think of this. Would a journey abroad be good for Serginho?

DOCTOR: Yes, that would be excellent! Excellent!

HERCULANO: *(Impatient.)* A boy who never leaves the cemetery! *(Anxious.)* So you'll help me. Your authority as a doctor will be enough. My aunts take what you say very seriously. We have relatives in Portugal. A word from you would clinch it.

Darkness on stage. Light on the AUNTS. HERCULANO is in the lighted area.

HERCULANO: I was with the doctor, and we talked about Serginho.

AUNT NO. 1: Why are you meddling in Serginho's life?

HERCULANO: *(Astonished.)* I'm his father!

AUNT NO. 2: *(Angry.)* But it was us that raised him.

HERCULANO: I know, auntie. No one disagrees. But it isn't that. It's that the doctor said it would be good for Serginho to take a journey.

AUNT NO. 1: *(Astonished.)* A journey?

AUNT NO. 3: *(To the others. A question.)* Do they want to take the boy away from us?

HERCULANO: *(Irritated.)* You keep saying boy, boy. He's an adult!

AUNT NO 2: A journey where?

HERCULANO: To Europe.

AUNT NO 1: What about us?

AUNT NO. 2: You're an evil person, Herculano, an evil person!

AUNT NO. 3: *(Sardonic.)* Let him speak!

HERCULANO: *(Desperate.)* Try and understand! It's for his health, his life! I'll miss him too, but it's a sacrifice I'm willing to make, like you.

AUNT NO. 1: *(Loud and angry.)* Who's talking about a sacrifice? What about our sacrifice?

HERCULANO: I realize you've been wonderful!

AUNT NO. 1: None of us ever married!

AUNT NO. 3: Serginho is all we have!

HERCULANO: Calm down, calm down! My God! This is crazy! Serginho can't live in a cemetery!

AUNT NO. 1: Yes he can! Why not? Serginho will never forget his mother, never!

AUNT NO. 1: *(Raising her voice.)* And you dare to talk about your wife's grave when you spent three days and nights in a whorehouse?

HERCULANO: *(Desperate.)* It's not true! It's not true! *(A change of tone. Breathless.)* The journey was the doctor's idea, not mine!

AUNT NO. 1: *(Almost spitting the words.)* That doctor's a communist!

HERCULANO: *(Surprised.)* He's our family doctor. He's a good doctor.

AUNT NO. 3: Can he really be a good doctor, a man who's intimate with his own nurse? A common mulatto?

Darkness on stage. Light on PADRE NICOLAU. HERCULANO appears.

HERCULANO: Padre Nicolau, I've come because … I would like you to help me. I need your help.

PADRE: *(Quick and malicious.)* Is it about a journey?

HERCULANO: *(Surprised.)* You already know about it?

PADRE: It would seem so.

HERCULANO: Have my aunts been here?

PADRE: Leave the questions to me.

HERCULANO: *(Painfully.)* Padre, can you help me?

PADRE: *(Mellifluous.)* I'm against this journey.

HERCULANO: You don't agree with it?

PADRE: *(Livelier.)* Because it means letting this boy out into the world? My son, don't you see it doesn't make any sense. You could lose that boy. He isn't ready to manage on his own. And another thing: Is this journey your idea?

HERCULANO: It isn't mine. It was the doctor's idea.

PADRE: *(More assertive.)* Ah, well, even worse.

HERCULANO: I don't understand. Why is it worse?

PADRE: Isn't the doctor active in politics?

HERCULANO: He's a socialist.

PADRE: Socialist, Communist, Trotskyite, they'll all the same. Believe me: only riff-raff like that need ideology as a justification. The boy should stay with his aunts.

Darkness on stage. Light on PATRÍCIO. HERCULANO appears. PATRÍCIO is drunk.

HERCULANO: I came here to appeal to you.

PATRÍCIO: I never said anything! I swear!

HERCULANO: Look, Patrício!

PATRÍCIO: *(Begging.)* Talk to me, but don't insult me!

HERCULANO: *(Begging.)* I didn't come to insult you. I'll pay the invoice for the car, the old rattletrap. But now I want to know the truth. Was it you who told my son about the three nights?

PATRÍCIO: *(Desperate.)* It wasn't me. It was your aunts who were checking your underwear!

HERCULANO: *(Furious.)* I couldn't care less about my aunts. *(Change of tone.)* But you don't need to confess. I just want you to do this: go back to Serginho and deny the whole story.

PATRÍCIO: Don't worry, don't worry about a thing! I'll tell him I was drunk. That I made it up! I'll tell him I'm a liar! I'll convince the kid! You deserve it right now, Herculano! Let me kiss your hand!

Darkness on stage. Light on GENI. HERCULANO enters. He's excited and unhappy.

HERCULANO: *(His anger contained.)* Did you go out?

GENI: *(Insolent.)* Why?

HERCULANO: Did you go out or not?

GENI: So what if I did!

HERCULANO: Geni, we agreed that …

GENI: *(Interrupting violently.)* I didn't agree anything!

HERCULANO: *(Strong.)* We did agree. Oh, yes, we did! You agreed! *(Louder and more desperate.)* I want to know where you went!

GENI: *(Angry.)* Who told you I went out? *(Furious.)* I know! It was the maid, that black woman, she's old and feeble minded. I hate that witch!

HERCULANO: She's not a witch! She raised me! She was a second mother to me! I have absolute confidence in her! You should know that!

GENI: I'm fed up! I'm fed up with all of it!

HERCULANO: *(Change of tone. Begging.)* Why did you go out?

GENI: I went to the cinema.

HERCULANO: *(Almost crying.)* Alone or with someone?

GENI: Who knows.

HERCULANO: *(Beside himself.)* Did you meet someone?

GENI: Are you jealous of me? Is that it? Are you surprised? A guy who only thinks of his son! And leaves me here in this place at the end of the world! A whole week without showing up!

HERCULANO: But I phone you, don't I?

GENI: *(Begins to cry.)* That's a real consolation! *(Violent.)* Do you forget that I'm young? *(Hysterical.)* I didn't die! The most decent women in the world can't live without a man!

HERCULANO: Geni, stop shouting!

GENI: *(Possessed.)* I'm in my own house and I can shout!

HERCULANO: You owe me an explanation because you went out against my orders!

GENI: *(Furious.)* I'm not a slave!

HERCULANO: *(Suffering.)* You know I'm trying to resolve our situation, our future, your future, Geni!

GENI: And so? It's talk, talk, talk! *(Change of tone.)* None of it stops you being a man to me and me being a woman to you. I don't sleep at night. I toss and turn in the bed until the sun comes up!

HERCULANO: *(His hand on his chest.)* I swear, I give you my word of honour the only thing I've been doing is organising my son's trip.

GENI is struck. Transfigured, she turns.

GENI: *(With new interest.)* When does your son leave?

HERCULANO: *(Looking down.)* He's not going.

GENI: *(Astonished.)* He's not going?

HERCULANO: I did everything I could. But he doesn't want to. The aunts don't want him to. No one wants it. I don't know what else to say, there isn't anything to say.

GENI approaches HERCULANO. Face to face.

GENI: *(With threatening sweetness.)* And if there's no trip, there's also no wedding, is that right? *(Shouting.)* Tell me!

HERCULANO: Listen. It isn't like that. What's happened is a delay. Just a delay. Maybe later.

GENI: *(Threatening.)* Go on, go on!

HERCULANO: *(Feebly.)* It's like this Geni. Give it time. Give it time.

GENI: *(Repeating, quieter and with false sweetness.)* Give it time. Give it time.

GENI explodes, turning around, holding her head.

GENI: Idiot, idiot! I thought I could get married. But a woman from the whorehouse doesn't get married! Everything is against me! And who knows if it isn't growing, now, right now, this very moment. *(GENI opens her blouse and holds her breast.)* Is that a lesion on my breast?

HERCULANO holds her.

HERCULANO: Listen, Geni, my love!

GENI: *(Through gritted teeth.)* You deserve to have your face busted!

HERCULANO: *(Unsure.)* Geni, I won't allow this!

GENI: Do you think you have the right to stop me doing anything? With me here playing the clown, having to satisfy myself! *(A bitter imitation.)* Wedding night! I'll deflower you! *(A change of tone from parody.)* You going to be a man now! Right now!

HERCULANO: *(Disorientated and insecure.)* I won't degrade myself. I'm leaving, Geni!

GENI: *(Triumphant.)* Go! You can go, but you leave by one door and I leave by the other. And then I'll do it with anyone, on the first street corner!

HERCULANO manages to take two paces. Stops and turns.

HERCULANO: *(A strangled voice.)* No, Geni, no.

HERCULANO embraces GENI, who remains rigid, upright, in erect profile. He slides down the length of her body to the floor and clings to her legs.

GENI: *(Slowly, her voice hoarse with hatred.)* Kiss my feet, like I kissed yours.

HERCULANO debases himself before GENI. He lowers his head and kisses her shoes. He sobs. GENI does not move. She has a moment of disgust. The stage is dark.

GENI: *(The recorded voice of GENI.)* And then the madness began. Three days and nights without stopping. I turned the mirror towards the bed. I took you into the garden. I told you to slap me, and bite me. I slapped you and bit you. I slapped your face again and again!

Light on GENI and HERCULANO. They are in bed. GENI face down. HERCULANO, half naked, puts on his shirt.

HERCULANO: My legs are shaky.

GENI: Give me a cigarette.

HERCULANO: They're finished.

GENI: There's one.

HERCULANO takes the pack.

HERCULANO: Yes, there's one.

HERCULANO passes the cigarette to GENI. He continues to dress and speak at the same time.

HERCULANO: Are you tired?

GENI: *(Exhaling smoke.)* It's that pain in my ovaries.

HERCULANO: It will pass. Get some rest. Sleep. Look, I'm going into the city and I'll be back tonight.

GENI: What for?

HERCULANO: Don't you want me to come back?

GENI: Come back. It's your house. *(Quick and assertive.)* But you can sleep by yourself.

HERCULANO: *(Astonished.)* Are you joking?

GENI: You're not sleeping with me.

HERCULANO: Are you serious, Geni?

GENI: That was the last time.

HERCULANO: Listen, my darling. We've just had a three day honeymoon. And then all of a sudden you ...

GENI: All of a sudden, yes. I was smoking that cigarette and I decided it's over. I'm leaving.

HERCULANO: Where to?

GENI: *(Violent.)* To the whorehouse! *(More moderate.)* That's where I belong, not here.

HERCULANO: *(Trying to take hold of her.)* My love ...

GENI: *(Furious.)* Stop that! And there's another thing: I want to be anyone's, but not yours. You can sleep with anyone you like, but not me.

HERCULANO: Geni!

HERCULANO is interrupted. Someone knocks loudly at the door.

AUNT NO. 1: *(Hoarse with fear.)* Open it! Open it! Open this door!

GENI: *(Astonished.)* Who's that?

HERCULANO: *(Panic stricken.)* It's my aunt! Stay there, don't move!

AUNT NO. 1: *(Still knocking.)* Open it you scoundrel!

HERCULANO is by the door.

HERCULANO: Auntie!

GENI covers herself with a wrap.

HERCULANO: Just a moment!

AUNT NO. 1: *(Maddened.)* Can you hear me Herculano?

HERCULANO: Go into the drawing room and I'll be right with you!

AUNT NO. 1: Your son is dying!

HERCULANO opens the door. AUNT No.1 enters violently. HERCULANO seizes her by her wrists.

HERCULANO: *(As if delusional.)* What was it? What happened to Serginho?

The AUNT is no longer angry.

AUNT NO. 1: *(Desperate.)* It was a low-life. A Bolivian.

HERCULANO: One thing at a time!

The AUNT detaches herself form her nephew with intense calm, and speaks.

AUNT NO. 1: I'll tell you. One thing at a time.

HERCULANO: *(Sobbing.)* Is Serginho hurt?

GENI: *(Hysterical.)* Tell us!

AUNT NO. 1: *(Slow and hoarse-voiced.)* Serginho found out you were here with a woman. A tramp. He wanted to see with his own eyes. He saw you and this ... *(She can't find the word.)* ... you two, naked, at night, in the garden, naked. You and this ... The boy ran away. He went into a café, in fact a bar. And for the first time in his life, he got drunk.

HERCULANO: *(Shouting.)* What happened?

AUNT NO. 1: *(Controlled but shaking.)* I'm telling you. One thing at a time. He got drunk. He got into a fight.

HERCULANO: But he's alive? He's alive?

AUNT NO. 1: They arrested the boy and they put him in a cell with a Bolivian criminal. And the other man was stronger than him. *(Exultant.)* And so *(With a real paroxysm.)* I won't say any more! I won't tell you! *(Recoils from GENI.)* That woman won't hear another word from me, not another word.

HERCULANO: But he's alive?

AUNT NO. 1: *(Incoherent, face to face with her nephew.)* Your son was raped! Raped! Is that what you'd like to know? *(Goes over to GENI and repeats to her.)* Raped! They raped the boy!

HERCULANO: *(Sobbing.)* No! No!

AUNT NO. 1: *(Change of tone. An almost sweet lament.)* The boy served as a woman for a Bolivian rapist! He yelled and he was raped! The guard saw it all but he didn't do anything. The guard saw it. The other prisoners saw it.

GENI: *(Clasping HERCULANO.)* I'm not leaving! I'll stay, I'll stay Herculano!

HERCULANO: *(To GENI.)* You bitch! You bitch!

AUNT NO. 1: *(Crazed.)* He's dying. In the hospital!

HERCULANO runs out, shouting. Then, like someone insane, the AUNT continues.

AUNT NO.1: *(Walking back and forth.)* When I was a little girl, I heard my father say, "A faggot, I'd kill him!" *(With sudden energy, to GENI.)* But the boy isn't like that. He's a saint. A saint!

GENI: *(Desperate.)* Madam, I know, I know! I know Serginho! He'll be OK. He's not going to die.

AUNT NO. 1: He should die. It would be better if he died. But I don't want him to die. Papa was always saying that: "A pederast, I'd kill him! I'd kill him." I didn't even know what a pederast was!

GENI: What happened to your nephew could happen to anyone!

AUNT NO. 1: It could happen to anyone.

GENI: It happens a lot in those prisons!

AUNT NO. 1: It happens. It happens. My father, if he'd been Hitler, he would have ordered all the pederasts to be killed. The guard saw it all. He was there and he saw it all. The other prisoners saw it. *(Fiercely.)* You're just a prostitute, but you have to believe me. That boy had never known a woman, never even felt desire. His underwear was spotless, no sign of sex at all.

Suddenly, the AUNT looks upwards. She speaks clearly, like a fanatic.

AUNT NO. 1: My boy was impotent. He was an angel.

END OF ACT 2

Act 3

HERCULANO enters the POLICE CAPTAIN's office. The CAPTAIN is speaking on the phone to his mistress. HERCULANO stops at the door.

CAPTAIN: *(Radiant.)* Right, right, I must be losing my mind! It's Tuesday today, Tuesday! And I was sure it was tomorrow your husband was on duty!

HERCLANO is close to the CAPTAIN's desk.

CAPTAIN: *(To his mistress.)* Just a moment my angel! No, no, just a moment! *(To HERCULANO.)* You can't just come in here like this! This isn't a whorehouse!

HERCULANO: *(Beside himself.)* Are you in charge here?

The CAPTAIN stands, furious.

CAPTAIN: Go and speak to the desk clerk!

HERCULANO puts both hands on the table.

HERCULANO: *(Shouting.)* I want to talk to the captain!

CAPTAIN: If you shout in here I'll have you locked up!

HERCULANO: *(Thumping his fists on the table.)* If you think you can take that tone with me you're mistaken! After what happened to my son, I'm not afraid of you or two hundred others like you! Do you know who I am? Do you?

Alarmed, the CAPTAIN speaks on the phone.

CAPTAIN: I'll talk to you in a moment my darling! I'll call you right away. What? Something's come up here. I'll call you in five minutes.

The CAPTAIN rings off. Turns back to HERCULANO.

CAPTAIN: I don't see anyone here between two and four. Only after five o'clock!

HERCULANO: *(Furious.)* You'll see me! CAPTAIN: Do you realize you're in a police station!

HERCULANO: *(Furious.)* Yes, in the very police station where they had their way with my son. An eighteen-year-old boy! I'm his father, his father! They raped him, downstairs in the cells.

CAPTAIN: *(Restrained.)* Yesterday. A Bolivian thief.

HERCULANO: *(Crazy.)* That's what they all say. A Bolivian thief. And so?

CAPTAIN: Go down and speak to the desk clerk.

HERCULANO: But it's you who are responsible!

CAPTAIN: You're speaking to someone in authority! I'll have you arrested for lack of respect.

Darkness on stage. Light on the AUNTS. HERCULANO appears.

HERCULANO: My son won't talk to me! He won't see me. Why?

AUNT NO. 1: *(Crying.)* He's ashamed, the poor child!

HERCULANO: But I'm his father!

AUNTO No. 2: Have you forgotten who's to blame?

AUNT NO. 3: Serginho doesn't want to see anyone. Not his father, not even his aunts. He only asks for Patrício.

HERCULANO: *(To himself.)* I can't believe my son hates me! I need him to forgive me! I can't live, I can't even die without my son's forgiveness!

Darkness on stage. Light on the police station.

HERCULANO: I'm not coming to complain. I'm really not. I've come with a gun to kill that Bolivian.

CAPTAIN: Do you have a gun licence?

HERCULANO: *(Crescendo, ignoring him.)* I'm going to fill that son of a bitch with bullets!

CAPTAIN: My friend, you need to calm down!

HERCULANO, in his anger, paces round in circles.

HERCULANO: I can't look my son in the face unless I kill that guy, kill him. *(Change of tone.)* But I get here and I find that he's been released. *(Shouting.)* The Bolivian thief has been released! Released! Are you police crazy?

CAPTAIN: Police! Police! Always the same thing!

HERCULANO: You're irresponsible!

Finally the CAPTAIN explodes and thumps his fist on the table.

CAPTAIN: Right! Now you listen to me! Listen to me! I'm not some kind of clown. I'm in charge here!

HERCULANO is silent.

CAPTAIN: This is nothing to do with the police! You don't know a thing about the justice system! The police arrest and justice releases! A lawyer came – one of those lawyers – with a habeas corpus. *(Breathless.)* The law is as full of holes as a Swiss cheese.

HERCULANO: *(Astonished.)* Don't you understand? It's my son! My son was raped in one of your cells! He's in hospital and who knows if they can stop the haemorrhage! Isn't anyone going to do something? Anything at all?

CAPTAIN: *(Acquiescing.)* Right, let's see. What would you like me to do? Come on, tell me, what? *(Shouting.)* I'm not the Justice System.

HERCULANO: But someone – someone has to do something! *(Shouting.)* We have to do something! Something!

CAPTAIN: Look, my friend! *(Assertive.)* We're on a budget! We don't have a proper jail, so we have to improvise a jail. We don't have any staff, and we don't have any space. Have you ever seen where we keep prisoners? It's worth a look. The other day, didn't you read it in the paper? They did the same thing to a blind guy, raped a blind guy. And he was blind, he smoked dope, but he was blind. Police and their budgets!

At this moment the phone rings. The CAPTAIN jumps.

CAPTAIN: *(Impatient.)* Hallo! Hallo! *(Radiant.)* It's me darling. I was calling you. Just a second. A second.

The CAPTAIN covers the phone and speaks to HERCULANO.

CAPTAIN: Go out there for a moment. Wait in the corridor. Wait there.

HERCULANO: I haven't finished yet!

CAPTAIN: You're really trying my patience! *(Furious.)* Get out! This is an important call. When I've finished, I'll call you. Get out!

HERCULANO leaves the lighted area. The CAPTAIN addresses the phone.

CAPTAIN: *(Radiant.)* My darling, there's a guy here who won't leave me alone. But listen, are you listening sweetheart? I've got a favour to ask you. A favour. It's this – wait for me, dressed, but with no panties.

The stage is dark. Light on PADRE NICOLAU. HERCULANO enters.

534

HERCULANO: Padre, there's a … an island where the children are born with cancer. After what happened to my son, I think, father *(Lowers his voice.)* I think that island is the way it should be.

PADRE: You must pray my son. Prayer is everything!

HERCULANO: *(Intense.)* I want to pray, I really do! But there's one thing I know. No amount of praying will change what happened in the jail. Sometimes I start imagining how it was. I can't get it out of my head, I can't. My son screaming. *(Change of tone.)* But Padre, a real scream sounds like an imitation. *(Delirious.)* Doesn't it? Someone who undergoes an amputation, yes, someone mutilated screams like nothing on earth. I once saw a boy who'd just lost both hands in a paper cutter. He screamed, as if he was imitating a scream, faking the pain of his wounded flesh.

Lights down. HERCULANO in the doctor's office.

HERCULANO: *(Appealing.)* Doctor, please tell me. I'm begging you, begging you not to just be formal. I need the truth!

DOCTOR: Would you like a cigarette?

HERCULANO: *(Impatient.)* Yes, I will!

The DOCTOR lights HERCULANO's cigarette.

DOCTOR: What's the question.

HERCULANO: Do you believe that what happened, that monstrosity, could it change him, do you understand me? Change the personality of my son?

DOCTOR: *(Beginning.)* My dear fellow …

HERCULANO: *(Impulsive.)* Don't answer straightaway. The question needs to be clearer. I need courage. *(In a flash.)* Do you think my son could cease being a man?

DOCTOR: Absolutely not! Why would he cease being a man? Your son is innocent. More innocent than you or I, because he was the one who was humiliated and here we are having a cigarette and chatting!

Darkness on stage. Light on the PADRE. HERCULANO appears.

HERCULANO: Think, Padre, just think! *(Change of tone.)* Am I taking too much of your time?

PADRE: I have a christening quite shortly, but we can talk.

HERCULANO: I'll be quick. When my wife … you know that I adored – adored! – my wife. When she died, I wanted to kill myself. Two days after the funeral, I found a revolver I'd hidden. I locked myself in my room. And I got as far as putting the barrel of the gun in my mouth. But then I had a vision of the most obscene penetration you can imagine. I'm sorry! I'm sorry! But that's what I saw at that moment – an obscene penetration. So, so I didn't kill myself *(Exploding.)* And then, they do this thing to my son! You'll tell me one thing has nothing to do with the other. *(Frightened.)* But in my head, the two things are mixed up together. I didn't kill myself because I was nauseated, the thought of sex sickened me!

PADRE: Forgive me, but I need to go.

HERCULANO: *(Impatient.)* Just one more thing! *(Stumbling over his words.)* I need you to tell me if my reasoning is correct. If it is. It's like this.

PADRE: Why don't you come by later on.

HERCULANO: Just one moment. I believe that if God exists, he exists. Yes, if God exists what is important is the soul. It's the soul isn't it?

PADRE: Go on.

HERCULANO: Or am I wrong? I mean to say, that the fact, the rape, is a horrible, miserable, stupid detail. The haemorrhage is also a detail, everything is a horrible detail.

The stage darkens. Light on GENI. HERCULANO enters.

HERCULANO: *(Astonished.)* Are you still here?

GENI: *(Sweet and sad.)* I was waiting for you.

HERCULANO makes a gesture, pointing.

HERCULANO: *(Shouting.)* Get out! Get out!

GENI: Herculano, I'm not going! You can insult me, you can kick me out but I'll come back. I'll come back Herculano!

HERCULANO: Do you want me to smash your face?

GENI: Do whatever you like. I don't care. *(Impulsively.)* You need me, Herculano!

HERCULANO: *(Exploding.)* You're such a cynic!

GENI: I don't leave a man when he's down! *(Anxious to convince him.)* No one knows me, but I know myself. I need someone to pity. My love is all about pity. I swear I'm dying of pity, Herculano! Pity for you and your son!

HERCULANO: Look Geni. You're to blame. Me too. But do you realize? You're the one who's worse. *(A fearsome shout.)* You're a prostitute. You belong in the whorehouse!

GENI: *(Sweet and violent.)* I belong here with you!

HERCULANO: I don't want you!

GENI: *(Crying.)* I'll be your servant, I'll be your son's servant! I'll wash the floors, but I won't leave. Herculano! I won't leave here until my life is finished! I don't want anything – listen Herculano, listen! I don't want anything except a plate of food and a corner to sleep in!

HERCULANO: You don't fool me. What's your plan? You've got a plan, what is it?

GENI: *(Fanatic.)* To live for you and for Serginho!

HERCULANO: Don't talk about my son! If you as much as open your mouth to mention my son …

GENI: *(Impulsive.)* Herculano, I need to see Serginho, right now.

HERCULANO: *(Shouting.)* Are you crazy?

GENI: *(Hysterical.)* Before it's too late! *(Low and ferocious.)* You can beat me to pulp but I'm going to talk to your son! I'm so sorry for your son and when I'm full of pity I'm a saint! *(Lowering her voice.)* Herculano, I spoke to your aunts! I just came from there!

Darkness on stage. Light on the AUNTS. GENI appears.

AUNT NO. 2: Get out of here or I'll call the police!

GENI: Madam, you don't know what I've come to say. I've come here …

AUNT NO. 3: Get out!

GENI: *(Desperately, to AUNT NO. 1.)* Madam, the lady who knows me, we spoke before. I have something important to say. *(To the other AUNT.)* Let me speak, and then I'll go away!

AUNT NO. 2: She was naked in the garden!

GENI: For the love of God!

AUNT NO. 3: A slut in our house!

AUNT NO. 1: Say it then! After what happened to Serginho nothing shocks me any more! You can even be naked!

AUNT NO. 2: Nothing shocks me, nothing, nothing at all!

AUNT NO. 1: Say it and get it over!

GENI: You can believe me. I am what I am, but I'm also different. *(To the AUNT she knows.)* I'm not like the others. You know, I'm going to die from a lesion on my breast.

AUNT NO. 3: *(Hysterical.)* If Serginho dies, I don't want an autopsy!

GENI: *(Lowering her voice.)* It was my mother's curse! I know it. First they'll be a lump. And then they'll be a lesion. It's a sure as day follows night.

AUNT NO. 3: No autopsy! No autopsy!

GENI: I need to see that boy! It has to be right away.

Darkness on stage. Light on HERCULANO. GENI appears.

GENI: Your aunts threw me out.

HERCULANO: For the last time! Either you go, or the person who calls the police will be me. And you'll leave here in handcuffs.

GENI: Herculano! If I don't speak to your son, he's going to die!

Darkness on stage. Transition to SERGHINO's room in the hospital. PATRÍCIO is at his bedside.

SERGINHO: *(A strangled voice.)* Patrício!

PATRÍCIO: I'm listening.

SERGINHO: I'm going to kill that woman.

PATRÍCIO: Geni?

SERGINHO: When I get out of here, I'll kill her, I'll kill her!

PATRÍCIO: *(Vacillating.)* Serginho, can I ask you something?

SERGINHO: *(Obsessive.)* I'll kill that woman!

PATRÍCIO: *(Uncertain.)* Do you still love him … do you still love your father?

SERGINHO: I don't have a father! I don't want a father like him!

PATRÍCIO: Serginho, I want to ask you a favour! A favour, Serginho! Are you listening?

SERGINHO: *(Vague and delirious.)* I don't have a father.

PATRÍCIO: Listen Serginho. Herculano is out there. Outside. And I promised.

SERGINHO: He can't come in here! I won't let him!

PATRÍCIO: Serginho, listen. He'll only come in if you want him to. If you let him. But there's a favour, a favour I'm asking you. Let your father come in for one minute. Then he'll go. Do this for me, do it for me, Serginho.

Pause.

PATRÍCIO: You can say what you want. Or don't say anything. Just be silent. It's up to you. But if you don't it's me that will suffer.

Silence. Then PATRÍCIO exits and HERCULANO enters. He stops in front of the bed.

HERCULANO: *(Low voiced, upset.)* Serginho, it's me. Your father.

There is no response. HERCULANO begins to cry.

HERCULANO: Look. I went to the police station to murder the bastard. I was going to hunt him down with a gun. Are you listening, son? I was going to pump six holes in him, like you'd kill a dog! *(Starts to cry again.)* But he wasn't there any more. He's been released. Habeas corpus. The bastard has been released!

Silence.

HERCULANO: Listen, son. I just spoke to the doctor. He promised me that in a few days you can come home. When you get out of here, we two, you and me, we'll hunt down that Bolivian. I've never seen him, so I could pass him in the street without recognizing him. But you'd know him. We'll kill the Bolivian bastard! I promise you – we'll do it together!

SERGINHO raises himself half-way.

SERGINHO: *(A hoarse voice, almost inhuman.)* Don't talk about that! Don't! *(Change of tone.)* What about your mistress? Why don't you talk about your mistress?

HERCULANO: Do you forgive me?

SERGINHO: Don't you dare talk about forgiveness. It was because of you, it was because of your mistress that "it" happened! And I lost my mother!

HERCULANO: Serginho, your mother died long before all this!

SERGINHO: Not for me she didn't! *(Places his hand on his breast.)* I used to go to the cemetery and talk – talk to my mother's grave. *(Fierce.)* I'm not crazy! You're the ones who are crazy! *(Radiant.)* At night, she used to come to my room. I couldn't sleep without a kiss from her. *(Change of tone.)* But after – after "it" happened, she didn't come any more. She's ashamed of me, she finds me loathsome. All because of you and your mistress.

HERCULANO: Serginho, I want to tell you something.

SERGINHO: Why did you come here?

HERCULANO: *(A crescendo.)* Listen, son. If someone told you I was going to marry that woman, it's a lie, it's defamation! The idea never occurred to me. She's not even my mistress! A prostitute isn't a mistress, she's a woman everyone uses – and they pay her for it! She could never be my wife, never! You have to believe me! You've never seen your father lie. *(His exultation fades.)* Serginho, a real man forgives his father!

SERGINHO: I'll never forgive you. The father thing is all over. I don't have a father any more!

HERCULANO: Don't you have anything else to say to me?

SERGINHO: *(Slow and furious.)* I'm now calling you father for the last time. Father, I shan't be going to your funeral!

Darkness on stage. Light on GENI and PATRÍCIO.

PATRÍCIO: You're an idiot! Get that idea out of your head!

GENI: Do this for me, Patrício!

PATRÍCIO: The boy wants to kill you, you stupid creature!

GENI: *(Fanatic.)* Patrício, I'm not going to die from a bullet or a knife!

PATRÍCIO: Don't give me that lesion story again!

GENI: If you'll take me, I'll give you all my jewellery!

PATRÍCIO: You dimwit! Herculano tried to bribe me too. Result – I went and told Serginho that you two were going to get married. It was me that took Serginho to see you two naked in the garden. Be careful when you're dealing with me!

GENI: I'll go on my own and to hell with you!

PATRÍCIO: Come here, Geni. You didn't realize it but you've given me an idea.

GENI: Like what?

PATRÍCIO: You're going to give me the portrait, that one, that really great one of you naked.

GENI: I don't give that portrait to anyone.

PATRÍCIO: Fine, then I don't take you to Serginho. He only does what I want. The kid's crazy. But it's a craziness that swings this way or that depending on my will.

Darkness on stage. HERCULANO is with the doctor.

HERCULANO: What surprises me, doctor, is that he didn't say a word about the Bolivian.

DOCTOR: The thing is, Herculano …

HERCULANO: What does it mean?

DOCTOR: It's obvious. It's a defence mechanism. Defence is normal and it's obligatory. The boy needs not to remember. He needs to forget.

HERCULANO: *(Desperate.)* I'm the one who can't forget it for a single minute. It's in my mind all the time. And in my dreams. Can you believe it if I told you that every single night I dream about the Bolivian?

DOCTOR: You're cultivating it, you're feeding this obsession. It's not just the boy who needs to forget, it's you as well, and your aunts, and all of us!

HERCULANO: But he hates me!

DOCTOR: Herculano! Don't give so much weight to a fleeting reaction. It's a reaction that as an adult and a father, you need to understand. Didn't I tell you? You're dramatizing everything!

HERCULANO: You're right. I'll leave now, doctor.

DOCTOR: Let me know what happens.

HERCULANO exits. The DOCTOR checks his notes. HERCULANO returns.

HERCULANO: I came back to tell you something. What pains me most, do you know what it is? *(In unbearable tension.)* At the police station, a cop told me. He told me that back in his own country, the Bolivian was the baritone in the church choir. Before he was a thief, or maybe when he was already a thief, he was singing mass. He sang in the jail as well. From what the policeman said, he was about thirty-three years old, filthy dirty, but handsome.

Darkness on stage. SERGINHO and PATRÍCIO.

PATRÍCIO: Serginho, there's only one person who's to blame and it's your father!

SERGINHO: And what about her?

PATRÍCIO: It was Herculano who was naked in the garden. And that woman, do you understand? She took off her clothes because that's her job. *(Low and diabolical.)* The dead see everything and so did your mother.

SERGINHO: *(Amazed.)* The dead see everything and so does my mother and she saw me in the jail when …

PATRÍCIO: Forget about the Bolivian.

SERGINHO: *(Slowly.)* Do you want me to kill my father?

PATRÍCIO: *(Sudden euphoria.)* Don't kill him. No. He's not going to die, no chance! Serginho, you hate your father, I hate my brother. We hate the same man. *(Quieter still, with a short heavy laugh.)* We mustn't forget the aunts, must we Serginho?

SERGINHO: The aunts!

PATRÍCIO: Did you ever notice they smell of decay?

SERGINHO: But I like the aunts.

PATRÍCIO: I don't dislike them. They're just boring. Let's leave it at that.

SERGINHO: I can see now I never liked my father. Even before mother died. I always hated him and I didn't realize it.

PATRÍCIO: Listen Serginho. In our family, I'm the louse. They treat me like a louse. But our time is coming. *(Breathing deeply.)* What you're going to do to your father is a lot worse than death.

SERGINHO: What's worse than death?

PATRÍCIO: Listen to my idea. I spent a sleepless night, just thinking about this: your father marries Geni.

SERGINHO: A prostitute?

PATRÍCIO: Yes, your father will be the husband and the prostitute will be his wife!

SERGINHO: His wife, like my mother?

PATRÍCIO: This marriage is just what we need and do you know why? Because you're going to make a cuckold of your father! Do you get it now?

SERGINHO: But that woman disgusts me!

PATRÍCIO: That's all been worked out. Do you understand? This isn't about pleasure, it isn't about desire, it's about vengeance! And you're the one who's going to insist they get married!

SERGINHO: No, no!

PATRÍCIO: *(Crazed.)* I'm giving the orders here! *(Change of tone.)* This is how it goes. The two of them get married. One day there's a family gathering. Everyone's there. Your father at one end of the table and you at the other. And then you say it, this one word will be enough: Cuckold. That's all. Nothing else.

The two look at the each other. Silence. PATRÍCIO takes the portrait.

PATRÍCIO: Now look at this picture. Look at it.

SERGINHO: *(Amazed.)* She had this photo taken. She was completely naked!

PATRÍCIO: Nice body. Look! Lovely breasts.

Darkness on stage. Light on SERGINHO. PATRÍCIO is not there and GENI enters.

GENI: *(Numb with fear.)* Are you better?

SERGINHO: *(Covers his face with one of his hands.)* It's you.

GENI: Patrício said I could come. He knew you were getting on well and that …

SERGINHO uncovers his face and for the first time, looks at GENI.

SERGINHO: *(Desperate.)* Are you laughing at me?

GENI: *(Also desperate.)* I'm not laughing, I'm crying!

SERGINHO: *(Furious.)* Crying? *(Crescendo.)* Why are you crying?

GENI: *(Exploding.)* Pity. It's pity!

SERGINHO: *(Surprised.)* Pity! *(Furious.)* Patrício sent you here knowing you're sorry for me? I want to know why you're sorry …

GENI: It isn't that! I say too much! Sometimes I say things I shouldn't!

SERGINHO: If you cry, and you're sorry, it's because you're thinking about what happened to me. You're thinking about "that"?

GENI: I'm not. I swear!

SERGINHO: Everyone who comes in here, all of them. Doctors, nurses, they all think the same thing.

GENI: *(Exploding.)* Maybe the others think it, I don't!

SERGINHO: Come here. Here!

SERGINHO takes GENI's hand.

SERGINHO: If you want to stay alive, never, never mention this. If you say a single word about …

GENI: You're hurting me.

SERGINHO: *(Changing tone, now caressing, now threatening.)* But I know you won't forget. *(Without a break.)* Go on, shut the door and come back. But listen, if you want, now is your chance to run away.

GENI shuts and locks the door and returns.

GENI: I'm staying.

SERGINHO: Sit here. Here on the bed.

GENI obeys.

SERGINHO: And now that we're alone, what if I strangled you, like this?

SERGINHO puts his hands round GENI's neck as if he were really going to strangle her.

GENI: *(With patient humility.)* I'm not afraid of you.

SERGINHO: *(Brusquely.)* You know he was released. That he's left the jail?

GENI: Who?

SERGINHO: Him! Him! *(As if he was talking to himself, not to GENI.)* He speaks Spanish! He speaks Spanish! I used to think Spanish was even more beautiful than Italian. *(Low voiced.)* I can't stand hearing anyone speaking Spanish ever again.

GENI clings to the boy.

GENI: Forget it! Don't think about it!

SERGINHO: *(Distressed.)* He's here.

GENI: *(Looking around her in panic.)* Where? Where?

SERGINHO: *(Distant.)* He's nearby. An animal knows, doesn't it? When it's going to rain? *(Intense.)* I know those things too. I know when he comes, when he's nearby, when he's really close. *(Stronger.)* If I open the window I see a man on the sidewalk, or on the corner. He's going round and round the hospital!

GENI: Serginho! Listen Serginho! There's no one there! The guy's a long way away!

SERGINHO: *(Violent.)* He's close. He's close. He's following me. I can feel it. *(More fearful.)* Maybe in the corridor.

SERGINHO falls on his knees with a low moan. GENI also falls to her knees. She takes the boy's face in her hands.

GENI: Sweetheart! I'm here!

SERGINHO: *(Sobbing.)* I don't know who said that Spanish is the language of a lover, the language of love!

GENI: You have to forget.

SERGINHO points vaguely. He appears delirious again.

SERGINHO: It's him again! He's coming, he's coming this way, towards the hospital! He's crossing the road, Geni!

GENI: You're delirious!

The recorded voice of GENI.

SERGINHO: *(Shouting.)* It's you! Why are you here?

GENI: I'm your friend!

SERGINHO: I'd like to smash your face in!

GENI: *(Radiant.)* Shame me! You can shame me! *(Laughing crying.)* I want to be shamed!

SERGINHO: *(Fierce.)* Take off your clothes!

GENI withdraws.

GENI: No, Serginho, no!

SERGINHO: Take them all off!

GENI: *(Eager.)* You're sick, you're weak! You'll hurt yourself!

SERGINHO: I want you naked! *(A desperate euphoria.)* It's not desire. I'm avenging my mother! It's revenge!

GENI is exultant.

GENI: It's revenge! Mine too! I'm taking my revenge too! *(Sobbing.)* I'm taking my revenge on … on nobody! *(A change of tone and she unbuttons her blouse.)* Look at my breasts – how pretty they still are!

SERGINHO: *(Hoarse with desire.)* Show me, I want to see.

GENI: *(Shows him her breasts, but turns her face away with sudden shame.)* Do you know, this makes me embarrassed. I don't know … embarrassed at you?

SERGINHO: *(Lowering his voice, in cruel desire.)* You're going to tell me what you do with my father. What you two do together. *(Resentful and spitting out the words.)* I want to do everything my father does with you.

GENI: *(Eager.)* Everything? *(A change of tone. Supplicating.)* Listen, whatever you want me to do, I'll do it. But there are some things a man does with a woman that disgust him, afterwards. *(Desperate.)* I don't want you to be disgusted by me!

SERGINHO: *(Malign.)* Has my father ever been disgusted by you?

GENI: *(Desperate.)* But your father isn't like you. You're different. *(Passes her hand through his hair.)* You're so young!

GENI embraces the boy, eager.

GENI: Sometimes, I'm disgusted by myself.

SERGINHO: *(Cruel.)* Why haven't you taken all your clothes off?

GENI: *(Anxious, like a girl.)* There's a lot of light in here. Can I turn the light off.

SERGINHO: *(Insulting.)* Do you turn it off with my father?

GENI: *(Shaking, feverish.)* If you'd rather we can leave it on. *(Without a break.)* Serginho, do you know I don't think the body of a woman is pretty?

SERGINHO: *(As if he was beating her.)* Go on! Talk! Talk!

GENI: *(Also exultant.)* When I see one of the girls at work naked, I feel sick! You can't imagine, really sick!

At the same time as she speaks, she takes off her shoes and starts to undress. SERGINHO interrupts her brutally.

SERGINHO: Don't take off your clothes! Why are you taking off your clothes?

GENI: You asked me to, you told me to!

SERGINHO: *(Furious.)* Did you think I was going to do something with you?

GENI: I'll tell you everything we do, everything, me and your father!

SERGINHO appears to be talking to someone invisible.

SERGINHO: I'm not betraying my father! A whore doesn't count as betrayal! *(Shouting.)* What are you anyway, yes, you?

GENI: *(Astonished.)* Me?

SERGINHO: Aren't you a whore? *(With a strangled voice.)* Tell me!

GENI: I am.

SERGINHO: *(Possessed.)* A what? A what?

GENI: *(Exploding.)* A whore!

SERGINHO, with triumphant cruelty, roars.

SERGINHO: Then get out of here! Get out! Get out!

GENI: *(Desperate.)* So I'll never come back?

SERGINHO: *(Low and breathless.)* Come back when you're married. Marry my father and come back as my father's wife, as his wife. *(Lowering his voice.)* And as my stepmother.

GENI runs away. SERGINHO falls on his knees, his head down. Darkness on stage. The doctor's office, HERCULANO is present.

HERCULANO: *(Euphoric.)* Doctor, do you believe in miracles?

DOCTOR: I believe in mankind.

HERCULANO: *(Emotional.)* That's right! That's right. So do I. In mankind. Yes. *(Lively.)* But forgive me. If they take life eternal away from man, he becomes just an animal on all fours, straight away.

DOCTOR: *(Laughingly.)* Then I'm a quadruped.

HERCULANO: *(Disconcerted.)* What's that? You have eternal life, even if you don't want it!

DOCTOR: *(With affectionate irony.)* Thank you so much. *(Without a break.)* But what's your miracle?

HERCULANO: First I'll tell you the story of two kisses. It goes like this: I once did my brother Patrício a favour. He kissed my hand. I admit I didn't understand and I found his kiss rather contemptible. OK. Then it was my turn. *(Eager.)* I've just kissed the hand of my own son.

DOCTOR: Serginho?

HERCULANO: Do you know why?

HERCULANO covers his face with one of his hands and weeps.

HERCULANO: I'm sorry, doctor.

DOCTOR: Don't be ashamed of crying.

HERCULANO: But just think, Serginho came today and asked me, almost insisted that I marry Geni. I suddenly got the sense that the child was me and he was the adult.

DOCTOR: What did you say?

HERCULANO: What did I say? Ah! I wept and I kissed my son's hand. And he knows all about Geni's past, he knows everything.

Lights down on them both. Transition to PADRE NICOLAU. HERCULANO enters.

HERCULANO: Padre, today I woke up with the wish to forgive.

PADRE: To forgive who and for what?

HERCULANO: I wasn't thinking of anyone in particular. An impersonal forgiveness, an indiscriminate one. To forgive the whole world, just like that.

PADRE: My son, don't be in haste to forgive. Mercy can also corrupt.

Darkness on stage. Light on the DOCTOR. HERCULANO returns.

HERCULANO: What I call a miracle is this sense of resurrection. Mine too. And Geni's. You don't know what kind of person she is. Her goodness, her tenderness! Even Patrício has completely changed!

DOCTOR: But when it comes to it, you attribute to a miracle something which is in fact to your son's credit. *(Without a break.)* And the marriage? Are you going through with it?

HERCULANO: I start on the paperwork tomorrow. *(Without a break.)* But Serginho was here yesterday. Now you can give me your opinion. What do you think?

DOCTOR: *(Categorical.)* It was quite different! Last time I couldn't examine the boy's chest. He was as ashamed as if he had breasts. But yesterday he took off his clothes and stepped totally naked on the scales. He's much more manly now.

HERCULANO: Isn't that a kind of resurrection?

DOCTOR: It's man. Always man, Herculano. There never was, never has been a absolute scoundrel, someone totally despicable. The most degraded of men has salvation within him.

HERCULANO: There's more. There's more. Serginho has even persuaded the aunts. They accept the marriage. They're discussing the trousseau with Geni.

DOCTOR: *(Putting his hand on his client's shoulder.)* Herculano, man is a formidable creature as you see. Whatever happened to your son, happened. But this monstrous event was the beginning of a whole new way of living. *(Livelier.)* A resurrection, as you say. Serginho saved himself, you saved yourself, and your aunts and Patrício.

HERCULANO: You can't live without God! You have to believe in God! Whether you want it or not, you are eternal!

Darkness on stage. The recorded voice of GENI.

GENI: A month later, we were married, Herculano. A civil and a religious ceremony. Serginho was one of the witnesses. In the church, I wanted to scream, to scream.

Light on stage. The three AUNTS are seated on a small bench.

AUNT NO. 2: *(Fearful.)* Geni has such lovely manners that she doesn't seem like a woman who ... *(Stops, fearful.)*

AUNT NO. 1: *(In authority. The leader among them.)* A woman who what? *(Threatening.)* I won't have this kind of talk in my presence ...

AUNT NO. 2: *(Frightened.)* I was talking very quietly.

AUNT NO. 1: *(Threatening.)* What were you saying about Geni?

AUNT NO. 3: Geni is family now.

AUNT NO. 2: *(Shaking with timidity.)* But I was going to say something nice about Geni. *(Trying to please.)* If you look at Geni you'd never think she was from the whorehouse...

AUNT NO. 1: Are you insane?

AUNT NO. 2: Me, insane?

AUNT NO. 1: *(Accusing.)* Yes, yes. You're the oldest of us. *(Rapid and assertive.)* Do you know what arteriosclerosis is? *(To AUNT NO.3.)* That's right isn't it?

AUNT NO. 3: You've got arteriosclerosis!

AUNT NO. 1: Geni didn't come from a whorehouse. Honestly. It was you that put that idea in your own head, because your memory is going. It's arteriosclerosis!

AUNT NO. 2: *(Almost voiceless, terrified.)* Don't put me away! I don't want to be locked up!

AUNT NO. 1: *(Assertive.)* Right. Then don't ever say, ever again, that Geni was from a whorehouse. Geni was a virgin when she married.

AUNT NO. 3: A virgin.

AUNT NO. 2: *(Sweet, humble and patient.)* Geni was a virgin when she married.

Darkness. Light on PATRÍCIO and SERGINHO.

PATRÍCIO: Is it time, Serginho?

SERGINHO: I didn't hear you.

PATRÍCIO: It's time to do it. When are you going to call your father a cuckold?

SERGINHO: *(Frivolous.)* I'll see.

PATRÍCIO: *(Quick.)* Are you scared?

SERGINHO: I'm not scared. But I need to see if I still hate him with the same hate.

PATRÍCIO: Now I've seen it all. You're a coward like your father. Act like a man!

SERGINHO: Patrício, this is my problem.

Light on GENI, in bed. SERGINHO appears and lies down next to her.

GENI: Sweetheart, don't bite me. Yesterday, the old guy asked me what the mark was on my arm.

SERGINHO: *(Laughing, almost mouth to mouth.)* What was your excuse?

GENI: I said he did it himself.

SERGINHO: Did he believe you?

GENI: What else could he do?

SERGINHO: You bite and scratch me too.

GENI: But you don't have anyone else. I don't want him to get suspicious. What would be the point?

SERGINHO: Do you know why I feel lousy with you? It might sound lousy but I feel you're cheating on me.

GENI: Don't say that. Not even as a joke. There's no woman more faithful than I am.

SERGINHO: Are you cheating on me with my father?

GENI: *(Intense.)* That's not cheating. The one who's cheated on is him. And anyway, who's to blame for that?

SERGINHO: Be careful, Geni.

GENI: Were you or weren't you? You wanted us to get married. I wanted to run away. I said – let's go. You didn't want to. You refused. And I ended up getting married because as your stepmother, I can be close to you. Even if we argued, I'd be close to you, always.

SERGINHO: *(Frivolous.)* Give it a rest! Do you sleep with the old guy? If you do, I can also cheat, what a joke!

GENI: *(Already in pain.)* Serginho, don't say that even as a joke. You know I'm the jealous type. I admit it. *(Without a break.)* What's that? Is it bloodstains?

GENI examines SERGINHO's back.

SERGINHO: It was you that did it!

GENI: You're saying the same as what I say to him!

SERGINHO: My little whore!

GENI: *(Lively.)* Have you got the guts to cheat on me?

SERGINHO: *(Laughing.)* Never!

GENI: Who knows, you might be thinking: I've cheated on her already and the silly bitch doesn't realize! I bet you've already cheated on me a whole lot! Serginho, I don't want to be cheated on!

SERGINHO: Why are you crying?

GENI: Look at me. These days, sometimes, I get the sense your thoughts are far, far away. You look at me without seeing me. Tell me, but no lying, what are you thinking about if it isn't me? If you admit it, I won't be angry. Who is she?

SERGINHO: You!

GENI: *(Crying.)* Liar! *(Intense.)* Have you ever cheated on me? Even for two minutes?

SERGINHO: Never!

GENI: Not even a kiss? Even without the rest of it, I think a kiss is a betrayal. I'm jealous of your kisses. *(Appealing.)* If you cheated on me, don't kiss me. *(Furious.)* Did you kiss someone else?

SERGINHO: *(Without a break. Harsh.)* Geni, there's something I have to tell you.

The recorded voice of GENI.

GENI: *(Anxious.)* Is it good or bad? I'm scared. I'm scared of everything. *(Trying to sound natural.)* What do you have to tell me?

SERGINHO: I'm going on a trip.

GENI: *(Astonished.)* Liar!

SERGINHO: It's true. I've agreed it all with my father. I asked him to keep it a secret. I wanted to tell you myself.

GENI: *(Stupefied.)* I can't believe it. *(Crescendo.)* I still can't believe it.

SERGINHO: Wait!

GENI: A trip where to?

SERGINHO: Europe. The United States.

GENI: *(Controlled.)* For how long?

SERGINHO: It depends.

GENI: No! Don't I have the right to know? It must be a long
trip! Six months, a year? *(Furious.)* I can't be away from
you for six months or a year! What are you hiding from
me? I want to know exactly how long.

SERGINHO: A year!

GENI: *(Like one possessed.)* I won't let you, I won't allow it! I'll
run away with you! I'm going with you!

SERGINHO: Geni, I'm travelling on the old guy's money!

GENI: *(Desperate.)* You're leaving me! You settled things with
the old guy and you want to dump me!

SERGINHO: Listen, Geni!

GENI: *(Crying.)* Serginho, I depend on you. You're everything
to me. I never had a love like this!

SERGINHO: Go on, talk. And then I'll talk.

GENI: I'm a different woman, because of you. I was worthless.
I changed. Didn't you see how I changed? I swear it! Do
you want to see something else? Yesterday I jumped out
of the car and a bottle of perfume I'd just bought fell.
Without meaning to, I said "merda". It isn't even a swear
word, but if you could imagine the shame I felt, the guilt.
Shame, guilt, for us, for our love. Since I've known love,
I don't want to be a whore any more, not ever!

SERGINHO: Can I talk, Geni?

GENI: I won't let you go! I'll make a scandal! I'll tell your
father that you're my lover! I'll destroy you. Or if you
want to go on a trip, at least wait until I'm dead. I'm going
to die early. A lesion is going to grow on my breast. When
I'm dead, you can go!

SERGINHO: I want to go, but with your consent. I want you to agree. Will you listen, Geni?

GENI: *(Crying.)* No, no!

SERGINHO: *(Starting to exult.)* Listen. I need to go on a trip. For me, it's a question of life or death. If you love me. Tell me: do you love me?

GENI: *(Sobbing.)* I can't live without you!

SERGINHO: *(Excited.)* Right. So you have to agree. Do you understand? I can't take any more. Do you want me to go crazy or put a bullet through my head? It's not a pleasure trip. I need to. I need to do it. *(Shouting.)* Can you understand that!

GENI: *(Breathless, uncertain.)* Why do you need to?

SERGINHO: *(Desperate.)* I have to spend some months away from here. Places where no one knows me or knows what happened to me. Paris or London, somewhere where I'm just another person like the others, the same as the others. I need to see people who don't know about me. It would be so wonderful to walk down the street and no one knows anything! Do you understand? I want to save myself.

GENI: *(Surprised.)* But you've already forgotten.

SERGINHO: *(A strangled voice.)* You think I've forgotten?

GENI: You've already bought a whole load of books in Spanish!

SERGINHO: *(Astonished.)* What are you implying?

GENI: *(Scared.)* Nothing! I'm not implying anything!

SERGINHO: *(Triumphant.)* This is how it is. you didn't forget. You mention the books in Spanish. Why? *(Starts to cry.)*

It's not just you that cries, I cry too! Geni, if you love me –
and I know you love me – let me go on this trip! *(Sobbing.)*
Tell me to go, say go, go!

SERGINHO falls to his knees, embracing GENI. She strokes his hair.

GENI: Go my darling, go.

Darkness. Light on the interior of GENI's house. PATRÍCIO enters.

PATRÍCIO: How are you Geni? It's me, Geni!

GENI opens the door of her bedroom, frightened.

GENI: How did you get in?

PATRÍCIO: *(Malign.)* Don't you recognise your brother in law?
(Without a break, a change of tone.) I got in by getting in.
(Change of tone. Another voice.) When I got here, the maid
was going out, she and someone else. So I came in, just
like that. Isn't this my brother's house?

GENI: You're drunk.

PATRICO: *(A heavy laugh.)* You despise me, don't you Geni?
(Stops laughing.) I don't care. I want to talk to you.

GENI: Oh, my God!

PATRÍCIO: *(Continuing.)* Just a chat.

GENI: Herculano isn't here.

PATRÍCIO: *(Cynical.)* I came because I know he's in Sao
Paulo. *(A smug laugh.)* Geni, I've got news for you, a real
bombshell!

GENI: Listen Patrício, come back tomorrow, another day. Go
away! I'm sleepy.

PATRÍCIO: *(Mellifluous and threatening.)* Sleepy Geni? *(Harsher.)*
I'm going to tell you something that will make you

sleepless for the rest of your life! *(He beats his chest, with sudden exultation.)* You'll never sleep again, even when you're dead!

GENI: *(Angry.)* Are you going to get out of my house?

PATRÍCIO: Your lover left, didn't he?

GENI instinctively looks around.

GENI: Shut up!

PATRÍCIO: Herculano isn't here, so I can talk. *(Without a break and eager.)* It was great to see you at the airport. Not a tear. Herculano was crying. What about you?

GENI: I'm going to sleep.

GENI wants to go back into the bedroom. PATRÍCIO quickly turns and blocks her way.

PATRÍCIO: I came here to tell you something and you're going to listen. It's something interesting about your lover. *(A sordid laugh.)* But if you don't want me to tell you I'll go away. I won't tell you. *(Faking.)* Good night, Geni.

Going through with the play-acting, PATRÍCIO takes two steps. GENI is anguished.

GENI: OK. But get it over with.

PATRÍCIO: *(Excited.)* Did you know that before leaving, Serginho gave me a load of money, a cheque?

GENI: *(Lights up.)* Serginho is such a good boy. So kind!

PATRÍCIO: *(With cruel joy.)* But it wasn't good will. No one is good to me. It was fear. I threatened to make a scandal at the airport.

GENI: Are you crazy?

PATRÍCIO: Drunk, yes. Crazy, no. *(Angry and without a break.)* You're the one who's crazy. You never suspected anything. I'm going to tell you something that will make you fall flat on your back. *(Angry.)* Serginho left with the Bolivian!

PATRÍCIO starts laughing, in crescendo.

PATRÍCIO: It's a honeymoon with the Bolivian. Their long honeymoon. Serginho will never come back, never.

GENI fills the stage with her howls.

GENI: No, no, no, no!

PATRÍCIO's voice crescendo's more. He roars the final curse.

PATRÍCIO: I'll see Herculano dead! I'll see him dead! Dead with cotton in his nostrils.

Darkness on stage. They all disappear. Light on the bed without love. For the last time, we hear the recorded voice of GENI.

GENI: Your son left. He left with the Bolivian. They were on the same plane. The same flight. I'm alone and I shall die alone. *(An outburst of hatred.)* I don't want my name on my gravestone. Don't put anything! *(Exultant and angry.)* And you, you old cuckold! Curse you! Curse your son, and your family of aunts. *(A crazed laugh.)* My regards to the butch aunt! *(A last scream.)* And a curse on my breasts!

The voice of GENI dissolves in a sob. The recording ends. Sounds of a tape rewinding. Only the empty bed is lit.

THE CURTAIN FALLS, SLOWLY, ON THE
ACT 3 AND FINAL ACT.